SO-BZB-306

PSEUDEPIGRAPHA OF THE OLD TESTAMENT
AS PART OF CHRISTIAN LITERATURE

STUDIA
IN VETERIS TESTAMENTI
PSEUDEPIGRAPHA

EDIDERUNT

M.A. KNIBB, H.J. DE JONGE

J.-CL. HAELEWYCK, J. TROMP

VOLUMEN DECIMUM OCTAVUM

M. DE JONGE

PSEUDEPIGRAPHA OF THE OLD TESTAMENT
AS PART OF CHRISTIAN LITERATURE

PSEUDEPIGRAPHA OF THE OLD TESTAMENT AS PART OF CHRISTIAN LITERATURE

THE CASE OF THE TESTAMENTS OF THE TWELVE PATRIARCHS AND THE GREEK LIFE OF ADAM AND EVE

BY

M. DE JONGE

BRILL
LEIDEN · BOSTON
2003

BS
1700
.J66
2003

This book is printed on acid-free paper

Library of Congress Cataloging-in-Publication Data

Jonge, Marinus de, 1925-
  Pseudepigrapha of the Old Testament as part of Christian literature : the case of the
testaments of the twelve patriarchs and the Greek Life of Adam and Eve / by M. De Jonge.
      p. cm. — (Studia in Veteris Testamenti pseudepigrapha ; v. 18)
  Includes bibliographical references and index.
  ISBN 90-04-13294-5 (alk. paper)
    1. Apocryphal books (Old Testament)—Criticism, interpretation, etc. 2. Testaments of
the Twelve Patriarchs—Criticism, interpretation, etc. 3. Life of Adam and Eve—Criticism,
interpretation, etc. I. Title. II. Series.

BS1700.166 2003
229'.91—dc21

                                                                                    2003052250

ISSN   0929-3523
ISBN   90 04 13294 5

© *Copyright 2003 by Koninklijke Brill NV, Leiden, The Netherlands*

*All rights reserved. No part of this publication may be reproduced, translated, stored in
a retrieval system, or transmitted in any form or by any means, electronic,
mechanical, photocopying, recording or otherwise, without prior written
permission from the publisher.*

*Authorization to photocopy items for internal or personal
use is granted by Brill provided that the appropriate fees are paid directly to The Copyright
Clearance Center, 222 Rosewood Drive, Suite 910, Danvers MA 01923, USA.
Fees are subject to change.*

PRINTED IN THE NETHERLANDS

TABLE OF CONTENTS

Preface VII

Introduction 1

PART ONE

THE "PSEUDEPIGRAPHA OF THE OLD TESTAMENT" AND EARLY
CHRISTIANITY. SOME GENERAL QUESTIONS

1. "Pseudepigrapha of the Old Testament": An Ill-Defined
Category of Writings.. 9

2. The "Pseudepigrapha of the Old Testament" as Witnesses
to the Authority of the Old Testament in the Early Church 18

3. Developing a Different Approach 29

4. The Christian Transmission of Pseudepigrapha. Some Cases.. 39

PART TWO

THE CASE OF THE TESTAMENTS OF THE TWELVE PATRIARCHS

5. Defining the Major Issues in the Study of the *Testaments of
the Twelve Patriarchs* 71

6. *The Testaments of the Twelve Patriarchs* as a Document
Transmitted by Christians.. 84

7. The *Testaments of the Twelve Patriarchs* and Related
Qumran Fragments... 107

8. Levi in the Aramaic Levi Document and in the *Testament
of Levi* 124

9. The Two Great Commandments in the *Testaments of the Twelve Patriarchs* 141

10. Light on Paul from the *Testaments of the Twelve Patriarchs*? The *Testaments* and the New Testament 160

PART THREE

THE CASE OF THE GREEK LIFE OF ADAM AND EVE

11. The Christian Origin of the Greek *Life of Adam and Eve* 181

12. The Washing of Adam in the Acherusian Lake (Greek *Life of Adam and Eve* 37:3) in the Context of Early Christian Notions of the Afterlife (coauthor: L. Michael White) 201

13. The Greek *Life of Adam and Eve* and the Writings of the New Testament 228

Bibliography 241

Index of References 257
Analytical Subject Index 272

PREFACE

This book appears fifty years after my first publication on the pseudepigrapha of the Old Testament. In 1953 my *The Testaments of the
Twelve Patriarchs. A Study of their Text, Composition and Origin*
(Assen: Van Gorcum) was accepted by the Faculty of Theology of
the University of Leiden as a thesis for the degree of Doctor of Theology. This first book was followed by many further publications on
the *Testaments* from my hand, often written in cooperation with others, who also contributed studies of their own (see, in particular,
chapters 5 and 6 below). During the last ten years I have also devoted
my time to other Old Testament pseudepigrapha, especially the *Life
of Adam and Eve*.

Over the years it has become increasingly clear to me that given
the fact that our primary textual witnesses are, in great majority, of
Christian provenance, this group of writings should, first of all, be
studied as part of early Christian literature. In 1953 I argued that the
Testaments of the Twelve Patriarchs are a Christian document incorporating Jewish traditions. Since then I have discovered that they are
just one example of many, although we are confronted with a specific
situation in each individual case. The title of the present volume
Pseudepigrapha of the Old Testament as Part of Christian Literature
contains a programme; it calls for a paradigm shift in pseudepigrapha
research.

Looking back on the past fifty-odd years many persons come to
mind who have helped me to develop my ideas. Without attempting
to be complete, I would like to mention the names of Professors J. de
Zwaan and T.W. Manson who guided my steps during the preparation of my thesis. Much later, during the years of preparation of a
new critical edition of the *Testaments* (that appeared in 1978), I could
work together with Henk Jan de Jonge, Harm W. Hollander and Theo
Korteweg, who started as assistants and became true collaborators.
Harm Hollander had a great share in the preparation of the commentary that followed in 1985. To remain in Leiden: during the past ten
years I worked together with Johannes Tromp on the *Life of Adam*

and Eve. With him I also had numerable discussions on other pseudepigrapha during the preparation of the present volume.

Wider afield there were during the years my colleagues in pseudepigrapha research Michael E. Stone (Jerusalem), Robert A. Kraft
(Philadelphia), George W.E. Nickelsburg (Iowa City) and Michael A.
Knibb (London) who, each in his own way, worked along similar
lines.

L. Michael White kindly agreed to the use in chapter 12 of an essay which we recently wrote together. I thank the editors of the *Studia in Veteris Testamenti pseudepigrapha* for accepting this book in
this series, started in 1970 by the late A.-M. Denis and myself, and
for much good advice. Johannes Tromp rendered valuable assistance
in preparing the final manuscript for the printer.

2318 VE Leiden, Libellenveld 19   M. DE JONGE

INTRODUCTION

I. THE PROBLEM

Much has been written on the pseudepigrapha of the Old Testament, particularly about those that are thought to be of Jewish origin. They have been studied as sources for the history and thought of Judaism in the time between 200 before to 100 after the beginning of the common era. They have especially been used as witnesses to the diversity of Judaism in that period—and, of course, also to throw light on the origins of the Jesus movement and early Christianity.

The pseudepigrapha were thus studied as Jewish writings, though transmitted by Christians (just like the writings of Philo and Josephus), sometimes interpolated by them or redacted more thoroughly, sometimes also seemingly free from contamination. Scholars were confident that they could reconstruct the original Jewish texts with the help of customary text-critical and literary-critical methods, and then use those original documents for historical investigations into the ideas of Judaism in the period around the beginning of the common era.

Fifty years of study of the *Testaments of the Twelve Patriarchs* have made me aware of the many pitfalls encountered by scholars who want to pursue the track back from a particular document, which has come down to us because Christians thought it worthwhile to copy it, to a possible early Jewish writing lying underneath, or at least to Jewish material incorporated in it. During the last decade investigations into the problems posed by the various recensions of the *Life of Adam and Eve* have corroborated this conclusion. The so-called pseudepigrapha of the Old Testament do not form a uniform collection. In fact there is not even consensus about the question which writings should be included in this category. The situation is different for each individual pseudepigraphon, but at the same time certain questions crop up always and everywhere.

The thesis of this book is that the so-called pseudepigrapha of the Old Testament have to be read primarily as writings transmitted by Christians over many centuries. They were transmitted because copyists regarded them as important and were of the opinion that they could function meaningfully in the communities for which they copied them. Transmission clearly presupposes the enduring relevance of what is transmitted. In early Christianity as well as in the Middle Ages, and even later, Christians all over the Christian world were interested in narratives, wisdom books, psalms, apocalypses, testaments, etcetera centring around figures known from the Old Testament (I use this term deliberately in this connection, and do not speak about the Hebrew or Jewish Bible). Are we able to say anything more about their importance, and about the nature of their authority? Only when we understand the function of these writings in the circles in which they were transmitted can the questions connected with the provenance of the material involved, and with the possible Christian adaptation of it, be answered satisfactorily. So much is clear: much careful analysis has to be carried out before a particular pseudepigraphon can be used as a source for our knowledge of early Judaism or of Christianity in the first century.

II. This Volume

This volume makes use of a number of essays written by the present author and published after 1990. All of them have been revised, and material has been rearranged in order to avoid repetition where possible; also some chapters have been added. All this has been done to present the main argument of this book as clearly and forcefully as possible.

Part One deals with questions of a general nature, affecting all pseudepigrapha of the Old Testament. Chapter 1 argues that the term "pseudepigrapha of the Old Testament" should be used as a literary category, comprising those writings that are concerned with the lives, activities and words of great figures of Israel's past. They are not necessarily Jewish; nor does their date of origin have to be restricted to the period between 200 BCE and 100 CE. In fact the great majority of these documents have come down to us because they were transmitted by Christians. And they were transmitted because Christians, having accepted the Old Testament as authoritative for their own communities, were interested in what otherwise could be known about the great men and women of the past (see chapter 2). This point

of departure leads to an approach to the Old Testament pseudepigrapha that differs from that found in many contemporary handbooks
and collections of pseudepigrapha. This approach is explained in
chapter 3 and illustrated in chapter 4 dealing with the Christian
transmission of eight documents. These documents are not
approached as Jewish writings, subsequently modified by Christians
during the transmission process, but they are consistently treated as
documents transmitted by Christians which may or may not be
shown to go back to an originally Jewish document.

Two other writings, the *Testaments of the Twelve Patriarchs* and
the *Life of Adam and Eve*, are dealt with in more detail in the following sections.

The six chapters in Part Two are concerned with the *Testaments of
the Twelve Patriarchs*. Chapter 5 outlines what I came, during the
period between 1950 and 1990, to regard as the major issues in the
study of this important pseudepigraphon, starting with the view
argued in my first book of 1953 that the *Testaments* should be read as
a Christian document acquainted with Jewish traditions. It is followed by chapter 6 that takes the *Testaments* seriously as a document
transmitted by Christians. Chapters 7 and 8 deal with the relationship
between the *Testaments* and related Qumran fragments, in particular
the Aramaic Levi Document. Chapter 9 discusses an important
ethical aspect: the views in the *Testaments* on the two great
commandments. The section ends with an essay on the use of the
Testaments in interpreting the New Testament, in particular the Letters of Paul.

Part Three discusses, in three chapters, the Greek version of the
Life of Adam and Eve and its place in early Christian thought.
Chapter 11 tries to prove that the picture given here of the transgression of Adam and Eve, their penitence and their sharing in
eternal life, bestowed on them by a merciful God, fits into the
interpretation of Genesis 3 in mainstream Christianity around 200 CE.
Chapter 13, written in cooperation with L. Michael White, deals with
one particular text, *GLAE* 37:3, which describes how Adam is
washed three times in the Acherusian Lake before being brought into
the presence of God and brought to Paradise. This element is shown
to be Christian. In the second part of the chapter it is compared to
other Christian traditions about the Acherusian Lake and the river
Acheron, influenced in turn by various Greek notions. And finally,

chapter 13, like the last chapter in the preceding part, deals with the use of the writing under discussion in the interpretation of the writings of the New Testament.

III. LIST OF EARLIER PUBLICATIONS USED IN THIS VOLUME

Chapters 1 and 2 go back to a contribution delivered at the fiftieth *Journées bibliques* in Louvain (2001): "The Authority of the 'Old Testament' in the Early Church: The Witness of the 'Pseudepigrapha of the Old Testament,'" (with an Appendix: "What do we mean by 'Pseudepigrapha of the Old Testament?'"), to be published in J.-M. Auwers and H.J. de Jonge (eds.), *The Biblical Canons* (BETL 163; Leuven: Peeters, 2003), 457-484.

Chapter 3 is new, but takes up some points raised earlier in "The so-called Pseudepigrapha of the Old Testament and Early Christianity," in P. Borgen and S. Giversen (eds.), *The New Testament and Hellenistic Judaism* (Aarhus: Aarhus University Press, 1995; reprint: Peabody, Mass.: Hendrickson, 1997), 59-71.

Chapters 4 and 5 were also especially written for this volume.

Chapter 6 goes back to "The Transmission of the Testaments of the Twelve Patriarchs by Christians," *VC* 47 (1993), 1-28.

For chapter 7 see "The Testaments of the Twelve Patriarchs and related Qumran Fragments," in R.A. Argall, B.A. Bow, R.A. Werline (eds.), *For a Later Generation. The Transformation of Tradition in Israel, Early Judaism and Early Christianity* (Festschrift for George W.E. Nickelsburg; Harrisburg, Pa.: Trinity Press International, 2000), 63-77.

An earlier version of chapter 8 "Levi in Aramaic Levi and in the Testament of Levi," appeared in E.G. Chazon, M.E. Stone and A. Pinnick (eds.), *Pseudepigraphic Perspectives: The Apocrypha & Pseudepigrapha in Light of the Dead Sea Scrolls. Proceedings of the International Symposium of the Orion Center for the Study of the Dead Sea Scrolls and Related Literature* (STDJ 31; Leiden: Brill, 1999), 71-89.

Chapter 9 is an abbreviated version of "The Two Great Commandments in the Testaments of the Twelve Patriarchs," *NovT* 44 (2002), 371-392.

Chapter 10 goes back to "Light on Paul from the Testaments of the Twelve Patriarchs?" in L.M. White and O.L. Yarbrough (eds.), *The Social World of the First Christians. Essays in Honor of Wayne A. Meeks* (Minneapolis, Fortress Press, 1995), 100-115.

Chapter 11 is an updated version of the essay "The Christian Origin of the *Greek Life of Adam and Eve*," that appeared in G.A. Anderson, M.E. Stone and J. Tromp (eds.), *Literature on Adam and Eve. Collected Essays* (SVTP 15; Leiden: Brill, 2000), 347-363.

Chapter 12 is a slightly abbreviated version of M. de Jonge and L.M. White, "The Washing of Adam in the Acherusian Lake (*Gr. Life of Adam and Eve* 37:3) in the Context of Early Christian Notions of the Afterlife," in J.T. Fitzgerald, T.H. Olbricht and L.M. White (eds.), *Early Christianity and Classical Culture: Comparative Studies in Honour of Abraham J. Malherbe* (NovTSup 110; Leiden: Brill, 2003), 605-631.

Finally, chapter 13 appeared earlier in a different form as "The Greek Life of Adam and Eve and the Writings of the New Testament," in A. von Dobbeler, K. Erlemann, R. Heiligenthal (eds.), *Religionsgeschichte des Neuen Testaments. Festschrift für Klaus Berger zum 60. Geburtstag* (Tübingen/Basel: Francke, 2000), 149-160.

PART ONE

THE SO-CALLED PSEUDEPIGRAPHA
OF THE OLD TESTAMENT AND EARLY CHRISTIANITY.
SOME GENERAL QUESTIONS

CHAPTER ONE

"PSEUDEPIGRAPHA OF THE OLD TESTAMENT":
AN ILL-DEFINED CATEGORY OF WRITINGS

The term "pseudepigrapha of the Old Testament" has become fashionable since the beginning of the twentieth century when two col-
lective works appeared in which this word played an important role.[1]
First *Die Apokryphen und Pseudepigraphen des Alten Testaments*,
two volumes edited by E. Kautzsch,[2] and somewhat later *The Apocrypha and Pseudepigrapha of the Old Testament* edited by R.H.
Charles (also in two volumes).[3] The titles of these two volumes betray the Christian viewpoint of these two scholars, and the distinction
"apocrypha-pseudepigrapha" their typically Protestant stance. The
Protestant "apocrypha of the Old Testament" are regarded as
"deuterocanonical" by Roman-Catholics, who use the term "apocrypha" for the books that Protestants call "pseudepigrapha."[4] But
whichever of the two terms is chosen, the question remains which
books should be classified as such. Kautzsch and Charles limited the
"pseudepigrapha of the Old Testament" to books written by Jews in
the period between 200 BCE and 100 CE, but not belonging to the
apocrypha of the church. Comparison between their collections
shows that already these two scholars did not entirely agree as to

---

[1] Much earlier, in the first decades of the eighteenth century, J.A. Fabricius published his
Codex Pseudepigraphus Veteris Testamenti, 2 vols. (Hamburg, 1713; second edition 1722-
1723).

[2] Tübingen: Mohr, 1900 (second edition 1921, reprinted by the Wissenschaftliche Buchgesellschaft, Darmstadt, 1961).

[3] Oxford: Clarendon, 1913 (several reprints).

[4] Compare the nineteenth century collection of J.-P. Migne, *Dictionnaire des Apocryphes*, 2
vols. (Paris, 1856 and 1858; reprint Turnhout: Brepols, 1989). In this collection Migne also
deals with the New Testament Apocrypha. In the *Corpus Christianorum* J.-C. Haelewyck
recently published a *Clavis Apocryphorum Veteris Testamenti* (Turnhout: Brepols, 1998). A.-
M. Denis, who published, successively, an *Introduction aux Pseudépigraphes grecs d'Ancien
Testament* (SVTP 1; Leiden: Brill, 1970), a *Concordance grecque des pseudépigraphes d'Ancien Testament* (Louvain-la-Neuve: Institut Orientaliste, 1987) and a *Concordance latine des
pseudépigraphes d'Ancien Testament* (Turnhout: Brepols, 1993), finally chose for the second
edition of his completely revised *Introduction* (published posthumously by J.-C. Haelewyck)
the title *Introduction à la littérature religieuse judéo-hellénistique*, 2 vols. (Turnhout: Brepols,
2000).

which writings should be counted among the Old Testament pseudepigrapha.

Others avoided the term "pseudepigrapha" or used it for a much
smaller number of writings. So, for instance, E. Schürer in the third
volume of his *Die Geschichte des jüdischen Volkes*, which is mainly
devoted to Jewish literature.[5] He spoke about "palästinisch-jüdische
Literatur" in general (beside the "hellenistisch-jüdische") and reckoned only some writings to the category "prophetische Pseudepigraphen." Later, in 1928, P. Riessler brought together a very large number of "ausserkanonische Schriften des Judentums" under the title
Altjüdisches Schrifttum ausserhalb der Bibel.[6] We may regard the
series of monographs that begin to appear in the 1970s under the title
Jüdische Schriften aus hellenistisch-römischer Zeit (JSHRZ) as the
successor to Kautzsch's two volumes.[7] It gives an extensive collection of books, divided into five groups: "Historische und legendari-
sche Erzählungen," "Unterweisung in erzählender Form," "Unterweisung in lehrhafter Form," "Poetische Schriften," "Apokalypsen."

Among other collections mention may be made of the French *La
Bible. Écrits Intertestamentaires*[8] of 1987. It gives translations of
nineteen "pseudépigraphes de l'Ancien Testament" preceded by
some "Écrits qoumrâniens" (taking up about a quarter of the book).
There also appeared in the 1980s the Italian *Apocrifi dell'Antico Testamento*[9] and the five volumes of the Spanish *Apócrifos del Antiguo
Testamento.*[10] Comparison of these last two collections shows that, as
might be expected, the problem of selection and limitation is also
there for those who prefer the term "apocrypha" to that of "pseudepigrapha."

In 1984 M.E. Stone edited the book *Jewish Writings of the Second
Temple Period* in the series "Compendia Rerum Iudaicarum ad No-

---

[5] Leipzig: Hinrichs, fourth edition 1909 (see especially pp. 258-370).

[6] Heidelberg: Kerle Verlag/W.Rühling (reprinted by the Wissenschaftliche Buchgesellschaft, 1966).

[7] Published by Gütersloher Verlagshaus Gerd Mohn.

[8] Editors: A. Dupont-Sommer and M. Philonenko (Bibliothèque de la Pléiade 337; Paris:
Gallimard, 1987).

[9] Originally two volumes, edited by P. Sacchi (Torino: Unione Tipografico-Editrice Torinese, 1981 and 1989); later three additional volumes appeared, see n. 26 below.

[10] Edited by A. Díez Macho and others (Madrid: Ediciones Cristiandad, 1983-1987).

vum Testamentum."[11] As its subtitle tells us, it deals with "Apocrypha, Pseudepigrapha, Qumran Sectarian Writings, Philo, Josephus." It classifies the sources according to literary genre (though differently from JSHRZ) or provenance. There is no special chapter devoted to the "pseudepigrapha"; the writings found near the Dead Sea are dealt with separately. Important for our purpose is what Stone says about the difference between the volume edited by him and the next, entitled *The Literature of the Sages*.[12] I quote:

> The volume on rabbinic literature comprises material relevant to the history of Jewish literature and thought transmitted within the Jewish tradition and in Semitic languages. The present volume includes material that was not transmitted by Jewish tradition. Part was preserved by the various Christian churches and part was uncovered by archeological chance (p. xix).

The discovery of a great number of writings, some of them already known earlier, near the Dead Sea has indeed considerably broadened and deepened our knowledge of the literature, history and the religious ideas of Judaism in the period around the beginning of the Common Era. It is very important that in this case we are likely to deal with documents hidden in the time of the Jewish war against the Romans, which consequently must have been written before that date. The discovery of the Qumran Scrolls meant a great boost for the research into the writings already known, including the pseudepigrapha; they could now be studied in a wider context and from new viewpoints.[13] Stone rightly stresses, however, that many of those, like

---

[11] Assen, Van Gorcum/Philadelphia, Fortress, 1984. The book appeared in the second section of "Compendia," devoted to Jewish Literature.

[12] *The Literature of the Sages. First Part* (ed. S. Safrai) appeared in 1987 (CRINT II, 3a).

[13] It should be noted, however, that the caves at Qumran yielded only a few apocrypha or pseudepigrapha already known before the discoveries near the Dead Sea. P.W. Flint in his contribution "'Apocrypha', Other Previously-Known Writings, and 'Pseudepigrapha' in the Dead Sea Scrolls," to P.W. Flint and J.C. VanderKam (eds.), *The Dead Sea Scrolls after Fifty Years. A Comprehensive Assessment* (Leiden: Brill, 1999), vol. 2. 24-66, mentions only Tobit, Sirach, the Epistle of Jeremiah (with a question mark), Psalm 151A and B, Psalm 154 and 155, *Enoch* and *Jubilees*. He rightly classifies a number of fragments of the Aramaic Levi Document, 4Q TNaph and some fragments that, according to some people, can be connected with Judah and Joseph, plus fragments connected with Kohath and 'Amram, among "material related to the *Testaments of the Twelve Patriarchs*" (note the "related to"!). An entirely different question is whether other Qumran documents should be reckoned to the "pseudepigrapha of the Old Testament." Flint refers here to M.J. Bernstein's essay "Pseudepigraphy in the Qumran Scrolls: Categories and Functions," in E.G. Chazon, M.E. Stone, A. Pinnick (eds.), *Pseud-*

the works of Philo and Josephus, were only transmitted by Christians. This basic fact should not be overlooked in the study of these writings, and in the use of the material transmitted by Christians, for the reconstruction of Jewish history and Jewish religious ideas in the period before 70 CE.

We shall have to pay special attention to two collections in English that may be regarded as successors to R.H. Charles's pseudepigrapha-volume. Its direct successor at the Clarendon Press, edited by H.F.D. Sparks, received the title *The Apocryphal Old Testament*.[14] This book serves as a companion volume to *The Apocryphal New Testament* by M.R. James,[15] published by the same publisher. Sparks expressly avoids the term "pseudepigrapha" and distances himself from Charles's view that the writings under discussion are Jewish, date from the "intertestamental" period, and are, as such, of great importance for our knowledge of the Judaism of the period and the background of early Christianity. Sparks does not want just to present background literature for students of the New Testament, nor can the writings involved be treated as that. Most of the books may indeed be of Jewish origin, he says, but often we find Christian elements as a result of interpolation or redaction. There are also Christian apocryphal texts that use Jewish material, and we must also allow for the likelihood that Christians, influenced by what they read in the Old Testament, composed writings of this kind of their own. Sparks writes: "Our single criterion for inclusion has been whether or not any particular item is attributed to (or is primarily concerned with the history or activities of) an Old Testament character (or characters)."[16] Not everything that satisfied this criterion could be included, but

---

epigraphic Perspectives. The Apocrypha and Pseudepigrapha in Light of the Dead Sea Scrolls (STDJ 31; Leiden: Brill, 1999), 1-26. Defining "pseudepigrapha" as "texts falsely attributed to an author (usually of great authority) in order to enhance their authority and validity," this author distinguishes between different uses of the term. Beside "authoritative pseudepigraphy" proper, there is "convenient pseudepigraphy" ("where the work is anonymous but individual voices are heard within it") and "decorative pseudepigraphy" ("where the work is associated with a name without a particular regard for content or to achieve a certain effect"—for these definitions, see pp.1-7 and p. 25). In this light Bernstein and Flint discuss a number of documents; a definitive, generally accepted classification is still outstanding.

[14] Oxford: Clarendon, 1984.

[15] First edition 1924, many times reprinted. Recently revised and expanded by J.K. Elliott, Oxford: Clarendon, 1993.

[16] See H.F.D. Sparks, "Preface," pp. ix-xviii; quotation p. xv.

Sparks tried to present at least the most important and interesting documents; he did not include writings (only) found at Qumran.

The second collection to be mentioned here are the two volumes *The Old Testament Pseudepigrapha*, edited by J.H. Charlesworth.[17] Volume 1 is devoted to "Apocalyptic Literature and Testaments," volume 2 to "Expansions of the 'Old Testament' and Legends, Wisdom and Philosophical Literature, Prayers, Psalms and Odes; Fragments of Lost Judeo-Hellenistic Works." Apart from the fragments just mentioned Charlesworth has included no less than fifty-two writings. Qumran documents are lacking, just as in the collection of Sparks. Charlesworth declares that he deliberately chose to present a large collection. He noticed, he says, a "consensus that the Pseudepigrapha must be defined broadly so as to include all documents that conceivably belong to the Old Testament Pseudepigrapha." After this he continues:

> The present description of the Pseudepigrapha is as follows: Those writings 1) that, with the exception of Ahiqar, are Jewish or Christian; 2) that are often attributed to ideal figures in Israel's past; 3) that customarily claim to contain God's word or message; 4) that frequently build upon ideas and narratives present in the Old Testament; 5) and that almost always were composed either during the period 200 B.C. to A.D. 200 or, though late, apparently preserve, albeit in an edited form, Jewish traditions that date from that period.

He adds:

> Obviously, the numerous qualifications ... warn that the above comments do not define the term "pseudepigrapha"; they merely describe the features of this collection.[18]

The fact that the word "pseudepigrapha" figures so prominently and is used as an inclusive—and at the same time elusive—term, is remarkable. Charlesworth retains it notwithstanding "the numerous qualifications." Also other publications from his hand show abun-

---

[17] Garden City, NY: Doubleday, 1983 and 1985. Among the many reviews I mention that by S.P. Brock in *JJS* 35 (1984), 200-209 and 38 (1987), 107-114. See also the reviews of the works of Sparks and Charlesworth together, by M.E. Stone and R.A. Kraft in *RSR* 14 (1988), 111-117.

[18] J.H. Charlesworth, "Introduction for the General Reader," p. xxv.

dantly that he is aware of the complexity of the situation.[19] His survey article "Pseudepigrapha of the Old Testament" in the *Anchor Bible Dictionary*[20] begins with the observation that many of these documents were composed by Jews, that others were expanded or rewritten by Christians, and that some are Christian compositions depending in various degrees on pre-70 Jewish documents or oral traditions. Nevertheless: however difficult it may be to determine in detail what is Jewish and what not, the importance of the entire collection lies for Charlesworth in its being "essential reading for an understanding of early Judaism (ca. 250 BCE to 200 CE) and of Christian origins."[21]

In stating this repeatedly and emphatically Charlesworth stands in the tradition starting with Kautzsch and Charles. Including so many extra writings in his selection does not make it easier, however, to substantiate this claim in each individual case. But quite apart from that, the case can be made that it makes at least as much sense to study these documents "as part of the continuous flow of Jewish and Christian creativity which in good part derives from preoccupation with the 'canonical books'," as Stone remarked in his review of Charlesworth's two volumes.[22] Stone refers there to an earlier article from his hand in which he rightly observes that documents for which there is no independent corroboration or other compelling evidence cannot, without more ado, be used as sources for our knowledge of Judaism in the period of the Second Temple. "Before the Pseudepigrapha and similar writings are used as evidence for that more ancient period, they must be examined in the Christian context in which they were transmitted and utilized."[23]

A very special and individual approach to the pseudepigrapha problem is found in J.-C. Picard's essay "L'apocryphe à l'étroit.

---

[19] See, for instance his *The Pseudepigrapha and Modern Research* (SBLSCS 7; Missoula MT: Scholars, 1976; second expanded edition 1981) and *The Old Testament Pseudepigrapha and the New Testament* (SNTSMS 54; Cambridge: Cambridge UP, 1985; new edition with new preface [pp. vii-xxiv], Harrisburg:Trinity International, 1998).

[20] *ABD* (New York: Doubleday, 1992), vol. 5, 537-540.

[21] See not only the article just mentioned but also *OTP*, vol. 1, pp. xxvii-xxix and *In the Crucible. The Pseudepigrapha as Biblical Interpretation*, in J.H. Charlesworth and C.A. Evans (eds.), *The Pseudepigrapha and Early Biblical Interpretation* (JSPSup 14; Sheffield: Sheffield Academic Press, 1993), 20-43.

[22] See note 17; quotation from p. 112.

[23] "Categorization and Classification of the Apocrypha and Pseudepigrapha," *Abr-Nahrain* 24 (1986), 167-177, quotation from pp. 172-173.

Notes historiographiques sur le corpus d'apocryphes bibliques."[24] He prefers to speak about a "continent apocryphe," one could say "an apocryphal world," in which people lived for a long time. His aim is to take account of the entire complex of apocryphal biblical traditions in Antiquity and in the Middle Ages (and even later), among Jews, Christians and Muslims.[25] These apocryphal traditions functioned as myths, as basic, foundational stories in the communities that transmitted them, orally and in writing, and naturally in many variants. They require a literary and historical as well as an ethnological approach. A purely text-critical or source-critical analysis of these writings, with a view to reconstructing their earliest form, and using this earliest form as evidence in the study of early Judaism or early Christianity, does not do justice to the apocryphal tradition as a complex process. Such a completely one-sided approach has also led to the formation of very limited collections of "pseudepigrapha of the Old Testament" (as in the case of Kautzsch and Charles), and similarly limited collections of "Apocrypha of the New Testament" (such as Hennecke-Schneemelcher). One can, of course, always consider including more or different documents in such collections, but what is really needed is a completely different approach to apocryphal literature.

Many comments could be made in the margin of Picard's characterization of pseudepigrapha research since the end of the nineteenth century as one-sided and reductionist. To me, at any rate, it would seem perfectly legitimate to attempt to reconstruct the first stages in a transmission process. In the case of the writings under discussion it makes sense to consider in which cases it is possible to trace the origins of this process back to Christian circles in the first two or three centuries, or even to Jewish groups around the beginning of the common era. In trying to achieve this goal it will be necessary to apply all the philological, literary and historical methods that are

[24] In *Apocrypha. Le champ des apocryphes* 1 (1990), 69-117. This essay was reprinted in J.-C. Picard, *Le continent apocryphe: Essai sur les littératures apocryphes juive et chrétienne* (Instrumenta Patristica 36; Steenbrugis: In Abbatia S. Petri/Turnhout: Brepols, 1999), 3-51. In this book, a posthumous collection of Picard's most important publications, one finds an introduction to Picard's ideas about the "apocryphal world" by Francis Schmidt (see pp. xix-xxviii).

[25] He praises the collections by J.A. Fabricius, who edited not only the *Codex pseudepigraphus Veteris Testamenti* mentioned in note 1, but earlier also a *Codex apocryphus Novi Testamenti*, Hamburg, 1703 (second edition 1719).

available—bearing in mind, of course, the great complexity of the
entire process of transmission. What is remarkable is Picard's positive assessment of the works of H.F.D. Sparks and J.H. Charlesworth, to which he refers briefly at the end of his essay. In their
approach he notices "une rupture définitive avec les présupposés trop
réducteurs et le réductionnisme méthodologique illustrés, au debut de
ce siècle, par les recueils de Kautzsch et de Charles."

Finally I would like to draw attention to a recent article by P.
Sacchi, which serves at the same time as the introduction to volumes
3 and 4 of the *Apocrifi dell'Antico Testamento*.[26] He continues to
prefer the term "apocrypha" to "pseudepigrapha." He accepts the
literary criterion that the writings concerned must be ascribed to
and/or have to deal with figures from the Old Testament. At the same
time, however, he would like to hold on to the Catholic interpretation
of the term "apocrypha," which in his view provides a clear historical
criterion. This term "has a precise historical meaning which can be
retained even nowadays ...: thus it is possible to define a corpus of
texts which cannot extend beyond the beginning of the second
century CE."[27] In the end Sacchi distinguishes between "intertestamental" apocrypha (Jewish, before 100 CE), Jewish Old Testament apocrypha (after 100), Christian Old Testament apocrypha
(after 100), and Jewish medieval (post-talmudic) apocrypha. Sacchi
regards the survival of the "genre" as interesting, and he does realize
that the apocrypha/pseudepigrapha were transmitted by Christians—
yet he is of the opinion that the distinctions he proposes are prac-
ticable and meaningful.

Summing up:

a. There is no consensus as to which writings should be regarded
as belonging to the "pseudepigrapha of the Old Testament," and this
is due to the different ways the term has been used in the past and in
the present. On the one hand, it is used for all documents in which
one or more biblical figures play an important role, but on the other
hand, a historical criterion is often applied, and the term is restricted

---

[26] See note 9. Published in 1999 and 2000 by Paideia in Brescia (which already in 1997 had
published volume 5, an appendix with the works of Jewish-Hellenistic writers from the
diaspora). Sacchi's article "Il problema degli apocrifi dell'Antico Testamento" appeared in
Henoch 21 (1999), 97-129.
[27] From the English summary on p. 129.

to writings dating from the period between about 200 BCE and 100 CE that are supposed to be of Jewish origin.

It is also important that only in a relatively restricted number of instances can one properly speak of "pseudepigraphy" as such (i.e., ascription of a writing to somebody else than the real author), and that, by contrast, also a number of books that were later incorporated in the Hebrew Bible/the Christian Old Testament and in the New Testament may be called "pseudepigrapha" in the literal sense.

b. Yet it remains meaningful to pay attention to those writings which have in common that they are concerned with the lives, activities and words of a great figure (or great figures) in the Old Testament. Students of early Judaism and early Christianity will concentrate on the earliest stages in the transmission of such writings, in early Christianity and, where this can be demonstrated, also among Jewish groups in the period around the beginning of the common era. In all cases it is important to keep in mind the great complexity of the transmission process.

CHAPTER TWO

THE "PSEUDEPIGRAPHA OF THE OLD TESTAMENT"
AS WITNESSES TO THE AUTHORITY OF THE OLD
TESTAMENT IN THE EARLY CHURCH

This essay will deal with the question of why the writings commonly classified among the "pseudepigrapha/apocrypha of the Old Testament" were transmitted by Christians and how they functioned in the Early Church. I want to argue that they are witnesses to the authority of the books of the "Old Testament" for (a considerable number of) Christians in the second century and later. The Christians who accepted these books as authoritative were interested in what could otherwise be known about Adam, Enoch, Moses, Elijah and other important figures. The words of these great figures from the past carried weight, their faith and righteous conduct were exemplary. Hence it makes sense and is worthwhile to study the "pseudepigrapha/apocrypha of the Old Testament" as part of the literature of early Christianity.

I. The Place of the Jewish Authoritative Writings among
Christians in the Second Century

In the writings that were later brought together in the "New Testament" the books that had authority for Jews are presented as authoritative for the followers of Jesus as well. Their status is not argued, it is simply taken for granted. In his contribution about the interpretation of Scripture in the New Testament, D.-A. Koch describes the situation as follows:

> Weder für Jesus von Nazareth noch für die frühen (palästinisch- oder
> hellenistisch-) judenchristlichen Gemeinden stellte sich die Frage nach
> der "Beibehaltung der Schrift" ... Da nirgends ein neuer Gott, sondern
> "nur" ein neues Handeln dieses Gottes proklamiert wurde, blieb die
> Schrift als umfassendes Zeugnis von Gottes Wirken und seinem ver-
> pflichtenden Willen notwendigerweise in Geltung—trat jetzt aber in

Wechselverhältnis gegenseitiger Interpretation mit dem Bekenntnis zu dem neuen Heilshandeln Gottes in Jesus Christus.[1]

Koch mentions here some matters that remained important also in the second century (and later). How can one demonstrate continuity in God's actions? How should Christians read and interpret the Scriptures? How do Christians, in discussions with Jews who refer to the same Scriptures, justify their point of view? How does one deal with the elements of discontinuity—eventually leading to the question: Can one really speak of a continuous acting and speaking of one and the same God?

Later Christians, in increasing numbers of non-Jewish descent, are more and more confronted with the necessity of self-defence in a Hellenistic milieu. How does the appeal to the Scriptures function in such a context? The debate between Christian and non-Christian philosophers becomes interrelated with that between Christians and Jews, and with inner-Christian discussions and controversies. In what follows some major issues will be indicated. Following Hans von Campenhausen[2] and John Barton[3] (and others) I shall pay special attention to the views of Marcion and those of Justin Martyr.

II. CANON AND TEXT

Many scholars have emphasized that questions concerning the fixation of a list of "biblical" books did not play an important role in the first three centuries CE. For Jews and Christians the important point was the appeal to "a collection of authoritative books." One does not yet feel the need for a precise description and exact delimitation of "an authoritative collection of books."[4] To formulate this differently: one possessed "Scriptures," but did not worry about the delimitation of a "canon."[5] We also do not note any friction between Jews and

---

[1] *TRE* 30 (1999), 457-471, p. 457.

[2] H. von Campenhausen, *Die Entstehung der christlichen Bibel* (BHT 39; Tübingen: Mohr [Siebeck], 1968)

[3] J. Barton, *The Spirit and the Letter. Studies in the Biblical Canon* (London: SPCK, 1997).

[4] This distinction is made by B.M. Metzger in his *The Canon of the New Testament. Its Origin, Development and Significance* (Oxford: Clarendon, 1987), p. 282.

[5] See Barton, *The Spirit and the Letter*, p. 9 (and *passim*, following A.C. Sundberg). For canon questions in Judaism and Christianity see, for instance, R.T. Beckwith and E.E. Ellis in M.J. Mulder and H. Sysling (eds.), *Mikra. Text, Translation, Reading and Interpretation of the*

Christians in this period about the question which books are
authoritative or not. In chapters 71-73 of his *Dialogue with Trypho*
Justin accuses the Jewish teachers of omitting crucial passages in the
Septuagint; the authority of the books as such is not a subject of
discussion.[6]

In this context it is interesting to look for a moment to the appeal
to the testimony of Enoch in Jude 14, where the words προεφήτευσεν
δὲ καὶ τούτοις ἕβδομος ἀπὸ Ἀδὰμ Ἑνὼχ λέγων are followed by a
quotation from *1 En.* 1:9 (known to us in an Ethiopic and a Greek,
plus a very fragmentary Aramaic, version).[7] Enoch, the patriarch
from the period before the Flood, was clearly a man of authority, also
for the author of the Epistle of Jude. But, in the words of Richard
Bauckham, "while this word [*scil.* προεφήτευσεν] indicates that Jude
regarded the prophecies in *1 Enoch* as inspired by God, it need not
imply that he regarded the book as canonical Scripture."[8] A. Vögtle
rightly adds that, in the case of the Epistle of Jude, one should not
use the term "canonical": "Er schrieb ja lange vor der Zeit, da 'inspi-
riert' und 'kanonisch,' 'Schrift' und 'Kanon' identische Begriffe
wurden."[9]

A key text in support of this view on the relation between "Scripture" and "canon" is Eusebius's report on Melito, bishop of Sardis
around 170 CE. In *H.E.* 4.26, 13-14 he tells us that a list of τῶν
ὁμολογουμένων τῆς παλαιᾶς διαθήκης γραφῶν can be found in the
preface of Melito's Ἐκλογαί. In this preface Melito addresses his
"brother Onesimus" who had asked him several times for ἐκλογαί

Hebrew Bible in ancient Judaism and Early Christianity (CRINT 2,1; Assen-Maastricht: Van
Gorcum/Philadelphia: Fortress, 1988), resp. "Formation of the Hebrew Bible," 39-86 and "The
Old Testament Canon in the Early Church," 653-690.

[6] See Ellis, "The Old Testament Canon," p. 655.

[7] For details see R. Bauckham, *Jude, 2 Peter* (WBC, 50; Waco TX: Word, 1983), pp. 93-
101 and A. Vögtle, *Der Judasbrief/Der zweite Petrusbrief* (EKK, 22; Solothurn-Düsseldorf:
Benziger/Neukirchen-Vluyn: Neukirchener, 1994), pp. 71-84. See also B. Dehandschutter in
J.J.A. Kahmann and B. Dehandschutter, *De Tweede Brief van Petrus en de Brief van Judas*
(Boxtel: KBS, 1983), pp. 138-139 and in his contribution "Pseudo-Cyprian, Jude and Enoch.
Some notes on 1 Enoch 1:9," in J.W. van Henten *et al.* (eds.), *Tradition and Re-interpretation
in Jewish and Early Christian Literature* (FS J.C.H. Lebram; SPB 36; Leiden: Brill, 1986),
114-120. Beside the quotation in v. 14 the epistle shows acquaintance with *1 En.* 6-16 in vv. 6-
7 and, very probably, with *Assumptio Mosis* in v. 9. Unfortunately, this passage is lacking in the
fragmentary Latin version of this document, the only one known. See also chapter 4, sections 7
and 8 below.

[8] *Jude, 2 Peter*, p. 95.

[9] *Der Judasbrief*, p. 85.

from the Law and the Prophets respecting the Saviour and the Christian faith in general. Onesimus had also asked for exact information concerning the number and the order of the "old books" (τῶν παλαιῶν βιβλίων). In order to give an answer to these questions, Melito travelled to the East, "the place where these things were proclaimed and done." There he accurately ascertained the books of the Old Testament (ἀκριβῶς μαθὼν τὰ τῆς παλαιᾶς διαθήκης βιβλία)—which he duly lists.

This is the first time the question of the number and the order of the Jewish writing that are authoritative for Christians was raised explicitly. Interestingly, not only Eusebius in his introduction, but also Melito himself uses, beside the expression "the old books," also the term "the books of the Old Covenant/Testament." From this time onwards this is a current expression among Christians for the authoritative writings taken over from Israel.[10]

The problem of the text(s) of the "Old Testament" available to Christians during the first two or three centuries, and the question of how they cited them, need not be solved here. In general they used the Septuagint, or Hebraizing recensions of the Greek translation. Deviations from the text and the textual variants now found in critical editions of the various books of the Septuagint can be explained by the use of local traditions, quotation from memory, or the desire to bring the witness of the Scriptures in agreement with that concerning God's revelation in Jesus Christ. A striking example is Justin's reproach to the Jews in *Dial.* 71-73 (already referred to). According to him the Jews have omitted sayings by Ezra and Jeremiah, as well as the words "from the wood" after "The Lord reigns" in Ps. 95(96):10 (cf. also *1 Apol.* 41,1-4). Justin follows here a christianized text, probably in a collection of proof-texts.[11]

It is difficult to be certain about the number of Christian communities or authors that will have had a complete collection of "old books" at their disposal. In the second century there certainly existed

---

[10] Zie *PGL*, p. 348, s.v. διαθήκη sub 3 (cf. p. 268, s.v. ἐνδιάθηκος) and von Campenhausen, *Die Entstehung der christlichen Bibel*, pp. 305-311 (with references to Clement of Alexandria and Origen). On the expression ἐπὶ τῇ ἀναγνώσει τῆς παλαιᾶς διαθήκης in 2 Cor. 3,14 see (still) H. Windisch, *Der zweite Korintherbrief* (KEK; Göttingen: Vandenhoeck & Ruprecht, 1924; Neudruck 1970), p. 121.

[11] See, among others, O. Skarsaune, *The Proof from Prophecy. A Study in Justin Martyr's Proof-Text Tradition: Text-Type, Provenance, Theological Profile* (NovTSup 56; Leiden: Brill, 1987), pp. 35-42.

collections of quotations ("florilegia," "testimonia-books"). A number of scholars have assumed Christian use of similar anthologies also for the first century (already in the epistles of Paul).[12]

III. THE GNOSTICS AND MARCION

Harnack's well-known thesis that the Gnostics, in a process of acute Hellenization of Christianity, would have rejected the "Old Testament," has proved no longer tenable. Von Campenhausen is of the opinion that the Gnostics were indeed very much interested in ancient writings, including the Scriptures of Judaism and the traditions connected with them.[13] In a considerable number of Gnostic documents we find expositions of "Old Testament" texts, particularly also of the first chapters of Genesis. Of course these writings and traditions are used critically, and judged by the standards of the Gospel as understood by the specific Gnostic authors. Also "spiritual" standards (derived from Hellenistic philosophy) are applied, but in general the reliability and authority of the Jewish Scriptures are not questioned.

Birger Pearson has described the situation as follows:

> The Bible ("Old Testament") was part of the Christian heritage, as it was of the Gnostic heritage. But there was considerable variety in the way Gnostic Christians looked upon it. Three basic attitudes emerged: 1) open rejection of the Old Testament; 2) whole-hearted acceptance of it; and 3) an intermediate position according to which the biblical text was inspired by the lower Creator or lesser powers, but nevertheless contained "spiritual truth" to be ferreted out by means of a spiritual (allegorical) exegesis. Authorization for this procedure was found in revelation attributed to the Saviour and various of his apostles"[14].

Marcion was far more radical. For him the only authoritative writings were the "Euangelion" (a thoroughly redacted version of the Gospel of Luke) and the "Apostolikon" (the epistles of Paul, that is the Corpus Paulinum without the Pastorals, also cleansed of supposed inter-

---

[12] See recently M.C. Albl, *'And Scripture Cannot Be Broken'. The Form and Function of the Early Testimonia Collections* (NovTSup 96; Leiden: Brill, 1999).

[13] *Die Entstehung der christlichen Bibel*, pp. 88-108.

[14] "Use, Authority and Exegesis of Mikra in Gnostic Literature," *Mikra* (ed. Mulder and Sysling), 635-652; quotation on p. 652. See also his "Jewish Sources in Gnostic Literature," in M.E. Stone (ed.), *Jewish Writings of the Second Temple Period* (CRINT 2,2; Assen: Van Gorcum/Philadelphia, Fortress: 1984), 443-481.

polations). These contained the revelation of the One, true God who had made himself known through Jesus Christ. According to Harnack, Marcion played a central role in the formation of the canon of the "New Testament," but Metzger adds a significant qualification: "It was in opposition to Marcion's criticism that the Church first became fully conscious of its inheritance of apostolic writings." He quotes with approval a statement by R.M. Grant: "Marcion forced more orthodox Christians to examine their own presuppositions and to state more clearly what they already believed."[15]

Marcion also forced his "orthodox" opponents to examine their presuppositions in their use of the Jewish authoritative writings. In an interesting chapter "Marcion Revisited" John Barton has argued that Marcion took the Jewish Scriptures very seriously indeed.[16] "The old Scriptures were, in fact, a Jewish book through and through, but they were a wholly reliable and trustworthy Jewish book." These Scriptures did not speak, however, of the good God, the Father of Jesus Christ, but contained the revelation of a lower Creator-god. Opposed to all allegorical interpretation, Marcion could in no way connect the message of the Jewish Scriptures with that in his "Euangelion" and "Apostolikon."

> For Marcion's gospel is the good news that mankind has been freed from the thrall of the Old Testament god; and unless one knows this (proscribed!) text, and also knows why it is wrong, one cannot properly welcome the gospel message.

In order to make this clear, and also to demonstrate the many contradictions and incongruities in the Scriptures of the Jews, Marcion wrote his *Antitheses*, for his followers a book of great importance and authority. This book, according to Barton, "provided the essential content of Marcionite faith by way of an interpretation of Scripture."

Over against Marcion and the Marcionites (some of them, like Apelles, even more radical than their master), "orthodox" Christians held on to the conviction that the One, true God can be found in both the ancient books of the Jews and in the Gospel(s) together with Epistles. This made further reflection on the hermeneutics of the "Old Testament" indispensable. To quote Barton again:

---

[15] *The Canon of the New Testament*, pp. 91-99; quotation on p. 99.

[16] *The Spirit and the Letter*, pp. 35-62; the following quotations are found on pp. 43, 51 and 65 respectively.

> In insisting on the identity of God the creator and God the redeemer, orthodox Christians found themselves necessarily committed to the Old Testament, which they restored to a more central role.

Below, in chapter 11, in an analysis of the *Greek Life of Adam and Eve*, I hope to demonstrate that this document, essentially a story about the life, death and departure of Adam and Eve, wants to show that the God who speaks and acts in Genesis 3 is the One, true God who is merciful to Adam and Eve and to all human beings who obey his commandments. As such it had its place in the inner-Christian discussion about the true interpretation of Genesis.

IV. JUSTIN MARTYR

According to von Campenhausen, Justin is the first Christian theologian with something like a "doctrine of Holy Scripture." As a man of authority in the church of Rome, around the middle of the second century, he is active on various fronts. He writes his first and his second *Apology* to make Christianity acceptable for Hellenistic philosophers and to secure a place for it within the structures of the Roman empire. He has to defend Christian ideas, as von Campenhausen puts it, "vor dem Richterstuhl der platonischen Überzeugung."[17] At the same time he does not shun the debate with the Gnostics and Marcion, and in this debate he employs arguments used of old in the discussions between Christians and Jews. Justin's most extensive work is his *Dialogue with Trypho*. As C.H. Cosgrove has argued, this book is not an apology directed against the Jews, even less a missionary treatise, but rather an inner-Christian attempt to clarify the position of the church in God's history of salvation, over against groups of judaizers as well as over against Marcion and the Marcionites.

> Indeed the main themes of the *Dialogue* are among the most serious faced by the church of the second century; the problem of the Mosaic law, that of the Old Testament as canon, and especially the question of Christian self-definition over against Judaism and yet in terms of the Old Testament.[18]

---

[17] *Die Entstehung der christlichen Bibel*, pp. 106-122; quotation on p. 115.

[18] C.H. Cosgrove, "Justin Martyr and the Emerging Christian Canon. Observations on the Purpose and Destination of the Dialogue with Trypho," *VC* 36 (1982), 209-232; quotation on p.

Reflecting on this problem Justin develops a view of the Bible at the centre of which is the question of the authority of the Scriptures taken over from the Jews.[19]

It is worthwhile highlighting a number of points from von Campenhausen's clear exposition of Justin's ideas concerning Scripture. Justin is firmly convinced that it is God himself who speaks in these writings, through his Logos or through the Spirit of prophecy. Their inspired status gives us the certainty that it is God whom we meet in every word contained in them. There are, therefore, no contradictions in the Scriptures, although Justin often has to go all out in order to solve problems with the help of allegorical and typological interpretation. In order to demonstrate the continuity in God's words ands actions he repeatedly uses the well-known scheme of prediction and fulfilment. Of this von Campenhausen says:

> Er stammt aus der älteren christlichen Tradition, dient jetzt aber in charakteristisch veränderter Zielsetzung weniger dazu, den Christusglauben vor der Schrift auszuweisen, als vielmehr umgekehrt, die bedrohte Autorität der Schrift aufs Neue zu begrunden."[20]

At the same time Justin is convinced that all truth found in the works of prominent Greek philosophers comes from God as well. He uses the argument found in the works of Hellenistic-Jewish apologists that those philosophers are dependent on the Bible. Plato derived his wisdom from Moses who, after all, lived many centuries earlier.[21] Chris-

218. Cosgrove's view is shared by Barton, see *The Spirit and the Letter*, pp. 56-57. Strikingly Cosgrove considers the possibility that the first Apology also served an inner-Christian purpose; in the end, however, he remarks: "… the problem of persecution faced by the second-century church demands that a real external dialogue be regarded as the primary focus of this work" (n. 41). Yet earlier, in n. 7, he says: "There were no doubt internal needs for self-definition and self-justification vis-à-vis the Hellenistic world as well." For a discussion of various views on the *Dialogue* see R.S. MacLennan, *Early Christian Texts on Jews and Judaism* (Brown Judaic Studies; Atlanta: Scholars, 1990), pp. 49-88 and S.G.J. Sanchez, *Justin Apologiste Chrétien. Travaux sur le Dialogue avec Tryphon de Justin Martyr* (CRB 50; Paris: Gabalda, 2000). MacLennan opts for "an apologetic essay written to Christians" (p. 84); Sanchez emphasizes: "Justin a décidé d'écrire un *dialogue* entre un Juif et un chrétien et non un *adversus Judaeos*" (p. 253).

[19] Justin does not develop a theory concerning the "New Testament"; see Cosgrove, "Justin Martyr," pp. 221-224, and, in a broader perspective, Barton, *The Spirit and the Letter*, pp. 79-91.

[20] *Die Entstehung der christlichen Bibel*, p.109.

[21] *Die Entstehung der christlichen Bibel*, p. 109, n. 162. Von Campenhausen mentions also Justin's doctrine of the λόγος σπερματικός. See also John G. Gager, *Moses in Greco-Roman Paganism* (SBLMS 16; Nashville-New York: Abingdon, 1972), pp. 76-79. As defenders of

tians have a strong case in their debates with Jews as well as gentiles. It may seem that they are mere newcomers in the history of humanity, but they are the ones to whom God has granted the right understanding of all he has revealed all through the ages. Justin takes great pains to prove this with a variety of arguments. At a certain moment in his discussion with Trypho he points to the testimonies of David, Isaiah, Zechariah and Moses, and asks:

> Do you acknowledge those, Trypho? They are laid down in your Scriptures, or rather in our Scriptures, not yours. For we believe in them, but you read them without understanding their meaning" (*Dial.* 29,2).[22]

In his controversy with the Gnostics and Marcion Justin wants to demonstrate that the entire Law comes from God, and that it contains nothing that is unworthy of him. There is also no reason to accuse him of inconsistency, arbitrariness or ignorance *(Dial.* 23,1-2; 30,1; 92,5).[23] Insofar as commandments show people how to lead a pious and righteous life, they are universally valid. Also commandments that can be explained as references to the mystery of Christ present no problem. But how are the many rules of the "ceremonial law" (to use a later term) to be reconciled with God's eternal will? Justin declares that these rules were intended for the Jews only, because of their σκληροκαρδία. They were additionally given to keep this people on the right track and to bring it to repentance. It is important to note how Justin stresses that a great number of God's commandments were meant for a particular period in history only.[24] He divides the history of salvation into three periods. The time of the righteous

---

Moses' priority vis-à-vis the Greeks, Gager mentions Aristobulus, Eupolemus, Artapanus, Philo and Josephus, and among Christians Justin, Tatian, Clement of Alexandria, Origen and Eusebius.

[22] R.L. Wilken, *The Christians as the Romans (and Greeks) Saw Them* in E.P. Sanders (ed.), *Jewish and Christian Self-Definition*, vol. 1 (London: SCM, 1980), 100-125, has pointed out that the Christians in their discussions with gentiles had to prove that the Jewish interpretation of the "Old Testament" was wrong. "Attempts to legitimate Christian religious claims had to deal not only with the philosophical objections of pagans, but with scriptural and historical arguments, offered by pagans (and Jews), but supported by the existence of a rival tradition of interpretation" (p. 123).

[23] See *Die Entstehung der christlichen Bibel*, 112-116 and, in more detail, also T. Stylianopoulos, *Justin Martyr and the Mosaic Law* (SBLDS 20; Missoula MT: Scholars, 1975).

[24] See especially Stylianopoulos, "Justin's Historical Interpretation of the Law," in *Justin Martyr and the Mosaic Law*, pp. 153-163; cf. pp. 51-67.

before Moses, the interim period of the extra regulations in the Mosaic law intended for Israel in particular, and the new dispensation inaugurated by Jesus Christ.[25]

Below, in chapter 6, section 3.3 and chapter 9, section 2.2.2, I shall argue that Justin's insistence on the fact that the faithful in the period before Moses (sometimes called "patriarchs") obeyed God without detailed regulations, together with his conviction that Jesus Christ has been given as an "eternal and definitive law" (*Dial.* 11,2) helps us to understand how the *Testaments of the Twelve Patriarchs* were understood by Christians in the latter part of the second century, and later. The *Testaments* bring to the fore the essential and abiding elements in God's commandments, and they announce that all who obey those, in Israel and among the gentiles, will have a share in God's kingdom after the coming of Christ.

V. READING THE "PSEUDEPIGRAPHA/APOCRYPHA" OF THE OLD TESTAMENT IN A CHRISTIAN CONTEXT

It makes sense, then, to study the "pseudepigrapha/apocrypha of the Old Testament" as part of the literature of early Christianity. Because, as we have seen in chapter 1, the great majority of these writings have come down to us as they were transmitted by Christians, it is even our first task to study them in this perspective. The next, important, problem is to determine whether a particular writing already existed in some form in Jewish circles before it was taken over (and perhaps interpolated or redacted) by Christians, or whether Christian composition, with or without the use of Jewish written or oral traditions, is the more likely option. Even in those cases where a Jewish document or Jewish material was adopted and handed down basically *without* Christian alterations, this was done in the firm belief that it belonged to the Christian heritage. The authoritative writings of Judaism have, from the beginning, been authoritative for the Jesus-movement—though, of course, the belief in Jesus' special

---

[25] "Der Gegensatz zum alten Gesetz ist für Justin nicht durch das Evangelium und den Glauben, sondern durch das vollkommene Gesetz bestimmt, das die Patriarchen gekannt und die Propheten verkündigt haben und das durch Jesus, den neuen Gesetzgeber, endlich vollkommen und mit erlösender Kraft verkörpert ist"—so von Campenhausen, *Die Entstehung der christlichen Bibel*, p. 117.

relationship to God, and in the meaning of his death and resurrection, provided it with a new hermeneutical key in interpreting them. An important facet of the history of Christianity in the first three centuries is the ongoing struggle for the right assessment of the value of these writings and their correct interpretation. Eventually they were incorporated into the Christian Bible as the "Old Testament." The interest in writings concerned with important biblical figures should be seen against this background.

To outsiders early Christianity, in all its variety, may have looked like a new movement. In the conception of those who accepted the Old Testament as part of the Bible, Christians were the ones who understood the right meaning of God's words and actions in world history, from Adam through Moses, the prophets and Jesus until the present day. From this perspective there was basic continuity between new and old. The problem was to demonstrate this in discussions with pagans (Hellenistic philosophers, for instance) and Jews; for this purpose Christians interpreted the writings of the past typologically and allegorically, and showed how words and events in the past had received their fulfilment in the new dispensation in which they were now privileged to live. Often, I think, this basic continuity was assumed rather than demonstrated; Old Testament passages were handed down, studied and meditated on for their own sake, as evidence of God's concern for humankind, all through the ages. This accounts for the difficulties faced by modern interpreters when they want to distinguish between (earlier) Jewish and (later) Christian elements in the "pseudepigrapha." Relatively little is exclusively Christian, and certainly we are not allowed to assume that all that is not overtly Christian is of Jewish origin.

CHAPTER THREE

DEVELOPING A DIFFERENT APPROACH

I. The Conventional Point of View

The approach to the "pseudepigrapha of the Old Testament" advocated in the present volume is still by no means common among scholars, nor (consequently) among those who are dependent on the work of specialists in the field. English-speaking persons, as well as the many who have English as their second language, will turn to the two volumes of Charlesworth's *The Old Testament Pseudepigrapha*, by far the richest collection of translations in English, with introductions and notes that are easily accessible. As we have seen in chapter 1, Charlesworth, though aware of the complexity of the transmission of the various writings and the problems of interpretation, continues the tradition started by E. Kautzsch and R.H. Charles in the beginning of the twentieth century. For Charlesworth and many others the chief importance of the so-called pseudepigrapha of the Old Testament lies in the fact that they help us to understand the great variety within Judaism around the beginning of the common era, the period of Jesus and the first Christians.

Those whose mother tongue or second language is German will consult the collection of documents (Apocrypha/Deuterocanonical Writings and Pseudepigrapha) in the monograph series "Jüdische Schriften aus hellenistisch-römischer Zeit". The title of the series, though no doubt appropriate in the case of a number of writings (such as the Apocrypha) presupposes that in the case of *all* of them a Jewish form of the document dating from the Hellenistic-Roman period can be reconstructed, and that their real importance lies in the fact that they can be used as sources for our knowledge of Judaism in the period concerned.

As the series was nearing completion the present editors, Hermann Lichtenberger and Gerbern S. Oegema have started a series of "Supplementa" with a number of comprehensive, up to date introductions to all the writings published in the five sections of the collection (see above, chapter 1), as well as a bibliographical volume and a comprehensive index. Three of those volumes have appeared so far, a Bibliography by A. Lehnardt, an Introduction to the first section by U. Mitmann-Richert and one to section 5 by G.S. Oegema.[1] A General Preface by Lichtenberger and Oegema formulates a program quite in line with the idea of the series: "Die Einführung bietet eine umfassende Einleitung in das jüdische außerqumranische und nichtrabbinische Schrifttum (mit Ausnahme von Philo und Josephus)" (vol. 1, p. IX).

U. Mittmann-Richert's volume deals with 3 Ezra, 1-3 Maccabees, Judith, the Additions to Esther and Daniel, the *Paralipomena Ieremiou, Vitae Prophetarum* and the *Fragments of Jewish-Hellenistic Historians*. In her opinion, all these writings, however different they may be, testify to the (variegated) spiritual resistance, in Palestine and the Diaspora, against the attacks on Jewish religion by Antiochus and enemies like him. They show an inner unity, centring around an orientation on the Jerusalem temple and obedience to the Law. But what about the *Vitae Prophetarum* and the *Paralipomena*, to be dated in the Roman period or perhaps even in the second century CE (*Paralipomena*)? "Auch diese Werke sind Dokumente der Glaubenserschütterung durch das gegen die Juden und ihren Tempel aufgebotene heidnische Machtarsenal und der in der nationalen Krise geübten Glaubensbewährung." The main difference between these documents and the other ones is that the danger of the destruction of the Jerusalem temple has now become a reality.[2] Particularly with regard to these two writings critical questions may be asked, directly related to their transmission by Christians. These will be discussed in the next chapter.

II. ANOTHER APPROACH

Critical objections against the traditional study of the "pseudepigrapha of the Old Testament" in the twentieth century have been voiced by several people. A review of those and suggestions for an

---

[1] A. Lehnardt, *Bibliographie zu den jüdischen Schriften aus hellenistisch-römischer Zeit* (JSHRZ 6,2; Gütersloh: Gütersloher Verlagshaus, 1999); U. Mittmann-Richert, *Einführung zu den historischen und legendarischen Erzählungen* (JSHRZ 6,1.1, 2000); G.S. Oegema, *Apokalypsen* (JSHRZ 6,1.5, 2001).

[2] See Mittmann-Richert, *Einführung*, 1-3 (quotation from p. 3).

alternative approach were given in the lectures and discussions during a meeting of the Seminar on "The Early Jewish Writings and the New Testament" during the SNTS conference at Tel Aviv in August 2000, which was devoted to the subject "Christianization of ancient Jewish writings." A report of that meeting can be found in the *Journal for the Study of Judaism* 32,4 (2001).[3] To two essays on special subjects, one by M.A. Knibb on *1 Enoch* and one by D.C. Harlow on *3 Baruch* we will return in the next chapter;[4] here it should be noted that the introductory sections of these articles provide useful general information. R.A. Kraft's "Setting the Stage and Framing some Central Questions" presents a particularly useful survey of the *status quaestionis* and some trenchant remarks about the possibilities of making real progress in this field.[5] His main thesis is formulated as follows:

> With most of the materials of interest for this study—"Jewish sources"—our main avenue of discovery starts in Christian contexts. That is, with rare exceptions provided mainly by discovery of ancient manuscripts (most notably the Dead Sea Scrolls) and by continuous Jewish transmission, our knowledge of "Jewish sources" relating to the period of Christian origins comes through Christian interests and transmission. While this fact is widely recognized, it is not always taken seriously in the study of those materials. For example, while we are often

---

[3] See the introduction by J.W. van Henten and B. Schaller, "Christianization of Ancient Jewish Writings," *JSJ* 32 (2001), 369-370.

[4] M.A. Knibb, "Christian Adoption and Transmission of Jewish Pseudepigrapha: The Case of *1 Enoch*," and D.C. Harlow, "The Christianization of Early Jewish Pseudepigrapha: The Case of *3 Baruch*" in *JSJ* 32 (2001), 396-415 and 416-444 respectively.

[5] See *JSJ* 32 (2001), 371-395. Here I may also mention the essays on the reception and editing of Jewish material in early Christianity (with much attention for the continuity in the process) collected in J.C. VanderKam and W. Adler (eds.), *The Jewish Apocalyptic Heritage* (CRINT 3, 4; Assen:Van Gorcum/Minneapolis: Fortress, 1996). S.G. Wilson, in his *Related Strangers: Jews and Christians 70-170 CE* (Minneapolis: Fortress, 1995), 94-109, analyzes what he calls "Christian adaptations of Jewish apocrypha" with a view to obtaining a fuller picture of Jewish-Christian relations in the years immediately after 70 and in the second century. A positive aspect of his approach is his insistence that the resulting texts should be read as "Christian products in a Christian context" (p. 95). At the same time, however, he approaches them as texts of Jewish origin adapted by Christians, following J.H. Charlesworth's essay "Christian and Jewish Self-Definition in Light of the Christian Additions to the Apocryphal Writings," in E.P. Sanders, A.I. Baumgarten and A. Mendelson (eds.), *Jewish and Christian Self-Definition, vol 2. Aspects of Judaism in the Graeco-Roman Period* (London: SCM, 1981), 27-55.

warned—quite appropriately—that the rabbinic Jewish sources are relatively "late" in their preserved forms and therefore can only be used
with great care and caution in the study of Christian origins, the same
sort of methodological circumspection seldom is voiced with regard to
the use of the "pseudepigrapha" and related materials, which are often
also relatively "late" as we find them in their preserved forms, and
have come to us through clearly Christian hands and interests. ...

This does not mean that it is impossible to use such materials to
"get back" to the earlier period that may be the focus of our interest,
any more than the rabbinic sources should be considered irrelevant or
impervious for such purposes. What it does mean is that similar care is
necessary in determining how to use these materials responsibly. They
are, first of all, "Christian" materials, and recognition of that fact is a
necessary step in using them appropriately in the quest to throw light
on early Judaism. I call this the "default" position—sources transmitted by way of Christian communities are "Christian" whatever else
they may also prove to be. (p. 372)

This point of view agrees fully with the approach advocated in the
present volume. It is endorsed by a statement by Michael E. Stone
made in an article of 1986 (already briefly referred to in Chapter 1):

Documents for which there is no independent early corroboration or
other compelling evidence can no longer just be used, with no more
ado, as sources for Judaism of the Second Temple period. Indeed,
some of them are undoubtedly just that; others, I am sure, are rework-
ings of Jewish documents or traditions from that period and contain
material of extraordinary importance for the study of Judaism and
Christian origins. The position here being maintained is not nihilistic;
it is a call for greater methodological sophistication, while making no
presuppositions as to the results thus obtained. Indeed, it is reasonable
to think that the antiquity of some works will be confirmed, while others will be shown to incorporate Jewish sources or traditions. Nonethe-
less, before the pseudepigrapha and similar writings are used as evidence for that more ancient period, they must be examined in the
Christian context in which they were transmitted and utilized.[6]

Kraft's essay of 2001 is the latest in a series of articles written over a
period of more than twenty-five years. It started with a programmatic
article "The Multiform Jewish Heritage of Early Christianity" of

---

[6] M.E. Stone, "Categorization and Classification of the Apocrypha and Pseudepigrapha,"
Abr-Nahrain 24 (1986), 167-77 (quotation on pp. 172-73).

1975,[7] and his contribution "Reassessing the Recensional Problem in Testament of Abraham" to the volume *Studies in the Testament of Abraham* edited by G.W.E. Nickelsburg (1976).[8]

In these articles Kraft emphasized first of all that we should use the terms "Jewish" and "Christian" as neutrally as possible, taking into account the great variety in Judaism and Christianity during the first centuries of the common era. We should also consider the possibility that for certain persons the distinction between "Christian" and "Jewish" was not very relevant—at least in certain respects. Although the so-called pseudepigrapha of the Old Testament were transmitted as literature for Christians, characteristically Christian interests and ideas were not always in evidence.

> Apparently the orientation of the various Christian users was flexible enough to allow some sort of positive status to these materials without causing serious conflict with "Christian" ideas.[9]

In many cases it is difficult to decide whether transmission entailed copying, redaction, interpolation or even composition. These processes may not even be mutually exclusive. Certainly we must never assume that "Christian" interest always betrayed itself by leaving "Christian" traces. "It should not be assumed that a document composed or compiled by a Christian will necessarily contain characteristically 'Christian' tenets."[10] The evidently Christian elements are usually found in "messianic" texts.

> Some Christians seem to have felt it important to have 'predictive' texts (especially apocalyptic) in which aspects of the career and func-

---

[7] It appeared in *Christianity, Judaism and other Greco-Roman Cults* (FS Morton Smith, ed. J. Neusner; Leiden: Brill, 1975), vol. 3, 174-199.

[8] SBLSCS 6; Missoula MT: Scholars Press, 1976, 121-137. See also Kraft's study on a related problem "Christian Transmission of Greek Jewish Scriptures: A Methodological Probe," in A. Benoît (ed.), *Paganisme, Judaïsme, Christianisme. Mélanges offerts à Marcel Simon* (Paris: Éd. E. de Boccard, 1978), 207-226. For the following survey of Kraft's approach, compare my "The So-called Pseudepigrapha of the Old Testament and Early Christianity," in P. Borgen and S. Giversen (eds.), *The New Testament and Hellenistic Judaism* (Aarhus: Aarhus University Press, 1995. Reprint Peabody, Mass.: Hendrickson, 1997), 59-71, especially 60-62.

[9] "Multiform Heritage," 179-180.

[10] "Recensional Problem," 135.

tion of their messiah were somehow noted, even if only cryptically or in passing.[11]

In many instances, however, Jewish and Christian ideas ran parallel. Homiletic and liturgical texts (of various types, especially prayers) could be used in Jewish and Christian communities; the same applies to paraenetic material. Moreover,

> many Christians still looked for a future eschatological/apocalyptic consummation, and thus helped maintain a continuity with similar pre- and non-Christian Jewish interests.[12]

Kraft also reminds us that the Greek form of the Jewish Bible was transmitted by Christians without Christian adaptations worth mentioning, at least as far as the earliest form of text is concerned. Also many pseudepigrapha were transmitted over a considerable period of time without noticeable adaptation (see e.g. the *Ethiopic Enoch* cycle). Other writings were redacted only superficially or interpolated in only a few places. We also find cases of thorough reworking of Jewish material and incorporation into Christian compilations without loss of a "Jewish" flavour. As examples are mentioned the cycle on Adam and Eve, transmitted in various forms in different Christian circles, the *Ascension of Isaiah*, and the *Sibylline Oracles*. In connection with this last collection Kraft says:

> The overtly Christian portions are themselves quite diverse in content and origin, and the total work provides an excellent example of how some types of literature were not "authored" in any normal sense of the word, but *evolved* in stages over the years.[13]

Finally, we should remember that a considerable number of fragments from Hellenistic-Jewish authors have only come down to us because Eusebius of Caesarea copied them for his *Praeparatio Evangelica*, composed in the beginning of the fourth century. Of course, shorter quotations and allusions are also found in the works of other Christian authors.

Repeatedly Kraft has demonstrated the necessity of systematically studying "Jewish" literature transmitted through Christian channels as part of the "Christian" heritage. There is yet another aspect of this

---

[11] "Multiform Heritage," 180.

[12] "Recensional Problem," 136

[13] "Multiform Heritage," 184-185.

complex matter requiring attention: In Christian circles this material circulated in a Greek form—often lost, and then only recoverable through ancient versions dependent on it—but it seems likely that in a number of cases it existed earlier in Hebrew or Aramaic.[14] But who translated it, and when and where? All along there must have been intensive contacts between Hebrew or Aramaic and Greek speaking Jews, but how the writings of interest to us were translated, we do not know. Moreover, it is extremely difficult to distinguish between translation Greek and the "biblical" Greek that Christians considered suitable for this type of literature.[15] In addition, the fact that certain sections incorporated in a writing may indeed go back to Semitic sources, whilst the rest may have been composed in a language inspired by the Greek Bible, is a source of further complication.

In 1994 Kraft returned to the subject in a contribution "The Pseudepigrapha in Christianity" to the volume *Tracing the Threads. Studies in the Vitality of Jewish Pseudepigrapha* edited by J.C. Reeves.[16] In this informative essay we again find a number of observations which would deserve further elaboration. For our purpose it is important that Kraft pays special attention to the transmission of the pseudepigrapha in the period before the tenth century. He observes that we know very little about the reception of these writings in "orthodox" and "heterodox" circles and about the milieux in which they were transmitted (apocalyptic movements? monasteries?). He remarks that we have only a few Greek manuscripts of the pseudepigrapha older than the ninth century. It seems that only in the later Byzantine period did scribes start to copy pseudepigraphical material on a larger scale. There are some, in themselves important, earlier sources (in particular in Coptic, Syriac and Latin), but Armenian, Ethiopic and Old Slavic manuscripts are, again, later. For each individual document the situation is different.

Following the way back to the earliest form of a writing remains a difficult task. One thing, however, Kraft wishes to stress:

> From my perspective, "the *Christianity* of the 'Pseudepigrapha" is not the hidden ingredient that needs to be hunted out and exposed in con-

---

[14] "Multiform Heritage," 194-196.

[15] "Recensional Problem," 127-135.

[16] SBLEJL 6; Atlanta: Scholars, 1994, 55-86. The article goes back, however, to a lecture held in 1976.

trast to a supposed native *Jewish* pre-Christian setting. On the contrary, when the evidence is clear that only Christians preserved the material, the Christianity of it is the given, it is the setting, it is the starting point for delving more deeply into this literature to determine what, if anything, may be safely identified as originally Jewish.[17]

With this last quotation we have come full circle. Also many other points listed above return in Kraft's most recent assessment of the situation. So he stresses again that Christians have treated "Jewish" materials in many different ways: they have copied or excerpted them faithfully, but also sometimes added interpolations; sometimes they have revised and redacted them thoroughly; they have even composed new documents on the basis of material provided by the Bible.

> If we really believe that Christians appropriated their selection of Jewish scriptures and saw themselves as legitimate owners and protectors—as standing and participating in the tradition—why should it be difficult to believe that Christians could produce "Jewish" sounding supporting materials?[18]

We should also take into consideration that the documents which interest us display a great variety of literary genres. We find, for instance, apocalyptic writings next to hymns and prayers, commentaries beside hagiographic and homiletic writings, historical surveys beside ethical treatises. One can well imagine that these texts functioned differently and were, therefore, transmitted differently.

All along we should take the great complexity of the transmission process very seriously. Most of these texts have been copied and translated for over a thousand years, and it is particularly difficult to reconstruct the initial stages of transmission. What did scribes and translators, living and working in very different situations, contribute to possible transformations of the text? In Chapter 6 the present author will sketch in some detail the situation with regard to the textual witnesses of the *Testaments of the Twelve Patriarchs*, and in Chapter 11 the many differences beween the Greek, Armenian/Georgian, Latin and Slavonic versions (and even those between the various groups of Latin witnesses) of the *Life of Adam and Eve* will be mentioned briefly.

---

[17] "The Pseudepigrapha in Christianity," 75.
[18] "Setting the Stage," 375.

Kraft repeatedly reminds us of the difficulty in determining what "must" be "Jewish" and what is "clearly" "Christian". Starting from the "default" position we may discover the use of older traditional material to support non-Jewish Christian interests and attitudes. Kraft, however, rightly remarks:

> One of the dangers here is the circularity of argument if it is suggested that something would have been "impossible" in pre- or non-Christian Judaism, or for that matter, "impossible" as a Christian claim (even when found in manuscripts transmitted by Christians)![19]

I may add: only where we are able to compare the use of traditional material in a particular writing with the use of the same, or similar, material in indubitably Jewish sources, can solid conclusions about the aim and provenance of our document be drawn. I demonstrate this in Chapter 8 where I compare the *Testament of Levi* in the *Testaments of the Twelve Patriarchs* and the Aramaic Levi Document, fragments of which are known from Qumran and elsewhere, and show that the *Testaments* convey a clear christological message. In Chapter 11 I show that the matter is considerably more complicated in the case of the Greek *Life of Adam and Eve* with a paraenesis that is neither overtly Christian nor clearly Jewish. Given the complex nature of this work, which may well incorporate many older traditions, individual parallels in other Jewish or Christian sources do not help us to determine its provenance. It can be argued that the *Life of Adam and Eve*, at least in its oldest form (represented by the Greek version) aims to emphasize God's mercy for Adam and Eve, and that its message was particularly important in the period around 200 CE, when Christianity wrangled about the correct interpretation of Genesis 3. It makes sense, therefore, to regard the *Life of Adam and Eve* as a Christian writing of that period. Theoretically, however, it could also have been meaningful in a different, possibly earlier, Jewish context.

Here again, Kraft puts a difficult methodological question. Speaking about the collection of writings called *1 Enoch* he notes that the *Parables* section is only known in Ethiopic, translated and transmitted by Christians. He writes:

---

[19] "Setting the Stage." 392.

there is no good reason not to consider that section as also Jewish in origin, but the evidence is not as decisive. And the danger of circularity in argumentation begins to become a factor. I can create a believable non-Christian Jewish context that could have produced this material, but must I do so? Should I do so?[20]

This question is an appropriate one, also in other instances.

The value of Kraft's expositions lies in the questions he poses and in his insistence that there are no easy answers and certainly no uniform solutions—as he illustrates by referring to many examples. Chapters 5 to 13 of the present volume will concentrate in detail on the problems posed by the *Testaments of the Twelve Patriarchs* and the *Life of Adam and Eve*. In the next chapter, however, I shall first discuss briefly a number of other writings, in order to illustrate the great variety of situations we encounter when we take the Christian transmission of the "pseudepigrapha of the Old Testament" seriously.

---

[20] "Setting the Stage," 387.

CHAPTER FOUR

THE CHRISTIAN TRANSMISSION OF PSEUDEPIGRAPHA.
SOME CASES

The study of the pseudepigrapha is beset with many difficulties, and each individual case is different. In view of the often complex situation with regard to the primary sources and the different skills required to analyze them properly, most scholars can only claim to have specialized knowledge of a limited number of documents. On the following pages I shall make use of the work of others and begin with a survey of recent work on the writings discussed. Of course, other books could have been added to the selection, and in every single case treated below problems could have been discussed in more detail. I hope, however, that my analysis of a number of cases illustrates sufficiently the issues involved in pseudepigrapha research that takes seriously that we have received these writings in a form transmitted to us by Christians—who considered them important enough to hand them down from generation to generation.[1]

There are two main questions: First, what primary sources do we possess, and what can we know of the oldest recoverable text, lying at the basis of the available manuscripts? In almost every case we are faced with transmission by Christians, and consequently also the archetype in question has to be treated as Christian, even if it does not reveal any distinctively Christian features. This leads to the second question: is there evidence for the existence of an earlier stage, or earlier stages, of the document, perhaps even a Jewish stage dating around the beginning of the common era? It is at this point that many scholars are too naïve. Assuming that "pseudepigrapha of the Old Testament" must, at least at an early stage, have been Jewish, they apply literary critical techniques in an effort to discover interpolations or traces of redaction. If these cannot be found the writing is re-

---

[1] Indispensable repertories of basic data (and the scholarly evaluation of those) for all pseudepigrapha are J.-C. Haelewyck, *Clavis Apocryphorum Veteris Testamenti* (Corpus Christianorum; Turnhout: Brepols, 1998) and the two very detailed volumes by A.-M. Denis (with collaborators, edited by J.-C. Haelewyck), *Introduction à la littérature religieuse judéo-hellénistique* (Turnhout: Brepols, 2000).

garded as Jewish and dated early. If there are, the overtly Christian traces are removed and the remainder is dubbed Jewish. After all that has been said in the previous chapter, it is clear that such analysis starts at the wrong end—with a Jewish writing whose existence still has to be proven.

Even where, as in the case of the *Assumption of Moses*, the text as it has come down to us seems to be an originally Jewish text of the first century CE, transmitted by Christians without alterations, we do not know the exact wording and content of that writing at that time (see section 8). The same applies in the case of *1 Enoch* where parts of the material transmitted by Christian hands in Greek and Ethiopic have been transmitted independently in Aramaic by Jews. Here we clearly have an early Jewish text; yet it is very difficult to establish the form of text current in Jewish and early Christian circles in the centuries around the beginning of the common era (see section 7).

Another illustration of the complexity of the situations we encounter is provided by the discussion of *4-5-6 Ezra* (see section 3). I have noted that the oldest recoverable text of *2 Baruch* and *4 Ezra* is Jewish, and I have, without further argument, adopted a date around 100 CE. Here we hear the voices of Jews seeking answers to the perplexing questions raised by the destruction of the Jerusalem temple in 70 CE. Also the *Paralipomena Ieremiou* describes the destruction of city and temple, followed, however, by a return from Babylon. Yet the present text speaks about this return in such a way that we may ask where its author is still concerned with actual punishment and return, or rather with the gathering of God's beloved in the heavenly Jerusalem. In section 4 I argue that removal of the patently Christian final section of the document does not leave us with a Jewish original still concerned with the issues of 70, or of those leading up to the Bar Kochba revolt, as is commonly thought. If the *Paralipomena* ever existed in a Jewish form, reconstruction of it remains very difficult. A similar situation exists in the case of the *Greek Apocalypse of Baruch* in which Baruch mourns the destruction of Jerusalem, but is shown on a heavenly tour that other issues are of far greater importance (section 5).

I begin my survey with the *Ascension of Isaiah*, part of which has, until recently, been treated in collections of Old Testament pseudepigrapha, as the *Martyrdom of Isaiah*, but has now, in its entirety, found a place in the "Series Apocryphorum" of the *Corpus Christia-*

norum. Pseudepigrapha of the Old Testament have been transmitted as Christian apocrypha; that is how they have come down to us.

I. ASCENSION OF ISAIAH

The *Ascension of Isaiah* consists of two main parts. Chapters 6-11 form the "Vision of Isaiah," which describes a journey by Isaiah through the seven heavens. In the seventh heaven the prophet sees how the Most High tells "the Lord Christ who will be called Jesus" (10:7) to descend to earth. Isaiah witnesses his descent, his miraculous birth from Mary, his life, death and resurrection, and finally his ascension, worshiped by the angels of the various heavens, until he sits down at the right hand of the Great Glory. This vision is preceded, in chapters 1-5, by an account of Isaiah's martyrdom; this includes another vision of the prophet in 3:13-4:22. After a short introduction in 3:13, which shows acquaintance with chapters 6-11, the vision proper concerns the life and death of Christ who is called "the Beloved," his ascension, the mission of his disciples and the corruption of the church and its leaders afterwards, and, finally, the descent of Beliar as king of this world, followed by the Second Coming and final victory of the Lord.

There is no doubt that the *Ascension of Isaiah* is Christian in its present form. Yet collections of "pseudepigrapha of the Old Testament" include a "Martyrdom of Isaiah" among the Jewish pseudepigrapha. So we find "Das Martyrium des Propheten Jesaja" by G. Beer in the collection by E. Kautzsch[2] (in the section "Pseudepigraphische Legenden"), and "The Martyrdom of Isaiah" in the collection by R.H. Charles, from the hand of the chief editor himself (in the section "Sacred Legends").[3] With many other scholars Beer and Charles regarded the account of Isaiah's death as a martyr found in *Asc. Is.* 1:1-3:12; 5:1-16 as basically Jewish. More recently, E. Hammershaimb treated "Das Martyrium Jesajas" in the series "Jüdische Schriften aus

---

[2] *Die Apokryphen und Pseudepigraphen des Alten Testaments,* vol. 2 (Tübingen: Mohr, 1900), 119-127.

[3] R.H. Charles, *The Apocrypha and Pseudepigrapha of the Old Testament,* vol. 2 (Oxford: Clarendon, 1913), 155-162. This contribution goes back to R.H. Charles, *The Ascension of Isaiah* (London: A. and C. Black, 1900), a book that exercised a great influence on later scholarship.

hellenistisch-römischer Zeit"[4] and M.A. Knibb the "Martyrdom and
Ascension of Isaiah" in the *Old Testament Pseudepigrapha* edited by
J.H. Charlesworth.[5] The position chosen by Knibb is interesting.
With some hesitation because of the difficulties to remove the "Martyrdom" from the "Ascension," he assumes a substantial Jewish sub-
stratum of a martyr's tale, which existed before being incorporated
into the present document. It was composed in Palestine, almost certainly in Hebrew, and not later than the first century CE. This "Martyrdom" presents a reasonably coherent narrative but there are obvious signs of Christian editing in 1:2b-6a, 7, 13; 2:9; 5:1a, 15-16.
These passages stem from the person who wanted to link the different sections of the final document together. Knibb remains cautious,
and concludes:

> It should, however, be observed that it cannot simply be assumed that
> the material left after the excision of these passages constitutes the ori-
> ginal Jewish "Martyrdom of Isaiah." The possibility of Christian re-
> working of what appears to be Jewish material needs to be kept in
> mind.[6]

In recent years scholarship on the *Ascension of Isaiah* has taken a different turn, chiefly by concentrating on the final stage of the document.[7] 3:13-4:22 and chapters 6-11 are considered as different but related Christian prophecies, attributed pseudonymously to Isaiah.
They are thought to have originated in Jewish-Christian circles in
Syria (Antioch), in conflict with church leaders, and aware of the
hostility of the Roman authorities towards the Christian movement.
Both visions are connected and framed by the story of Isaiah's martyrdom, centering around the struggle between true and false prophe-

---

[4] This contribution is the first in the second section called "Unterweisung in erzählender
Form" (JSHRZ 2,1; Gütersloh: Gütersloher Verlag, 1973), 15-34.

[5] Vol. 2 (Garden City, New York: Doubleday, 1985), 143-176. It was followed by "The
Martyrdom of Isaiah" in M. de Jonge (ed.), *Outside the Old Testament* (Cambridge Commentaries on Writings of the Jewish and Christian World, vol. 4; Cambridge: C.U.P., 1985), 178-
192.

[6] "The Martyrdom of Isaiah," 180.

[7] See Jonathan Knight, *The Ascension of Isaiah* (Guides to Apocrypha and Pseudepigrapha;
Sheffield: Sheffield Academic Press, 1995) who refers *inter alia* to R.G. Hall, "*The Ascension
of Isaiah*: Community, Situation, Date and Place in Early Christianity," *JBL* 109 (1990), 289-
306 and publications by a number of Italian scholars. The publications and views of these
scholars are conveniently summed up by E. Norelli in his *Ascension du prophète Isaïe* (Apocryphes. Collection de poche de l'AELAC; Turnhout: Brepols, 1993).

cy. No doubt traditional material about the persecution of Isaiah and other prophets has been used, but we are unable to prove the existence of an earlier coherent Jewish "Martyrdom of Isaiah" later incorporated into the Christian document.[8]

The most recent edition of the *Ascension of Isaiah* (presenting critical texts of all available versions (Ethiopic, Greek, Coptic, Latin, Slavonic), and a full commentary can now be found in the volumes 7 and 8 of the "Series Apocryphorum" of the *Corpus Christianorum*.[9] It is interesting that this authoritative text edition with commentary forms part of this series. The moral to be drawn from this story of research is that this pseudepigraphon of the Old Testament should first of all be treated as a Christian writing.

II. Vitae Prophetarum

The *Lives of the Prophets* are known to us in Greek and in a number of ancient versions (Latin, Syriac, Armenian, Georgian, Ethiopic, Arabic, Slavonic and Hebrew). This writing was not included in the collections of Kautzsch and Charles; the first to translate it was P. Riessler, who was able use the edition by Th. Schermann (1907) which has not been surpassed so far.[10] The situation changed only in the 1980s. D.R.A. Hare was responsible for the translation, notes and introduction of the *Lives* in the *Old Testament Pseudepigrapha*.[11] A.M.

---

[8] E. Norelli, *Ascension du prophète Isaïe*, 73-74: "Il est vain et illusoire de faire remonter à un écrit juif et indépendant l'histoire du martyre d'Isaïe contenue dans la première partie de l'Ascension. En effet cette histoire est racontée d'une manière qui s'adapte parfaitement aux exigences polémiques actuelles des prophètes qui ont produit l'Ascension."

[9] P. Bettiolo, A. Giambelluca Kossova, C. Leonardi, E. Norelli, L. Perrone, *Ascensio Isaiae. Textus. Commentarius* (Turnhout: Brepols, 1995). E. Norelli, the author of the commentary, published the French translation in *Ascension du prophète Isaïe* and also, with different notes, in F. Bovon and P. Geoltrain (eds.), *Écrits apocryphes chrétiens*, vol. 1 (Bibliothèque de la Pléiade 442; Paris: Gallimard, 1997), 499-546.

[10] P. Riessler, *Altjüdisches Schrifftum ausserhalb der Bibel* (Heidelberg: Kerle Verlag/W. Rühlig, 1928), 871-880; 1321-1322. Th. Schermann, *Prophetarum Vitae Fabulosae* etc. (Leipzig: Teubner, 1907) and *Propheten und Apostellegenden nebst Jüngerkatalogen des Dorotheus und verwandter Texte* (TU 31,3; Leipzig: Heinrichs, 1907). In 1946 C.C. Torrey published *The Lives of the Prophets. Greek Text and Translation* (SBLMS 1; Philadelphia). A new edition (including the versions) in the "Series Apocryphorum" of the *Corpus Christianorum*, prepared by a team of scholars led by M. Petit and F. Dolbeau, has been announced in the *Bulletin de l'AELAC* 2 (1992), 10-13.

[11] Vol. 2, 379-399.

Schwemer wrote the volume in JSHRZ.[12] D. Satran published an interesting monograph *Biblical Prophets in Byzantine Palestine. Reassessing the Lives of the Prophets*,[13] in which he raises a number of fundamental questions which also occupy us in the present chapter.

The Greek version exists in seven recensions; it cannot be proved that it goes back to a Hebrew or Aramaic original. As their basic text all modern scholars use the oldest textform, the first anonymous recension transmitted in a seventh century addition to the Codex Marchalianus, Vat. gr. 2125, a copy of the prophetical books of the Bible. Many scholars, including Hare and Schwemer, regard the *Lives* as a Jewish text, probably written in Palestine, and dating from the first century CE. Satran disagrees; he is of the opinion that the document is a Christian composition dating from the fourth or fifth century, which (as is evident from the number and diversity of the textual witnesses) became very popular in the Eastern and Western churches. For the purpose of our discussion in the present chapter it is helpful to compare Schwemer's arguments with those put forward by Satran.[14]

According to A.M. Schwemer the literary form of the *Lives* corresponds to that of short biographies in Graeco-Roman literature, for instance those in the *Metamorphoses* of Antoninus Liberalis (second century CE). She notes that only a few passages in the *Lives* are overtly Christian and explains these as later Christian interpolations, to be compared with later insertions in the other recensions of the Greek text. Comparing the legend of Isaiah's martyrdom in the *Lives* with that in the *Ascension of Isaiah,* and the account of the stoning of Jeremiah in the *Lives* with that in the *Paralipomena Ieremiou,* she finds that the *Lives* reflect an earlier stage of the tradition, and the other two writings contain clearly Christian expansions. Next, the geographical data of the *Lives* reflect the political and cultural situation in the Hasmonean and Roman period. Also the picture of the

---

[12] A.M. Schwemer, *Vitae Prophetarum* (JSHRZ 1,7, 1997), 539-658. This volume has very detailed notes; it goes back to the author's *Studien zu den frühjüdischen Vitae Prophetarum*, 2 vols (TSAJ 49-50; Tübingen: Mohr [Siebeck], 1995-1996) containing no less than 914 pages. Compare also U. Mittmann-Richert, *Einführung zu den historischen und legendarischen Erzählungen* (JSHRZ 6, 1,1), 156-171.

[13] SVTP 11, Leiden: Brill, 1995.

[14] Schwemer discusses Satran's work at several occasions in her books. Satran could use Schwemer's dissertation lying at the basis of the two volumes in the TSAJ-series, but states: "... the advanced state of my own manuscript no longer allowed a proper assimilation and assessment of her findings" (p. 19, n. 52).

prophets in the *Lives* corresponds with descriptions of Jewish prophets in the first century by Josephus and other sources. Of only six out of the twenty-two prophets is it reported that they died a violent death; this theme was clearly not very important for the author(s). Much attention, however, is paid to the places where the prophets were buried. Schwemer follows Jeremias in pointing to Jesus' words in Luke 11:47, par. Matt. 23:29, depicting his adversaries as building the tombs of the prophets killed by their ancestors.[15] This is taken as an indication for a first century date of the *Vitae Prophetarum*.

Like others D. Satran takes the text of the first anonymous recension as a starting point. for the simple reason that it provides the earliest form of text available. As we have just seen, it is found in a seventh century addition to the Codex Vat. gr. 2125. This fact, combined with the evidence of Syriac witnesses and the use of the *Vitae* by Isidore of Seville (ca. 560-636) in his *De ortu et obitu patrum*, points to the existence of an ample textual tradition (in Greek, Syriac and Latin) at the close of the sixth century. We know much about the dissemination of the *Lives* in various parts of the Christian world since then, but the history of the writing before that date is difficult to trace.[16] The text in the Codex Marchalianus presents "an amalgam of traditions, oral and written, from a broad expanse of time. Consequently we must attempt an assessment of the *Lives of the Prophets* as a complex document reflecting successive elements of authorial, editorial or scribal activity."[17]

Here, as in the case of other writings, working back from the existing Christian text presents many difficulties. Satran agrees with R.A. Kraft when the latter insists that it is wrong to assume that passages written by Christians will necessarily contain characteristically "Christian" content. It is also rash to assume that not overtly Christian passages must be regarded as Jewish.[18] As an example Satran

---

[15] See J. Jeremias, *Heiligengräber in Jesu Umwelt (Mt 23,29; Lk 11,47). Eine Untersuchung zur Volksreligion der Zeit Jesu* (Göttingen: Vandenhoeck & Ruprecht, 1958).

[16] *Biblical Prophets in Byzantine Palestine*, 9-16; 29-33. Compare A.M. Schwemer: "Man weiß wenig über die Tradierung der VP im 2. und 3. Jh. n.Chr.; deshalb ist ja der Spätansatz ihrer Entstehung, wie ihn Satran vertritt, so verlockend" (*Vitae Prophetarum*, 554). She adds, however: "Daß jüdische Pseudepigraphen erst nach Jahrhunderten wieder auftauchen, ist der Normal- und kein Sonderfall" (*ibid.*).

[17] *Biblical Prophets in Byzantine Palestine*, 68.

[18] See pp. 31-32, referring to some of the earlier articles of Kraft summarized in the previous chapter.

mentions the story of the penitence of King Nebuchadnezar in the *Vita* of Daniel, where Daniel prescribes an ascetic diet of "soaked pulse" for the king, comparable to that which a monk would take on as a penitential discipline during the Lenten period.[19] At first glance the terminology does not strike us as Christian, yet this particular diet forms a typical element in Byzantine piety. Here, as elsewhere in the *Lives*, we find a Christian element deeply embedded in the fabric of the text. Of course, Satran does not deny the possibility of the incorporation of early Jewish traditions in the *Lives*, but he insists that the mere incorporation of such material tells us very little of the essentially Jewish or Christian character of the document as a whole. A considerable part of the post-biblical heritage was common to Judaism and Christianity. In short: "the identification and isolation of Christian elements in the *Lives*... is neither a practical nor an efficacious manner of restoring an originally Jewish text."[20]

Late Roman and early Byzantine society emphasized the importance of holy men in a multifaceted role (intercessor, healer, miracle worker, spiritual guide). The *Lives of the Prophets*, close (in form and content) to early fifth century collections of the lives of the monks of Egypt and of Syria, form a link between contemporary holy men and biblical prophets. Hagiography and "sacred geography" go hand in hand—sparked off by the intense fascination with the land of Palestine and by pilgrimage to holy sites since the time of Constantine. The consistent attention to the burial sites of the prophets in the *Lives* should be explained in the context of the Christian "cult of the saints" between the third and sixth centuries, rather than in connection with popular piety centering on the graves of the prophets in first century Palestine, for which Satran can find little or no hard evidence.[21]

Satran did not succeed in convincing Schwemer, who emphasizes the difference between the *Lives* and Christian hagiographical writings from the period indicated by Satran. The *Lives* are short and simple, and they do not glorify the prophets; they are thoroughly Jewish, and the few Christian elements can be removed easily. They

---

[19] See Satran, *Biblical Prophets in Byzantine Palestine*, 89-91. The Greek term ὄσπρια used here is found in the Old Greek version of Dan. 1:12, 16.

[20] See pp. 75-76. Compare also my study "Christelijke elementen in de Vitae Prophetarum," *Nederlands Theologisch Tijdschrift* 16 (1961-1962), 161-178.

[21] See, in particular, Satran's chapter 4, "Context, Genre and Meaning"(pp. 97-117).

reflect the first century background of Jesus' words in Luke 11:47, par. Matt. 23:29. In this matter Schwemer sides with Jeremias. Jeremias's approach is carefully analyzed by P.W. van der Horst in his Franz-Delitzsch-Vorlesung of 2000.[22] In this essay he tries to prove that, contrary to what Satran asserts, there is a context in first century Judaism for basic elements in the Lives. Although there is no document of clearly Jewish origin that states unambiguously that Jews built tombs for biblical holy persons which were the object of pilgrimage, and where miracles could be expected and intercession could be asked for, there is a lot of circumstantial evidence pointing in that direction. The data about burial sites in the *Vitae Prophetarum* derive from Jewish traditions, possibly even of first century Palestinian provenance. And as to the writing as a whole: it could be a Christian document incorporating this Jewish material, but for Van der Horst its sustained attention to tribal affiliation and the fact that not a single tomb of New Testament personalities is mentioned—not even that of the prophet John the Baptist—point to a Jewish origin.

The discussion is likely to go on for some time, particularly about the historical alternative: a first century Jewish context or a fourth or fifth century Christian one. Yet literary questions should be settled before we can turn to the historical ones. Satran has rightly emphasized that we know the *Lives* in the form they received after a crucial Christian redactional stage in the fourth or fifth century. We should be careful in our attempts to reconstruct earlier stages, or to delimitate earlier embedded traditions, particularly because it is not at all easy to distinguish between what is undoubtedly Christian and what is certainly Jewish. To return to Van der Horst's argumentation for a moment: Why could not the attention to the tribal affiliation of the prophets be a matter of "antiquarian interest" on the part of a Christian author?[23] And why would Christians wanting to write about the lives of the prophets not restrict themselves to the heroes of the Jewish Scriptures, adopted as the Old Testament of Christianity? Assuming that the *Vitae Prophetarum* go back to an original Jewish docu-

---

[22] *Die Prophetengräber im antiken Judentum* (Münster: Institutum Judaicum Delitzschianum, 2001). An English version "The Tombs of the Prophets in Early Judaism" can be found in P.W. van der Horst, *Japheth in the Tents of Shem. Studies on Jewish Hellenism in Antiquity* (Leuven: Peeters, 2002), 119-138.

[23] So Satran, *Biblical Prophets in Byzantine Palestine*, 109.

ment of the first century CE, in any event remains a hazardous undertaking.

III. 4-5-6 EZRA

4 Ezra is a Jewish apocalypse commonly dated about 100 CE. Like the Syriac Apocalypse of Baruch (2 Baruch) to which it is in some way related, it uses the fall of Jerusalem in 587 BCE as a fictional setting. The brokenhearted and troubled "Baruch" and "Ezra" challenge God's justice and dispute with him or his angels, receive apocalyptic visions, and eventually become the agents of God's consolation of his people. Pondering the events of 70 CE the apparently Jewish author raises the questions "Why?" and "Whither?" The first question refers to the problem of theodicy, the second relates to the future of Israel as God's covenant people after the disaster.[24] Both writings have come down to us through the hands of Christians, but show no signs of significant "Christianization" during the transmission process. *2 Baruch* 1-77, i.e. the apocalypse proper, is extant in only one Syriac manuscript dating from the sixth or seventh century; the *Letter of Baruch* that follows in chapters 78-87 is known in more manuscripts.[25] *4 Ezra* has had a much wider circulation in early Christianity, particularly in the Western Church, where it became connected with *5* and *6 Ezra*. For our present purpose it is worthwhile drawing attention to some features of the Christian transmission of this writing.[26]

4 Ezra is generally thought to have been composed in Hebrew and to have been translated into Greek. We have, indeed three quotations in Greek Christian authors, and there are eight versions made from the Greek (Latin, Syriac, Ethiopic, Georgian, Arabic [two], Armenian and Coptic). All these versions can be assumed to have been made in

---

[24] Here I have taken over a few characterizations by G.W.E. Nickelsburg in his *Jewish Literature between the Bible and Mishnah* (Philadelphia: Fortress, 1981), 280-281.

[25] There is also an Arabic translation of the entire *2 Baruch* and a Greek fragment of 13:11-14:3.

[26] I follow here T.A. Bergren, "Christian Influence on the Transmission History of 4,5 and 6 Ezra," in J.C. VanderKam and W. Adler (eds.), *The Jewish Apocalyptic Heritage in Early Christianity* (CRINT 3,4; Assen: Van Gorcum/Minneapolis: Fortress,1996), 102-127, going back to his *Fifth Ezra: The Text, Origin and Early History* (SBLSCS 25; Atlanta: Scholars, 1990) and *Sixth Ezra: The Text and Origin* (New York/Oxford: Oxford U.P., 1998). For 4 Ezra see M.E. Stone, *Fourth Ezra* (Hermeneia; Minneapolis: Fortress, 1990).

a Christian milieu. A number of Christian phrases are found, such as *revelabitur filius meus Iesus* in the Latin version of 7:28, where the earliest recoverable text seems to read "for my Messiah will be revealed."[27] Comparison between the versions allows us to detect such modifications and to go back to a stage at which they were not present.

The transmission history of the Latin version is particularly complex. At some point, apparently in the Latin tradition, the text of *6 Ezra* came to be associated with that of *4 Ezra*; in certain manuscripts it was attached at the end of *4 Ezra*. Its full text is attested only in Latin, but this is a translation of the Greek.[28] Later also *5 Ezra*, known only in Latin,[29] became connected with *4 Ezra*, in some cases at the end of *4-6 Ezra*, at a later stage at the beginning, resulting in the sequence *5-4-6 Ezra* that occurs in many Latin manuscripts and in editions of the Vulgate; for the whole often the designation *2 Esdras* is used. It can be argued that *5 Ezra* became associated with *4-6 Ezra* around 450 CE; this means that the association of *4 Ezra* and *6 Ezra* may go back to 400 CE at the latest. To connect *4 Ezra* and *6 Ezra* the end of *4 Ezra* (14:49-50), reporting Ezra's assumption to heaven, was omitted, and possibly also the beginning of *6 Ezra*, which is anonymous in its present form, was removed. *5 Ezra* and *4 Ezra* are both attributed to an "Ezra," and there are indications that *5 Ezra* knew *4 Ezra*, with which it shares themes and images.

6 Ezra consists of a series of predictions of impending doom for the world at large, and for certain countries in particular, because of the iniquity that prevails everywhere. Egypt, Assyria, Babylon (= Rome) and Asia are singled out for special mention. The final section (16:35-78) exhorts God's people to remain faithful to his commandments, to persevere in persecution and to believe in God's final triumph over evil. The eschatological language and imagery make it difficult to determine the provenance and date of the document. In

---

[27] This is, however, the only patently Christian phrase in the Latin version. In the Syriac and Georgian versions, as well as in the Coptic fragment there are none, in the Ethiopic version again only one. Several Christian textual elements are found in the two Arabic versions and the Armenian one contains a large body of Christian material.

[28] A small Greek fragment of *6 Ezra* 15:57-59 is found in Oxyrhynchus papyrus 1010; see Bergren, *Sixth Ezra*, 58-59,

[29] According to Bergren, *Fifth Ezra*, chapter 7 (pp. 382-312) the original language of *5 Ezra* must remain an open question. Greek and Latin are the likeliest possibilities, the former is probably slightly preferable.

15:43-16:16 imagery from the Apocalypse of John is used in the description of the evil deeds and the fate of "Babylon"—and of Asia as an imitator of Babylon. Both will be severely punished for their sins and completely destroyed. These literary parallels with the Book of Revelation are for Bergren an indication of the Christian provenance of *6 Ezra*. A number of details in the description of the persecutions in 16:68-74 lead him to connect the writing with persecutions of Christians by the Romans during the reigns of the emperors Decius, in the middle of the third century CE, and Diocletian in the beginning of the fourth. If the passage 15:28-33 refers to the battles between Odaenathus of Palmyra and the Persian king Shapur around 260-267 CE, *6 Ezra* would have been written some time between 270 and 313 (the year of Constantine's accession to the throne), possibly in the Eastern part of the Roman empire, for instance in Asia. But here, again, the wording of the passage is such as to make it difficult to connect it with specific events.

Much, then, remains uncertain with regard to *6 Ezra*. We do not know whether it circulated independently before being joined to *4 Ezra*, and if so, in what form and under what name. In their present place these two final chapters, written at a time of crisis, urge readers to stand firm and to look out for God's help. He is sure to triumph in the end and all will be set right for those who remain faithful—as is also evident from Ezra's words in the preceding chapters.

5 Ezra is concerned with Israel's disobedience to God's commandments and her punishment and rejection. God complains: "What will I do for you, Jacob? You were (Sp.: He was) unwilling to obey me, Judah! I will go over to another nation and will give it my name, and they will certainly keep my statutes" (1:24).[30] This is taken up in 2:10-11:

> This says the Lord to Ezra: "Tell my people that I have prepared for them to eat, and I will give them the kingdom of Jerusalem, which I was going to give to Israel. And I will take for them the glory of Israel (litt.: them) and I will give to them the eternal dwelling places that I had prepared for Israel (litt.: them)."

---

[30] Here, and in the following quotations, I follow Bergren's translation of his reconstruction of the Latin text, which is primarily based on the Spanish recension (Sp.); see *Fifth Ezra*, 401-405.

Here the new nation is called "my people" and it is said to inherit everything originally preserved for Israel. *5 Ezra* ends, in 2:42-48, with a vision in which Ezra sees a large crowd on Mount Zion, singing hymns of praise to the Lord. A tall young man places crowns on the heads of all people. An *angelus interpres* states that these people are "those who have laid aside mortal clothing and donned the immortal, and confessed the name of God." The young man is "the son of God, whom they confessed in the mortal world" (quotations from vv. 45 and 47).

There are a number of textual parallels between *5 Ezra* and Matthew (for instance in *5 Ezra* 1:30-33 and Matt. 23:34-38), and there is a striking agreement between *5 Ezra*'s overall view on the history of salvation and that of the first gospel. Particularly in chapters 21-25 Matthew emphasizes the church's inheritance of Israel's privileges. Precisely in 21:33-44 where God's vineyard is given to "other tenants who will give (God) the produce at the harvest time" (v. 41), it is made clear that the new people have to produce the same "fruits of the kingdom" as were expected from (the leaders of) Israel (v. 43). In the same way *5 Ezra* 1:24 stresses that the coming people will keep God's statutes. And 2:40, a little before the final vision, announces: "Mount Zion, receive your number. Bring to completion your people clothed in white, who serve you with obedience, because they have fulfilled the law of the Lord" (cf. Matt. 5:17-20).

On the basis of these and other texts. G.N. Stanton has argued that the author of 5 Ezra was steeped not only in the Old Testament, but also in the Gospel of Matthew.[31] Just as in the case of Matthew the events of 70 CE led to a prolonged discussion and polemical debate with Judaism, *5 Ezra* may reflect the aftermath of the Bar Kochba revolt of 132-135 CE, the outcome of which was even more traumatic for Judaism and for Christian communities still in close contact with Jews. Bergren, who cautiously speaks only of "historical probabilities," is less specific about a possible date, but agrees that *5 Ezra* must have been written in a period where there was still lively debate, and where the relationship between Judaism and Christianity

---

[31] "5 Ezra and Matthean Christianity in the Second Century," *JTS* N.S. 28 (1977), 67-83; reprinted in *A Gospel for a New People. Studies in Matthew* (Edinburgh: T & T. Clark, 1992), 256-277.

was still viewed in terms of continuity rather than diametric opposition.[32]

Whether *5 Ezra* ever circulated independently before being connected with *4 Ezra*, and whether its author knew *4 Ezra*, remain disputed. In its present form and position it is a Christian introduction to the Jewish apocalypse, "acting as a prism through which *4 Ezra* is to be read and providing an interpretative key whereby its contents are made relevant to a new and different audience."[33]

IV. PARALIPOMENA IEREMIOU

The *Paralipomena Ieremiou* ("Matters omitted from Jeremiah the Prophet"), neglected in the pseudepigrapha collections of Kautzsch and Charles but included in the more recent ones, have received ample attention from scholars during the last decade; Jean Riaud and Jens Herzer published monographs and Berndt Schaller was responsible for the volume in the JSHRZ series.[34]

Notwithstanding this recent detailed work (particularly Schaller's volume in the JSHRZ series is a mine of information) uncertainty remains as to the document's purpose and provenance. The *Paralipomena* are known in many Greek witnesses, belonging to a longer and two shorter recensions, as well as in Ethiopic, Armenian, Slavonic and Rumanian translations. The original language of the *Paralipo-*

---

[32] *Fifth Ezra*, 24-26.

[33] B.W. Longenecker, *2 Esdras* (Guides to Apocrypha and Pseudepigrapha; Sheffield: Sheffield Academic Press, 1995), 118.

[34] J. Riaud, *Les Paralipomènes du prophète Jérémie: Présentation, texte original, traduction et commentaires* (Cahiers du centre interdisciplinaire de recherches en histoire, lettres et langues 14; Angers: Université Catholique de l'Ouest, 1994; J. Herzer, *Die Paralipomena Jeremiae: Studien zur Tradition und Redaktion einer Haggada des frühen Judentums* (TSAJ 43; Tübingen: Mohr [Siebeck], 1994); B. Schaller, *Paralipomena Jeremiae* (JSHRZ 1,8; Gütersloh: Gütersloher Verlagshaus, 1998), 659-777. In 1996 these three scholars read papers at the "Early Jewish Writings" seminar during the meeting of the *Studiorum Novi Testamenti Societas* at Strasbourg—published a few years later in the *Journal for the Study of the Pseudepigrapha* 22 (2000). Here Riaud and Herzer give un update of their views. At the end of the volume one finds a useful annotated bibliography by Schaller (pp 91-118). In a short reaction to the paper by Riaud (pp. 45-49), the present author raises some critical questions about the view (shared by all three authors) that the *Paralipomena* are a Jewish document taken over and edited by Christians. A number of points from this article return below.

mena is Greek;[35] the longer recension is considered the primary one. Unfortunately there is still no critical edition.[36] The writing clearly uses traditional material (partly known from other sources such as the *Syriac Apocalypse of Baruch*), but it fails to weld it together into a really coherent story. The various episodes highlight different aspects of the destruction of Jerusalem and the temple and of the promise of a return from Babylon; the lack of coherence and focus makes it difficult to determine the purpose of the authors/editors of the document as it lies before us, or of the people who transmitted it in an earlier form. It has recently been suggested, for instance, that the author(s) belonged to a Jewish Christian baptist group with syncretistic esoteric features.[37] The writing has also been connected with a Johannine type of Gnostic Christianity.[38] Many scholars regard the main body of the text (1:1-9:9) as a Jewish composition dating from the first third of the second century CE, perhaps from between the beginning of the reign of Hadrian and the beginning of the Bar Kochba revolt (118-132). Later the clearly Christian section 9:10-32 was added by Christians who made Jeremiah, the hero of the story, a herald of "Jesus Christ, the light of all the ages, the inextinguishable lamp, the life of faith" (v. 13).

Jeremiah is, indeed, the central figure, who plays a prominent role at the beginning and at the end of the story. He witnesses the fall of Jerusalem, consigns the vessels of the temple service to the earth and throws the keys of the temple to the sun, before being dragged off to Babylon with the people (1:1-4:5). Baruch stays behind in a tomb outside the city (4:6-11). The next episode centers around Abimelech, earlier sent out by Jeremiah to get figs from the estate of Agrippa. It tells about his return to the city after a sleep of 66 years; he does not recognize it and is informed about what has happened (chapter 5). An angel brings him to Baruch who, at the command of

[35] So B. Schaller in his "Is the Greek Version of the *Paralipomena Jeremiou* Original or a Translation?" *JSP* 22 (2000), 51-89.

[36] There is a provisional edition by R.A. Kraft and A.E. Purintun, *Paraleipomena Jeremiou* (SBL Texts and Translations, Pseudepigrapha Series 1; Missoula MT; Scholars, 1972), which should be used together with Schaller's textcritical notes in JSHRZ 1,8.

[37] See M. Philonenko, "Simples observations sur les Paralipomènes de Jérémie," *RHPR* 76 (1996), 157-177. This thesis is rejected by J. Herzer in his "Paralipomena Jeremiae—eine christlich-gnostische Schrift?" *JSJ* 30 (1999), 25-39.

[38] B. Heininger, "Totenerweckung oder Weckruf *(Par. Jer.* 7, 12-20)? Gnostische Spurensuche in den Paralipomena Jeremiae," *SNTSU* A 23 (1998), 79-112.

another angel of the Lord, sends an eagle with a letter and fifteen still fresh figs from Abimelech's basket to Jeremiah in Babylon (6:1-7:12). There the eagle descends on a corpse about to be buried and revives it; the eagle delivers the letter which is read to the people, and Jeremiah sends a letter back. Abimelech's figs are distributed to the sick among the people (7:13-32). The *Paralipomena* end with a brief report of the return of Jeremiah and the people. Jeremiah tells those who return that they should love the Lord and forsake the works of Babylon. This means that those who are married to Babylonian men and women have to leave their spouses behind. Some refuse to take that step and build a city of their own, Samaria (chapter 8). In chapter 9 Jeremiah officiates as highpriest in the temple, bringing sacrifices during nine days, concluding on the tenth day with a special sacrifice and a prayer. Directly after that prayer he "becomes as one whose soul has departed." When the people want to bury him this is forbidden by a voice from heaven. His soul returns to his body after three days, and the prophet announces the coming of Jesus Christ after 477 years. The people get angry and want to stone him. Jeremiah, however, still has to disclose to Baruch and Abimelech all the (further) mysteries he has seen. A stone receives the shape of Jeremiah and becomes the target of the stones of the people until Jeremiah has fulfilled his mission and is fatally hit by the stones himself. Baruch and Abimelech bury him and put the stone on his grave with an inscription: "This is the stone that was the helper of Jeremiah."

In chapter 9 we find many overtly Christian phrases.[39] There is an evident reference to Isaiah's death as a martyr, as depicted in the *Ascension of Isaiah* (9:20, cf. *Asc. Is.* 3:9, 13; 4:13-15; 5:1-16[40]). This grand finale of the *Paralipomena* should be analyzed in detail, also with regard to possible links with earlier parts of the narrative. Then the question will arise whether the Christian redaction restricted itself to an addition at the end of the document (either from vers 10 onwards, or somewhat earlier), or whether a redactor's hand is also visible at other places. Herzer and Schaller deny any further Christian

---

[39] Commentators note a significant number of parallels with the Johannine writings in the New Testament.

[40] Compare also the announcement of the mission of the twelve apostles in 9:18 and *Asc Is.* 3:17; 11:22.

redaction,[41] but they both fail to take into account that Christian redactors/authors do not restrict themselves to overtly Christian statements, and that in a number of cases phrases may be Jewish as well as Christian.

Let us take one significant example: in 9:5 Jeremiah, in his final prayer, does not mention the safe return to Jerusalem, but prays for help from Michael, the archangel of righteousness who will bring the righteous into the heavenly city. We may compare this with 4:8 where "return to the city" stands parallel with "having life,"[42] or 5:34 where Abimelech concludes his conversation with an old man who has informed him about the fate of Jerusalem with the wish: "May God illumine your way to the city above, Jerusalem."[43] Surprisingly, chapter 8, which is concerned with the separation between the true servants of God in Jerusalem and those who build Samaria, ends with a message of Jeremiah to the people of Samaria: "Repent, for the angel of righteousness is coming and will lead you to your exalted place" (8:9).

The return of the people to Jerusalem, under the leadership of Jeremiah—according to chapter 9 herald of the Son of God who is to come—becomes the symbol of the gathering of the "beloved" people (3:8) in the heavenly Jerusalem. Even the Samaritans who repent will be allowed to enter that city. The fact that in chapter 8 the question of mixed marriages arises is often taken as a proof of typical Jewish concerns and hence of Jewish provenance. But the emphasis is on the issue of "forsaking the works of Babylon" (6:13-14, 22; 7:32; chapter 8), which may have had a wider meaning for a Christian redactor. Perhaps the promise to the Samaritans in 8:9 may be connected with Jesus' words to the Samaritan woman in John 4:21,"The hour is coming when you will worship neither on this mountain nor in Jerusalem" (cf. also vv. 22-23).

In conclusion: there is a case to be made for a much more thoroughgoing Christian redaction of the *Paralipomena* than is common-

---

[41] See Herzer, *Die Paralipomena Jeremiae*, 171-176 and Schaller, *Paralipomena Jeremiou*, 666 n. 15.

[42] A Johannine phrase.

[43] The figs of Abimelech, that do not rot away but remain fresh, can still help the sick when the return to Jerusalem is imminent (7:32, cf. 3:15). They symbolize the life given to the true servants of God (6:5-7). Compare also the revival of a dead person in Babylon by the messenger-eagle in 7:17.

ly accepted. The conglomerate of Jewish traditions found in this writing may have served another purpose before a Christian editor remoulded it to convey his message, but also in this case it is difficult to establish the content and wording of the earlier Jewish document. And, finally, if the emphasis is no longer on an actual return to Jerusalem or a rebuilding of the city and the temple, it becomes difficult to determine its date; there is no longer any reason to situate the *Paralipomena* at the beginning of the second century.

V. The Greek Apocalypse of Baruch

The most recent study of the provenance and transmission of the *Greek Apocalypse of Baruch* is D.C. Harlow's essay "The Christianization of Early Jewish Pseudepigrapha: The Case of *3 Baruch*,"[44] already mentioned in the previous chapter. It refers back to the author's monograph *The* Greek Apocalypse of Baruch (3 Baruch) *in Hellenistic Judaism and Early Christianity*.[45]

In his article Harlow formulates the matter that interests us in this chapter as follows:

> Are the distinctly Christian elements of *3 Baruch* original to the work, or were they added later? More to the point, can a determination of their compositional status even settle the issue of origin? ... the answer to the first question is 'Later'; the answer to the second, 'No'. ... a work lacking in overt Christian formulations need not be Jewish at all.[46]

His argumentation is as follows: The *Greek Apocalypse of Baruch* is known in Greek and in a Slavonic translation made from the Greek.[47] The Slavonic text lacks the explicitly Christian elements found in the Greek, but it contains its own explicitly Christian elements which are largely independent of the Greek. In both cases the Christian elements appear to be later additions. Nevertheless, it remains pos-

---

[44] *JSJ* 32 (2001), 416-444.

[45] SVTP 12; Leiden: Brill, 1996. Compare J. Riaud, "Quelques réflexions sur l'*Apocalypse grecque de Baruch* ou *III Baruch* à la lumière d'un ouvrage récent," *Sem* 48 (1999), 89-99.

[46] *JSJ* 32 (2001), 423-424.

[47] For the Greek see the edition by J.-C. Picard, *Apocalypsis Baruchi Graece* (PVTG 2; Leiden: Brill, 1967), 61-96. For the Slavonic see H.E. Gaylord, "3 (Greek Apocalypse of) Baruch," in Charlesworth (ed.), *The Old Testament Pseudepigrapha*, vol 1, 653-679. Gaylord prints translations of the Slavonic and the Greek on opposite pages.

sible that *3 Baruch* is an original Christian composition, progressively Christianized, however lightly, in the course of its transmission.

3 Baruch begins with Baruch mourning over the destruction of Jerusalem. An angel appears and urges him to stop bothering God with prayers for the salvation of Jerusalem. The angel will show him "other mysteries greater than these" (1:6, cf. v. 8). An account of a heavenly journey follows. The angel conducts Baruch on a guided tour of five heavens. After arriving at the fifth heaven, they meet Michael, who in his heavenly liturgy ascends to, and descends from, the presence of God, presumably in a higher heaven. The emphasis is on individualized eschatology and ethical universalism. Chapters 2-16

> reinforce the message by setting Baruch's initial concern in the broader framework of God's sovereign control over both the cosmos and the fate of humanity, and by replacing the initial opposition of Israel versus the nations with that of those who have good works versus those who do not.[48]

If the description of Baruch's situation in chapter 1 (and also the introduction to the book) may be taken as reflecting the situation of the time of writing, the author must have been concerned to minimize the significance of Jerusalem's destruction and to discourage hope for its restoration. This seems to reflect a Jewish answer to a Jewish problem in the time after 70 CE. Harlow has to admit, however, that if chapter 1 is no more than a literary device to introduce the heavenly tour (as Martha Himmelfarb has argued)[49] there is no compelling reason to assert an original Jewish authorship.

In his book Harlow showed how *3 Baruch* could be meaningfully read as a Jewish text, but equally well as a Christian one.[50] In his recent article he concludes that it remains difficult to say with any certainty whether it fits best in Hellenistic Judaism of the Diaspora or in Byzantine and later Christianity, and he adds:

> Most interpreters have situated it meaningfully in the former context, but the later setting(s) may prove the more secure framework when

---

[48] *JSJ* 32 (2001), 427-428.

[49] *Ascent to Heaven in Jewish & Christian Apocalypses* (New York/Oxford: Oxford U.P., 1993), 32.

[50] *The Greek Apocalypse of Baruch*, chapter 3 (pp. 109-162) and chapter 4 (pp. 163-205).

this and other pseudepigrapha are further studied as part of the literary heritage of Christianity.[51]

I agree, also in view of the resemblance between the attitude towards the return to Jerusalem in the *Paralipomena Ieremiou*, and that towards the destruction of the city in the *Greek Apocalypse of Baruch*.[52]

VI. JOSEPH AND ASENETH

This writing combines two stories: the first, and principal, one (in chapters 1-21) tells about the meeting between the Egyptian Aseneth and Joseph, resulting in Aseneth's conversion to the service of the God of Israel, their marriage and the birth of Manasseh and Ephraim. It is followed by a second story (in chapters 22-29) about an unsuccessful attempt by Pharaoh's son, aided by the sons of Bilhah and Zilpah (especially Gad and Dan), to ambush Aseneth, who is defended by the sons of Leah (especially Levi and Simeon) and Benjamin. The son of Pharaoh is killed, his father dies of heartbreak, and Joseph is left regent of all Egypt.

Joseph and Aseneth did not find a place in the early twentieth century collections of Old Testament pseudepigrapha of Kautzsch and Charles. The first modern edition was that by P. Batiffol in 1889-90, but its editor regarded it as a Christian composition.[53] It was included in Riessler's *Altjüdisches Schrifttum*.[54] Much later, research on the document received a major impetus from two studies: first, C. Burchard's *Untersuchungen zu Joseph und Aseneth. Überlieferung— Ortsbestimmung*[55] and, second, M. Philonenko's *Joseph et Aséneth. Introduction, texte critique, traduction et notes*.[56] Burchard was invited to write the section on Joseph and Aseneth for *The Old Testament Pseudepigrapha*[57] and the volume in the series "Jüdische

---

[51] P. 443.

[52] This would, of course, require further study. Harlow speaks briefly about the *Paralipomena* on pp. 90-93; 169-171; 201-202; 204-205 of his book and in n. 28 of his article.

[53] "Le livre de la prière d'Aséneth" in P. Batiffol, *Studia Patristica: Études d'ancienne littérature chrétienne*, vols 1-2 (Paris: Leroux, 1889-90), 1-160.

[54] Pp. 497-538; 1303-04.

[55] WUNT 8; Tübingen: Mohr (Siebeck), 1965.

[56] SPB 13; Leiden: Brill, 1968.

[57] Vol. 2, 177-247.

Schriften aus hellenistisch-römischer Zeit."[58] For that purpose he composed a preliminary edition of the text.[59] He also wrote a number of detailed studies, later brought together in his *Gesammelte Studien zu Joseph and Aseneth* of 1996.[60] Philonenko did not publish any further contributions to the study of this writing; his edition of the text formed the basis of some later translations.[61]

The past decade has seen a remarkable new interest in *Joseph and Aseneth*. The following books may be mentioned: R.D. Chesnutt, *From Death to Life: Conversion in Joseph and Aseneth*;[62] A. Standhartinger, *Das Frauenbild im Judentum in der hellenistischen Zeit: Ein Beitrag anhand von 'Joseph und Aseneth'*;[63] G. Bohak, *Joseph and Aseneth and the Jewish Temple in Heliopolis*;[64] and R.S. Kraemer, *When Aseneth met Joseph: A late Antique Tale of the Biblical Patriarch and His Egyptian Wife, Reconsidered*.[65] These studies, and the opinions of many other scholars, have been analyzed and assessed by E.M. Humphrey in her *Joseph and Aseneth* of 2000.[66]

Many problems raised by these recent studies cannot be discussed here. In what follows I shall concentrate on those connected with the history of the text, and those of provenance and date. As to the text: *Joseph and Aseneth* was written in Greek; it is known in a number of Greek manuscripts, divided into four different families, plus some important ancient versions (Syriac, Armenian, Latin [two], Slavonic). Burchard opted for an eclectic text, mainly based on family *b*, consisting of some Greek witnesses together with the Syriac, Armenian and the two Latin versions. Philonenko reconstructed a much shorter

---

[58] JSHRZ II,4 (1983).

[59] Easily accessible in A.-M. Denis, *Concordance grecque des Pseudépigraphes d'Ancien Testament* (Louvain-la-Neuve: Université Catholique de Louvain. Institut Orientaliste, 1987), 851-859 and in *Gesammelte Studien* (see following note), 161-209. See now also C. Burchard, *Joseph und Aseneth kritisch herausgegeben* (PVTG 5; Leiden: 2003).

[60] SVTP 13; Leiden: Brill, 1996. Here one finds, on pp. 321-459 (plus xix-xxiii) an updated version of his very informative survey of basic evidence "Der jüdische Asenethroman und seine Nachwirkung. Von Egeria zu Anna Katharina Emmerick oder von Moses aus Aggel zu Karl Kerényi" (originally in ANRW I,20.1 [1987], 658-667).

[61] It was taken up in *La Bible. Écrits intertestamentaires* (Bibliothèque de la Pléiade 337; Paris: Gallimard, 1987), cxxii-cxxv, 1559-1601 and used by (among others) D. Cook for his translation in *The Apocryphal Old Testament* (ed. H.F.D. Sparks), 465-503.

[62] JSPSup 16; Sheffield: Sheffield Academic Press, 1995.

[63] AGAJU 26; Leiden: Brill, 1995.

[64] SBLEJL 10; Atlanta: Scholars, 1996.

[65] New York: Oxford U.P., 1998.

[66] Guides to Apocrypha and Pseudepigrapha; Sheffield: Academic Press, 2000.

text, primarily based on family *d*, consisting of two Greek manuscripts plus the Slavonic version. Most scholars followed Burchard,
but recently Standhartinger and Kraemer have argued for the priority
of the shorter text, regarding the longer text as the result of later expansion.

This has led Burchard to reconsider his position.[67] After some hesitation, he has maintained his earlier opinion, that a process of abbreviation is much more likely than gradual expansion. He notes that
a long form of *Joseph and Aseneth* is attested by the Syriac version
as early as the sixth century, whereas the oldest witness of the short *d*
text is MS B of the eleventh century. Another argument in favour of
the abbreviation theory is that in places where the long and the short
text overlap the sequence of phrases is essentially the same; also that
practically the entire short text is contained in the longer. Next, in
narrative texts unprotected by canonical status one often finds
abbreviations in passages where the narrative flow is slow. Burchard
proceeds to show that this is indeed the case in *Joseph and Aseneth*.
And as to Standhartinger's thesis that the short text portraying
Aseneth as a self-confident and emancipated young lady is likely to
be earlier than the longer which turns her into an obedient daughter
who later lives the life of a virtuous married woman, Burchard asks
whether the short text could not be a revision effected in Byzantine
times by a scribe impressed by the stance of Byzantine upper class
women.[68]

Turning now to the problem of provenance, we should take note of
Burchard's reminder that the entire tradition of *Joseph and Aseneth*,
except perhaps the Syriac version, goes back to an archetype in
which the writing was preceded by a homily on Joseph ascribed to
Ephraem Syrus (306-377 CE).[69] It will not be much older than the
Syriac version. All available textual evidence, then, takes us back to,

---

[67] See, for instance, his "Zum Stand der Arbeit am Text von Joseph und Aseneth," in M.
Becker and W. Fenske (eds.), *Das Ende der Tage und die Gegenwart des Heils* (FS H.-W.
Kuhn; AGAJU 44; Leiden: Brill, 1999), 1-28 and "The Text of *Joseph and Aseneth* Recon-
sidered" (forthcoming in *JSP* 2003 and kindly put at my disposal by the author).

[68] Alternatively, a later Christian author may have regarded Aseneth as an allegory of the
soul united with Christ, or as a model of virginity. The abbreviator may also have been interested in Joseph rather than in Aseneth.

[69] The combination of these two writings is found in witnesses belonging to families *a*, *b*
(including the Armenian version) and *d*, and also in a palimpsest that is a close ally to *c*.

say, a fifth century Christian archetype.[70] This raises the question whether *Joseph and Aseneth* is a Christian writing or a Jewish one, perhaps later interpolated or redacted by a Christian hand. Here, again, we are confronted with the situation that a text may be Christian as well as Jewish, and that the only way to arrive at a decision, is to look for distinctively Jewish or Christian elements. Anyone, Jewish or Christian, who read Genesis 41 in his Bible and wondered how the exemplary Joseph could marry a gentile woman, and who was interested in the relation between Joseph and his brothers between the definitive settlement of Jacob and his family in Egypt and the meeting after Jacob's death in Gen. 50:15-21, may have decided to compose a narrative explaining what happened.

The book was written in Greek and presupposes the Septuagint or a similar ancient Greek version. It depicts Aseneth as a model proselyte and the mother of all proselytes. If the document is Egyptian as it seems to be, the most likely theory is that it was written by an Egyptian Jew in the period between 100 BCE and 100 CE.[71] Efforts to determine more precisely the milieu in which *Joseph and Aseneth* originated have been numerous, but have not led to a generally accepted result.[72] But if the document is of Jewish origin, the fact remains that the oldest recoverable text is Christian, and much later; consequently one should consider the possibility of Christian interpolation/redaction in the intermediate period. Burchard, who admits that there may have been Christian touching up, denies that there is any literary critical proof of such changes or interpolations—but there is certainly room for a more differentiated approach.[73] This is found in Kraemer's recent study *When Joseph met Aseneth*. She sets out to demonstrate that *Joseph and Aseneth* is not a tale of conversion, but a late antique tale of adjuration of an angel by a woman. This leads her

---

[70] See "Zum Stand," 26; "The Text of *Joseph and Aseneth* reconsidered" (forthcoming); and earlier "Der jüdische Asenethroman," 560-561 (338-339). On pp. 558-559 (336-338) of "Der jüdische Asenethroman" Burchard mentions a possible dependence on *JosAs* on the part of the "Passion of Irene" (perhaps to be dated in the fifth century at the latest); cf. also Kraemer, *When Joseph met Aseneth*, 235-237.

[71] The *terminus ad quem* is the revolt under Trajan (115-117 CE).

[72] See the survey in Humphrey, *Joseph and Aseneth*, 48-63.

[73] See "Der judische Asenethroman," 643 (421) and "The Text of *Joseph and Aseneth* Reconsidered," both times referring to T. Holtz, "Christliche Interpolationen in "Joseph und Aseneth," *NTS* 14 (1967-8), 482-497, now also in T. Holtz, *Geschichte und Theologie des Urchristentums. Gesammelte Aufsätze* (eds. E. Reinmuth and C. Wolf; Tübingen: Mohr [Siebeck], 1991), 55-71.

to a search for parallels in Jewish, pagan and Christian texts. Her conclusion is that the present writing, exalting the God of Joseph, is Christian rather than Jewish, is conversant with haggadic interpretation, and shows the influence of Jewish mysticism as well as of solar henotheism and neoplatonic cosmology and theurgic practice. Kraemer dates the shorter version around 300 CE, the longer version some time after; in her opinion the arguments for locating the author in Egypt are weak. Whether the details of Kraemer's reconstruction of the milieu in which Joseph and Aseneth originated are convincing, I leave to the judgement of specialists; her cautious approach with regard to Jewish or Christian provenance is certainly to be applauded.[74]

The question of the presence of Christian elements in the earliest recoverable text of our writing deserves renewed further investigation. Exclusively Christian elements may be absent, but there are at least a number of phrases that are Christian as well as Jewish, and very little, if anything, can be considered as exclusively Jewish.[75]

---

[74] See, for instance, her chapter 9, "The Authorial Identity of Aseneth reconsidered," 245-285.

[75] A few examples: *First*, 8:5 describes a man who worships God (ἀνὴρ θεοσεβής) as one "who will bless with his mouth the living God and eat blessed bread of life and drink a blessed cup of immortality and anoint himself with blessed ointment of incorruptibility." Aseneth is promised bread, cup and ointment (15:5; cf. 8:9) and, in fact, receives them (as is explained by the angel) when she is fed a piece of supernatural honeycomb (16:16; cf. 19:5 and 21:21). Before, she has given up blessing dead and dumb idols, eating from their table bread of strangulation and drinking from their libation a cup of insidiousness, and anointing herself with ointment of destruction (8:5; cf. 21:13-14). Here we may compare 1 Cor. 10; 11:17-34 and John 6. *Second*, there is the rule, formulated by Levi in 23:9, "We are men who worship God, and it does not befit us to repay evil for evil." This rule is enforced by Aseneth and Levi in 28:(5), 14. and 29:3. Here Rom. 12:17; 1 Thess. 5:15 and 1 Pet. 3:9 may be mentioned. In chapter 29 Levi's attitude towards the son of Pharaoh resembles love of one's enemy as prescribed in Matt. 5:43-48 and par. One should also note Levi's command to Benjamin in 29:4,"put your sword back into its place (cf. Matt. 26:52; John 18:11). *Third*, Joseph is called "(the) son of God" (6:3, 5; 13:13), his "firstborn son" (18:11; 21:4, cf. 23:10). This may first of all characterize him as a supremely righteous man (cf. 16:4; 19:8; 21:4; 23:10 and Wisd. 2-5), superior to the firstborn of Pharaoh. But if Christians are not responsible for this terminology, they may have read it later as a reference to Joseph as figure of Jesus Christ. Likewise, in 4:7 Joseph is described as "a man who worships God, and self-controlled ... a man powerful in wisdom and experience and the spirit of God is upon him and the grace of God (is) with him." 19:11, however, goes a decisive step further when Joseph, kissing Aseneth three times, gives her "spirit of life," "spirit of wisdom," and "spirit of truth."

VII. 1 ENOCH

1 Enoch was for a long time only known in an Ethiopic version and through a number of Greek fragments.[76] Later, eleven fragmentary Aramaic manuscripts were found in Cave 4 at Qumran: seven of them (4Q201-202; 204-207; 212) covering parts of the *Book of the Watchers* (the traditional name for chapters 1-36), the *Book of Dreams* (chapters 83-90) and the *Epistle of Enoch* (chapters 92-105), and four (4Q208-211) covering parts of the *Astronomical Book* (chapters 72-82). The manuscripts range in date from the beginning of the second century BCE to the time of Herod, and provide evidence for an unambiguously Jewish text of *1 Enoch*. Nearly all these fragments are small and their text has to be reconstructed with the help of the Greek and Ethiopic versions. Our knowledge of this Jewish evidence is, therefore, limited. We can also not be sure how much of the Enochic corpus extant in Ethiopic (the most complete collection available) was at one time extant in Aramaic. It is uncertain whether the *Book of Giants* (represented by a number of fragments) should be counted among the Qumranic Enoch collection. What is undisputed, however, is that the *Book of Parables* (chapters 37-71) has left no traces at Qumran. As this book is not extant in Greek either, we have to rely on the Ethiopic version alone for our knowledge of it.

We do not know when and where the Greek version was made, nor whether all sections available in Aramaic were translated at the same time. About 25 percent of the Ethiopic text is also found in a Greek form. The most substantial portions are found in the Codex Gizeh (Codex Panopolitanus) of the sixth century (containing 1:1-32:6) and a Chester Beatty-Michigan Papyrus of the fourth (containing 97:6-104:13 and 106:1-107:3). In both cases parts of the Enochic corpus were copied together with Christian works.[77]

---

[76] In this section I follow M.A. Knibb, "Christian Adoption and Transmission of Jewish Pseudepigrapha: The Case of *1 Enoch*," *JSJ* 32 (2001), 396-415. See also the extensive introduction to G.W.E. Nickelsburg's commentary on 1 Enoch, of which the first volume has now appeared: *1 Enoch 1. A Commentary on the Book of 1 Enoch, Chapters 1-36; 81-108* (Hermeneia; Minneapolis: Fortress, 2001), 1-125. On the person and the book of Enoch in Early Christian literature, see J.C. VanderKam, "1 Enoch, Enochic Motifs and Enoch in Early Christian Literature," in VanderKam and Adler (eds.), *The Jewish Apocalyptic Heritage*, 33-101.

[77] There are also extracts from the *Book of the Watchers* in the *Chronographia* of Georgius Syncellus († 810).

The Ethiopic is a daughter version of the Greek, made by Christians; Knibb dates it to the fifth or sixth century. Unfortunately, the manuscripts at our disposal are much younger. In the list of 49 pre-1900 manuscripts given by Nickelsburg there are only six that can be dated to the fifteenth or the sixteenth century.[78]

Knibb concludes: "The textual evidence for *1 Enoch* is disparate in origin, character and extent, and it raises a problem, namely which text should be used for purposes of translation, and particularly, for interpretation and comment."[79] The Aramaic is too fragmentary and the Greek gives substantial parts of the *Book of the Watchers* and the *Epistle*, but not of other sections. The Ethiopic may contain Christian elements, and in any case the evidence for its text is no earlier than the fifteenth century. Commentators who want to establish the earliest recoverable form of text have no alternative to weighing very carefully all available evidence for each individual passage. This "pseudepigraphon of the Old Testament" is undoubtedly Jewish in origin, but it is very difficult to establish the form of text current in Jewish and early Christian circles in the centuries around the beginning of the common era.

A number of ancient Christian authors show familiarity with Enochic books and even quote from them.[80] For these authors the antediluvian saint of whom Scripture said that he "walked with God; then he was no more because God took him" (Gen. 5:23) was a person of great authority as a prophet. The earliest Christian writer to appeal to him, the author of the Epistle of Jude, introduces his quotation from *1 En.* 1:9 in v. 14 with the words: "It was about these (i.e., the people who in v. 4 are called 'intruders ... who long ago were designated for this condemnation as ungodly') that Enoch in the seventh generation from Adam prophesied..." (NRSV). God's appearance with myriads of holy ones to execute judgment, announced in the beginning of the *Book of the Watchers*, is here said to refer to the imminent parousia of the Lord Jesus Christ, who will execute

---

[78] *1 Enoch 1*, 16-17

[79] "The Case of *1 Enoch*," 404.

[80] VanderKam discusses references to *1 Enoch* in Jude, pseudo-Barnabas, (Athenagoras), Clement of Alexandria, Tertullian and Origen (pp. 35-54). See also section 6.3 "Early Christianity" in the Introduction to Nickelsburg's commentary (pp. 82-108), which ends with a survey of 1 Enoch's function in the Ethiopian Church—the only section of Christendom to accord canonical status to the book (cf. also Knibb, "The Case of *1 Enoch*," 413-415).

judgment on all ἀσεβεῖς, particularly those in the communities addressed in this epistle. Jude 14 presents *1 En.* 1:9 in a special form, and commentators (those on *1 Enoch* as well as those on the Epistle of Jude) differ in their assessment of the relation between this form and the text forms found in Ethiopic, Greek and Aramaic. It is certain, however, that Jude quotes from a writing (the *Book of the Watchers* separately, or as part of a larger corpus) current in certain Jewish apocalyptic circles which was also regarded as relevant and authoritative in early Christian groups looking out for Jesus' parousia at God's final intervention on earth.

Nickelsburg, in his comment on 1:9, remarks: "It is uncertain to what extent NT passages about Jesus' parousia may have been affected by this text, as well as by Son of Man traditions."[81] The designation of Jesus as "Son of Man" is very important in early Christianity, and its relationship with the description of a heavenly vice-regent of God called Righteous One, Elect One, Anointed One and Son of Man in the *Book of Parables*, has been the subject of endless discussion. For many scholars, including Nickelsburg, the picture of Jesus as the Son of Man shows influence from the specific interpretation of Daniel 7 in the *Parables* (as well as from traditions in other Jewish sources). The *Parables*, generally considered to represent the latest major stratum in the Enochic corpus, are consequently dated in the second half of the first century CE.[82] This is still early enough to explain similarities between the *Parables* and the gospels, and late enough to explain their absence among the scrolls found at Qumran. We shall do well to remember, however, that this part of *1 Enoch* is only known to us in a late Ethiopic form transmitted by Christians.

VIII. THE ASSUMPTION OF MOSES

The Epistle of Jude not only quotes prophetic words of Enoch in v. 14, it also refers to a dispute between Michael and the devil concerning the body of Moses in v. 9, where we read: "Not even the archangel Michael, when he was disputing with the devil for posses-

---

[81] *1 Enoch 1*, 149. On what follows see also pp. 7; 83-86 and Nickelsburg's articles "Enoch, First Book of," *ABD* 2, 508-516 and "Son of Man,"*ABD* 6, 137-150. The second volume of the Hermeneia commentary will contain a detailed commentary on 1 Enoch 37-71.

[82] See also Knibb, The Case of *1 Enoch*," 407.

sion of Moses' body, presumed to condemn him in insulting words, but said: 'May the Lord rebuke you!'" (REB).[83] This dispute is also mentioned by Gelasius Cyzicenus, in his *Historia Ecclesiastica* II,21,7 where he reports on discussions of the bishops during the Council of Nicea. I quote: "In the Book of the Assumption of Moses, the archangel Michael, in a discussion with the devil, says: 'For by his Holy Spirit, all of us have been created' and further he says: 'God's spirit went forth from his face and the world came into being.'" Here two enunciations of Michael, introduced in a way similar to the one in Jude 9, are explicitly attributed to the "Book of the Assumption of Moses." That same book is referred to by Gelasius in *Hist. Eccl.* II,17,7. Here the phrase καὶ προεθεάσατό με ὁ θεὸς πρὸ καταβολῆς κόσμου εἶναί με τῆς διαθήκης αὐτοῦ μεσίτην corresponds to the "therefore, he has devised and invented me (*excogitavit et invenit me*), I who have been prepared from the beginning of the world to be the mediator (*arbiter*) of his covenant" found in the fragmentary Latin text containing the parting words of Moses to Joshua which is found in the sixth century palimpsest Milan Bibl. Ambr. C 73 Inf.[84]

Early Christians were clearly interested in various aspects of the dispute between Michael and the devil over Moses' body. The first of them known to us is the author of the Epistle of Jude. He contrasts Michael, who leaves it to the Lord to judge the devil, with the ungodly intruders in the community, who "flout authority, and insult celestial beings" (v. 8, REB). Unfortunately the ending of the *Assumption of Moses* is lacking in the fragmentary Latin text of the Biblioteca Ambrosiana, so that we do not know the full story. However, as J. Tromp has argued, the *Assumption of Moses* "is likely to

---

[83] In this section I follow mainly Johannes Tromp in his *The Assumption of Moses. A Critical Edition with Commentary* (SVTP 10; Leiden: Brill, 1993). I am grateful to Dr. Tromp for putting a recent article, "Origen on the Assumption of Moses," at my disposal, and discussing some relevant issues with me.

[84] It is commonly called "The Assumption of Moses" (a designation to be preferred to "Testament of Moses" used by some scholars). Gelasius' quotation is found in 1:14. Further possible quotations from *As. Mosis* were assembled by A.-M. Denis in his *Fragmenta pseudepigraphorum quae supersunt graeca* (PVTG 3; Leiden: Brill, 1970), 63-67. For a critical discussion of those see J. Tromp, *The Assumption of Moses*, 270-285. In 1993 the latter regarded only the three quotations by Gelasius and the one by Jude as certain. In his recent article he has added a phrase in Origen, *De Principiis* II,2.1 (preserved in Rufinus' Latin translation), *Michahel archangelus cum diabolo disputans de corpore Moysi ait a diabolo inspiratum serpentem causam extitisse praevaricationis Adae et Evae.*

have narrated the end of Moses' terrestrial life as a death followed by the burial of his body by Michael and the ascent of a spiritual part of his person to heaven, possibly accompanied or transported there by the archangel."[85] It may safely be assumed that at some moment the devil appeared and made objections to what was happening. The archangel's words in reply must, however, have effectively put the accuser to shame—and a number of these words survive in quotations. There is nothing to suggest that this story about Moses' death was not composed and handed down by Jews, before being taken over by Christians, among them the author of the Epistle of Jude, already at the end of the first century CE.

The part of the *Assumption of Moses* that has been preserved is a copy of a Latin version of a Greek original made by an unknown translator (a Christian?), probably in Italy.[86] It contains little that could be useful for Christian believers. The central figure, Moses, is portrayed as mediator between God and Israel, "prepared from the beginning of the world" (1:14; cf. 3:12), and as an advocate and intercessor for the people (11:17; 12:6). He prophesies what will happen to Israel after his death. Israel's history will be a history of transgression and repentance, divine punishment and mercy, culminating in the coming of the kingdom of God. "And then his kingdom will appear in his entire creation. And then the devil will come to an end, and sadness will be carried away together with him. Then the hands of the messenger, when he will be in heaven, will be filled, and he will then avenge them against their enemies" (10:1-2). This decisive turn of events will take place after a time of cruel repression, in which a man from the tribe of Levi, the mysterious Taxo, and his sons decide to die rather than to transgress the commandments of the God of their fathers. "For as we shall do this and die," Taxo says, "our blood will be avenged before the Lord" (9:7).

Much remains cryptic in chapters 9 and 10 (as in the preceding descriptions of earlier events), but very little is offered that could be interpreted in a Christian sense. As Herod's reign and death are the last recognizable historical events referred to (in 6:2-6), the writing will probably have to be dated not too long after that.[87] The *Assumption of*

---

[85] *The Assumption of Moses*, 285.

[86] The codex came to the Ambrosiana from the Abbey of Bobbio, founded by Columbanus in 612.

[87] J. Tromp, *The Assumption of Moses*, 116-117.

Moses, as it has come down to us, is a Jewish text handed down by Christians seemingly unaltered.

CONCLUSION

The brief discussions in this chapter have shown the complexity of the problems encountered in the analysis of the history of transmission of a number of "pseudepigrapha of the Old Testament" by Christians, and in a few cases also by Jews. There is much we cannot determine with certainty, and will perhaps never know, unless new manuscript evidence comes to light. It has also become clear, I hope, that the approach advocated in this and the previous chapter is the right one. Rather than starting from the assumption that the Old Testament pseudepigrapha are original Jewish documents of which the text can easily be recovered by deleting occasional Christian elements, our research has to start with the primary sources at our disposal. We should then fully take into account that most of them were transmitted in Christian contexts, and that we are held to work our way backwards—often from Byzantine times to the period of early Christianity and, if possible, further back to an earlier Jewish document or to Jewish traditions or sources embedded in the Christian writing in its earliest recoverable form. But much may have happened in the period between, say, the third century CE and the origin of the archetype reflected by the extant manuscripts, and it is far from easy to distinguish between what is "Christian" and what can only be regarded as "Jewish."

In chapters 5 to 10, which follow, I shall report on the situation with regard to the *Testaments of the Twelve Patriarchs*. It will become clear that even in the case of the much studied *Testaments* many problems remain open, even though there is no doubt that they are a Christian document. The same applies, *mutatis mutandis*, to the *Greek Life of Adam and Eve*, treated in chapters 11-13.

PART TWO

THE CASE OF
THE TESTAMENTS OF THE TWELVE PATRIARCHS

CHAPTER FIVE

DEFINING THE MAJOR ISSUES IN THE STUDY OF THE
TESTAMENTS OF THE TWELVE PATRIARCHS

During the greater part of the twentieth century a majority of scholars regarded the *Testaments of the Twelve Patriarchs* as a Jewish writing which had a complicated literary history in Judaism and was finally transmitted by Christians in an interpolated form. There were considerable differences of opinion with regard to the reconstruction of Jewish stages in the literary history of the document as well as to the delineation of the passages interpolated or redacted by Christians as is apparent already in the writings of F. Schnapp and R.H. Charles who introduced, translated and interpreted the *Testaments of the Twelve Patriarchs* in the highly influential collections *Die Apokryphen and Pseudepigraphen des Alten Testaments* and *The Apocrypha and Pseudepigrapha of the Old Testament*, respectively.[1] Nevertheless, the *Testaments* were generally studied as part of Jewish "intertestamental" literature, later also called the literature of the Second Temple period. What made some people question this approach and argue for a Christian origin of the *Testaments*, at least in their present form?

There is no need to give a survey of the history of scholarship on the *Testaments*. But for the purpose of this volume it will be helpful to describe the way the present author and a number of his colleagues travelled during the second half of the previous century, and to sketch how they learned to define the major issues in the study of the *Testaments* more adequately during that period.[2] Here, as far as the con-

---

[1] See chapter 1. Earlier Schnapp wrote his *Die Testamente der Zwölf Patriarchen untersucht* (Halle: Alex Niemeyer, 1884) and Charles his *The Greek Versions of the Twelve Patriarchs* (Oxford: Clarendon, 1908) and *The Testaments of the Twelve Patriarchs Translated from the Editor's Greek Text* (London: A. and C. Black, 1908). On Charles, see also chapter 9, section 1, below.

[2] For earlier surveys of the issues in the research on the Testaments from my hand see "The Interpretation of the Testaments of the Twelve Patriarchs in Recent Years," *Studies* (see note 4), 183-192; "The Testaments of the Twelve Patriarchs: Central Problems and Essential Viewpoints," in W. Haase (ed.), *Aufstieg und Niedergang der römischen Welt* II. 20. 1 (Berlin-New York: De Gruyter, 1987), 359-420; "The Main Issues in the Study of the Testaments of the

tribution of those connected with the University of Leiden is concerned, some stages can be distinguished, marked by a number of publications. There was, first, the research leading up to the present author's Leiden dissertation of 1953, with the title *The Testaments of the Twelve Patriarchs. A Study of their Text, Compostion and Origin*.[3] After a considerable time, in 1975, there appeared a volume of studies, written by him and those who worked with him on a new edition of the Greek text of the *Testaments*. These *Studies on the Testaments of the Twelve Patriarchs. Text and Interpretation*[4] were mainly preparatory studies for the projected edition, but some contributions dealt with questions of composition and origin. The next major step forward was the publication in 1978 of *The Testaments of the Twelve Patriarchs. A Critical Edition of the Greek Text*, by M. de Jonge in cooperation with H.W. Hollander, H.J. de Jonge and Th. Korteweg.[5] This edition called for a new commentary, to replace that of Charles of 1908, based on his text that appeared in the same year. The new commentary was prepared by H.W. Hollander and M. de Jonge, and appeared in 1985.[6] Finally, a number of individual articles on the composition and origin of the *Testaments*, written by M. de Jonge between 1980 and 1990, were brought together by H.J. de Jonge in a volume of essays published in 1991.[7]

Twelve Patriarchs," *Collected Essays* (see note 7), 147-163 and "The Testaments of the Twelve Patriarchs: Christian and Jewish. A Hundred Years after Friedrich Schnapp," *Collected Essays*, 233-243. For a clear introduction to previous and recent research on the Testaments see R.A. Kugler, *The Testaments of the Twelve Patriarchs* (Guides to the Apocrypha and Pseudepigrapha; Sheffield: Academic Press, 2001), 11-40. H.D. Slingerland's book *The Testaments of the Twelve Patriarchs: A Critical History of Research* (SBLMS 21: Missoula MT: Scholars, 1977) is less helpful (see my review in *JSJ* 9 [1978], 108-111). It should be noted that H.J. de Jonge in his "Die Patriarchentestamente von Roger Bacon bis Richard Simon (mit einem Namenregister)," *Studies*, 3-42 is the only author to give a (very interesting) analysis of the study of the Testaments in the period between the middle of the thirteenth to the beginning of the eighteenth century.

[3] Assen: Van Gorcum, 1953; second edition 1975 [Further referred to as *Dissertation*].

[4] SVTP 3; Leiden: Brill, 1975 [referred to as *Studies*].

[5] PVTG 1,2; Leiden: Brill, 1978 [*Edition*].

[6] SVTP 8; Leiden: Brill, 1985 [*Commentary*]. Thanks to a research grant H.W. Hollander could devote two full years to the preparation of this commentary.

[7] *Jewish Eschatology, Early Christian Christology and the Testaments of the Twelve Patriarchs. Collected Essays of Marinus de Jonge* (ed. H.J. de Jonge; NovTSup 63; Leiden: Brill, 1991) [*Collected Essays*].

I. THE STUDY OF THE TEXT

My dissertation of 1953 was intended as an examination of Charles's interpolation theory and concentrated, therefore, on questions of composition and origin. But its first chapter is rightly devoted to text-critical matters. At the time everyone had to start with Charles's edition of 1908 already mentioned, a storehouse of information concerning the Greek manuscripts and ancient versions (and about related Aramaic and Hebrew documents as well). In this edition, as in his commentary, Charles had confidently bracketed the Christian passages as interpolations, and very many scholars writing about the *Testaments* simply accepted his conclusions in the matter. The results of a new examination of Charles's theories concerning the text were highly critical and led to the conclusion that a completely new edition was called for.

First, Charles was able to use nine Greek manuscripts which he divided into two families. Three of those formed family α, in which Cod. Vat. Gr. 731, ff. 97r.-166v. of the XIIIth century ($=c$) was the principal witness. The other six formed family β, divided into two subgroups; here Cambridge Univ. Library MS Ff. I.24, ff. 203r.-261v. of the Xth century ($=b$) was considered to be the best representative. For Charles the most important of those two families was α, and he used c as the basis of his text.[8] A closer examination, however, provided ample evidence that Charles's assessment of the evidence was wrong, and that J.W. Hunkin had been right when, as far back as 1915, he showed that the α-group was little more than a free recension of the β-text.[9] R. Sinker had made a good choice when he chose the Cambridge MS as his text in his edition of the *Testaments* in 1869.[10]

A second important feature of Charles's edition was his abundant use of the Armenian version. Following F.C. Conybeare[11] and W.

---

[8] His theory that α and β went back to two lost Hebrew recensions has not found many adherents. In fact, his frequent efforts to interpret passages in the *Testaments* by translating them back into Hebrew have met with scepticism.

[9] "The Testaments of the Twelve Patriarchs," *JTS* 16 (1915), 80-95.

[10] *Testamenta XII Patriarcharum* (Cambridge: Deighton Bell and Co, 1869). Sinker used two manuscripts and later published collations of another two in *Testamenta XII Patriarcharum. Appendix* (Cambridge: Deighton Bell and Co, 1879).

[11] "On the Jewish Authorship of the Testaments of the Twelve Patriarchs," *JQR* 5 (1893), 375-398.

Bousset[12] he was of the opinion that this version, which in general gives a shorter text, could be used for the detection of Christian interpolations and the reconstruction of a Jewish original. Here again, I tried to show that the readings of the Armenian were often secondary—and this applies also where they present a shorter text—and that neither its variants, nor other variants in the Greek manuscripts, could bring us nearer to an earlier Jewish text.[13] Whatever literary-critical arguments could be adduced for assuming Christian interpolations, there was certainly no text-critical evidence to support this thesis.

The conclusion, therefore, had to be that, though Charles's edition was indispensable, it gave a completely one-sided picture of the relationships between the primary witnesses to the text. After a number of years I published a preliminary edition of the text, consisting of the diplomatic text of MS *b* plus a short apparatus with the most important variants, taken from Charles's edition.[14] Finally, in 1978 the Leiden *editio maior* mentioned in the previous section was published, based on fifteen Greek MSS (three of them fragmentary). The *stemma codicum,* going back to an important article of H.J. de Jonge,[15] shows two families: the first, family I, consists of MS *b* with MS *k* (=Cod. Venet. Marc. 494 [=331], ff. 263r.-264v.; this manuscript gives only extracts), whereas family II consists of all the other witnesses.[16] The new edition made use of the Armenian version, but only in a restricted number of cases where its evidence had proved important for the reconstruction of the text.[17]

---

[12] "Die Testamente der XII Patriarchen, 1. Die Ausscheidung der christlichen Interpolationen," *ZNW* 1 (1900), 141-175.

[13] See, earlier, the criticism of Bousset's and Charles's textual criticism in N. Messel, "Ueber die textkritisch begründete Ausscheidung vermeintlicher christlicher Interpolationen in den Testamenten der Zwölf Patriarchen," in *Festschrift W.W. Baudissin* (BZAW 33 (1918), 355-374. Messel's criticism, like that by J.W. Hunkin a few years before, was neglected by later interpreters.

[14] *Testamenta XII Patriarcharum edited according to Cambridge University Library MS Ff. 1.24, fol. 203a-261b with short notes* (PVTG 1; Leiden: Brill, 1964). A second revised edition with an updated introduction appeared in 1970.

[15] "Die Textüberlieferung der Testamente der Zwölf Patriarchen," *Studies* 45-62.

[16] Appendix 1 of the edition (pp. 181-191) lists all the differences between the two families and indicates the preference for a particular reading. Where no preference is stated, the text of family I is followed.

[17] Seven such instances are listed in Appendix II (pp. 193-206) together with Armenian variants found in *T.Levi, T.Issachar, T.Zebulun* 6-9 and *T.Joseph,* supplied by M.E. Stone or taken from his *The Testament of Levi. A First Study of the Armenian MSS of the Testaments of*

The edition was preceded by a number of exploratory essays in the *Studies*-volume of 1975 which, apart from discussions of text-critical issues, provided interesting insights into the history of the Christian transmission of the text. They will be referred to several times in sections 1 and 2 of chapter 6.

II. THE COMPOSITION OF THE TESTAMENTS

Schnapp and Charles both assumed Christian interpolations in a Jewish document, though they differed in the delimitation of these interpolations. They also detected Jewish interpolations. Schnapp, for instance, removed all apocalyptical passages and tried to prove that the original *Testaments* had only contained descriptions of the particular sins or virtues of the patriarchs and the exhortations connected with them. Charles, concentrating on the passages dealing with the future, distinguished, like Bousset before him, between pro-Levi passages in an original pro-Hasmonean document dating from the reign of John Hyrcanus, and anti-Levi passages, added around the middle of the first century BCE, when the Pharisaic group responsible for the original document became dissatisfied with Hasmonean rule.

This literary critical approach to the *Testaments* remained popular until far into the second half of the twentieth century. The complicated structure of individual testaments and certain features in all testaments which were considered mutually incompatible, led to complex theories of several redactions and stages of composition which were internally consistent. I shall not go into detail here because, as will be explained presently, I do not accept the basic presuppostions of this approach.[18] I just mention the principal proponents. The views of J. Becker, in his *Untersuchungen zur Entstehungsgeschichte der Testamente der Zwölf Patriarchen*,[19] became very influential because he contributed the volume on the *Testaments* to the German series *Jüdische Schriften aus hellenistisch-römischer Zeit*.[20] Next there are

---

the *XII Patriarchs in the Convent of St. James*, Jerusalem (Jerusalem: St. James Press, 1969) and *The Armenian Version of the Testament of Joseph* (SBLTT Pseudepigrapha Series; Missoula MT: Scholars 1975). See further chapter 6, section 2.2.

[18] See the survey by Kugler, *The Testaments of the Twelve Patriarchs*, 31-34.

[19] AGJU 8; Leiden: Brill, 1970.

[20] JSHRZ 3,1; Gütersloh: Gütersloher Verlagshaus Gerd Mohn, 1974 (second edition 1980), 16-163.

two massive volumes by A. Hultgård, with the title *L'eschatologie
des Testaments des Douze Patriarches*.[21] And, finally, we should
mention J.H. Ulrichsen, *Die Grundschrift der Testamente der Zwölf
Patriarchen. Eine Untersuchung zu Umfang, Inhalt und Eigenart der
ursprünglichen Schrift*.[22] These very detailed studies have not led to a
consensus. On the contrary, the vast and often irreconcilable
differences put forward, make us wonder whether such a literary
critical approach (sometimes, as in the case of Becker and Hultgård,
still backed up by text critical remarks) will ever lead to acceptable
results.[23]

The criteria of those who tried to reconstruct the earlier stages in
the compositional history of this writing are those of all literary critics. In 1980 I mentioned "unevennesses, doublets, sudden transitions
as to form and content, all other signs of inconsistency."[24] I added:

> It is not at all evident, however, that modern critics, applying modern
> standards of consistency, are in a position to determine whether there
> are inconsistencies or not. And if inconsistencies exist, they are hardly
> more understandable if ascribed to the activities of a redactor or inter-
> polator than if the so-called original author is responsible for them.

The same applies *mutatis mutandis* to the application of form-critical
criteria. In my dissertation I described, for instance, two "patterns"
found in the eschatological passages of the *Testaments*. I called them
Sin-Exile-Return passages and Levi-Judah passages. Here one recog-
nizes a standard pattern but at the same time a great variety of appli-
cations. "Forms" lead their own lives, and may be used for different
purposes and in different contexts.

I concluded:

---

[21] Vol. 1 *Interprétation des textes*; vol. 2 *Compostion de l'ouvrage, textes et traductions*
(Acta Universitatis Upsalienses: Historia Religionum 6 and 7, Uppsala 1977 and 1982 [Dis-
tributor: Almqvist & Wiksell, Stockholm]).

[22] Acta Universitatis Upsaliensis: Historia Religionum 10, Uppsala 1991.

[23] For criticism of the views of Becker and Hultgård see also my surveys of research
mentioned in n. 2 above. On Becker see also "Testament Issachar als 'typisches Testament',"
Studies, 291-316. For reviews of Hultgård's two volumes see *JSJ* 10 (1979), 100-102 and *JSJ*
14 (1983), 70-80; on Ulrichsen's study see *JSJ* 23 (1992), 295-302.

[24] In "The Main Issues in the Study of the Testaments of the Twelve Patriarchs", *NTS* 26
(1980), 508-524; now in *Collected Essays*, 147-163. The quotations below are found on pp.
155-156 of *Collected Essays*.

In the case of the *Testaments* it is important to pay every attention to the ways in which these forms were made to serve the purpose of the author(s) of this particular writing. We may not assume, for instance, that purer or more complete forms were extant at an earlier stage of the *Testaments*, but were spoiled by additions or other editorial activities of later redactors. Particularly if the author(s) of the *Testaments* brought together as much traditional material concerning the sons of Jacob as he (they) could find, in order to use it for their particular purpose, we must allow for the possibility that form criticism, like literary criticism, can serve only a limited purpose. Literary seams (of all sorts) may be signs of compilation as much as of anything else. At the moment an author (authors) decided to put together admonitions, exemplary stories about the sons of Jacob and predictions concerning the future within the framework of a collection of twelve testaments, this process of compilation necessarily implied the use of material that varied in form and content. However neatly it was put together, some sutures were bound to remain. We should note, but not over-emphasize them.

Nevertheless, these considerations do not enable us to solve once and for all the question whether the now Christian *Testaments* ever existed in (an) earlier form(s). It may be difficult to prove that the *Testaments* are the outcome of a thorough, and to a considerable degree consistent, Christian redaction and to determine its contents, but we cannot prove conclusively that the *Testaments*, as we have them now, were *composed* in Christian circles in the second half of the second century CE.[25]

That is the reason why, from 1953 onwards, the present author has concentrated on the comparison of the biographical, eschatological and paraenetical elements in the *Testaments* with parallel and related material of Jewish and Christian provenance. The central issue was and is: How did the redactor(s)—or rather compositor(s)—mould together the traditional elements which he (they) shared with others and his (their) personal contributions to a consistent whole, serving a particular purpose? What was the purpose of the *Testaments* in their final form?

---

[25] We may also not exclude the possibility of later additions to the Christian document, between the third and the eighth century. These, too, are difficult to detect (see further, chapter 6, section 3.2 below).

When, during the research for my dissertation, I tried to define traditional elements in the various testaments and to determine the ways these had been used to support and to illustrate the teachings of the document as a whole, I was able to start with the Hebrew and Aramaic material printed by Charles in three valuable appendices in his edition of the *Testaments*. They were Aramaic fragments of a Levi document found in the Cairo Genizah, partly parallel with a Greek fragment inserted in the Greek MS. Athos, Koutloumous 39 (= *e*, dating from the XIth century) after *T.Levi* 18:2; a medieval Hebrew *Testament of Naphtali*; and the late *Midrash Wayissaʻu* which gives a tale of Judah's exploits in battle, parallel to the description of a war against the Canaanites in *T.Judah* 3-7, and of those in a war against Esau and his sons in *T.Judah* 9 (similar parallels are found in *Jub.* 34:1-9 and 37:1-38:14 respectively). Also the notes in Charles's commentary on the *Testaments* often provided useful stepping stones for more detailed investigations. Besides *Jubilees*, also the targumim on Genesis and *Midrash Bereshit Rabbah* supplied many useful parallels. One could never point to direct literary dependence one way or the other, but the use of common traditional material could be demonstrated, particularly in cases where individual testaments had elements not found in any of the others.

To mention a few examples: The Aramaic and Greek Levi material proved the existence of (an) earlier text(s) about Levi, clearly also used by the author(s) of the present *T.Levi*, that could be shown to have used this material for his (their) own, Christian, purpose. The two visions found in *T.Naphtali* 5-7 and in the Hebrew *Testament* also point to a common source (nearer to the latter than to the former). This was clearly hostile to Joseph, whereas in the present testament, part of a document in which Joseph is the paradigm of virtue, all passages which could throw an unfavourable light on this son of Jacob are omitted or changed.[26] The analysis of the Joseph passages in the various testaments, and in *T.Joseph* in particular, showed the important part played by this patriarch in the paraenesis of the *Testa-*

---

[26] So also later the very detailed analysis in T. Korteweg, "The Meaning of Naphtali's Visions," in *Studies*, 261-290.

ments.[27] For instance, in *T.Joseph* we find two blocks of (different) biographical material, in chapters 3-9 and in chapters 11-16, introduced by chapters 1-2 and leading up to paraenesis in 2:7; 10:1-11:1 and 17:1-18:4. In chapters 3-9, highlighting Joseph's struggle with Potiphar's wife one finds traditional motifs current in Hellenistic novels.[28] Another interesting testament is that of Issachar. It praises the patriarch as a farmer working hard "in singleness of heart". This clearly goes back to the LXX-version of Gen. 49:14-15 which extols Issachar as a hard-working farmer, and not to the Hebrew text that is quite different. Parallel to this, Zebulun, a full brother of Issachar, and born directly after him, is depicted in his testament as a hard-working fisherman, always ready to help people in need.

Research after 1953, by many scholars, has led to a much fuller picture of the relationship between the extremely variegated traditional material (of Jewish, Hellenistic and also Christian provenance) and the teachings of the *Testaments* as a whole. The evidence collected until about 1985 can be found in the introductions to the individual testaments and the notes on specific passages in the *Commentary* by Hollander and De Jonge published in that year.

III. THE TESTAMENTS AND THE DEAD SEA SCROLLS

In my dissertation I did not discuss the documents found near the Dead Sea in 1947 and subsequent years. In fact, only some of the finds in Cave 1 had been published and Cave 4, which (as became apparent later) was to yield the most relevant evidence, was only discovered in the summer of 1952. I soon realized, however, that the Qumran material was potentially important; some scholars who were studying what had been published already, cautioned me that my theory of a Christian origin of the *Testaments* would be refuted the moment a fragment of the *Testaments* would surface at Qumran (as they considered likely). In the end it turned out that in essentials the outcome of the 1953 analysis of the use of traditional material in *T.Levi*

---

[27] This was later demonstrated at great length by H.W. Hollander in his *Joseph as an Ethical Model in the Testaments of the Twelve Patriarchs* (SVTP 6; Leiden: Brill, 1981). See also chapter 9 below.

[28] See M. Braun, *History and Romance in Graeco-Oriental Literature* (Oxford: Blackwell, 1938), 44-95, who especially points to material of the Phaedra-tradition.

could be upheld, also after more Levi-fragments (and related material) became available. In chapters 7 and 8, written after all available fragments had been published, I have described my present position. For the purpose of the present chapter, however, it may be good to sketch some of the stages on the way.

Already in 1952 A. Dupont-Sommer connected the picture of the ideal priest in *T.Levi* 17-18 with the Teacher of Righteousness, a central figure in the community that handed down the Scrolls.[29] In 1960 M. Philonenko, in his *Les interpolations chrétiennes des Testaments des Douze Patriarches,*[30] developed this thesis, and tried to show that what had been regarded as Christian (by all scholars dealing with the *Testaments*) should be regarded as Essene. In the end, Dupont-Sommer's and Philonenko's claims were rejected by the great majority of their colleagues, if only because it soon became clear that the Qumran community was particularly concerned with detailed exposition of the Law, and was strictly observant, an interest not found in the *Testaments*.[31]

In 1957 A.S. van der Woude, in his Groningen dissertation (which became influential in later discussion), brought up the *Testaments of the Twelve Patriarchs* in his analysis of the messianic expectations of the Qumran community.[32] He showed that this community expected a priestly Messiah (from Levi) and a royal, Davidic Messiah (from Judah); the evidence available in 1957 did not suggest a change of messianic ideas in the course of the community's existence. Van der Woude found the same expectations in the Levi-Judah passages in the *Testaments*, and regarded it as extremely likely that the Aramaic "Urschrift" of the *Testaments* was written by (a) member(s) of the Qumran community. Of course, I tried to prove that he was wrong as far as the *Testaments* were concerned, and emphasized the great var-

---

[29] See "Le Testament de Lévi (XVII-XVIII) et la secte juive de l'Alliance," *Sem* 4 (1952), 33-53 and also *Nouveaux aperçus sur les manuscrits de la Mer Morte* (Paris: Adrien-Maisonneuve, 1953), 63-84.

[30] Cahiers de la RHPR 35; Paris: Presses Universitaires de France, 1960.

[31] My discussion of Philonenko's book can be found in "Christian Influence in the Testaments of the Twelve Patriarchs," *NovT* 4 (1960), 182-235; later reprinted in *Studies*, 193-246.

[32] *Die messianischen Vorstellungen der Gemeinde von Qumrân* (Assen: Van Gorcum, 1957).

iety in the use of the Levi-Judah pattern in the *Testaments* (as, indeed, of other patterns used in the expectations of the future).[33]

An important step forward was the publication by J.T. Milik, in 1955, of an Aramaic prayer of Levi that, surprisingly, ran partly parallel to another addition in the Greek MS *e* of the *Testaments* (at *T.Levi* 2:3).[34] Later Milik also drew attention to 4Q fragments concerning Levi's son and grandson Kohath and 'Amram which proved to be important for a better understanding of the fragments of the Aramaic Levi document already known—still the source that helped us most to understand the traditional material on Levi used by the author(s) of *T.Levi,* and of the *Testaments* as a whole.[35] No indications came to light that the *Testaments*, in whatever form, were written or copied at Qumran. For a further discussion of the relationship between the *Testaments* and documents found at Qumran, see chapters 7 and 8 below.

IV. SOME ADDITIONAL REMARKS ON THE ESCHATOLOGICAL PASSAGES

A few remarks on the passages concerning the future are in order. Particularly these passages have occupied literary critics trying to reconstruct earlier stages of composition of the *Testaments* in order to use them as illustrations for different Jewish messianic ideas in the period of the second temple. The great diversity in these passages does indeed present difficulties—also for those who do not see these passages as the outcome of general growth, and do not regard the

---

[33] See the essay mentioned in n. 31. Later, of course, the discovery of new fragments led to much discussion of the variety in the expectations concerning the future in the Scrolls. With regard to the relation between the *Testaments* and Qumran Van der Woude finally changed his mind. See, for instance, the tenth edition of T.C. Vriezen and A.S. van der Woude *De Literatuur van Oud-Israël*, completely revised by Van der Woude (and published posthumously by F. García Martínez and E. Noort), that appeared under the title *Oudisraëlitische en Vroegjoodse Literatuur* (Kampen: Kok, 2000). Here Van der Woude discusses the *Testaments* on pp. 485-488; on p. 488 he writes: "Ondanks bepaalde overeenkomsten met de inhoud van sommige Qumrângeschriften is een Esseense herkomst van de Testamenten onwaarschijnlijk."

[34] "Le Testament de Lévi en araméen. Fragment de la grotte 4 de Qumrân," *RB* 62 (1955), 398-406. See my discussion in "Notes on Testament of Levi II-VII" in *Studies*, 247-260.

[35] See, for instance, my "The Testament of Levi and 'Aramaic Levi'," in F. García Martínez and E Puech (eds.), *Mémorial Jean Carmignac, RevQ* 49-52; vol. 13 (1988), 367-385; reprinted in *Collected Essays* 244-262. There I also discussed other fragments connected by Milik with the *Testaments*.

patently Christian phrases as later interpolations, but notice that the latter were essential elements in the document's teaching about God's final intervention in the history of Israel and the world.

In 1953 I devoted a long chapter to these passages; the analysis given there was updated and refined in a section of the Introduction to Hollander's and De Jonge's commentary.[36] Four types can be distinguished: the most important are the Sin-Exile-Return passages and the Levi-Judah passages; less prominent were the Saviour passages and Resurrection passages. Although some common features are evident, particularly in the case of the first two types, there is also an astonishing diversity within each category, both with regard to details in terminology and to the application in particular contexts. The same can be said about the combinations of Sin-Exile-Return passages with Levi-Judah passages, with one another and with Saviour and Resurrection passages. It is also difficult to explain why distinctively Christian elements appear in so many different ways and places.

We shall have to admit that there is much we do not know, and will perhaps never know, about the previous history of the *Testaments*. What we can and should do, however, is to take them seriously in their present Christian form. In 1986, dealing (again) with the thesis about the expectation of two Messiahs in the *Testaments*, put forward by Van der Woude and others, I tried to show that there is more consistency in the expectations concerning the future than is often thought. Two features stand out: (a) the patriarchs predict a central role for the tribes of Levi and Judah; but (b) wherever a "human agent of divine deliverance" comes into the picture, there is only one: Jesus Christ.[37] Here we should emphasize one other important aspect: Although Israel's refusal to accept Jesus Christ is mentioned several times (particularly with regard to the sons of Levi in *T.Levi*), there is all along a great concern for Israel's final salvation, and the definite promise that Israel will share in this salvation if it obeys God's commandments and/or believes in Jesus Christ.[38]

---

[36] See *Dissertation*, 83-96 and *Commentary*, 51-67.

[37] "Two Messiahs in the Testaments of the Twelve Patriarchs?" in J.W. van Henten, H.J. de Jonge *et al.* (eds.), *Tradition and Re-Interpretation in Jewish and Early Christian Literature* (FS J.C.H. Lebram; SPB 36; Leiden: Brill, 1986), 150-162; reprinted in *Collected Essays*, 191-203.

[38] See "The Future of Israel in the Testaments of the Twelve Patriarchs," *JSJ* 17 (1986), 196-211; reprinted in *Collected Essays*, 164-179.

This last element in particular helps us to understand how the final words of the sons of Jacob in the *Testaments* could be of importance for early Christian readers, who read their "Old Testament" and lived alongside Jews. As I shall argue in chapter 6, sections 3.3 and 3.4, the picture becomes even clearer if we analyze the paraenetical passages in the *Testaments*, and note how some authors in the second and early third century emphasize the continuity between the obedience to God's commandments expected from the believers in the time before Moses and that expected from believers (Jewish and non-Jewish) in the time after the coming of Jesus Christ. The authors of the *Testaments* use the authority of the sons of Jacob to convince their readers that Israel will be saved if it really obeys God's commandments—as interpreted by Christians after the example of Jesus Christ—and if it turns to the saviour of Jews and Gentiles.

CHAPTER SIX

THE TESTAMENTS OF THE TWELVE PATRIARCHS AS A DOCUMENT TRANSMITTED BY CHRISTIANS

In this paper I intend to take seriously that the *Testaments* have come down to us as a writing transmitted by Christians. It is particularly concerned with the history of the transmission of the *Testaments of the Twelve Patriarchs* in the early Church. It is, however, because also Christians from later ages were interested in these writings that they have come down to us at all. Therefore we shall start with the medieval witnesses, and work our way back to the first centuries of the common era.

I. THE TESTAMENTS OF THE TWELVE PATRIARCHS IN THE MIDDLE AGES

As we have seen in the preceding chapter the Greek manuscripts, our primary witnesses to the text of the *Testaments*, date from the end of the tenth century (Cambridge, Univ. Library, Ff I.24, ff. 203r.-261v. = *b*) up to the eighteenth century (Mt. Sinai, Monastery of St. Catherine, Cod. Gr. 2170 (= 608), ff. 8r.-88r. = *j*, the last of a series of three closely related manuscripts in this monastery, and the Modern Greek translation in Bibl. Acad. Bucharest, Cod. Gr. 508 (341), ff. 7r.-120r. = Ngr).[1] It is obvious that we have to look in the Greek codices for indications why the text was transcribed. But first we have to give our attention to the data relating to the transfer of the oldest manuscript of the Greek text, the codex *b* just mentioned, to the West and its translation into Latin.

1.1 *Robert Grosseteste (ca. 1170-1253) and the* Testaments of the Twelve Patriarchs

Around 1242 Robert Grosseteste, bishop of Lincoln, translated the *Testaments* from Greek into Latin, with the assistance of a certain

---

[1] For details see the Leiden *Edition*. (For the references *Dissertation, Edition, Studies, Commentary* and *Collected Essays* used in this chapter, see chapter 5, notes 3-7.)

Nicholas the Greek. Shortly before, he had sent John of Basingstoke to Greece with the purpose of tracking down the Greek *Testaments*. In the Leiden volume *Studies on the Testaments of the Twelve Patriarchs* H.J. de Jonge has given extensive information on this,[2] and the present author has been able to supply some additional information in a recent study.[3]

For the present purpose I concentrate on two clearly related data: the reports on the finding of the *Testaments* and their translation in the Chronicle of Grosseteste's contemporary Matthew Paris[4] as well as in the colophon which occurs already in a thirteenth-century manuscript of the Latin translation[5] and must have been added at a very early date—possibly already by Nicholas the Greek, like Matthew attached to the Abbey of St. Albans. Some matters are brought emphatically to the fore there.

In the first place, attention is repeatedly drawn to the many and distinct prophecies concerning Christ which are to be found in the *Testaments*. Matthew Paris mentions the "manifestas quae in eisdem patent de Christo Prophetias"[6] and the colophon "luculentae ('clear, reliable') prophetiae, quae in hoc scripto, luce clarius, coruscant ('glow, sparkle')." Matthew Paris adds that the *Testaments* are indisputably "de substantia Bibliothecae." "Bibliotheca" is a designation of the Bible current in the Middle Ages. In his opinion, the *Testaments* clearly contained "biblical material." Of course they did not as such belong to the canonical writings, but as to their substance they certainly ranked among them.

Why had these important witnesses concerning Christ remained hidden for such a long time? The colophon blames this on the Jews, and speaks about "invidia Iudaeorum, qui ea propter evidentissimas et manifestissimas, ac crebras de Christo prophetias, quae in iis scribuntur, diu occultaverunt," and Matthew Paris uses much the same

---

[2] "La bibliothèque de Michel Choniatès et la tradition occidentale des Testaments des XII Patriarches" and "Additional notes on the history of MSS. Venice Bibl. Marc. Gr. 494 (*k*) and Cambridge Univ. Libr. Ff. 1.24 (*b*)" in *Studies*, 97-106; 107-115.

[3] "Robert Grosseteste and the Testaments of the Twelve Patriarchs," *JTS* N.S. 42 (1991), 115-125.

[4] Matthaeus Parisiensis, *Chronica Majora* (ed. H.R. Luard), IV, 232-233 and V, 284-287.

[5] For details see the article mentioned in n. 3, pp. 118-119.

[6] *Chron. Maj.* V, 285.

terms.[7] That explains why many learned and wise men in the Church never quoted the *Testaments*. We owe it to the Greeks, "omnium scriptorum diligentissimi investigatores," that this writing has been translated from Hebrew into Greek[8] and was preserved over a long time so that now, thanks to Robert Grosseteste, it could radiate its glorious light, intended "ad robur fidei Christianae et ad majorem Judaeorum confusionem."[9]

Robert Grosseteste *cum suis* evidently used the *Testaments* to make abundantly clear to Jews and all possible adversaries of the true doctrine that salvation is to be expected exclusively from Jesus Christ and from the true Church that abides by Scripture. As early as 1253 Vincent of Beauvais incorporated excerpts from the *Testaments* in his *Speculum Historiale* because of their extremely clear and utterly beautiful prophecies concerning Christ, "quas nuper transtulit magister robertus grossum caput, lincolniensis episcopus de greco in latinum."[10] Bonaventura, too, in his Commentary on the *Sententiae* from 1250-1252[11] already quotes from the *Testaments* in Grosseteste's Latin translation, which in view of the number of transmitted manuscripts (no less than fifteen from the thirteenth century alone) must have been very popular from the start.

---

[7] "Testamenta duodecim Patriarcharum....quae per multa tempora incognita et abscondita fuerunt per invidiam Judaeorum, propter manifestas prophetias de Salvatore in eis contentas" (*Chron. Maj.* IV, 232).

[8] One has to assume translation from Hebrew into Greek if one starts from the thesis that the *Testaments* reproduce the words of Jacob's sons. Compare the introduction to the *Testaments* in Mt. Sinai, Monastery of St. Catherine, Cod. Gr. 547 (= 770), ff. 1r.-70r. (s. XVII) = *h* and also in the codices *i* (no known number; ff. 1r.-38r.; s. XVII?) and *j* (Cod. Gr. 2170 [= 608], ff. 8r.-88r; s. XVIII): Ἰωάννου τοῦ ποτε ἑβραίου εἴδησις τῶν διαθηκῶν τῶν ιβ' υἱῶν τοῦ πατριάρχου Ἰακὼβ μεταφρασθεῖσα ἀπὸ ἰουδαικῶν διαλέκτου εἰς ἑλληνικήν. For further data see the Leiden *Edition*, XIX-XXI. Cf. Oxford, Selden sup. ff. 232a.-262a. from the fourteenth century, which does not mention Grosseteste's name. S.H. Thomson, *The Writings of Robert Grosseteste Bishop of Lincoln 1235-1253* (Cambridge: Cambridge University Press, 1940), 43: "The rubric reads: secundum translationem Johannis Crisostomi de hebreo in grecum." See also the Middle Dutch manuscripts mentioned in n. 23.

[9] Thus Matthew Paris, *Chron. Maj.* IV, 233. The colophon speaks of the prophecies, which "in maiorem confusionem Iudaeorum et omnium haereticorum et inimicorum Ecclesiae gloriosius prorumpant."

[10] See on this H.J. de Jonge, "Les fragments marginaux dans le MS. *d* des Testaments des XII Patriarches," in *Studies*, 87-96.

[11] *Commentaria in Quattuor Libros Sententiarum* IV = *Opera Omnia* IV (ed. Quaracchi, 1899), Dist. XXIX, Qu. II, p. 703.

Highly interesting, finally, are two references to the *Testaments* in Roger Bacon's *Opus Majus* from 1266-1268,[12] in which he elaborates Matthew Paris's brief remark "quae constat esse de substantia Bibliothecae." In Pars II, cap. XVI he says that patriarchs and prophets have written other books beside those that are included in the Holy Scripture; books which, though not incorporated in the canon, have been used by "sancti et sapientes Graeci et Latini" right from the beginning of the Church.[13] Indeed did not Jude, for instance, already use Enoch in his Epistle (vv. 14-15)? We may, therefore, assign authority to the prophecies concerning Christ which proved to be correct. Elsewhere, in Pars VII, pars IV,[14] he says: if one objects that those writings are apocryphal and that therefore their authorship is not established, one should remember: "hoc non tollit veritatem quia libri hi recipiuntur a Graecis, Latinis, et Judaeis." The addition "Judaeis" here deserves special attention. Much as the Jews may have tried to suppress the witness of their patriarchs, in the final analysis the Christians are dependent on their tradition. In a letter from 1231 Grosseteste quotes St. Augustine's exegesis of Ps. 58:12 in the Vulgate, in which this Church Father argues that it is not allowed to kill the Jews, because they "portant codices nostros, de quibus prophetatus et promissus est nobis Christus." Indeed, Grosseteste continues, "ac per hoc sunt testes fidei Christianae contra infidelitatem Paganorum."[15]

1.2 *Indications of the importance of the* Testaments *in Greek manuscripts*

In a great number of Greek manuscripts we find additions in the margin, and occasionally also in the text, which, contrary to the equally frequent omissions,[16] give us information on the intention of the

---

[12] On Bacon see H.J. de Jonge, "Die Patriarchentestamente von Roger Bacon bis Richard Simon (mit einem Namenregister)" in *Studies*, 3-42.

[13] *Opus Majus* (ed. J.H. Bridges), Suppl. Vol., 71-72.

[14] *Opus Majus* (ed. J.H. Bridges), Vol. II, 391.

[15] *Roberti Grosseteste Episcopi quondam Lincolniensis Epistolae* (ed. H.R. Luard), Epistola V (pp. 33-38).

[16] Relatively many MSS. omit passages. In a number of cases it is a matter of copying errors, but generally speaking this is not so. The copyists did not go about in a systematic way; probably they simply thought the expositions of the *Testaments* too long-winded. In Ms. *g* (= Patmos, Mon. Joh. Theol. Ms. 411, ff. 178r-220v; saec. XV) which contains many abbreviations, the writer now and then vents his feelings. He leaves out two lists of spirits in *T.Reub.*

scribes involved. Frequently[17] we find in the margin the gloss περὶ χριστοῦ, not surprising after what just has been remarked about Grosseteste c.s. In Ms *m* (= Ankara, Türk Tarih Kurumu, Ms Gr. 60, pp. 339-482) dating from the second half of the sixteenth century we find at the end of the *Testament of Benjamin* (therefore at the end of the *Testaments*) the note:

> καὶ προσπάγητε πάντα πρὸς νόμον κυρίου καὶ κριτοῦ τῶν ἀπάντων, ἵνα εὕρητε αὐτὸν ἵλεων, ὅταν ἥξῃ ἐξ οὐρανοῦ καὶ γεννηθήσεται ὥσπερ νήπιον ἐκ γυναικός· καὶ αὐτὸς διδάξει ἡμᾶς πᾶσαν διδαχὴν πνευματικὴν ἐν ταπεινώσει, καὶ παθὼν παρὰ τῶν Ἰουδαίων ἕως μέχρι ἀναληφθῆναι εἰς τοὺς οὐρανοὺς καὶ πάλιν ἐρχόμενος μετὰ δόξης κρῖναι τὸν Ἰσραὴλ ἐν δικαιοσύνῃ καὶ ἀληθείᾳ.

> And be in everything connected with the law of the Lord and the Judge of the universe, that you will find him merciful when he comes from heaven and is born of a woman as a small child. And he will teach you all spiritual teachings in humility, and, having suffered on the part of the Jews until his assumption into the heavens, return with glory to pass judgment on Israel in justice and truth.

This passage substitutes a much more extensive testamentary final passage in *T.Benj.* 10:2-11 (in which the response of the patriarch's descendants to Jesus as human being on earth and his future judgment figure prominently) as well as chapter 11 (in which "a beloved of the Lord" of Benjamin's seed comes on the scene). It is followed by and abridged version of the final chapter *T.Benj.* 12, which also occurs in virtually the same form in Ms *d* (= Cod. Vat. Gr. 1238, ff. 350r-379v; saec. XII). *T.Benj.* 11, by the way, has, for obvious reasons, in another manuscript, *l* (= Athos, Laura I 48 [cat. no. 1132], ff.

2:2-9; after the introduction to the first list in *T.Reub.* 2:1 about "what I saw about the seven spirits of deceit when I repented" he writes: ἀρκεῖ μοι εἰς διδασκαλίαν ὑμῶν. Comparable is the omission of a passage in *T.Napht.* 2:2-8 about the correlation between body and spirit, ending in 2:9 with the exhortation to abide by the order of creation. The scribe of *g* makes Naphtali declare καὶ ἐποίουν τὰς ἐντολὰς αὐτοῦ (Jacob is meant) κατὰ τάξιν, and then adds καὶ ἕτερά τινα πολλὰ φυσιογνωμικά, before continuing with an adapted version of v. 9. According to *L.Sc.J., s.v.* φυσιογνωμία is "the science or art of judging a man by his features." For details, here and elsewhere, see the Leiden *Edition*.

[17] Except in Mss. *b* and *d*, to be discussed presently, also in *c* (Cod. Vat. Gr. 731, ff. 97r.-166v.; saec. XIII), and *hij*, the three manuscripts of the Monastery of St. Catherine in the Sinai, already mentioned.

204r—276r; saec. XVI-XVII) the marginal note περὶ τοῦ ἁγίου ἀπο-
στόλου Παύλου· καὶ γὰρ ἐκ τῆς φυλῆς αὐτοῦ ἦν.[18]

It is relevant here to dwell for a moment on three manuscripts: *b*
(the one used by Grosseteste); *d*, just mentioned, a manuscript from
Calabria written in 1195[19]; and *k* (= Venice, S. Marc. Cod. Gr. Z. 494
(= 331]), a manuscript containing excerpts from the *Testaments* on ff.
263r.-264v., and dating from the middle of the thirteenth century.

In the case of *b* attention should be called to four marginal notes.
T.Reub. 6:8 carries προφητεία περὶ χῦ; *T.Sim.* 6:7 προφητεία περὶ τῆς
ἐνσάρκου οἰκονομίας, *T.Levi* 2:10 περὶ τοῦ χῦ and *T.Levi* 4:1 πε<ρὶ>
τῆς σταυρώσεως τοῦ χῦ λέ<γεται>. It is possible, though not abso-
lutely certain, that these glosses stem from the author of the manuscript himself.[20]

An interesting case is *d*. Not only did the writer of the text add
περὶ τοῦ χριστοῦ in the margin some thirty times, but in addition to
this we find four Greek *marginalia* by a later hand, consisting of quotations of *T.Reub.* 6:8, 11-12; *T.Jud.* 23:5; 24:1-2; *T.Gad* 7:1; 8:1;
T.Ash. 7:2-3, 3-4; the text of these quotations does not precisely correspond with the text of these passages in the manuscript itself. As to
their contents, all four *marginalia* are of Christological purport. In all
four cases a (partial) Latin translation has been added by the same
hand. The Latin text of these translations agrees with the Latin excerpt from the *Testaments* incorporated in the *Speculum Historiale* of
Vincent of Beauvais, mentioned in the preceding section. H.J. de
Jonge, who has carried out a thorough investigation into the matter,
concludes that the choice and the extent of the marginal notes (not
the text itself) are determined by the Latin fragments in Vincent of
Beauvais's book. Vincent, as we have seen was above all fascinated
by the "apertissimae atque pulcherrimae de christo prophetiae" in the
Testaments.[21]

Finally there are the fragments in *k*. First rather long ones, with a
general introduction, from *T.Reuben, T.Simeon* and *T.Levi*, but with

---

[18] So, too, the copy of *l*, Athos Laura K 116 (cat. no. 1403). *d* has Παῦλος and *k* (see
below) περὶ τοῦ ἁγίου Παύλου.

[19] On *d* see H.J. de Jonge, "Les fragments marginaux dans le MS. *d*."

[20] Annotation of H.J. de Jonge at the collation: "Glosses of—perhaps—the writer of the
MS. himself." The handwriting is in any case related.

[21] For a great number of further details see H.J. de Jonge's article "Les fragments marginaux dans le MS. *d*."

T.Judah things begin to change. Although the introduction announces that the testament is concerned with courage and avarice, the excerpt proper is limited to *T. Jud.* 21:7-end in an abridged version, characterised as περὶ τῆς βασιλείας τῶν υἱῶν αὐτοῦ. Nothing has been taken over from *T.Issachar*, for, as the introduction tells us, οὗτος οὐδέν τι περὶ τοῦ χριστοῦ ἐφθέγξατο. All of the other seven excerpts restrict themselves to the eschatological passages at the end of the *Testaments*; the introductions briefly mention the paraenesis in the testament concerned, and then announce what the patriarch had to say about the Christ. Interestingly the final exhortation about the "pure disposition" in *T.Benjamin* 8 is incorporated.[22] It is clear that the scribe of these excerpts, or possibly already the writer of his *Vorlage*, was first of all interested in the Christological passages.

Summarizing: the data in the Greek manuscripts known to us point in the same direction as the reports about Grosseteste and his contemporaries. All users of the *Testaments* were concerned with references to Christ.

1.3 *The ethical exhortations in the* Testaments

The *Testaments* are, however, distinctly a paraenetic writing, as is evident from their structure and design. Could so obvious a fact have escaped the scholars in the Middle Ages and later? This is a point that clearly requires further investigation.

As H.J. de Jonge pointed out to me, the East Middle Dutch translation (from Latin) of the *Testaments*, which we have in three mutually independent manuscripts,[23] has clearly been transmitted with

---

[22] Only the introductions to *T.Dan* and *T.Benjamin* do not mention that the patriarch spoke περὶ τοῦ χριστοῦ. At *T.Dan* 5:8 there is a marginal note εἰς βαβυλῶνα λέγει clearly written by the writer of the MS, just as the interesting remark at *T.Jud.* 25:1 (speaking about the resurrection of Abraham, Isaac and Jacob along with Jacob's twelve sons): ὅτε ἀνέστη ὁ χριστὸς συναναστήσας αὐτούς. Of many more such additions it cannot be established that they stem from the writer himself. At the end of *T.Benjamin* the writer continues with a quotation from Gen. 49:17-18 LXX and a short commentary on this. In a different handwriting there is in the margin an addition περὶ τοῦ ἀντιχριστοῦ.

[23] Nijmegen, Gemeentearchief, Weeshuis Ms. 956, pp. 3a-50a; Ms. 957, pp. 3a-63a and Deventer, Athenaeumbibliotheek Ms I,42 (101D6), f. 247r-v (fragment, two pages of the introduction in two columns, see Catalogue 1892). See also Amsterdam, Universiteitsbibliotheek, VJ 17, mentioned by T. Mertens (see n. 25).The beginning in Ms. 957 (cf. 956) reads: "Here begin the testaments of the twelve patriarchs the children of the patriarch Jacob after the translation by St John Goldenmouth from the hebrew language into the greek language and from the greek language into the latin language and finally from the latin language into the

paraenetic intentions. This is evident from the short prologue and epilogue with which the translator provided the writing. Thus he says, at the end:

> Here end the sermons and the testaments of the twelve patriarchs children of Jacob the patriarch which they made at the very end of their lives in which they narrate a part of their lives with a variety of good examples and teaching which they taught to their children and commanded to practise.[24]

We may take it for granted that this translation was made in circles of adherents of the Modern Devotion, a movement that has produced a vast body of literature in the vernacular aimed at the *praxis pietatis*. In one of the manuscripts (Nijmegen, Gemeentearchief, Weeshuis no. 957) we find, besides the *Testaments*, the text of a Dutch translation of *De spiritualibus* ("Van der opclimminghen") from the hand of Gerard Zerbolt van Zutphen († 1398, a prominent pupil of Geert Grote).[25]

There is yet another Dutch translation, made in 1538. Its oldest Dutch printing dates from 1541, published by Albertus Palfraet in Deventer. All of its five or six printings between 1541 and ca. 1550 appeared in Overijssel, in the East of the Netherlands; after 1551 the translation appears in all sorts of editions in the Southern Nether-

---

dutch language" ("Hier beginnen die testamente der xij patriarchen kinder Jacobs des patriarchen na oversettinge sancte Iohans guldenmoint van ebreuscher tongen in grixser tongen ende van grixser tongen in latijnscher tongen ende ten lesten van latijnscher tongen in duytscher talen"). For John Chrysostom see also n. 8.

[24] "Hier eyndet die sermone ende die testamente der xij patriarchen Jacobs kinder des patriarchen die si maecten inden lesten eynde oers leuens daer si in seggen een deel van oren leuen mit menigerhande goeden exempel end leer die si oren kinderen leerden end beualen te doen"—see L. Sormani, *Inventaris van de Archieven van het Borger-kinderen-Weeshuis, het Arme-kinder-Weeshuis en de beide Weeshuizen te Nijmegen* (Nijmegen, Drukkerij Gebr. Jansen, 1951), 302. Besides, (in MSS. 956 and 957) also in the introduction: "... ende prophentierden hem toecomende dinghen, die naemaels gheschien solden, van oen ende van oren naecomelijnghe" (E.T.: "... and prophesied things that would happen to them, things that afterwards were to happen, to them and their progeny").

[25] T. Mertens, "Geestelijke testamenten in de laatmiddeleeuwse Nederlanden. Een verkenning van het genre," in G.R.W. Dibbets and P.W.M. Wackers (eds.), *Wat duikers vent is dit! Opstellen voor W.M.H. Hummelen* (Wijhe: Uitg. Quarto, 1989), 75-89, points out that many spiritual testaments from the late Middle Ages are known, also in particular from the circles of the Modern Devotion. On pp. 86-88 he gives a list of them (with on p. 86 a reference to MS. Amsterdam, Universiteitsbibliotheek VJ 17 of the *Testaments*, according to H.J. de Jonge a copy after the printed edition of 1540).

lands.[26] C.C. de Bruin and H.J. de Jonge have associated them with the chiliastic movement of David Joris (active in the Netherlands between ca. 1528 and 1540). This would explain why this translation was put on the index of prohibited books.[27]

In any case the readers of this second translation were not only interested in the paraenetic parts but also in the prophecies in the *Testaments*. On the title page of the edition that appeared in 1544 with Pieter Warnerszoon in Kampen we read: "The testaments of the XII patriarchs Jacob's children, how each before his end taught his children (to live in) the fear of the Lord and exhorted (them) to live a God-fearing life. Also how each particularly through the prophetic spirit witnessed to Christ the true Messiah (clearer than light). In which are contained much magnificent teaching and many consoling promises by Christ very consoling and altogether inducive to a God-fearing life."[28] It is significant that precisely the second half of this passage (from "Also how each..." onward) is omitted on the title pages of the three printings of the *Testaments* by Plantijn, dating from 1561, 1564 and 1566.[29] Plantijn—also, by the way, the printer of the Index (1570)—evidently thought it well-advised to omit the reference to the prophetic spirit.

These forms of reception of the *Testaments*, in the Netherlands and elsewhere, deserve more attention. One could, for instance, assume with good reason, that in the monasteries in which the *Testaments* were transcribed, in the East as well as in the West, the ethical content of this writing was well received. But within the scope of this paper we have to go back from the Middle Ages to, in the end, the

---

[26] See A. Welkenhuysen, "Plantijns drukken van de Testamenten der XII Patriarchen (1561, 1564, 1566) in hun 'boekhistorische' context," *De Gulden Passer* 66-67 (1988-1989), 505-515, see especially p. 509.

[27] A. Welkenhuysen, "Plantijns drukken," 514. Compare the article by I.M. Veldman and H.J. de Jonge mentioned in the next note, p. 179.

[28] "Die testamenten der XII patriarchen Jacobs kinderen, hoe een yeghelick voer sijnen eynde sijn kinderen gheleert totter vreesen Godts ende Godtsalighen leven vermaent heeft. Oock hoe een yeghelick bysonder doer den propheetschen ghyest van Christo den waeren Messia (claerder dan dat licht) gethuyghet. Daer inne veel schooner leer ende troestlicker toeseggingen van Christo begrepen sint seer troestelick ende tot eenen waren Godtsalighen leven gants dienstelick." See I.M. Veldman and H.J. de Jonge, "The Sons of Jacob: the Twelve Patriarchs in Sixteenth-century Netherlandish Prints and Popular Literature," *Simiolus* 15 (1985), 176-196, esp. p. 178, n. 10 and the picture on p. 186.

[29] Reproduced in facsimile by A. Welkenhuysen.

early Church. What can be said, on the basis of the transmission in the Middle Ages, about that in the preceding period?

II. PRIOR TO THE TENTH CENTURY

2.1 *The transition from uncial to minuscule*

Our oldest Greek textual witness Ms. *b* dates from the end of the tenth century. As the Leiden research has established, it belongs, together with Ms. *k,* to one small family, called family I. All other textual witnesses (including the Armenian, Slavonic and Serbian translations) belong to family II. How old, then, is the archetype of the tradition known to us?

H.J. de Jonge, who, in the volume *Studies on the Testaments of the Twelve Patriarchs* (1975), made a substantial contribution to the reconstruction of the *stemma codicum* employed in the Leiden *Edition*,[30] also devoted an important article to this question.[31] On the basis of an examination of thirteen passages showing different readings in family I and family II, he concludes that the *Testaments* were transcribed not once but twice in the ninth century, when the transition was made form uncial to minuscule. In fact, the variants concerned can best be explained on the basis of a wrong or at least divergent reading of uncial script. If the *Testaments* were transcribed from uncial to minuscule script twice, the odds are that also two different uncial manuscripts were used. And if this is the case, the archetype of the textual tradition known to us must go back beyond the ninth century. How far back it is impossible to establish.

2.2 *The Armenian translation*

The next question to be considered is whether the translations from Greek into other languages help us to trace an older stage of textual tradition. In the case of the *Testaments of the Twelve Patriarchs* efforts have been made to go farther back by means of the Armenian translation, known in more than fifty manuscripts and clearly very popular in the Armenian church. In an article from 1969 C. Burchard

---

[30] "Die Textüberlieferung der Testamente der Zwölf Patriarchen," *ZNW* 63 (1972), 27-44 reprinted in *Studies*, 45-62.

[31] "The Earliest Traceable Stage of the Textual Tradition of the Testaments of the Twelve Patriarchs," *Studies*, 63-86.

dated the translation to the sixth or seventh century on the strength of the kind of Armenian employed,[32] and M.E. Stone concurred.[33] To prove this, however, turned out to be far from easy.

The earliest Armenian manuscripts date from the tirteenth century,[34] and the oldest list of sacred writings mentioning the *Testaments* is that of Johannes Sarkawag of Hatbat (1045/55-1129?). Burchard says that Johannes knew the *Testaments* in Armenian, but M.E. Stone believes it quite possible that he quoted a list of Greek writings.[35] If this is so he cannot be adduced as an indubitable witness for the Armenian text of the *Testaments*.

The place of the Armenian translation (A) in the *stemma codicum* is reasonably certain.[36] It belongs to fam. II and, like *eafchij*Ngr and the Slavonic translation, it has an abridged, secondary text in *T.Zebulun*.[37] It does not share many other secondary readings in that group, but shows many points of similarity with (manuscripts belonging to) subfamily *gldm*Fm^d; consequently A has to be situated between these two subfamilies. The oldest witness for the short version of *T.Zebulun* is *e* (= Ms. Athos, Koutloumous 39 [cat. no. 3108], ff. 198r-

[32] "Zur armenischen Überlieferung der Testamente der zwölf Patriarchen" in C. Burchard, J. Jervell and J. Thomas, *Studien zu den Testamenten der Zwölf Patriarchen* (BZNW 36; Berlin: Töpelmann, 1969), 1-29.

[33] "New Evidence for the Armenian Version of the Testaments of the Twelve Patriarchs," *RB* 84 (1977), 94-107, esp. p. 102. This article (as well as that mentioned in n. 41) can now be found in M.E. Stone, *Selected Studies in Pseudepigrapha and Apocrypha with Special Reference to the Armenian Tradition* (SVTP 9; Leiden: Brill, 1991), 131-144 (see esp. p. 139). C. Burchard, who has done much work on the Armenian version of *Joseph and Aseneth*, has shown that in many Armenian manuscripts the translations of *Joseph and Aseneth* and the *Testaments* are found together. In a recent essay "Character and Origin of the Armenian Version of *Joseph and Aseneth*," in V. Calzolari Bouvier, J.-D. Kaestli and B. Outtier (eds.), *Apocryphes arméniens: transmission-traduction-création-iconographie* (Publications de l'Institut romand des sciences bibliques 1; Lausanne: Éditions du Zèbre, 1999),73-90, he argues that the Armenian version of *Joseph and Aseneth* was not made in the sixth or seventh century, but in the tenth or eleventh. He does not give an explicit view on the date of the Armenian version of the *Testaments*, although he refers to the discussion summarized in the present section.

[34] S. Lazarro 346 (1220); Jerusalem 1925 (1269); Erevan 1500 (1282/3); Bodl. Arm. e 30 (s. XII); see Burchard, "Zur armenischen Überlieferung," pp. 13-14.

[35] See M.E. Stone, "Armenian Canon Lists III—the Lists of Mechitar of Ayrivank' (c. 1285 CE," *HTR* 69 (1976), 289-300 and "New evidence," 102, with the conclusion : "It seems safer, therefore, to abandon the use of this list as a witness to the existence of the Armenian version of the Testaments in the eleventh century."

[36] See, for what follows, M. de Jonge, "The Greek Testaments of the Twelve Patriarchs and the Armenian Version," *Studies*, 120-139.

[37] See M. de Jonge, "Textual Criticism and the Analysis of the Composition of the Testament of Zebulun," *Studies*, 144-160.

229v), a manuscript dating from the eleventh century. It is not certain when the abridgment was made, but as regards the Greek material it need not have been before the tenth or eleventh century. In 1975 I therefore concluded, referring to H.J. de Jonge's argument concerning the transliteration from uncial to minuscule script:

> The Armenian translation is very unlikely to be earlier than the IXth century. We should be cautious, therefore, to put the Armenian translation in the VIth or VIIth century on the basis of the impression made by its language alone. Surely the possibility may not be excluded that some scribe at a later date deliberately used classical or classicizing language for a writing like the *Testaments* which purported to come from ancient times. What we really need is unequivocal early external evidence for A. [38]

Research has, of course, continued. Two persons in particular who have contributed to it deserve special mention. I briefly mention A. Hultgård, who in his *L'eschatologie des Testaments des Douze Patriarches* II,[39] 11-52, extensively discussed the textual problems of the *Testaments* with special attention for the position of the Armenian translation. He assumes four textual types: *bk, gldm, eafnchij*SNGr and A, which independently go back to archetypes from the third or fourth century. For the reconstruction of the archetype we need all four types, and consequently also the Armenian version[40]; obviously they existed already before the ninth century—even though Hultgård cannot adduce evidence for transliteration in the case of *gldm* and *eafnchij*, and his arguments for the dependence of A on a Greek text written in uncials are not convincing.

In any case he considers A as very important for the reconstruction of the oldest Greek text. In agreement with M.E. Stone, he says that in general the Armenian version offers a shorter text and occasionally redacts radically; this will have been so right from the beginning of the translation in the fifth or sixth century, and will have

---

[38] *Studies*, p.138.

[39] A. Hultgård, *L'eschatologie des Testaments des Douze Patriarches II. Composition de l'ouvrage. Textes et traductions* (Acta Universitatis Upsaliensis. Historia Religionum 7; Uppsala 1982). See my review in *JSJ* 14 (1983), 70-80.

[40] Crucial is his preference for the shorter text in *T.Zebulun*; the longer one is, in his opinion, secondary. For that reason for him the most important dividing line is not that between *bk* and the other groups, but that between *bk* and *gldm* on the one hand and *eafnchij*SNgr and A on the other.

continued subsequently. All the same Hultgård uses singular Armenian readings whenever it suits him; as I have tried to demonstrate
elsewhere, his textcritical analysis is not very precise, methodically
speaking; and now and then he handles criteria of internal criticism in
a very subjective manner.

Later, M.E. Stone drew attention to an interesting new Armenian
witness.[41] In the oldest Armenian manuscript on paper, Erevan, Matenadaran no. 2679, dating from 981, we find on ff. 251r-252r excerpts
from the *Testaments*. Though unimportant as to their literary value
for lack of a clear line and purpose, these excerpts are very important
from the point of view of textual history and textual criticism. This
"Epitome" (as Stone calls it) gives a text that is not directly dependent on that of any of the other witnesses which can be divided into
four textual types.[42] Stone concludes:

> Since the *Epitome* is as old as the oldest Greek witness, its ancestor must
> be older, perhaps notably older than that. This implies that the *Vorlage* of
> Armenian on the Greek stemma is most likely of the eighth century or
> earlier and in any case no later than the early ninth century at the very
> latest.[43]

It is clear that the first half of the ninth century just fits in with H.J.
de Jonge's reconstruction of the transliteration process, whereas an
earlier dating leads to considerable difficulties. Yet Stone, on stylistic
grounds, is very much inclined to assume an earlier date. He gives no
details but refers to the judgment of archbishop Norair Bogharian,
"one of the great scholars of Armenian of the generation" who, in a
conversation, "pointed to the absence from *Testament of Levi* of the
stratum of Armenian vocabulary that entered the language as a result
of the influence of the stylistic aberrations of the Philo-Hellene
school of the late fifth and early sixth centuries."[44] We therefore have
to allow for a translation made in the fifth century, but Stone remains

---

[41] "The *EPITOME* of the Testaments of the Twelve Patriarchs," *Revue des Études Arméni-
ennes*, N.S. 20 (1986-1987), 69-107; reprinted in Stone, *Selected Studies*, 145-183. See also a
second article "The Epitome of the Testaments of the Twelve Patriarchs in Matenadaran No.
2679," *Mus* 108 (1995), 265-277.

[42] As has been demonstrated by Hultgård and Stone. See also M.E. Stone, "The Armenian
Version of the Testaments of the Twelve Patriarchs. Selections of Manuscripts," *Sion* 49
(1975), beside "New Evidence," mentioned in n. 33.

[43] "The *EPITOME*," 75 (151).

[44] "The *EPITOME*," 76 (152).

cautious, aware of having to assume more than two transliterations in that case. He knows that this is extremely difficult to prove; but, he says, what cannot be demonstrated may for all that have taken place.

My conclusion is that we have to wait for unequivocal quotations from or allusions to the *Testaments* in the writings of early Armenian authors. With all due respect, it would seem to me that arguments on the strength of vocabulary or style are tenuous, because this kind of narrative and exhortative literature, in which moreover the sons of Jacob are purported to speak, has its own peculiar style and vocabulary.

In conclusion there is one other point deserving to be mentioned briefly. The Armenian version shows the tendency to shorten the text, even more so than the Greek manuscripts that have abbreviations. The textcritical rule *lectio brevior potior* certainly does not hold good for the *Testaments*, in any case not where divergencies of this kind are concerned. Needless to say that this means that even where we have to do with redacted Christian passages the shorter, less "Christian," Armenian text is not closer to the original.[45]

III. BACK TO THE TESTAMENTS OF THE TWELVE PATRIARCHS IN THE SECOND CENTURY

3.1 *The* Testaments *between the third and the eighth century*

The first Christian author to quote the *Testaments* is Origen in his homilies on Joshua (transmitted in Latin only).[46] While not considering them canonical ("sed in aliquo quodam libello, qui appellatur testamentum duodecim patriarcharum, quamvis non habeatur in canone"), he yet thinks that they have sensible things to say. Referring to *T.Reub.* 2-3, he continues: "talem quendam invenimus sensum, quod per singulos peccantes singuli satanae intelligi debeant." Origen

---

[45] As I tried to show in my dissertation (see chapter 5.1 above). I should also like to draw attention to an observation J. Jervell made in his "Ein Interpolator interpretiert. Zu der christlichen Bearbeitung der Testamente der Zwölf Patriarchen" (pp. 30-61 in the volume mentioned in n. 32). Jervell remarks that the Armenian version thoroughly modifies the pronouncements in the *Testaments* on the salvation of the nations and Israel. "Die armenische Übersetzung ist deshalb eine spätere christliche Übersetzung und Bearbeitung, für die das Verhältnis Israel und die Völker ohne Belang ist, für die die Testamente das Schicksal der Menschen überhaupt darstellen, m.a.W. Universalismus" (p. 40).

[46] *In Librum Jesu Nave Homiliae* 15,6 (ed. W. Baehrens, G.C.S., *Origenes VII 2*, Leipzig 1921).

clearly attributes at least some authority to the *Testaments*. On the strength of this reference we have to consider the beginning of the third century as *terminus ad quem* for them. On the basis of parallels (to be discussed presently) with other authors from the last half of the second century and the beginning of the third (Justin, Irenaeus, Hippolytus), it is likely that they came into being at the end of the second century.

The reference in Origen is unmistakably vague as to the content of the passage involved; the same applies to that to *T.Napht.* 2:8 in Jerome, *Tractatus de Psalmo* 15.[47] These references give us no certainty as to the exact contents of the *Testaments* known to both authors. Are there possibilities to give a more specific picture of the developments between ca. 200 and ca. 700 (assuming that the present textual tradition in any case goes back to an eighth century archetype)?

One thing is certain: textual criticism leaves us in the lurch at this point. For instance: at the end of *T.Dan* 7 verse 3 is plainly a later addition. After the conclusion of the testament in 7:2 with the words "and his sons buried him, and afterwards they brought up his bones (to bury them) near Abraham, Isaac and Jacob," the text continues with the words: "But, as Dan prophesied to them, that they would forget the law of their God, and be alienated from the land of their inheritance and from the race of Israel and their family and offspring, so it came to pass." This is clearly a gloss, but all the same it is present in the entire manuscript tradition, and as to its contents not completely without parallel in the *Testaments*, witness *T.Ash.* 7:6: "Therefore you will be scattered as Gad and Dan, my brothers, who will not know their lands and tribe and tongue." If we consider this verse as a later addition, we do so on the strength of the conviction that this verse does not fit in the composition pattern of the *Testaments*. We cannot ascertain when this gloss found its way into the text.

As was argued in chapter 5, several things are bound to remain unclear if we try to reconstruct the previous history of the *Testaments*. They consist of farewell discourses, with a distinct beginning and a

---

[47] Ed. G. Morin, *Anecdota Maredsolana* III 3, Oxoniae 1903, now in C.C.L. 78, Turnhout 1958, p. 376: "In libro quoque Patriarcharum, licet inter apocryphos computetur, ita inveni: ut quomodo fel ad iracundiam, sic renes ad calliditatem et ad astutiam sint creati. Πανουργία autem id est calliditas..." Cf. *T.Napht.* 2:8 ... χολὴν πρὸς πικρίαν ... νέφρους εἰς πανουργίαν.

distinct end, devoted to the paraenesis of the moribund patriarch to his children and grandchildren; they are illustrated with biographical material and end in prophecies concerning the future of the patriarchs' children and grandchildren. Occasionally we come across a great amount of haggadic material, as in the case of Levi—for which we have a parallel document—or in the case of Judah, where we find traditions about wars of Jacob's sons with the Canaanites, transmitted in *Jubilees* and elsewhere. In *T.Joseph* that (just like *T.Levi* and *T.Judah*) is considerably longer than the other nine testaments, there are two cycles of stories, one about Joseph and Potiphar's wife (chapters 3-9) and one about Joseph's arrest and captivity (chapters 11-16). We may rightfully assume that the contents of the *Testaments* were also determined by the tradition material available in written and/or oral form. But since we often cannot resort to external witnesses, we can at times only conjecture about the sources; nor can we determine how it reached the *Testaments*. This certainly applies to the time before the end of the second century. But, strictly speaking, there is even the possibility that there were *later* additions to the biographical material to the *Testaments* in the third century or later.

3.2 *The Christological passages*

We now turn to the eschatological/Christological passages. In view of the results of our analysis of the medieval transmission, it is obvious that we would have to look there for possible later additions. Transcribers will often have been unable to resist the temptation to dot the i's and cross the t's. Again, the problem is, however, to prove they did so, and to date these additions.

Earlier I have pointed out that in spite of everything there is considerable coherence and consistence in the pronouncements on the future, and on the role of Jesus Christ in that future.[48] But at the same time we come accross divergencies (in all the various types of passages about the future) and unexpected turns. May these perhaps also, at least partly, be explained as commentaries or additions from different periods to existing Christian *Testaments*? In theory, yes! Yet we have to admit that this offers little help in practice since, here too, it is only with great caution that we are allowed to apply our modern criteria of consistency. We find, for instance, both "adoption-

---

[48] See chapter 5, section 4.

ist" and "patripassionist" pronouncements in the *Testaments*. Thus in *T.Levi* 16:3 we read about "a man who renews the Law in the power of the Most High," whom the sons of Levi will call a deceiver (πλά–νος). *T.Levi* 18:6-7 and *T.Jud.* 24:2 refer to the story of Jesus' baptism in the Jordan. But in *T.Levi* 5:2 God announces that he himself is going to live in the midst of Israel , and 4:1 gives a description of the mighty things that are going to happen "at the suffering of the Most High." *T.Jud.* 22:2 mentions "the coming (παρουσία) of the God of righteousness," but shortly afterwards we read in 24:1 "and from my seed a man will arise like the sun of righteousness, walking with the sons of men in meekness and righteousness, and no sin whatever will be found in him."

It remains a moot question whether one is allowed to apply strict dogmatic standards to the *Testaments* such as have been refined in later theological debates. Implicitly referring to nineteenth-century discussions about the possibility of either a Jewish Christian origin of the *Testaments* or a gentile Christian one (a distinction very current at the time[49]), I concluded in 1953 (on the basis of these and many other examples) that the author could freely employ "adoptionist" and "patripassionist" utterances because he was not aware of their one-sidednesses and liabilities. I also pointed out the great variety in Christology in the second century, when what later was to be called "heterodox" and "orthodox" could still occur side by side in the work of one author. "It must ... be borne in mind that in c. 200 A.D. the dogmatic controversy about the nature of Christ, and the attempts to create a well-defined Christological terminology, had only just started."[50] Moreover, the *Testaments* were concerned with paraenesis for a broad public rather than with Christology for connoisseurs; also the available oral and written tradition was of influence,[51] as were various Old Testament motifs. The exact terminology the patriarchs used was less important than the fact that they announced whom the church

---

[49] See the survey in H.D. Slingerland, *The Testaments of the Twelve Patriarchs: A Critical History of Research* (SBLMS 21; Missoula, Montana: Scholars Press, 1977), 8-15.

[50] *Dissertation*, 125.

[51] So also A. Hultgård; after having pointed out a number of parallels between Christological pronouncements in writings from the second century and those in the *Testaments*, he concludes: "Puis, comme le rédacteur chrétien développe ou refond un texte antérieur, il est légitime de supposer une influence de la terminologie du texte primitif. Le caractère différent de certains passages christologiques des Testaments peut ainsi être expliqué" (*L'eschatologie* 2. 235).

professed as its Lord and Master. Given this variety in Christology from the start, it is impossible to use Christological variants for tracing later additions (not to mention redactions) in the *Testaments*.

To bring this matter to a close: in view of the many references to Jesus Christ and the particular attention paid to Israel's response to him and to the way in which Israel could participate in the salvation brought about by him, we cannot but posit that to the author(s) of the *Testaments* the words of the patriarchs were important as an announcement of their own situation. Continuity in the history of salvation was assumed; the Jewish Scriptures were taken very seriously and concomitant traditions were readily adopted. Both the writings of the Old Testament and the traditions connected with them, were interpreted in a Christian fashion.[52]

In order to situate the *Testaments* in the early church more precisely we shall have to pay special attention to the earliest forms of exegesis of Scripture. In this connection I have examined the work of the first commentator of the Bible whose writings are known to us, Hippolytus of Rome, and in particular his commentary on Genesis 49 and Deuteronomy 33.[53] This investigation did not result in a great amount of direct parallels—but it did (among other things) lead to the important insight that to Hippolytus and his readers Jesus was obviously to be connected with Levi as well as with Judah. And furthermore it became clear in the course of this study with how great an inventiveness biblical data were interpreted in such a way that they could throw light on Christian ideas. Exegetical treatises like those of Hippolytus show early Christianity as a community reading and interpreting Scripture—often very much *ad hoc* and unsystematically.

It is an interesting point that the *Testaments* pay special attention to the relationship between Israel and Jesus as the redeemer of non-Jews and Jews. In the next section more will be said about this.

---

[52] See on this H.W. Hollander and M. de Jonge, *Commentary*, §8 "The Testaments in the early Christian Church" (pp. 67-82); M. de Jonge, "The Pre-Mosaic Servants of God in the Testaments of the Twelve Patriarchs and in the writings of Justin and Irenaeus," *VC* 39 (1985), 157-170 and "Hippolytus' 'Benedictions of Isaac, Jacob and Moses' and the Testaments of the Twelve Patriarchs," *Bijdragen* 46 (1985), 245-260. See now my *Collected Essays*, 263-276 and 204-219 respectively.

[53] See the article on Hippolytus mentioned in the preceding note and also "Two Interesting Interpretations of the Rending of the Temple-veil in the Testaments of the Twelve Patriarchs," *Bijdragen* 46 (1985), 350-362 (= *Collected Essays*, 220-232).

3.3 *The function of the ethical exhortations in the* Testaments *within early Christianity*

First and foremost, the *Testaments* give ethical instructions, to be followed by the descendants of the patriarch till the end of time. The ethics of the *Testaments* show influence of the Psalms and Wisdom books of the LXX, especially those only transmitted in the Greek Bible. The Cynic-Stoic philosophers offer many parallels. This has been shown convincingly by H.W. Hollander in his study on Joseph as a typical "good man" and as ethical model in the *Testaments*.[54] At the end of his very detailed investigation Hollander observes that he has not found unambiguously Christian elements, and concludes: "In any case, the question whether the *Testaments* are originally Christian and Jewish will have to be studied also in the context of the analysis of early Christian paraenesis in its interplay with Hellenistic and Jewish ethics" (p. 97). This analysis was subsequently carried out during the preparation of the *Commentary* just mentioned. Beside the biblical references this lists consistently all Hellenistic, Hellenistic Jewish and early Christian parallels that could be found.[55]

In the chapter on "The Common Ethic" in his *Between Athens and Jerusalem*[56] J.J. Collins arrives at the same conclusion. "Ultimately the ethics of the Testaments cannot be pinpointed as the product of a specific situation. They are of interest for our purpose as material which seems to have accumulated and circulated in Hellenized Jewish circles over two hundred years and was eventually taken over by Christianity." Here and in other writings originating from the Diaspora, the specific and exclusively Jewish elements are pushed into the background, and current philosophical-ethical notions have been adapted to an overall Jewish religious scheme of reference. On this

---

[54] See his *Joseph as an Ethical Model in the Testaments of the Twelve Patriarchs*, "Conclusion" (pp. 93-97).

[55] See also Hollander's essay "The Portrayal of Joseph in Hellenistic Jewish and Early Christian Literature," in M.E. Stone and T.A. Bergren (eds.), *Biblical Figures Outside the Bible* (Harrisburg, Pa: Trinity Press International, 1998), 237-63. Here he discusses the *Testaments* in the section "The Reception of the Joseph story in Early Christian Literature" together with the New Testament and 1 Clement.

[56] J.J. Collins, *Between Athens and Jerusalem. Jewish Identity in the Hellenistic Diaspora* (New York: Crossroad, 1983), 137-174. The quotation in the text is from p. 156. A revised edition of this book was published by Eerdmans, Grand Rapids in 2000.

point we may compare *Gesetz und Paränese* by K.-W. Niebuhr,[57] in which he searches for "Katechismusartige Reihen für die Gesetzes-paränese" and draws the conclusion that it is not only in the *Testaments* that we find a "geprägte paränetische Tradition des Frühjuden-tums," but also in Philo, *Hypothetica* 7, 1-9, in Josephus, *Contra Apionem* 2, 190-219 and in Pseudo-Phocylides.

Personally, I have over the last few years learned to emphasize the fact that in the field of ethics there has been a considerable measure of continuity between Hellenized Judaism and certain circles in early Christianity.[58] All sorts of utterances in the *Testaments* are simply Jewish as well as Christian, and totally acceptable to the non-Jewish and non-Christian Hellenistic fellow-citizens of the author(s) and readers of the *Testaments*.

I tried to show this in my essay "Rachel's Virtuous Behavior in the Testament of Issachar."[59] Here I discussed the pronouncement in *T.Iss.* 2:1 on sexual continence (ἐγκράτεια), also within marriage, and the thesis in 2:3 that sexual intercourse ought to be practised with the purpose of begetting children rather than for the lust of pleasure (φιληδονία). There are interesting parallels here in statements of philosophers (e.g. Musonius Rufus and Seneca), of Josephus in his description of the Essenes in *B.J.* 2, 119-166, of Philo (very numerous), and also in Christian sources from the second century, specifically in the Sentences of Sextus. Others, too, in particular Clement of Alexandria, offer a lot of material on this subject.

Particularly with regard to the ethics of the *Testaments* we do well to approach with utmost caution the thesis that what is not manifestly Christian stems from an earlier Jewish version of the *Testaments*. We are not free to regard the ethical pronouncements in the *Testaments* as expressions of an "open" type of Judaism from which early Christianity should have originated. The *Testaments* prove that there has been continuity between Hellenistic-Jewish and Christian paraenesis; it is not impossible that also ethical pronouncements only received

---

[57] Karl-Wilhelm Niebuhr, *Gesetz und Paränese. Katechismusartige Weisungsreihen in der frühjüdischen Literatur* (WUNT II 28; Tübingen: J. C.B. Mohr, 1987).

[58] As, of course, has been known all along to readers of the Epistle of James, the Shepherd of Hermas and other Christian writings such as the Sentences of Sextus.

[59] Published in D. Balch *et alii* (eds.), *Greeks, Romans and Christians. Essays in Honor of A.J. Malherbe* (Minneapolis: Fortress and Augsburg, 1990), 340-352—now in my *Collected Essays,* 301-333. See also my earlier article "Testament Issachar als 'typisches' Testament," in *Studies*, 290-316, esp. 311-314.

their present form at the final moulding of the *Testaments* in Christian circles.[60]

The continuity between the ethics of the patriarchs and that of the believers in the time after Jesus Christ is strikingly supported theologically, i.e., with respect to the history of salvation, in the words of early Christian thinkers like Justin, Irenaeus and Tertullian.[61] In the light of their statements on the faith of the patriarchs and their obedience to God in the time before Moses, and on the concentration on the Decalogue and the two great commandments as their summary after the coming of Christ, it becomes clear why exactly the paraenetical testaments of Jacob's sons should become authoritative for Christians of the second century and later. The *Testaments* indicated what God's commandments really were and are about; then, in the days of Jacob's sons, as well as now, in the time after Jesus Christ whose coming they predicted. In the time after the patriarchs Moses had been commissioned to issue extra commandments for the obstinate Jews, but these were only intended for Israel, and valid only for a restricted period. The coming of Jesus Christ, as bringer of salvation for Jews and gentiles, had rendered them superfluous. The descendants of the patriarchs should give heed to this: they, too, should accept and obey this saviour and concentrate on the essential commandments.

At the end of the *Testaments*, in *T.Benj.* 10:4-10, we read how at the last judgment Enoch, Noah, Shem, Abraham, Isaac and Jacob will rise from the dead together with the twelve sons of Jacob, "worshipping the King of heaven appearing on earth in the form of a humble man." All people will rise and be judged according to their response to this saviour, gentiles as well as Israelites. But the sons of Benjamin should know:

> But you, if you walk in holiness before the face ot the Lord,
> you will again dwell safely with me;
> and all Israel will be gathered together unto the Lord (v. 11).

---

[60] On this see also my essay "Die Paränese in den Schriften des Neuen Testaments und in den Testamenten der Zwölf Patriarchen. Einige Überlegungen" in H. Merklein (ed.), *Neues Testament und Ethik. Für Rudolf Schnackenburg* (Freiburg-Basel-Wien: Herder, 1989), 538-550, also in my *Collected Essays*, 277-289.

[61] See my article "The Pre-Mosaic Servants of God in the Testaments of the Twelve Patriarchs and the Writings of Justin and Irenaeus," mentioned in n. 52; compare H.W. Hollander and M. de Jonge, *Commentary*, §8.3 (pp. 71-76).

In Justin, *Dial.* 45,4; 80-81; 130,1-2 we find a similar description.

> We gentiles will rejoice with his people; I mean: along with Abraham, Isaac and Jacob and the prophets, indeed of all that people who live agreeable to God (130,2).[62]

3.4 *The purpose of the* Testaments

Viewed against the background of what has just been said, the function and purpose of the *Testaments of the Twelve Patriarchs* in early Christianity becomes a little clearer. They formulate how in the time after Jesus Christ God's commandments have to be obeyed, indeed what was God's intention throughout the history of salvation. By this they take up a clear stand in the inner-Christian discussion about the validity of God's Law. But for Israel, too, it is this obedience that really matters; this is the message contained in the summons by the fathers of the twelve tribes, who also announce the salvation in Jesus Christ to Israel. The author(s) of the *Testaments* was/were clearly anxious about the fate of Israel; he/they wanted to urge the Jews to accept the message of Jesus Christ and to let themselves be persuaded by it. To this end he/they strikingly chose the form of a paraenetical tract rather than that of a polemic, apologetic or missionary writing. We do not know to what extent Christians who put forward the point of view defended in the *Testaments* were successful in convincing the Jews with whom they entered into debate or dialogue. So much is clear, however: the Christian circles responsible for the *Testaments* were genuinely concerned with the salvation of the Jews. In their thinking about and their contacts with their Jewish brethren they let themselves be guided by the ideas expressed in this writing.

In any case, the *Testaments* cannot simply be classified as "Adversus Judaeos" literature[63]—which probably is a misnomer anyway. Likewise, the Gospel of Matthew and Justin's *Dialogue with Trypho*, mentioned by G.N. Stanton in his article "Aspects of Early Christian-Jewish Polemic and Apologetic,"[64] cannot (or only from a very one-

---

[62] I return to the question of the ethics of the *Testaments* in chapter 9.

[63] See H. Schreckenberg, *Die christlichen Adversus-Judaeos-Texte und ihr literarisches und historisches Umfeld (1.-11. Jh.)* (Europ. Hochschulschriften 23, Bd. 172: Frankfurt a.M.-Bern-New York-Paris: Peter Lang, ²1990).

[64] *NTS* 31 (1985), 377-392; published again in his *A Gospel for a New People. Studies in Matthew* (Edinburgh: T.&T. Clark, 1992; 232-255.

sided point of view) be considered as writings levelled against the Jews.

Finally I may point to the interesting assessment of the evidence by Georg Kretschmar.[65] He regards the *Testaments* as a Christian composition from the second century, at a later stage more than once interpolated by Christians (an in itself plausible supposition, but very hard to prove, as I have argued above). Kretschmar classifies the *Testaments* among the "crypto-Christian writings." He emphasizes that they were composed in Christian circles which could formulate, and recognize, their convictions in texts attributed to authors of Old Testament times. In these parting words of the sons of Jacob the message concerning Christ was contained, not in an overtly missionary fashion, but hidden, in the form of allusions and promises, only really understandable for insiders. In Kretschmar's view the *Testaments* stem from Hellenistic-Jewish Christian circles that put much emphasis on the continuity in the history of salvation. The process of interpolation, assumed by Kretschmar, shows, according to him, that the *Testaments* were also used by communities of a different background, and remained authoritative for mainstream Christians of later generations.

Summa summarum: continuing study of the function of *Testaments of the Twelve Patriarchs*—and other "pseudepigrapha of the Old Testament"—in the early Church remains necessary. It is likely to result in an increasingly differentiated picture of the relations between various groups of Jews and various groups of Christians in the second and third centuries—and probably also later, in the period after Constantine when Christianity took up a central position in the Roman Empire.

---

[65] "Die Kirche aus Juden und Heiden. Forschungsprobleme der ersten christlichen Jahrhunderte," in J. van Amersfoort and J. van Oort (eds.), *Juden und Christen in der Antike* (Kampen: Kok, 1990), 9-43, esp. 31-35. The author refers to an earlier article "Die Bedeutung der Liturgiegeschichte für die Frage nach der Kontinuität des Judenchristentums in nachapostolischer Zeit" in M. Simon (ed.), *Aspects du Judéochristianisme* (Paris: Presses Universitaires de France, 1965), 113-137, esp. 123-125 where he discusses *T.Levi* 8.

CHAPTER SEVEN

THE TESTAMENTS OF THE TWELVE PATRIARCHS
AND RELATED QUMRAN FRAGMENTS

After the short introduction about "The Testaments and the Dead Sea Scrolls" in chapter 5, it is now time to survey all the evidence published to date. However fragmentary it may still be, it is worthwhile to look at it in detail. (1) First, the numerous fragments of an Aramaic Levi Document link with those from the Cairo Genizah and the Greek fragments connected with them. (2) Next, there is the fragment of a document in which Naphtali tells about his mother Bilhah. (3) A few more fragments have been connected with an Aramaic *Testament of Judah* and an Aramaic *Testament of Joseph,* but these ascriptions are far from certain. (4) Finally, there are the fragments connected with Levi's son Kohath and his grandson 'Amram. These last fragments may compared to the Aramaic Levi Document, as well as some other texts in one way or the other related to the patriarchs. The present chapter discusses all relevant data and ends with the conclusion that there is no indication of the existence of a writing with the final words of all sons of Jacob directed to their children. The next chapter will concentrate on the Aramaic Levi Document and compare its picture of Levi with that in the *Testament of Levi* in the *Testaments of the Twelve Patriarchs.*

I. FRAGMENTS OF AN ARAMAIC LEVI DOCUMENT[1]

As we have seen, R.H. Charles rendered scholarship a great service by printing the text of Cairo Genizah fragments from the Cambridge University Library and the Bodleian Library in Oxford in Appendix III (pp. 244-256) of his edition of the *Testaments of the Twelve Patriarchs.* He also provided the text of the partly overlapping addition found at *T.Levi* 18:2 in the eleventh century Greek manuscript Athos Koutloumous 39 (= *e)* of the Testaments (plus that of a small Syriac

[1] For more details see chapter 8 below.

fragment). Important in themselves,[2] these fragments drew comparatively little attention until nearly fifty years later, when J.T. Milik published a great number of small fragments under the siglum 1Q21[3] and a larger "Prayer of Levi" from a manuscript found in cave 4, corresponding to yet another addition in the same Greek manuscript, found at *T.Levi* 2:3.[4] These publications made clear that the fragments from the Cairo Genizah and those found at Qumran represented slightly different forms of one document. After 1955 not much happened[5] until, finally, J.C. Greenfield and M.E. Stone published all available Qumran fragments in the series Discoveries in the Judean Desert.[6] They assign the fragments to six different manuscripts: 4Q213, 4Q213a, 4Q213b, 4Q214, 4Q214a, 4Q214b, and call the writing under discussion "Aramaic Levi Document" (avoiding the word "testament"). A little earlier R.A. Kugler edited the same fragments but assigned them, like Milik before him, to two manuscripts, 4Q213 and 4Q214.[7] In his book Kugler also tried to reconstruct the entire document (which he calls "Aramaic Levi") on the basis of all available sources, and he compared the "Levi-Priestly Tradition" in it with that found in *Jub.* 30:1-32:9 and the *Testament of Levi*.[8]

However fragmentary the evidence (still) is, there is much more to compare in the case of the *Testament of Levi* than in the rest of the *Testaments of the Twelve Patriarchs*. It may be regarded as certain that *T.Levi* is directly or indirectly dependent on a written source

---

[2] See the analysis of the composition of the *Testament of Levi* in my dissertation, *The Testaments of the Twelve Patriarchs: A Study of their Text, Composition and Origin* (Assen: Van Gorcum, 1953; 2d ed., 1975), 38-52.

[3] D. Barthélemy and J.T. Milik, *Qumran Cave I* (Oxford: Clarendon, 1955), 87-92.

[4] "Le Testament de Lévi en araméen. Fragment de la grotte 4 de Qumrân," *RB* 62 (1955), 398-406.

[5] Milik also published a small fragment in *The Books of Enoch. Aramaic Fragments of Qumrân Cave 4* (Oxford: Clarendon, 1976), 23-24. See note 12 below.

[6] *Qumran Cave 4. XVII. Parabiblical Texts, Part 3* (ed. G.J. Brooke *et al.*; DJD 22; Oxford: Clarendon, 1996), 1-72.

[7] *From Patriarch to Priest. The Levi-Priestly Tradition from* Aramaic Levi *to* Testament of Levi (SBLEJL 9; Atlanta: Scholars, 1996). For a chart of corresponding identifications of the 4Q Levi-fragments by Greenfield and Stone, and Kugler see A. Aschim in an appendix to his review of Kugler's book, *JBL* 117 (1998), 353-355.

[8] Or rather, a (Jewish) "Original Testament of Levi"; he did not discuss the present Christian *Testament*. In his recent *The Testaments of the Twelve Patriarchs* (Sheffield: Sheffield Academic Press, 2001), 38, however, he writes: "My own experience with developing theories regarding the transitional stages between a work like *Aramaic Levi* and the *Testaments* reveals the difficulty of achieving sufficient agreement to make the undertaking particularly valuable."

identical or very similar to the Aramaic Levi Document (hereafter ALD). This also explains why *T.Levi* differs so much from the other eleven testaments, in structure as well as in content. At the same time comparing *T.Levi* with ALD brings out interesting Christian elements in the testament, which are structural rather than incidental and can, therefore, not be eliminated as later interpolations.

With regard to the reconstruction of ALD many uncertainties remain. First is the matter of the exact wording of the earliest stage of the document. Where the Qumran fragments and the Cairo Genizah texts overlap, they often do not have an identical text; comparison with the Greek texts brings additional difficulties. The very existence of these Greek additions to an eleventh century Greek manuscript of the *Testaments of the Twelve Patriarchs* raises many questions. How, and in what form, did this material reach the Christian scribe of the manuscript, or one of his predecessors? When was this text translated from Aramaic (or Hebrew), and by whom (a Jew or a Christian)? Because nothing is left of the beginning and the end of ALD we cannot determine its literary genre, and it is therefore better not to refer to it as a "testament." It is, however, in all likelihood related to 4QTQahat and 4Q'Amram, which contain instructions (and visions) supposedly handed down in priestly circles through the generations; I return to these texts below.

The fragmentary nature of the evidence makes it sometimes difficult to determine the order of the fragments within ALD. As was already clear from the material in Charles's Appendix III there is a continuous text providing parallels for the end of *T.Levi* 8 to the end of *T.Levi* 13, excluding *T.Levi* 10. We find the end of a vision (cf. chapter 8); a report of journeys to Bethel and to Isaac and Isaac's instructions to Levi concerning his priestly duties (much longer than those found in *T.Levi* 9); a biographical account of Levi and his descendants (cf. chapters 11-12) and a long speech by Levi on the value of wisdom (cf. chapter 13). New material, particularly in connection with the wisdom speech, has come to light, but as far as this section of ALD is concerned, the picture has not changed.

Much more disputed is what preceded this section. *T.Levi* has two visions, one in chapters 2-5, one in chapter 8. In between we find the Shechem episode in chapters 6-7. This episode follows Levi's appointment to the priesthood by the Most High (5:1-2) and the command by an angel to execute vengeance on Shechem because of

Dinah (5:3-7). This episode precedes the vision of Levi's investiture by seven angels (chapter 8). It has often been assumed that the "Prayer of Levi" (first edited by Milik, present in what is now called 4QLevi[b] ar 1-2 and the Greek addition to MS *e* at *T.Levi* 2:3) which ends with the introduction to a vision, pointed to the existence of two visions in ALD as well. Of a Shechem narrative only little remains (in columns a and b of the Cambridge Cairo Genizah fragment). Probably two new fragments (4QLevi[b] ar 3 and 4), dealing with a woman who has discredited the name of her father and adding a blessing for the pious of the Levitical line, should be added here (cf. *Jub.* 30:5-17). Greenfield and Stone raised doubts about the place of the "Prayer of Levi" in ALD but did not come up with a new suggestion.[9] Kugler, however, is of the opinion that there was only one vision in ALD, placed after the Shechem incident and before the journeys of Jacob and family to Bethel and to Isaac.[10] This solution, in my opinion, raises at least as many problems as it wants to solve.[11]

Can we say anything about what followed after Levi's teaching on wisdom corresponding to *T.Levi* 13? Some small fragments, now called 4QLevi[a] ar 3-5, announce the sins of the speaker's sons. Because of a supposed reference to Enoch Milik suggested a parallel to the Sin-Exile-Return passage in *T.Levi* 14.[12] The parallel is not at all close and the reading "Enoch" is far from certain.[13] The suggested place of these fragments consequently remains doubtful.

There is considerable doubt about the assignment of 4Q540 and 4Q541 to ALD, tentatively suggested by E. Puech,[14] but rejected by Greenfield and Stone, as well as by Kugler.[15] They would, in Puech's

---

[9] "The Prayer of Levi," *JBL* 112 (1993), 247-266.

[10] *From Patriarch to Priest*, 47-50, 68-87.

[11] See chapter 8, section 2.3.

[12] *The Books of Enoch*, 23-24.

[13] See Greenfield and Stone, *Qumran Cave 4. XVII*, 20-23.

[14] "Fragments d'un apocryphe de Lévi et le personnage eschatologique. 4QTestLévi[cd](?) et 4QAJa," in J. Trebolle Barrera and L. Vegas Montaner (eds.), *The Madrid Qumran Congress: Proceedings of the International Congress on the Dead Sea Scrolls, Madrid 18-21 March, 1991* (STDJ 11,2; Leiden: Brill, 1992), 2.449-501. He also mentions J.T. Milik's suggestion to link 4Q548, commonly assigned to the 'Amram document, with *T.Levi* 19:1 (see p. 491, n. 48). Cf. also G.J. Brooke, "4Q Testament of Levi[d](?) and the Messianic Servant High Priest," in M.C. de Boer (ed.), *From Jesus to John. Essays on Jesus and New Testament Christology in Honour of Marinus de Jonge* (JSNTSup 84; Sheffield: Sheffield Academic Press, 1993), 83-110.

[15] *From Patriarch to Priest*, 51-52. See also M.A. Knibb, in F. García Martínez and E. Noort (eds.), "Perspectives on the Apocrypha and Pseudepigrapha. The Levi Traditions," *Per-*

view, provide parallels to some clauses in *T.Levi* 17-18. Now it is likely that *T.Levi* (16:1), 17:1-11 gives extracts of a source with a story of the priesthood according to jubilees and weeks, but it is impossible to reconstruct the *Vorlage*.[16] Puech finds a parallel between 17:7-10 and 4Q540. In this fragment we find the number 52, which Puech supposes to refer to a number of weeks; of the accompanying noun only a final *nun* is readable, however. This he connects with *T.Levi*'s picture of seven jubilees, with a return to the land in the fifth week. *T.Levi* 17:10 also mentions a renewal of the house of the Lord, and this may, in Puech's view, correspond to "he will rebuild (?) [like] a servant of God [with] his g[oods], an[other] sanctuary w[hich] he will consecrate [for him (?)]" (line 5 of the fragment). The reconstruction of this line remains uncertain[17] and, apart from that, all of this remains highly speculative.

The fragment 4Q541 9 i speaks of a priestly figure who will atone for all the children of his generation. Of him it is said: "His word is like the word of the heavens, and his teaching according to the will of God. His eternal sun will shine and its fire will burn in all the ends of the earth; above the darkness it will shine. Then, darkness will vanish [fr]om the earth, and gloom from the dry land" (lines 3-5).[18] Puech points here to the description of the eschatological high priest in *T.Levi* 18: 2-4, 9 (as well as to 4:3). M. Philonenko gladly hails this as another piece of evidence in favour of the Essene origin of the Testaments.[19] It is, however, not as simple as that.

The only thing we can say with certainty is that *T.Levi* 18 and the fragment under discussion give a similar description of an ideal priest. We may also compare 1QSb iv 27 (in the blessing of the

---

spectives in the Study of the Old Testament & Early Judaism. A Symposium in Honour of Adam S. van der Woude on the Occasion of His 70th Birthday (VTSup 73; Leiden: Brill, 1998), 197-213, esp. pp. 207-209.

[16] See H.W. Hollander and M. de Jonge, *The Testaments of the Twelve Patriarchs: A Commentary* (SVTP 8; Leiden: Brill, 1985), 174-177.

[17] F. García Martínez and E.J.C. Tigchelaar, *The Dead Sea Scrolls Study Edition* (2 vols.; Leiden: Brill, 1997-1998), 2. 1079 translate" [...] the sun [...] ... a sanctuary [...] he will consecrate [...].'

[18] Translation García Martínez and Tigchelaar, *The Dead Sea Scrolls Study Edition,* 2. 1081.

[19] "Son soleil éternel brillera (4QTestLévi^c-d(?) ii 9," *RHPR* 73 (1993-94), 405-408, especially 405-406: "Soulignons que la présence de ces précieux fragments ne confirme absolument pas le charactère chrétien des Testaments des Douze Patriarches, mais invite, tout au contraire, à reconnaître l'origine essénienne de ce pseudépigraphe."

priests) "… may he make you hol[y] among his people, like a lumi-
nary […] for the world in knowledge, and to shine on the face of the
many."[20] The coming priest will be like Levi himself, to whom the
angel who accompanies him during his first vision says: "You will
light up as a bright light of knowledge in Jacob, and you will be as
the sun to all the seed of Israel" (4:3).[21] Exactly here, in *T.Levi* 18:2-4
and 4:4, the particular stance of the *Testaments* regarding the priesthood comes out.

Levi will be as the sun—a blessing will be given to him and to all
his descendants—but only until the coming of God's son whom
Levi's sons will kill (4:3-4). It is concerning God's son that Levi
should instruct his sons (4:5-6). Levi warns his descendants in no less
than three Sin-Exile-Return (S.E.R.) passages; the first in chapter 10;
the second in chapters 14-15 (where the children of Levi are called
"the lights of heaven," "darkened through ungodliness," see 14:3-4);
and in chapter 16. The section 17:8-11 again follows the S.E.R. pattern in vv. 8-10. Return and renewal of the temple are, however, followed by the arrival, once again, of sinful priests (v. 11). After
vengeance from the Lord and failing of the priesthood (18:1) the
Lord will raise a new priest whose "star will rise in heaven as a king,
lighting up the light of knowledge as by the sun of the day; he will be
magnified in the world until his assumption" (v. 3). Nowhere do we
find that the new priest will be from the tribe of Levi (contrast the
king from Judah in *T.Judah* 24); it is clear he cannot be a descendant
of Levi, after what was said in 4:4, underlined by the word of the
Most High in 5:2: "Levi, I have given you the blessings of the
priesthood until I come and sojourn in the midst of Israel." In *T.Levi*
18 (and elsewhere) Jesus is meant, as is also clear from the reference
in v. 7 to the story of his baptism (Mark 1:9-11 and par). One should
respect these differences (and resist the temptation to remove those as
later interpolations in the *Testaments*, as many have done before
knowing about 4Q541).

We should do all we can to reconstruct the Aramaic Levi Document, but we should be wary to assign to that writing every fragment
with a parallel to *T.Levi*. It should also be noted that the other twenty-

---

[20] Translation García Martínez and Tigchelaar, *The Dead Sea Scrolls Study Edition*, 1. 107.

[21] The imagery used here is, of course, also used with others than priests, see Hollander and
de Jonge, *Commentary*, 142 (note on 4:3).

three fragments of 4Q541 cannot be connected with any text in *T.Levi*.[22] Moreover, it is not certain that it is Levi who announces the future priest in this fragment.[23] Puech opts for Levi as speaker, and mentions the possibility that 4Q540-541 belonged to a testament. 4Q541 fragment 24 ii, preserving what appears to be the conclusion of the document, gives final admonitions and promises to a son. Line 2 speaks of mourning, and M.A. Knibb has suggested that this may concern the death of the speaker, referred to as "your father" in line 5.[24]

II. 4Q215: A FRAGMENT OF A TESTAMENT OF NAPHTALI?

As long ago as 1956 J.T. Milik announced the discovery of parts of a *Testament of Naphtali* in Hebrew.[25] He said that it had no connection with the medieval *Testament of Naphtali*, but contained a genealogy of Bilhah in a larger form than that found in Greek *T.Napht.* 1:6-12. Much later, in 1976, he quoted in passing only two lines, corresponding to *T.Napht.* 1:12.[26] Only recently the three fragments of the genealogy (4Q215) have been published by M.E. Stone, in volume 22 of Discoveries in the Judaean Desert.[27] Stone discovered that four other fragments with an apocalyptical text, commonly also assigned

[22] So also Kugler, *From Patriarch to Priest*, 51

[23] As Puech, on pp. 485-491 of his article, reminds us, J. Starcky, "Les quatre étapes du messianisme à Qumrân," *RB* 70 (1963), 492 thought that the fragments under discussion belonged to a Testament of Jacob, addressed to Levi. See also A. Caquot, "Les testaments qoumrâniens des pères de sacerdoce," *RHPR* 78/2 (1998), 3-26, esp. p. 13.

[24] See his "Messianism in the Pseudepigrapha in the Light of the Scrolls," *DSD* 2 (1995), 181-184 and also "Perspectives on the Apocrypha and Pseudepigrapha: The Levi Traditions," 209.

[25] See note 1 on p. 407 of his "'Prière de Nabonide' et autres récits d'un cycle de Daniël. Fragments araméens de Qumrân 4," *RB* 63 (1956), 406-415. Compare p. 97 of his "Écrits pré-esséniens de Qumrân: d'Hénoch à 'Amram," in M. Delcor (ed.), *Qumrân. Sa piété, sa théologie et son milieu* (BETL 46; Paris-Gembloux: Duculot/Leuven: University Press, 1978), 91-106.

[26] *The Books of Enoch*, 198.

[27] "215. 4QTestament of Naphtali," *Qumran Cave 4. XVII. Parabiblical Texts, Part 3*, 73-82. Now easily accessible in García Martínez and Tigchelaar. *The Dead Sea Scrolls Study Edition*, 1. 454-457. Preliminary edition in M.E. Stone, "The Hebrew Testament of Naphtali," *JJS* 47 (1996), 311-332, later followed by M.E. Stone, "Some Further Readings in the Hebrew Testament of Naphtali," *JJS* 49 (1998), 346-347. See also R.H. Eisenman and M. Wise, *The Dead Sea Scrolls Uncovered* (Shaftesbury: Element, 1992), 156-160, and G.W. Nebe, "Qumranica I: Zu unveröffentlichten Handschriften aus Höhle 4 von Qumran," *ZAW* 106 (1994), 307-322, especially 315-322.

to the same testament, really belong to a different document, now labelled "4QTime of Righteousness" (4Q215ᵃ). Stone has also devoted an interesting article to 4Q215 entitled "The Genealogy of Bilhah,"[28] in which he discusses the relationship between this document (which he continues to designate as *Testament of Naphtali*), the Greek testament belonging to the *Testaments of the Twelve Patriarchs*, and a passage in *Midrash Bereshit Rabbati* compiled by Rabbi Moses the Preacher in Narbonne in the eleventh century. He enters into a discussion with M. Himmelfarb who already in 1984 asked attention for the parallels between the medieval midrash and the Greek *Testament*.[29] She had, at that time, concluded that the parallels between the midrash and the testament were "not the result of independent Jewish transmission of these traditions, but of R. Moses' use of parts of the *Testaments* as a complete Christian document."[30] With 4Q215 in hand, Stone is able to show that the relationship between the midrash and 4Q215 is closer than that between the midrash and Greek *T.Napht.* 1:9-12, so that we may conclude that "one or another form of an apocryphal Hebrew or Aramaic Naphtali document which had existed in the period of the Second temple was available to R. Moses the Preacher in Narbonne in the eleventh century."[31]

All three texts make Bilhah the daughter of a brother of Deborah, Rebekah's nurse mentioned in Gen. 35:8. In the Greek the brother is called Rotheus, in 4Q215 'Achiyot, in *Bereshit Rabbati* 'Achotay. Taken captive, he is bought free by Laban who gives him his servant Aina (the Greek manuscripts differ here) to wife; 4Q215 has here Channah, and this seems to be the original name behind the Chavah of *Bereshit Rabbati*. All three texts then relate how Channah first gives birth to Zilpah (who is named after the village/town in [or: to] which Rotheus was taken captive, and to Bilhah. In all three sources the name "Bilhah" is explained by a play of words on the root *bhl* (to

---

[28] *DSD* 3 (1996), 20-36. Compare also his "Warum Naphtali? Eine Diskussion im Internet," *Judaica* 54 (1998), 188-191.

[29] "R. Moses the Preacher and the testaments of the Twelve Patriarchs," *AJS Review* 9 (1984), 55-78. The relevant passage is found on p. 119 of C. Albeck (ed.), *Midrash Bereshit Rabbati* (Jerusalem, 1940).

[30] "R. Moses the Preacher," 78.

[31] "The Genealogy of Bilhah," 36. The question of how traditions found in the pseudepigrapha reached authors and compilers of medieval midrashim is worthy of further investigation; the articles by Himmelfarb and Stone give some intersteing considerations.

hasten); immediately after her birth Bilhah is eager to drink with her mother.

After a blank of one line 4Q215 tells how Laban gave Channah and her two daughters to Jacob after he had come to him on his flight from Esau. Zilpah was given to Leah and Bilhah to Rachel and in due course Bilhah gave birth to "Dan [my] brother"—and to Naphtali himself, we may add, although the text breaks off at this crucial point. *Bereshit Rabbati* has a similar addition to the genealogy proper, but the Greek has no parallel here. The Greek attaches the genealogical remarks in 1:9-12 to the story of Naphtali's birth in 1:6-8 (cf. Gen. 30:1-3, 7-8).

In two respects Greek *T.Napht.* 1:9-12 is more explicit than the related material. First it tells that Bilhah was born on the same day as Rachel (v. 9). Next it emphasizes that "Rotheus was of the family of Abraham, a Chaldean, god-fearing, freeborn and noble" (v. 10). It is apparently important to make clear that all sons of Jacob, also those born from slave women, are related to Abraham on their paternal as well as their maternal side.[32] This explains the interest in these particular genealogical details—although this sentence is absent in 4Q215 and *Bereshit Rabbati*. The details appear in the *Testaments* because their author(s) had access to this traditional material; yet it does not seem to be directly relevant for the purpose of the Greek *Testament of Naphtali*.

In 4Q215 the author repeatedly refers to Bilhah as "my mother," and because in the last readable line we meet "Dan [my] brother" the document must be ascribed to Naphtali. But was it a testament? Stone points to the Hebrew *Testament of Naphtali* which in the section dealing with visions by Naphtali is more original than the Greek *Testament of Naphtali* (cf. *T.Naph* 5-7). It must, therefore, go back to a much earlier document on which both the Greek and Hebrew *Testaments* draw independently. The Hebrew testament we know does not have anything comparable to the genealogy of Bilhah under discussion, yet "it is possible that the Qumran fragment dealing with Bilhah's genealogy is derived from the same original document."[33]

---

[32] See H.W. Hollander and M. de Jonge, *Commentary*, 299, referring to some remarks by L. Ginzberg. See also this commentary for what immediately follows.

[33] "The Genealogy of Bilhah," 33.

Hence Stone continues to speak of a Qumran TestNaphtali, and 4Q215 is (still) called 4QTNapht.

Here I tend to disagree with him, and I would suggest to drop the "T" and to speak of 4QNapht. For one thing, not all Naphtali traditions need to come from one source, and for another, the common source of the Hebrew and Greek *Testaments* need not have been a testament. Indeed, the version of the two visions of Naphtali found in the Hebrew *Testament* has preserved a number of elements lacking in the Greek *Testament* that must have been present in the original document underlying both testaments. Stone rightly refers to Th. Korteweg's important essay of 1975, in which he argues this in great detail.[34] Korteweg, however, cautiously speaks of "the haggadic tradition which underlies both, and which may, or may not already have taken the form of a 'testament' itself"[35]—and rightly so. There is still another point to consider. The Hebrew text edited by Charles in Appendix II (pp. 239-244) of his edition of the *Testaments*, and based on Oxford MS. heb. d.11,[36] presents itself as *ṣww't nptly*; this is translated by Charles as "the Testament of Naphtali" and by E. Kautzsch as "der letzte Wille Naphtalis."[37] In his study of the testament as literary genre E. von Nordheim classifies this writing as a "testament" only after some hesitation.[38] There is, in fact, also a

---

[34] See his "The Meaning of Naphtali's Visions," in M. de Jonge (ed.), *Studies on the Testaments of the Twelve Patriarchs. Text and Interpretation* (SVTP 3; Leiden: Brill, 1975), 261-290. See already pp. 52-57 in my dissertation (see note 2). J. Becker, *Untersuchungen zur Entstehungsgeschichte der Testamente der zwölf Patriarchen* (AGJU 8; Leiden: Brill, 1970), 105-113, defends the priority of the Greek version; so also A. Hultgård, *L'eschatologie des Testaments des Douze Patriarches* (Acta Universitatis Upsaliensis, Hist. Rel. 7; Uppsala, 1982), 2. 128-135 (who, however, assumes that the Hebrew has kept some elements lost in the Greek). J.H. Ulrichsen, *Die Grundschrift der Testamente der zwölf Patriarchen* (Acta Universitatis Upsaliensis, Hist. Rel. 10; Uppsala, 1991), 145-155 follows de Jonge and Korteweg.

[35] "The Meaning of Naphtali's Visions," 280.

[36] He adds variants from two further manuscripts taken from an earlier edition by M. Gaster, "The Hebrew Text of One of the Testaments of the Twelve Patriarchs," *Proceedings of the Society of Biblical Archaeology* 16 (1893-1894), 33-49, 109-117.

[37] *Die Apokryphen und Pseudepigraphen des Alten Testaments* (Tübingen: Mohr, 1900), 2. 489-492. The meaning "testament" for *ṣww'h* is post-talmudic; M. Jastrow, *A Dictionary of the Targumim, the Talmud Babli and Yerushalmi, and the Midrashic Literature* (repr. New York: Pardes, 1950), 2. 1265a gives as meaning "command, order, verbal will."

[38] *Die Lehre der Alten. I Das Testament als Literaturgattung im Judentum der hellenistisch-römischen Zeit* (ALGHJ 13; Leiden: Brill, 1980), 104-114. It should be borne in mind that von Nordheim in his search for the characteristics of testaments assigns great importance to the testaments in the *Testaments of the Twelve Patriarchs*.

second version of the Hebrew *Testament* which bears the title "Haggadah on the Sons of Jacob." A. Hultgård has analysed it at some length in an appendix to the second volume of his *L'eschatologie*.[39] Though it is generally shorter than the version printed by Charles it gives essentially the same text—but it does not call it a "testament." This, again, raises the question whether the common tradition behind the *Testament of Naphtali* and the Hebrew document called "Testament" or "Haggadah" was a testament.[40]

III. FRAGMENTS ATTRIBUTED TO A TESTAMENT OF JUDAH AND TO A TESTAMENT OF JOSEPH

In 1978 J.T. Milik published some fragments which he thought he could ascribe to a *Testament of Judah* and a *Testament of Joseph*.[41] As in other cases, transcription, reconstruction of lost words or clauses and identification are interrelated, and his solutions have not gone unchallenged.

In the case of 4Q538 we have an episode in the story of Joseph and his brothers in Egypt, told by one of the brothers. Milik thinks that Judah is the speaker (cf. *T.Jud.* 12:11-12), but in view of the "... on my neck and hugged me" in line 6 of fragm. a, which can be compared with Gen. 45:14, other have thought of Benjamin.[42] There is, however, nothing parallel in the *Testament of Benjamin,* nor in any other passage in the *Testament*s. Milik also connected 3Q7, fragments 6 and 5+3 with *T.Jud.* 25:1-2.[43] Here, there is, again, very little

[39] See pp. 288-296. This second version is found in MS Parma 563 De Rossi only; it was printed in S.A. Wertheimer, *Batei Midrashot* (second edition by A.J. Wertheimer; Jerusalem: Mosad Harav Cook, 1954), 1. 199-203.

[40] As in the case of *Midrash Bereshit Rabbati*—and that of *Midrash Wayissa'u*—one would like to know more about the history of the transmission of the Second Temple material down to the Middle Ages.

[41] See his "Écrits préesséniens," 97-102.

[42] So K. Beyer, *Die aramäischen Texte vom Toten Meer* (Göttingen: Vandenhoeck & Ruprecht, 1984), 187 and F. García Martínez and A.S. van der Woude, *De rollen van de Dode Zee* (2 vols.; Kampen: Kok, 1994-1995), 2. 378-380, going back to F. García Martínez, "Estudios Qumránicos 1975-1985: Panorama Crítico (III)," *EstBib* 46 (1988), 325-374, especially 326-330.

[43] The 3Q fragments were published in M. Baillet, J.T. Milik and R. de Vaux, *Les "Petites Grottes" de Qumrân* (DJD 3; Oxford: Clarendon, 1962), 99. Later M. Baillet tentatively added twenty very small fragments belonging to 4Q484, see *Qumrân Grotte 4. III* (DJD 7; Oxford: Clarendon, 1982), 3.

to go on—only the name "Levi" and the mention of "the angel of the presence" can be used to establish a link with the passage in *T.Judah*; but the collocation of these words may just as well have to be explained differently.

The situation is only a little less controversial in the case of 4Q539, in which Milik finds parallels to *T.Jos.* 15:1-2, 16:4-5, and 17:1-2. In the tiny fragment 1, he connects the letters *mp* with the name Μέμφις found in *T.Jos.* 3:6; 12:1; 14:1-5; 16:1. Fragments 2 a-b (probably) refer to the Ishmaelites, and they mention a mourning of Jacob; this may be connected with the beginning of chapter 15 in the *Testament of Joseph.* Directly after this "minas" are mentioned and the number "eighty"; to this may be compared the story in chapter 16 about complicated negotiations between eunuchs sent by the "Memphian" (v.1) or "Egyptian (v.5) woman" and the Ishmaelites about Joseph. In v. 4 the woman is prepared to give as much as two minas of gold, in v. 5 her negotiator gives eighty pieces of gold (cheating his mistress by telling her that he had given a hundred). If these readings are right, particularly the second parallel is interesting.

One of the striking features of the *Testament of Joseph* is that it has two paraenetical themes and illustrates them with two different stories, one about Joseph and the Egyptian woman (3:1-9:5) and the second about Joseph's slavery and imprisonment (11:2-16:6). It has always been likely that the author(s) of the *Testaments* used a special source for the second part of *the Testament of Joseph*.[44] Although there is no reason to assume that 4Q539 formed part of that particular source, it could point to the existence of a similar written tradition about the selling of Joseph.

Neither in the case of 4Q538 nor in that of 4Q539 there is any indication that we are dealing with parts of a testament. In the case of the latter one has pointed to the fact that "my sons" and "my loved ones" are addressed in fragm. 2, line 2 (cf. "my son[s]" in line 6), but such an address is fitting also in other contexts than that of a testament.

Recently T. Elgvin has drawn attention to 4Q474 and suggested that it may be part of a Joseph apocryphon or even a testament.[45] It is

---

[44] For details see H.W. Hollander and M. de Jonge, *Commentary,* especially 362-365, 372-373, 393-394 and, in more detail, H.W. Hollander, *Joseph as an Ethical Model in the Testaments of the Twelve Patriarchs* (SVTP 6; Leiden: Brill, 1981).

[45] "4Q474—A Joseph Apocryphon?" *RevQ* no 69, vol. 18 (1997), 97-107.

a poorly preserved text that mentions Rachel and refers a few times to a beloved son, which in Elgvin's eyes may be Joseph. He tentatively reconstructs line 2 as a rephrasing of Gen. 37:3-4 and 48:22 so as to read "she rejoi]ced(?) in a son loved by hi[s fath]er above all [his brothers(?)." Next he uses Gen. 30:24 to reconstruct line 4: "... to] ask the Lord that [He g]i[ve her another(?)] son[..." These lines then, would reveal parallels with *T.Jos.* 1:2, 4; 10:5; 11:1 and *T.Benj.* 1:4-5—not surprisingly, because they deal with the same subjects and depend on the same or similar Bible passages. There is no parallel with 4Q539 (nor with the so-called "Apocryphon Joseph" preserved in 4Q371-373).

Elgvin then goes a step further by positing that lines 1-7 form a narrative introduction and lines 8-14 are part of prophecies by Joseph to his descendants. If so, the fragment could be called a testament. His principal argument is the use of a verb in the second person plural in line 4, translated as "you [as]ked(?)" (compared with the "and there they cried out to the Lord" found only in the Armenian version of *T.Jos.* 19:4).

Elgvin's transcriptions and reconstructions are very ingenious, but remain extremely tentative, as he himself admits time and again. This may be a text concerning Rachel and Joseph but there is no connection with the *Testaments of the Twelve Patriarchs*.

IV. FRAGMENTS CONNECTED WITH KOHATH AND ʿAMRAM

Reviewing what we have found so far, we conclude that 4Q215 confirms the existence of a source from which the genealogical material in *T.Napht.* 1:9-12 was taken. Next, 4Q539 may provide evidence about a written tradition about the selling of Joseph that, in some form, was used in the composition of *T.Jos.* 11:2-16:6. In neither case is it clear that the author(s) of the *Testaments of the Twelve Patriarchs* knew and used a testament.

The (relatively) rich material belonging to an Aramaic Levi Document proved very important; it shows that the *Testament of Levi* is dependent on a source identical or similar to ALD. ALD has testamentary features, but is not a testament.[46] M.A. Knibb rightly

---

[46] At the end of the biographical section in ALD (v. 81 according to the numbering introduced by Charles) we find: "and all the days of my life were one hu[ndred and thir]ty seven

calls it "an autobiographical narrative which includes significant passages of instruction."[47] He compares it with the first-person sections of the Genesis Apocryphon, the fragmentary "Apocryphon of Jacob" (4Q537)[48] and 4Q538 mentioned above. One may add, of course, 4Q215 and 4Q539.

On the other hand, 4Q540-541 may have belonged to a document giving final admonitions of Levi; this, however, cannot be proved beyond doubt.

At this point it may be helpful to look at 4QTQahat ar (= 4Q542)[49] and 4Q'Amram ar (4Q543-548)[50] which give final instructions by Levi's son and grandson to their children. We should note that both are mentioned in the biographical section ALD 62-81 (see especially vv. 67-68 and 74-77).[51] It is also remarkable that ALD does not only mention how Levi hands down general admonitions concerning true wisdom and righteous behaviour (vv. 82-84; 88-99), but also reflects the notion that priestly instructions were handed down from generation to generation. In ALD vv. 12-13 Isaac instructs Levi, and in vv. 22, 50, this patriarch refers to the example and teaching of Abraham (cf. *Jub* 21:10); in v. 57 he mentions the book of Noah as the source for Abraham. We may compare *Jub.* 45:16 that tells that Jacob gave all his books and the books of his fathers to Levi.[52]

Here 4Q542 fragm. 1, ii 9-13 ties in with: "And now, to you, 'Amram, my son, I comma[nd...] and [to] your s[on]s and to their

---

years and I saw my th[ird] generation before I died." A strange remark, as it is not made by an author reporting the death of the patriarch, but by the patriarch himself. Moreover it is followed in v. 82 by an introduction to a speech given earlier by Levi, when his brother Joseph died. The text of this speech is given *in extenso* in the following verses. It exhibits a number of testamentary features, but is clearly not a farewell speech. Was this second speech added later? And how did the ending of ALD take up the information in v. 81—compare *T.Levi* 12:6-7; 19:4? We simply do not know.

[47] "Perspectives on the Apocrypha and Pseudepigrapha: The Levi Traditions," 209.

[48] I note that García Martínez and van der Woude, *De rollen van de Dode Zee*, 2.376 write that though parallels point to Jacob as the central figure in this document, it cannot be excluded that Levi is the one who reports a vision.

[49] See E. Puech, "Le Testament de Qahat en araméen de la Grotte 4 (*4QTQah*)," *RevQ* nos. 57-58, vol.15 (1991), 23-54.

[50] Eisenman and Wise, *The Dead Sea Scrolls Uncovered*, 151-156 and K. Beyer, *Die aramäischen Texte vom Toten Meer. Ergänzungsband* (Göttingen: Vandenhoeck & Ruprecht, 1994), 85-92.

[51] Compare also 4Q559, fragm. 2 and 3.

[52] *Jub.* 7:38-39 mentions the succession from Enoch to Noah (cf. also *1 Enoch* 81:5-82:3) and 10:14 (cf.17) that from Noah to Shem.

sons; I command [...] and they have given to Levi, my father, and which Levi, my father, has giv[en] to me [...] all my writings as witness that you should take care of them [...] for you; in them is great worth, in their being carried on with you." This may be compared to i 7-8: "Hold on to the word of Jacob, your father and hold fast to the judgments of Abraham and to the righteous deeds of Levi and of me ..."[53]

Of 4Q'Amram the beginning has been preserved, even twice, in 4Q543 fragm. 1 as well as in 4Q545 fragm. 1 col. i. Here we read how 'Amram addresses his sons and calls Aaron in particular. Especially important is that we possess the *incipit* of this writing: "Copy of the words of the visions of 'Amram, son of Kohath, son of Levi. All that he revealed to his sons and that he ordered them on the day of his death ..." The writing is concerned with the final instructions of the patriarch before his death. The verb *pqd* is used here (as in 4QTQahat ii 9, 10 and in ALD vv. 82-84). It corresponds with Hebrew *ṣwh* used in the Bible for instructions before death (e.g. in Gen. 49:33; 2 Sam. 17:23 and 2 Kgs 20:1).[54] Next, the initial words resemble those in the beginning of the individual testaments in the *Testaments of the Twelve Patriarchs*, e.g. *T.Levi* 1:1: "A copy of the words of Levi, which he enjoined on his sons before his death."

We should note that the initial words highlight 'Amram's visions (compare those of Levi). Interestingly, one of the visions took place when 'Amram was in Hebron, with his father Kohath, to build the tombs of their fathers, and had to stay there because of a war between Egypt and Canaan (4Q544 fragm. 1 and 4Q545 fragm. 1 col. ii). This is also mentioned in *Jub.* 46:9-11 and echoed in *T.Sim.* 8:2 and *T.Benj.* 12:3. Again we find a tradition known and used by the author(s) of the *Testaments*.[55]

4Q542 does not speak about visions but concentrates on exhortations to follow the instructions of the fathers; obedience to God will lead to eternal blessings, disobedience to divine punishment. A few times (fragm. 1, i 4, 5, 12) the gift of Kohath and the fathers before him is called "inheritance" (*yrwtt'*). In lines i 11-13 we read: " ... because you have kept and carried on [the] inheritan[ce] which your

---

[53] Transl. García Martínez and Tigchelaar, *The Dead Sea Scrolls Study Edition*, 2. 1083.

[54] And, of course, to the word ἐντέλλομαι, very frequently used in the *Testaments of the Twelve Patriarchs*.

[55] For details see Hollander and de Jonge, *Commentary*, 127-128, note on *T.Sim.* 8:2.

fathers gave you, truth, and justice, and uprightness, and perfection, and purit[y, and ho]liness and the priest[ho]od, according to a[l]l that I commanded you ..."[56]

4QTQahat and 4Q'Amram would deserve to be analysed in greater detail, but what has been said above may suffice to establish a close link between these two documents and ALD (and possibly also with 4Q540-541). They represent a chain of priestly instructions, accompanied by promises of blessings and threats of divine punishment. Whether we call these instructions "testamentary" and these writings "testaments" (this remains dubious in the case of ALD) is, to a large extent, a matter of definition. Particularly since E. von Nordheim's study of 1980 mentioned above, it has become fashionable to speak of "testament" as a specific literary genre.[57] Scholars have found it difficult, however, to agree on its characteristics. It should also be borne in mind that, on the one hand, a number of writings called διαθήκη are not farewell-discourses spoken before dying, and that, on the other, such discourses are only seldom called "testament"; strictly speaking only the *Testaments of the Twelve Patriarchs* and the *Testament of Job* qualify.

V. No Testaments of the Twelve Patriarchs at Qumran

Three "testamentary" writings with priestly instructions by Levi, his son and his grandson, handing down what their fathers told them, plus autobiographical narratives by Naphtali, Joseph and perhaps Benjamin, are all we have found. The Dead Sea Scrolls do not provide any indication of the existence of a writing with the final words of all sons of Jacob directed to their children. We do find references to the twelve sons of Jacob and the twelve tribes of Israel. In 4Q252, 253, 254, 254a we have fragments of a "Commentary on Genesis," which deals, among other things, with the Blessings of Jacob in Genesis 49. There is also the "Apocryphon of Joshua" (4Q378-379) that in 4Q379 fragm. 1 speaks about the twelve sons of

---

[56] Transl. García Martínez and Tigchelaar, *The Dead Sea Scrolls Study Edition*, 2. 1083. I note in passing "and you will give me among you a good name" in line 10, cf. 4Q541 24 ii 5, and the announcement of future joy for Jacob, Isaac and Abraham in line 11, cf. *T.Levi* 18:14.

[57] See note 38, and my article "Testamentenliteratur" in *TRE* 33 (2001), 110-113.

Jacob and their tribes, singling out Levi as "the beloved."[58] In general, however, the Scrolls, in all their diversity, seem to focus their attention on Levi and his descendants.

---

[58] One should note that 11QTemple, cols. xxiii-xxv describes the sacrifices of the twelve tribes (cf. 4Q365, fragm. 23) and connects the names of the sons of Jacob with the gates of the temple in cols. xxxix-xli (cf. 4Q365ᵃ fragm. 2, col. ii, and also 4Q554 fragm. 1, cols. i-ii).

CHAPTER EIGHT

LEVI IN THE ARAMAIC LEVI DOCUMENT
AND IN THE TESTAMENT OF LEVI

This chapter is devoted to a comparison of the picture of Levi in the Aramaic Levi Document and that of the patriarch in the *Testament of Levi*. I shall not deal here with many of the problems connected with the reconstruction, translation and interpretation of ALD, but make critical use of the results of others, while I deal with the question to what extent the recently published material sheds new light on the genesis of *T. Levi*. It will become clear that the new material at our disposal helps us to see things more clearly, but that our knowledge is still fragmentary. As so often, our arguments are like little pieces of string, each too short to reach our goal; we have to tie the strings together in order to formulate an acceptable theory. Connecting the arguments within the framework of an overall theory remains a subjective activity.[1]

I. THE TESTAMENT OF LEVI

1.1 The collection of farewell-discourses of the sons of Jacob that bears the title *Testaments of the Twelve Patriarchs* forms a unity. The opening and closing passages of the individual testaments are structured in the same way. In the body of each testament we usually find the description of one or more episodes of the patriarch's life. The biographical details serve as illustrations for the exhortations that follow. The exhortatory passages give a spectrum of virtues and vices, together with general admonitions to obey the law of God and the commandments of the individual patriarch. At the end of each testament we find (a) prediction(s) of the future. There are many variations within this general framework, depending on the narrative ma-

---

[1] See also M. de Jonge and Joh. Tromp, "Jacob's Son Levi in the Pseudepigrapha of the Old Testament and Related Literature," in T.A. Bergren and M.E. Stone (eds.), *Biblical Figures Outside the Bible* (Minneapolis: Fortress, 1997), 203-236.

terial available (in or outside the Bible), and there is also a great diversity in the predictions regarding the future.

This description also fits *T.Levi*. Compared to the other eleven this testament shows, however, a relatively great number of specific elements. Many of these can be explained by comparing the testament with the availabe Aramaic and Greek fragments of the Levi-document under consideration. At the same time this comparison reveals a number of features that are peculiar to *T.Levi*. They are structural rather than incidental, and cannot be removed as later interpolations. They reveal that the present *T.Levi*, though acquainted with the material found in the Levi-fragments and therefore different from the other testaments, looks at Levi, called to the priesthood by God himself, from a Christian point of view.

1.2 *T.Levi* focuses on Levi's priestly office and that of his descendants. It is of central importance for Israel but it is limited in time. The Most High, seated on his throne of glory, tells Levi: "Levi, I have given you the blessing of the priesthood, until I come and sojourn in the midst of Israel" (5:2; cf. 4:4; 8:14). Repeatedly the future sins of the sons of Levi are announced, especially those against Jesus Christ (4:4 and chapters 10; 14-15 and 16).[2] Chapter 17 describes the decline of the priesthood.

Chapter 18 announces the arrival of a new priest, sent by God, who introduces a new era. Levi, predicting this arrival in very special terms, tells that he will share in the joy about his coming, together with Abraham, Isaac and Jacob (*T.Levi* 18:14). He says also that "His star will arise in heaven, as a king, lighting up the light of knowledge as by the sun of the day" (v. 3, cf. the description of his own office in 4:3), without mentioning that the new priest will be of his own tribe, whereas the corresponding passage in *T.Jud.* 24:1 predicts: "a man will arise from my seed like the sun of righteousness." In both cases Jesus, a descendant of Judah and often referred to as "Son of David," is meant. In *T.Levi* 2:10-11 we hear that the one "who will redeem Israel" to be announced by Levi will come from Levi and Judah. Levi and Judah are mentioned together in many other testaments, the one representing the priesthood and the other the kingship. Even Judah,

---

[2] One should note that *T.Levi* 1:1 announces that Levi's parting words to his sons are concerned with "all that they would do and that would befall them until the day of judgment."

in his testament (*T.Jud.* 21:1-6a) declares that the former is more important than the latter. A number of testaments connect the coming of a future deliverer with these two tribes, but in particular with Judah. This leads to a complex picture which I have analyzed elsewhere.[3]

In the Epistle to the Hebrews Jesus is called priest and high priest, but as one appointed by God as "priest for ever, according to the order of Melchisedek" (Ps. 110:4, repeatedly referred to in Hebrews). He is superior to Levi and the Levitical priests (see especially Hebrews 7). The approach found in Hebrews did not encourage early Christians to emphasize connections between Jesus and Levi. But because Jesus was regarded as king and (high) priest the two could be linked—as, for instance, in Hippolytus' commentary on Genesis 49 and Deuteronomy 33.[4]

1.3 Our oldest Greek manuscripts tell us that Levi's testament deals with "the priesthood and arrogance"[5] and that covers its contents pretty well. Its main biographical item is Levi's action together with Simeon at Shechem—in fact the only story in the Bible in which Levi plays a significant role (Genesis 34). It is introduced in *T.Levi* 2:1-2 and recorded and commented upon in 6:3-7:4. It returns in the list of biographical data in chapters 11-12, where we read in 12:5 "I was eight years when I went to the land of Canaan, and eighteen years when I killed Shechem, and at nineteen years I became priest...." There is a close connection between the "zeal" displayed by Levi at Shechem and his call to the priesthood. The Shechem story is prededed by a complex vision in which Levi makes a heavenly journey ending with an encounter with the Most High who appoints him priest (2:5-5:2). It is followed by an only slightly less complex vision in which seven men in white clothing carry out the actual investiture (8:1-17). The two visions are connected and corroborate each other. In 8:18-19 we read: "and when I awoke I under-

---

[3] See "Two Messiahs in the Testaments of the Twelve Patriarchs?" in J.W. van Henten *et al.* (eds.), *Tradition and Reinterpretation in Jewish and Early Christian Literature. Essays in Honour of Jürgen C.H. Lebram* (SPB 36; Leiden: Brill, 1986), 150-162, reprinted in *Jewish Eschatology, Early Christian Christology and the Testaments of the Twelve Patriarchs. Collected Essays of Marinus de Jonge* (ed. H.J. de Jonge; NovTSup 63; Leiden: Brill, 1991), 191-203. See also chapter 5, section 4.

[4] See "Hippolytus' 'Benedictions of Isaac, Jacob and Moses' and the Testaments of the Twelve Patriarchs," *Bijdragen* 46 (1985), 245-60; reprinted in *Collected Essays*, 204-219.

[5] See the title in *bldmef* διαθήκη Λευὶ περὶ ἱερωσύνης καὶ ὑπερηφανίας.

stood that this (vision) was like the former. And I hid this also in my heart and I did not tell it to anybody on earth."

The first vision is preceded by a prayer of Levi in 2:3-4. Pasturing the flocks at Abelmaul Levi "sees" the wickedness of men and asks God to be saved. The prayer is followed by an express command by the angel who has accompanied Levi on his heavenly journey, to execute vengeance on Shechem because of Dinah. Levi is assured of the angel's assistance and receives a shield and a sword (5:3-7). Levi takes this to heart (6:1-2) and acts accordingly (6:3-7:4).

After the second vision we hear that Levi, Judah and Jacob visit Isaac, and that Isaac blesses Levi according to his visions (9:1-2). Jacob goes to Bethel (cf. Gen. 35:1-5), receives a vision concerning Levi's priesthood and brings tithes of everything through Levi (9:3-4). After the entire family has moved to Hebron, Isaac instructs Levi repeatedly in the law of the priesthood (9:5-14). Some rules are mentioned specifically; they form a very mixed set.

Chapter 10 deals, quite unexpectedly, with predictions of the future sins of Levi's sons, using the Sin-Exile-Return (S.E.R.) pattern that is often found in the *Testaments* and that is, surprisingly, repeated in chapters 14-15 and 16.[6] This deliberate repetition of the S.E.R. pattern shows how much importance was attached to the future sins of Levi's descendants and their punishment. Only 16:5 mentions future bliss in a clearly Christian phrase: "(among the Gentiles you will be for a curse and for dispersion) until he will again visit (you) and in pity receive you through faith and water."

Between the first S.E.R. passage in chapter 10 and the second one in chapters 14-15 we find a list of biographical details concerning Levi and his children and grandchildren in chapters 11-12. A paraenetical passage in chapter 13 follows, which emphasizes study of the law and obedience to it. "Wisdom in the fear of the Lord with diligence" cannot be taken from a person, even when he loses everything he possesses and goes into exile. The example of Joseph is expressly mentioned. Chapter 13 is the only straightforward exhortatory passage in T. Levi; it does not refer to Levi's priesthood or that of his sons.

---

[6] For a detailed treatment of these chapters see my "Levi, the Sons of Levi and the Law in Testament Levi X, XIV-XV and XVI" in J. Doré *et al.* (eds.), *De la Tôrah au Messie. Mélanges H. Cazelles* (Paris-Tournai: Desclée & Cie, 1981), 513-523; published again in *Collected Essays*, 180-190.

Chapter 17 describes the story of the priesthood according to jubilees. It is very brief and reads like a bad abstract from a larger text. It ends with a description of the seventh jubilee according to the S.E.R. schema, followed by a reference to new sins of the priests and their punishment by the Lord, the extinction of the priesthood and the arrival of a new priest (chapter 18)

T.Levi ends with the usual closing passage in which, remarkably, Levi's descendants are introduced as "we" (chapter 19). After Levi's summons to choose between darkness and light, the law of the Lord and the works of Beliar, we read: "And we answered our father saying: Before the Lord we will walk, according to his law" (v. 2). One may note that Justin in his *Dialogue with Trypho* (116:3) calls the Christian community "the true highpriestly race of God." Christians bring pure offerings to the Lord among all the nations, in accordance with Mal. 1:11.[7] Apparently the author expects his Christian readers to identify themselves with Levi's descendants.

II. THE ARAMAIC AND GREEK LEVI-FRAGMENTS

2.1 It is helpful to begin with some introductory remarks, partly repeating what was said in the previous chapter:

2.1.1 The Aramaic and Greek fragments dealing with Levi are of very diverse provenance. According to M. Beit-Arié the Genizah material was written before 1000 CE.[8] We have the text of ten columns, wholly or in part. On the basis of an autopsy of the Bodleian and Cambridge material and comparison with the Greek texts from Mount Athos, R.A. Kugler concluded that, originally, there must have been three double leaves with altogether 24 columns.[9]

As to the fragments found at Qumran: First there are those assigned to 1Q21, assembled by Milik. Next there is the material from Cave 4 classified as 4Q213 and 4Q214, now divided over six manuscripts by J.C. Greenfield and M.E. Stone, all dated to about the mid-

---

[7] See pp. 260-62 in "The Testament of Levi and 'Aramaic Levi'," *Collected Essays*, 240-262).

[8] This is mentioned in J.C. Greenfield and M.E. Stone, "Remarks on the Aramaic Testament of Levi from the Genizah," *RB* 86 (1979), 214-230; see p. 216.

[9] See his *From Patriarch to Priest. The Levi-Priestly Tradition from Aramaic Levi to Testament of Levi* (SBLEJL 9; Atlanta: Scholars, 1996), 231-233: "Appendix 2. A Reconstruction of the Cairo Genizah Manuscript."

dle of the first century BCE or slightly earlier. 4Q540 and 4Q541, tentatively called 4QTest. Levi^{c,d} by E. Puech, probably did not belong to ALD, as we have seen.[10]

The Greek fragments are found in an eleventh century manuscript, but the shape and the date of the *Vorlage* of these additions to the regular text of *T. Levi* cannot be determined. The first addition to *e,* at *T.Levi* 2:3, consists of a prayer of Levi, with an introduction and a closing sentence. It forms a unity and is inserted just before the mention of a similar prayer in *T.Levi* 2:4. Did the scribe still know its original context? Does the same apply to the addition in *e* to *T.Levi* 5:2 which may also belong to the earlier Levi document? The last insertion, at *T.Levi* 18:2, has a proper beginning corresponding to *T.Levi* 9:1, but breaks off unexpectedly with the birth of Levi's son Merari (cf. *T.Levi* 11:7).

The small Syriac fragment published by R.H. Charles (British Library Add. MS. 17,913[11]) corresponds to part of Cambridge Genizah fragment, col. d.

2.1.2 Notwithstanding this diversity of provenance these fragmentary texts are witnesses to one single underlying text. When arranged in parallel columns they show overlap in numerous cases. There is clearly no direct literary dependence one way or another between the existing witnesses. Yet they may be used to correct and to supplement each other, and to reconstruct the underlying text, although there is likely to remain a considerable degree of doubt as to its original *Wortlaut,* due to the numerous orthographical and grammatical variants and differences in wording. The presence of a number of Aramaic fragments at Qumran makes it certain that the text at the basis was not only non-Christian but also pre-Christian. Most scholars date it to the third century BCE.[12] Some have argued in favour of the theory that the original language was Hebrew,[13] but it seems difficult to prove this conclusively.

---

[10] See chapter 7, section 1.

[11] See W. Wright, *Catalogue of Syriac Manuscripts*, vol 2 (London: British Museum, 1871), 997. The manuscript contains extracts of a great variety of writings and is dated A.D. 874.

[12] See Kugler, *From Patriarch to Priest*, 131-135 for a survey of recent opinion.

[13] See, for instance, P. Grelot, "Notes sur le Testament de Lévi," *RB* 86 (1956), 391-406, and Greenfield and Stone, "Remarks on the Aramaic Testament of Levi," 228.

In view of all this one may call the underlying document Aramaic Levi or, as Greenfield and Stone have suggested, Aramaic Levi Document (ALD). Because we do not have any remains of the beginning or the ending of the document it is difficult to determine its literary genre. It is not advisable to use the word "testament" in the title.[14]

2.1.3 Most scholars are of the opinion that *T.Levi* is directly or indirectly dependent on a written source identical or very similar to ALD; the alternative, dependence of both documents on a common source or oral tradition, has not much to recommend it.[15] In practice this has meant that the order of the available fragments of ALD and the structure of the document have been determined by comparison with *T.Levi*. Kugler has protested against this procedure and advocated a different structure as far as the first part of ALD is concerned.

2.2 After these introductory remarks we may proceed to a survey of the contents of ALD on the basis of the available fragments. Apart from the very fragmentary text on columns a and b of the Cambridge fragment (dealing with the Shechem episode), the Cairo Genizah and Athos material gives a continuous text, providing parallels for the end of *T.Levi* 8 to the end of *T.Levi* 13, with the exception of *T.Levi* 10. That is: they give the end of a vision; the story of the journey to Isaac, to Bethel and again to Isaac; and Isaac's instructions to Levi (compared to those in *T.Levi* 9 these are extremely lengthy and detailed). This is followed by a biographical account concerning Levi and his descendants ending with verse 81 that tells us: "And all the days of my life were one hun[dred and thir]ty seven years and I saw my th[ird] generation before I died." Levi's speech on the value of Wisdom pronounced earlier, in the year his brother Joseph died, follows in vv. 82-95.[16]

Chapter 10, the first of the three S.E.R. passages in *T.Levi* dealing with the sins of the sons of Levi, is a deliberate addition on the part

---

[14] On the relation between ALD and 4QTQahat and 4Q'Amram see chapter 7, section 4.

[15] For a review of current opinion see Kugler, *From Patriarch to Priest*, 28-33, 171-174.

[16] It is interesting to see how *T.Levi* avoids the awkward transition between v. 81 and v. 82. In 12:6-7 it reads: "And behold, my children, you are a third generation. Joseph died in (my) hundred and eighteenth year." In 13:1 the hortatory address follows as part of the present farewell speech. The mention of the year of Levi's death is found at the end, in 19:4, as part of the closing remarks of the author of the testament. We should note that the reference to the year of Joseph's death in 12:7 (still) comes unexpectedly; it would seem that this is a clear indication that *T.Levi* follows a *Vorlage* (at least) very similar to ALD. See also chapter 7, n. 47.

of the author of this testament who wanted to stress that point, important in his picture of the Levitical priesthood.

The new finds at Qumran have yielded additional material overlapping and supplementing the Genizah and Athos texts (with the exception of Cambridge cols. a and b)—as Greenfield and Stone as well as Kugler have shown. Numerous details still have to be discussed and a close analysis, particularly of the speech on Wisdom, for which there is relatively much new material, is called for. The point I want to make now is that there is still no reason to doubt that *T.Levi* and ALD run parallel here.

Some small fragments called 4Q Levi[a] ar 3-5 (so Greenfield and Stone) do not have anything in common with other known fragments, but ever since J.T. Milik suggested that they may correspond to the beginning of the second S.E.R. passage in *T.Levi* 14,[17] they have been put after the Wisdom speech.[18] Important elements in this text are the announcement of sins of the sons of the speaker and a supposed reference to Enoch (corresponding to that in *T.Levi* 14:1). I note, however, that Greenfield and Stone[19] are not at all sure that Milik's reading of that name is warranted. In that case the suggested place of these fragments is even more doubtful than it always has been.

2.3 We now turn to the remaining texts: the Cambridge fragments dealing with what happened at Shechem, the fragments with the Prayer of Levi plus the introduction to a vision, first edited by Milik (now called 4Q Levi[b] ar 1 and 2), and a piece of text dealing with a woman who has desecrated the name of her father, adding a blessing for the pious from the Levitical line (4Q Levi[b] ar 3 and 4).

Although there is no direct link with other fragments of ALD or with *T.Levi* the third piece of text seems to have to be connected with the story of Dinah and so will have to be placed somewhere after what remains of the narrative of the Shechem episode in columns a and b of the Cambridge fragment. Greenfield and Stone[20] as well as

---

[17] In *The Books of Enoch. Aramaic Fragments of Qumrân Cave 4* (Oxford: Clarendon, 1976), 23-24, cf. *HTR* 64 (1971), 344-345.

[18] It should be noted that Kugler, though more cautious in restoring the text resulting from the fragments than Milik, and adding another *caveat* about reconstructing ALD on the basis of *T.Levi*, follows Milik at this point—see his *From Patriarch to Priest*, 53, 118-130.

[19] *Qumran Cave 4. XVII*, 22.

[20] *Qumran Cave 4. XVII*, 33-35.

Kugler[21] point to *Jub.* 30:5-17, forbidding intermarriage with Gentiles. This discourse comes immediately after a short account of what happened at Shechem; it is followed by vv. 18-20 which promise an eternal blessing for Levi and his descendants because of Levi's zeal for the law of the Lord.

Scholars have usually put 4Q Levi[b] ar 1-2, together with the corresponding Athos text, before the fragmentary Cambridge text on Shechem, assuming that ALD, like *T.Levi,* recounted two visions, one before and one after the events at Shechem. The first vision in *T.Levi* 2-5 is a very complicated one, with undoubtedly Christian elements, and its counterpart in ALD may have been much simpler. But given the agreement in order elsewhere there did not seem to be reason to doubt a parallel sequence here too.

There are positive indications: the answer of the angel in *T.Levi* 4:2-3, 5 seems to be an answer to Levi's prayer in ALD rather than to that in *T.Levi* 2:4. In *T.Levi* the vision is situated at Abelmaul and ALD speaks about Abel-main. There is one accompanying angel in both documents and in both cases the gates of heaven are opened; ALD unfortunately breaks off at this point, but *T.Levi* describes here a heavenly journey of the patriarch.

And as to the end of the vision recorded prior to the journey of Levi with Jacob's family to Bethel: here we hear of seven angels, both in *T.Levi* and in ALD (represented by Bodleian col. a 1-13 supplemented with some small new fragments). At the end, in *T.Levi* 8:18-19, Levi says that after this vision he understood that this was like the former, and that he hid this also in his heart (cf. 6:2, at the end of the first vision). The corresponding passage in ALD has been translated: "The one vision is even as the other"—following the (first ever) translation of Charles who, however, seems to be influenced by the parallel in *T.Levi*. Greenfield and Stone translate: "Then I said: 'this is a vision, and thus I am amazed that I should have a vision at all'" (v. 7).[22] The text continues: "And I hid this too in my heart"—which may still implicitly refer to a first vision, as in *T.Levi*.

---

[21] *From Patriarch to Priest*, 78-80, 83-85.

[22] See Appendix III, "The Aramaic and Greek fragments of a Levi Document," in Hollander and de Jonge, *Commentary*, 457-469, especially 461-462.

Greenfield and Stone[23] have questioned the usual view by pointing out that the prayer of Levi in ALD seems to suppose a situation at which Levi's children are present, fitting a farewell scene, but not the one presupposed in *T.Levi* 2. Next, the washing ceremony before the prayer will be an action of Levitical purification. This may mean that Levi's prayer followed his consecration. Greenfield and Stone do not, however, propose a specific order for this part of ALD.[24]

Kugler's solution is a very radical one.[25] He tries to prove that ALD had only one vision, after the Shechem incident and before the journey of Jacob and his family to Bethel. Neither the usual arguments for a two vision theory nor the suggestions made by Greenfield and Stone are compelling; at all points he offers alternative interpretations and translations. In favour of his hypothesis he cites[26] ALD vv. 78-79 (Cambridge col. d 15-18), "...and I was eighteen when I killed Shechem and destroyed the workers of violence. I was nineteen when I became a priest." He notes that this runs parallel to *T.Levi* 12:3 (already mentioned above), "... and (I was) eighteen years when I killed Shechem, and nineteen when I became priest." In Kugler's view the authors of *T.Levi* should have adjusted this statement, because in its story the patriarch is already elevated to the priesthood before Shechem. But they did not, in my view because for them it was the actual investiture in *T.Levi* 8 that counted. I fail to see why the author of ALD, too, could not have written the biographical note after recounting two visions.

Another argument is supplied by Kugler's reconstruction of the Cairo Genizah document. It leads him to calculate an eight-column gap between the end of Cambridge a-b (with what remains of the Shechem narrative) and Bodleian a (the end of a vision). In that gap he situates Levi's prayer and one vision. The fragmentary text about

---

[23] "The Prayer of Levi," *JBL* 112 (1993), 247-266, especially 248-255, and earlier "Two Notes on the Aramaic Levi Document," in H.W. Attridge *et al.* (eds.), *Of Scribes and Scrolls. Studies on the Hebrew Bible, Intertestamental Judaism and Christian Origins presented to John Strugnell* (Lanham: University Press of America, 1990), 153-161.

[24] M.E. Stone and E. Eshel, who are currently preparing a commentary on ALD, are now of the opinion that the purification is somehow consequent on the Shechem incident; for details, see M.E. Stone, "Aramaic Levi Document and Greek Testament of Levi," in S.M. Paul *et alii* (eds.), *Emanuel. Studies in Hebrew Bible, Septuagint and Dead Sea Scrolls in Honour of Emanuel Tov* (Leiden: Brill, 2003), 429-437.

[25] See *From Patriarch to Priest*, 47-50, 68-87. For a more recent statement see his *The Testaments of the Twelve Patriarchs* (Sheffield: Sheffield Academic Press, 2001), 48-50.

[26] On this see expecially *From Patriarch to Priest*, 52-59.

intermarriage, already tentatively situated after the Shechem incident, can well be explained as part of an angelic speech to Levi connected with the vision (cf. *Jubilees* 30).

This reconstruction is quite ingenious, as are Kugler's attempts to disprove the arguments of those scholars who assume two visions.[27] I want to suggest that Kugler, though cautious at every step he takes, simply wants to prove too much. Given the fragmentary state of the evidence we are unable to prove that the new non-Genizah evidence has to be fitted in the gap just indicated (assuming that Kugler has rightly assessed the size of the gap). It is still possible to put part of the material before the Shechem episode and to assume that the order of events in ALD and in *T.Levi* was similar, if not identical. Definite proof one way or the other does not seem possible; in the meantime there is something to be said in favour of proceeding on the assumption that, given the situation elsewhere, *T.Levi* and ALD run parallel here too.[28]

2.4 Our knowledge of ALD remains fragmentary like the document itself. Yet we may say a few things about its portrayal of Levi. Levi is a priest who receives very detailed instructions concerning sacrifices (vv. 13-61), though not exactly those mentioned in the relevant sections of the Law of Moses. In the "Prayer of Levi" (vv. *6, *18) and in the final passages of Isaac's instructions (vv. 48-50, 58-61) his offspring join him in the priesthood, and share in its eternal blessing.

In the prayer great emphasis is placed on Levi's holiness, purity, wisdom and knowledge. He prays to be guarded from the unrighteous spirit, fornication and pride. He asks that God may show him the holy spirit and grant him counsel and wisdom, knowledge and strength (vv. *7-*8). Further, Isaac's priestly instructions begin with

---

[27] I mention his arguments briefly: The "from Abel-main" in ALD would seem to indicate that Levi received the vision elsewhere; the one angel mentioned in the beginning may be the first of the seven mentioned in the end. The opening of the heavens may be part of a dream on earth. In lines 12-13 of Bodleian col. a one should not translate "I hid this also in my heart," but "I hid this very thing in my heart" (a strained translation of the words *'p dn* in the text). The mention of Levi's sons in the Greek text of the prayer is the result of mistranslation. The purification ceremony before the prayer may be Levi's cleansing after being contaminated by the corpses at Shechem.

[28] See also M.A. Knibb in his "Perspectives on the Apocrypha and Pseudepigrapha. The Levi Traditions," in F. García Martínez and E. Noort (eds.), *Perspectives in the Study of the Old Testament & Early Judaism. A Symposium in Honour of A.S. van der Woude on the Occasion of His 70th Birthday* (VTSup 73; Leiden: Brill, 1998), 197-213, especially pp. 205-207.

an exhortation to remain holy and to shun sexual impurity (vv. 16-18). Levi's final prayer is: "Make me a participant in your words to do true judgment for all time, me and my children for all the generations of the ages" (v. *18). V. 59 in the priestly instructions ends with "blessing will be pronounced by your seed upon the earth."

In the instructions pronounced by Levi in the year of Joseph's death, the emphasis is on reading, writing and teaching of wisdom. Here Joseph is the primary model for Levi's children (v. 82 and following verses). Warnings against the future sins of Levi's descendants will have accompanied the exhortations, though it is difficult to determine their exact place in ALD.

ALD, as well as 4QTQahat and 4Q'Amram, clearly originated in priestly circles which stressed purity and the instructive role of the priesthood (cf. Deut. 33:8-11; Mal. 2:4-9). Somehow there is a connection between Levi's calling to the priesthood and his exploits at Shechem, but in view of the very fragmentary state of our evidence exactly at that point, it is difficult to make out the exact nature of that connection.[29]

III. LEVI IN ALD AND T. LEVI

3.1 It is now time to return to the picture of Levi in *T.Levi* and to ask again to what extent it was influenced by that found in ALD. As indicated in section 1, the present *T.Levi* is "structurally" Christian; but it does acknowledge the special position of Levi and his tribe, as (high) priests, judges, scribes and teachers of the Law, in the time before the arrival of Jesus Christ. And its description of the role played by Levi and his descendants is without any doubt closely related to that found in the Aramaic and Greek fragments discussed in section 2.

The question then arises, how do we explain those differences between *T.Levi* and ALD, particularly those which are more likely to go back to the *Vorlage* from which the Christian authors of *T.Levi* worked, than to these authors themselves?[30] If we put the question

---

[29] Some scholars have found indications that royal prerogatives are connected with Levi (1Q 21, fragm. 1; Bodl. col. a, vv. 4-6; ALD v. 67 in the Greek and Aramaic; perhaps also a few phrases in the newly discovered part of the Wisdom speech, now numbered vv. 99-100 by Kugler); for details see Kugler, *From Patriarch to Priest*, 131-134.

[30] For a full picture we would have to analyse *Jubilees* 30-32 as well. This analysis cannot be undertaken here, but cf. de Jonge and Tromp, "Jacob's Son Levi."

this way we realize how little we know about that *Vorlage*. First, we do not know exactly what ALD contained and how it was structured. Next, the authors of *T.Levi* may have had ALD before them in a form that differed from the one we try to reconstruct on the basis of the existing fragments. Let us look, for instance, at the Greek fragments in MS *e* for a moment. We know next to nothing about the *Vorlage* from which they were taken. But if these fragments survived until the eleventh century, there is a chance that a much fuller Greek document could be used by those responsible for the *Testaments* at the end of the second century. Such a document may have had its own development separate from and independent of that represented by the other witnesses to ALD.[31] Yet, with this restriction, we will find that comparison of *T.Levi* with ALD sheds more light on the testament.

3.2 The first vision, in *T.Levi* 2:1-6:2, is without any doubt a composite passage.[32] It may be divided into two or three sections, preceded by an introduction in 2:3-5, which mentions a prayer of Levi and a subsequent sleep and vision. In 2:6-4:1 we have a (very complex) description of seven heavens, an announcement of Levi's future task and a prediction of judgment; direct parallels in ALD are lacking. In 4:2-6 we hear of the answer to Levi's prayer, which, as we have seen, corresponds to the prayer in ALD rather than to 2:4. It is directly followed, in 5:1-6:2, by the account of a meeting of Levi with the Most High, his calling to the priesthood and a command by the angel to execute vengeance on Shechem because of Dinah. It all ends with Levi's waking up; he blesses the Most High and the angel, and returns to his father.

In all sections we find clearly Christian elements. In 2:10-11 a Levi-Judah passage announces a future redeemer; through Levi and Judah, God will appear among men. In the sixth heaven angels offer "a reasonable and bloodless" offering to God (3:6). And although the

---

[31] We should note that there are two quotations from a Levi document in Greek in the letters of the Egyptian monk Ammonas (second half of the fourth century CE). There is some similarity in subject matter with the Prayer of Levi as found in MS *e* of the *Testaments*. Whether Ammonas quotes from a divergent Greek version of ALD or from a related Levi document must remain open. For details see J. Tromp, "Two References to a Levi Document in an Epistle of Ammonas," *NovT* 39 (1997), 235-247.

[32] See my "Notes on Testament of Levi II-VII," *Studies,* 247-260, and the relevant section in Hollander and de Jonge, *Commentary,* 131-145.

blessing of Levi includes his offspring, it will be restricted to the period before "the Lord will visit all the nations in the tender mercies of his son for ever." In fact, Levi's sons "will lay hands upon him to do away with him" (4:2-6; cf. 5:2).

5:1-6:2 link up with 6:3-7:4, describing Levi's role in the events at Shechem. Levi is clearly depicted as a warrior-priest executing God's judgment on Shechem (5:3-4, cf. 6:8). The Christian authors of *T.Levi* would not have dwelt at such length on Levi's role at Shechem, both in 5:1-6:2 and in 6:3-7:4, if this had not been in their *Vorlage*. Because what they found went back to the biblical account in Genesis 34, and clearly formed part of the tradition concerning Levi's activities, they saw no reason to change the narrative as it stood.[33]

A second vision follows in chapter 8. The verses 1 and 18 underline that it corresponds with the former (cf. also 8:19 and 6:2). The repetition drives home the point of Levi's special exalted status. Also in the second vision there is a clear reference to the coming of Jesus Christ (8:11-15).

We now turn to Isaac's instructions to Levi about the priesthood in *T.Levi* 9:6-14, corresponding to vv. 14-61 in ALD. There is no doubt that this part of *T.Levi* gives some sort of extract of the very detailed instructions in ALD (although it abbreviates so much that we cannot be certain it knew them exactly in that form). After "the law of the Lord" in general, Isaac teaches Levi "the law of the priesthood" in particular; five types of offerings are mentioned (vv. 6-7). Then follows the extract that emphasizes purity in vv. 9-11, but says very little about sacrificing (vv. 12-14). In fact, Levi is warned against "the spirit of impurity ($\pi o \rho v \epsilon i \alpha$)" which, in due time, "will defile the holy things by your seed" (we should remember that a S.E.R. passage denouncing the sins of Levi's offspring follows in chapter 10). As a priest Levi will have to take for himself a wife who has no blemish, and has not been defiled, and is not of a race of strangers and gentiles" (v. 10).

The present text of *T.Levi* can be explained as the result of abbreviation and redaction of a text like that in ALD by its Christian authors. Of course the authors of *T.Levi* acknowledged that the priest

---

[33] Note, however, the parallel between 6:11 and 1 Thess. 2:16, too close to be coincidental; see chapter 10, section 5.2 below.

Levi had cultic functions, and that priests were subject to strict marriage laws. They did not go into details with regard to the rules concerning sacrifices, no longer relevant for their audience. They did emphasize the danger of πορνεία, however, a sin repeatedly denounced in *the Testaments,* especially in *T.Reuben* and *T.Judah.*

Next, a few remarks about *T.Levi* 13, a chapter with general exhortations, parallel to ALD vv. 81-95 (plus some text in new fragments). Again there is general agreement that the former knew the latter, but abbreviated and redacted it heavily. The most striking feature is that ALD stresses "truth" and "wisdom," whereas *in T. Levi* the law of God and wisdom (subordinate to it) occupy a central position. In both cases the exhortations are general rather than specific and relevant for any audience, Jewish, Christian, or even pagan.

How do we explain the emphasis on the Law in *T.Levi* 13 (vv. 1, 3, 4, cf. 19:1; 9:6)? Is this an indication of a Jewish *Vorlage* of the present *T.Levi,* different from the ALD-text we know? This is a not unlikely supposition. As Greenfield and Stone have remarked, "it is difficult to imagine a context in which a Christian translator would have replaced 'wisdom' with 'Law'."[34] They are right; yet the Christian authors of *T.Levi* maintained the word νόμος. For them the patriarchs belonged to the period before Moses, but they had observed God's law in their lives, before Moses had been ordered to issue extra-commandments especially for the Jewish people. These patriarchs had the necessary authority to exhort Israelites and Gentiles to live in the true obedience to God—also after the coming of Jesus Christ, as a new lawgiver who had summed up all that is righteous and pious in the two great commandments of love to God and love to one's neighbour.[35]

Finally: As we have seen, it is very difficult to say anything with certainty about the relationship between *T.Levi* and ALD after *T.Levi* 13. There are very few specific similarities between 4Q Levi[a] ar 3-5 and *T.Levi* 14-15. Moreover *T.Levi* applies the S.E.R. pattern in these chapters, as in chapters 10 and 16—bringing home the opposition of Levi's descendants against Jesus Christ, and their punishment. It is likely that *T.Levi* (16:1) 17:1-11 gives extracts from a larger story of

---

[34] "The First Manuscript of *Aramaic Levi Document* from Qumran," *Mus* 107 (1994), 257-281, especially 259, n. 7.

[35] See chapter 6, sections 3 and 4.

the priesthood according to jubilees and weeks, but that story is changed so drastically that reconstruction of the *Vorlage* is impossible—and 4Q540, fragment 1 is of little help here. And as to the much discussed chapter *T.Levi* 18, here 4Q541, fragment 9 i 2-4, speaking about a new priest, says a number of things about him that are parallel to *T.Levi* 18:2-4, but the similarities are few and of a general nature (see the use of the imagery of light and darkness). As elsewhere, the Christian phrases in *T. Levi* 18 (such as vv. 6-7) are found in strategic places. Efforts to reconstruct a pre-Christian version of this chapter have proved a challenge to many scholars,[36] but it should first of all be read in the light of chapters 2-3, 4 and 8 and in the context of Levi's overall view on the Levitical priesthood, as outlined in section 1.

Some Conclusions

a. The Levi-fragments found at Qumran form a welcome addition to the medieval Aramaic material from the Cairo Genizah already known to us and to the Greek text fragments preserved in two additions in the Greek MS *e*.

b. Eventually all available texts go back to one document (ALD), although they display a number of divergencies where they overlap.

c. Thanks to the fact that we now have fragments from Qumran, we may be certain that this material represents a text current before the beginning of the common era.

d. Our evidence still remains fragmentary, and differences will remain with regard to the reconstruction of the oldest accessible form of text and its structure. On the whole it seems advisable to let *T.Levi* help determine the order of the fragments.

e. The particular features of *T.Levi* within the *Testaments of the Twelve Patriarchs* can best be explained by assuming that it used, beside other (written) traditions, the text represented by the various fragments—in some, perhaps a Greek, form. Its exact *Vorlage* cannot be determined. There is no reason to posit a Jewish intermediate stage between ALD and *T.Levi*.

g. The redactional activity of the Christian author(s) of the *Testaments* in general and *T.Levi* in particular was at the same time con-

---

[36] See the list in Kugler, *From Patriarch to Priest*, 215, n. 155.

servative and drastic. A number of elements in the *Vorlage* were preserved, others were redacted heavily; all were fitted into a specific Christian framework. Levi's appointment as priest was acknowledged, but the failing of the Levitical priesthood received much attention. The priest expected to introduce a new era would not be a son of Levi.[37]

[37] I thank Dr. J. Tromp for helpful comments on an earlier draft of this essay.

CHAPTER NINE

THE TWO GREAT COMMANDMENTS
IN THE TESTAMENTS OF THE TWELVE PATRIARCHS

In (nearly) all individual testaments we find biographical, paraeneti-cal and eschatological elements. The references to the life of the pa-triarch, and/or that of Joseph, the paradigm of virtue, and the predic-tions of what will happen when God intervenes in the future, serve to illustrate and underscore the admonishments of the sons of Jacob. In this chapter I shall discuss the views of the *Testaments* on the two great commandments, to love God and to love one's neighbour, and on forgiveness as supreme example of love to one's fellow-man.

I. THE TESTAMENTS OF THE TWELVE PATRIARCHS:
JEWISH OR CHRISTIAN?

1.1 Is this paraenesis "Jewish" or "Christian," or is it wrong to think here in terms of "either—or"? In a number of earlier studies I have argued that the *Testaments* are an important witness to the continuity in ethical thought between Hellenistic-Jewish and Early Christian circles.[1] John J. Collins once wrote in his *Between Athens and Jeru-salem. Jewish Identity in the Hellenistic Diaspora*:[2] "The ethics of the *Testaments* resemble those of the Diaspora writings we have seen in their tendency to ignore the distinctive elements of Judaism and em-phasize those which would be acceptable to sophisticated gentiles." He points out that "despite numerous references to the law (*nomos* and *entolè* are used sixty times), the ethics are presented in broad moral terms." Collins realizes, of course, that the *Testaments* are Christian in their present form, but he regards it as important that "the sense of Jewish identity is reinforced by the choice of Jewish pseudonyms." But is it right to speak of *Jewish* pseudonyms? The sons of Jacob had also "patriarchal" authority for early Christians, as

---

[1] See chapter 6, section 3.3 above.

[2] New York: Crossroad, 1983. The quotations in the text are from p. 161 and p. 162. See also p. 183 in the second, revised and expanded, edition, published by Eerdmans, Grand Rapids in 2000.

Justin Martyr clearly tells us,[3] and we cannot simply assume that the Christian redaction (or composition?) of the *Testaments* was only concerned with references to Jesus Christ and other exclusively Christian statements.

One example: in *Testament of Benjamin* 3 the readers are exhorted to follow the example of "the good and holy man Joseph." In the *Testaments* Joseph is pictured as outstanding in his love for his brothers and in his willingness to bear sufferings in order not to put them to shame. In this chapter he is said to have asked his father Jacob to pray for his sons that God would not reckon to them whatever evil they had devised regarding him. The chapter ends, in verse 8, with a reference to "the Lamb of God and Saviour of the world," and it is said that "a blameless one will be delivered up for lawless men and a sinless one will die for ungodly men." Earlier I have argued that there is little point in only regarding the evidently Christian statements in v. 8 as Christian.[4]

> It does not make much sense to put a specific label to the remaining part of chapter 3 or to the description of the good man in chapters 3-8 as a whole, and call it "Jewish" or "Christian." It may have functioned in a Hellenistic-Jewish and a Christian context; at some stage the picture inspired someone to draw a parallel between this Joseph and Jesus Christ.

Not necessarily at the very last stage, I would like to add. One cannot remove the overtly Christian passage as an interpolation, assume that all the rest is Jewish, hence non- or even pre-Christian, and then use the *Testaments* to illustrate the Jewish milieu that influenced Jesus and his followers. This is exactly what R.H. Charles did nearly a century ago, and why (particularly) the *Testaments* were so important to him.

1.2 Because Charles has exercised such a great influence on subsequent research on the pseudepigrapha in general, and on the views of later generations on the *Testaments* in particular (even unto the

---

[3] See chapter 6. We return to this below.

[4] See "Test. Benjamin 3:8 and the Picture of Joseph as 'A Good and Holy Man'" in *Jewish Eschatology, Early Christian Christology and the Testaments of the Twelve Patriarchs. Collected Essays of Marinus de Jonge* (ed. H.J. de Jonge; NovTSup 63, Leiden: Brill, 1991), 290-300. The quotation in the text is found on pp. 292-293.

present day), it may be helpful for our purpose to look for a moment
to his views on the ethics of the *Testaments*. In 1908 he published his
edition of the text of the *Testaments* and his commentary on that document.[5] In 1913 he was responsible for the section on the *Testaments*
in the second volume of his *The Apocrypha and Pseudepigrapha of
the Old Testament*.[6] It is worthwhile to quote some characteristic
statements of his on the ethics of this book.

There is no doubt that among all the "pseudepigrapha of the Old
Testament" which he studied closely Charles felt especially attracted
to the *Testaments*, above all because of their ethics. In §1 of the
Introduction to his *Commentary*, "The Book and its Fortunes," he
speaks of "many laborious but happy years of research" (p. xviii),
and in his *Edition* he ends §1 of the Introduction with the words: "the
time has at last arrived for this book, so noble in its ethical side, to
come to its own" (p. ix). For Charles the *Testaments* were a Jewish
document interpolated by Christians. "Only a score of years ago Grabe's view that the Christian clauses were interpolations was rehand-
led in a treatise by a young German scholar Schnapp" (*Commentary*,
p. xviii).[7] Also the pre-Christian *Testaments* do not form a unity. On
the basis of an analysis of the eschatological passages Charles attempts to prove that an originally pro-Maccabean document dating
from the last years of John Hyrcanus was interpolated with additions
emanating from bitter opponents of the Maccabean dynasty. But,
however important the *Testaments* may be for our knowledge of the
messianic expectations in the two centuries before the beginning of
the common era,

> the main, the overwhelming value of the book lies not in this province,
> but in its ethical teaching, which has achieved a real immortality by in-
> fluencing the thought and diction of the writers of the New Testament,
> and even those of our Lord. This ethical teaching, which is indefinitely
> higher and purer than that of the Old Testament, is yet its spiritual

---

[5] *The Greek Versions of the Testaments of the Twelve Patriarchs* (Oxford: Clarendon, 1908)
and *The Testaments of the Twelve Patriarchs Translated from the Editor's Greek Text* (London: A. and C. Black, 1908).

[6] Oxford: Clarendon, 1913. The *Testaments* are found on pp. 282-367.

[7] He refers to J.E. Grabe, *Spicilegium SS. Patrum et ut Haereticorum I*, Oxoniae, 1698, with
on p. 134 the much quoted sentence "...Testamenta XII Patriarcharum à Judaeo olim scripta, à
Christiano autem interpolata..."; and to F. Schnapp's dissertation *Die Testamente der Zwölf
Patriarchen untersucht*, Halle 1884.

child, and helps to bridge the chasm that divides the ethics of the Old
and New Testaments (*Commentary*, p. xvii).

Charles returns to this topic in the last section of the Introduction to
his *Commentary* where he discusses the teaching of the book.[8] Here
we read on pp. xciv-xcv:

> We now see the importance of our text. It shows that pre-Christian Ju-
> daism possessed a noble system of ethics on the subject of forgiveness.
> By the early school of the Chasidim, or the pious ones of the Psalms,
> the best elements of the Old Testament had been taken up, studied and
> developed, and the highly ethical code of conduct deduced therefrom
> had been carried out in actual life by these ancient Quietists. But when
> Pharisaism, breaking with the ancient ideals of its party, committed it-
> self to political interests and movements, and concurrently therewith
> surrendered itself more and more wholly to the study of the letter of
> the Law, it soon ceased to offer scope for the further development of
> such a lofty system of ethics as the Testaments attest, and so the true
> successors of the early Chasids and their teaching quitted Judaism and
> found their natural home in the bosom of primitive Christianity.

In his introduction to the *Testaments* in volume II of his *The Apocrypha and Pseudepigrapha of the Old Testament* Charles repeats
much of what he wrote five years earlier. Important for our present
purpose is what he adds about the Christian elements in the book, all
of a dogmatic nature, according to him. Other English scholars have
wrongly suggested that also the ethical passages common to the *Testaments* and the New Testament must have been interpolated. Charles
underlines the differences between the dogmatic and the ethical statements:

> But these scholars have failed to observe the characteristic differences
> between the two sets of passages in question. In the case of the first we
> have *dogmatic Christian statements* interpolated in *a Jewish work at
> variance not only with the teaching and character of that work as a
> whole, but also at variance with their respective contexts*. But in
> regard to the second, we have ethical sayings and teachings, *which are
> in harmony not only with the spirit of the book as a whole, but also
> with their respective contexts*. The ethical teaching, while very much

---

[8] See § 27, following on §§ 25-26 (pp. lxxv-xcii) dealing with the influence of the
Testaments on Patristic literature and on the New Testament respectively. The preceding § 24
dealing with their influence on Jewish literature remains, significantly, limited to one page
only.

loftier than that of the Old Testament, is yet its true spiritual child, and, though not so pure and sublime as that of the N.T., is a product of the school that prepared the way for the N.T." (p. 291, italics by Charles).

For Charles the paraenesis of the *Testaments* formed an essential link between the ethical teaching of the Old Testament and that of the New. Historically, Jesus and his followers were the true successors of the early school of the Chasidim that produced the *Testaments* in their original form.

1.3 Charles's view on the *Testaments* and their place in the history of early Judaism rests on his confidence that the Christian elements in the text could be exactly delineated and removed as interpolations, and that also Jewish interpolations in an earlier Jewish *Grundschrift* could be distinguished. In both respects he has been followed by a number of scholars during the last century, whose operations resulted, however, in widely different reconstructions.[9] As we have seen, literary criticism of this sort is of only limited value in the case of texts like the *Testaments*. Its criteria for separation are unevennesses, doublets, sudden transitions as to form and content, in short: all signs of inconsistency. But it is by no means certain that modern standards of consistency are applicable here: what clearly strikes us as inconsistent, did not hinder the interpolator/redactor, or later readers, who for ages read and transmitted the text as we now have it. And in the case of the so-called Christian interpolations, one should be extra-critical of Charles's application (and non-application!) of the scissors-and-paste method, because, as was argued above, it is not always evident how we should distinguish between Jewish and Christian statements.

II. The Testaments on the Two Great Commandments

2.1 We shall now turn to the statements in the *Testaments* about the commandments to love God and to love one's neighbour, and ask what light they can shed on the question of the provenance and the transmission of the *Testaments*. Charles, comparing Matt. 22:37-39

---

[9] See chapter 5, section 2 above.

and *T.Dan* 5:3 states: "Our text (*scil. T.Dan* 5:3) is thus the first literary authority which conjoins the two great commands of love to God and love to our neighbour." A little later he says, referring to the fact that in Luke 10:25-27 it is a scribe who connects the two commandments: "... that the two great commandments were already conjoined in the teaching of the scribes at the time of our Lord, we may reasonably infer from our text, which was written 140 years earlier, and from the account in Luke."[10]

A number of later scholars have followed Charles in regarding the *Testaments* as the earliest witness to a combination of the two great commandments.[11] But what if we reject the theory that Christian elements can be removed as interpolations and are equally sceptical towards distinguishing later Jewish additions to a "Grundschrift"?[12]

2.2.1 The *Testaments* purport to give the last words of the twelve sons of Jacob. Their final instructions constitute their spiritual legacy —received from their fathers and to be handed down by their descendants to further generations. This is brought out nowhere more clearly than in one of the last chapters in the last testament, that of Benjamin. I quote *T.Benj.* 10:2-5:

> Therefore, my children, know that I am dying,
> Therefore, you must do truth and righteousness each one to his neighbour
> and justice unto preservation
> and keep the law of the Lord and his commandments.
> For I teach you these things instead of any inheritance.
> And do you also, therefore, give them to your children for an everlasting possession;
> for so did Abraham and Isaac and Jacob.
> They gave us all these things for an inheritance, saying:
> Keep the commandments of God,
> until the Lord will reveal his salvation to all nations.

---

[10] *Commentary*, lxxix and xcv.

[11] So still J.H. Ulrichsen, *Die Grundschrift der Testamente der Zwölf Patriarchen* (Acta Universitatis Upsaliensis: Hist. Rel. 10; Uppsala 1991), 284: "Die TP bieten wahrscheinlich die älteste Kombination dieser Gebote." He refers here to the "Grundschrift" he has reconstructed.

[12] For a detailed exposition of the passages concerned I may refer to Hollander and De Jonge, *Commentary*.

What Benjamin, like Abraham, Isaac and Jacob, teaches ἀντὶ πασῆς κληρονομίας can be summed up as "the law of God and his commandments," "the commandments of God," or more specifically as "doing truth and righteousness each one to his neighbour and justice unto preservation." At the end of the chapter, v. 11 speaks of "walking in holiness before the face of the Lord." The *Testaments* deal with a great many virtues, and warn against scores of vices, illustrating them with concrete examples from the lives of the patriarchs, but regularly they summarize their paraenesis in more general terms.[13] The very first summary, that in *T.Reub.* 3:8, for instance, also speaks about the "truth," and about "the law of God" together with "the admonitions of his fathers."[14] It is in such summarizing statements that we find the references to the two great commandments, jointly, or separately (as in *T.Benj.* 10:3).

The admonitions of the fathers that convey the commandments of God to their children and future generations are clearly set in the situation of Genesis, not in that of Exodus with the formal proclamation of the law by Moses on Mount Sinai. In *T.Zeb.* 3 we are told that Joseph's brothers bought sandals from the money they received by selling Joseph. What happened to them wearing these sandals is in v. 4 connected with the law on the Levirate marriage in Deut. 25:5-10 (LXX), introduced with the words "therefore it is written in the writing of the law of Enoch."[15] In *T.Levi* 10:5 "the book of Enoch" is referred to for the prediction that the house which the Lord will choose will be called Jerusalem. Also in other "Sin-Exile-Return" passages Enoch is mentioned as an authority. In *T.Zeb.* 9:5 Zebulun refers to the writing of his fathers as a source of information concerning the future, and in *T.Ash.* 7:5 Asher mentions "the tables of heaven."[16] To these tables he also refers in 2:8-10 when he describes people who combine wickedness with fasting. He calls them half-clean, but in reality unclean, and he compares them with swine and

---

[13] Some examples: "the law/the commandments of God," *T.Levi* 14:4; *T.Jud.* 13:1; 18:3; 26:1; *T.Iss.* 4:6; 5:1; *T.Zeb.* 5:1; 10:2; *T.Dan* 5:1; *T.Gad* 3:1; *T. Ash.* 6:3; *T.Jos.* 11:1; 19:6; *T.Benj.* 3:1; "truth," *T.Reub.* 3:8-9; 6:9; *T.Dan* 5:2; *T.Gad* 3:1 (here with "righteousness"); "to fear the Lord," *T.Levi* 13:1, 7; *T.Zeb.* 10:2: *T.Dan* 6:1; *T.Jos.*11:1; "to walk in simplicity," *T.Levi* 13:1; *T.Iss.* 4:6; 5:1; "wickedness…goodness," *T.Ash.* 3:1-2; *T.Benj.* 7:1; 8:1; cf. *T.Dan* 6:10. *T.Benj.* has "the good man" and "the good mind" as central themes.

[14] See also *T.Jud.* 13:1; *T.Zeb.* 10:2; cf. *T.Levi* 10:1; *T.Jud.* 1:4; *T.Jos.* 3:3.

[15] The variant "in the writing of the law of Moses" in MSS *chij* is, of course, secondary.

[16] See Hollander-De Jonge, *Commentary*, Introduction §4.4.1.

hares. Because he cannot refer to Lev. 11:1-8 or Deut. 14:6-8, he concludes with the words: "For God has said so in the tables of heaven."[17] We may add that nowhere in the *Testaments* typically Jewish precepts as the observance of the circumcision or dietary laws are advocated.[18]

2.2.2 *T. Benjamin* 10 not only characterizes and summarizes the ethical teaching of the *Testaments*, it also establishes a clear connection between obedience to the teaching of the patriarchs and receiving, together with them, a share in the salvation that God "will reveal to all the nations." We cannot, of course, deal here with the many, variegated and complex passages in the *Testaments* speaking about the future, that have sparked off so much controversy in the past. Let us just note that in this final testamentary chapter in *T. Benjamin*, which is clearly Christian,[19] it is said that when God reveals his salvation to all the nations Enoch, Noah and Shem, as well as Abraham, Isaac and Jacob will have a share in this. All sons of Jacob will rise with them, each over his own tribe (cf. *T.Jud.* 25:1-2; *T.Zeb.* 10:2). Indeed all people will rise, and all will be judged, Israel and the gentiles, and the criterion will be belief in Jesus Christ, in whom God appeared on earth. In the concluding verse 11 the author(s) states categorically:

> But you, if you walk in holiness before the face of the Lord,
> you will again dwell safely with me;
> and all Israel will be gathered together unto the Lord.

This view on the future of Israel and the gentiles agrees in many ways with that found in Justin Martyr's *Dialogue with Trypho*.[20] We

---

[17] Cf. the reference to Genesis 34 in *T.Levi* 5:4.

[18] On seeming discrepancies, to be explained by the fact that the author(s) of the *Testaments* consistently maintain(s) the once chosen pseudepigraphical stance, see my discussion with H.D. Slingerland, who has found typically Jewish, even Levitical, elements in statements about the law in the *Testaments*, in my *Collected Essays*, 257-262; 288-289.

[19] See also chapter 9 and chapter 11 (on the Benjaminite Paul). One should read these chapters without trying to remove the clearly Christian passages (which are very extensive in the final chapters of the *Testaments*) as interpolations. Charles greatly overrated the importance of the Armenian version here (see Hollander and De Jonge, *Commentary*, 412) and, as so often, mixed up textual criticism and literary criticism.

[20] See the discussion of this point in chapter 6, section 3.3, and compare "The Future of Israel in the Testaments of the Twelve Patriarchs," in *Collected Essays*, 164-179. See also H.W. Hollander, "Israel and God's Eschatological Agent in the *Testaments of the Twelve Patriarchs*," in P.W. van der Horst (ed.), *Aspects of Religious Contact and Conflict in the Ancient World* (Utrechtse Theologische Reeks 31; Utrecht: Faculteit der Godgeleerdheid, 1995), 91-104.

may point, for instance, to *Dial.* 80-81 where Justin expresses agreement with Trypho when the latter expects a rebuilt Jerusalem in which Christians "will be gathered and rejoice with Christ, together with the patriarchs and the prophets and the saints of our race, or even of them who became proselytes, before your Christ came" (cf. also *T.Benj.* 9:2). In *Dial.* 45:1 Justin says:

> Since they who did the things that universally, and naturally, and eternally are good, are pleasing to God, so shall they also be saved by means of this Christ of ours, in the resurrection equally with the righteous who were before them, Noah and Enoch and Jacob and any others there may be, together with those who recognize this Christ as the Son of God.

This includes, of course, the Jews insofar as they have kept the eternal and universal commandments found in the law of Moses (see 45:2-3). This law, however, contains a great number of extra regulations of a temporary nature and binding upon Jews only. No righteous person before Moses kept them, and since the coming of Jesus Christ we live in a new dispensation in which the eternal and universal commandments are, again, the only ones that are valid (*Dial.* 44-46; 11:2; 12:1-3; 14:1-8 etc.). The *Testaments* and Justin in his *Dialogue* are thus in agreement not only with regard to their expectation of God's definitive intervention in the future, but also in their views on the ethical commandments in force during the period of the "patriarchs" and after the coming of Jesus Christ (Justin uses the word "patriarchs" repeatedly to denote the righteous in the period before Moses). In *Dial.* 93:1 Justin declares that God has exhibited among every race of men the things that are righteous at all times and at all places; in 93:2 he adds that Jesus Christ has rightly declared that all righteousness and piety (πᾶσαν δικαιοσύνην καὶ εὐσέβειαν) are fulfilled in the two main commandments: to love God and to love one's neighbour.

2.3.1 As expected, we do not find any direct references either to Deut. 6:4-5 or to Lev. 19:18. For the relationship to God and the relationship to one's neighbour various terms are used. "To love one's neighbour" is only found in *T.Iss.* 5:2; *T.Benj.* 3:3-4; but cf. *T.Iss.* 7:6; *T.Dan* 5:3; *T.Zeb.* 8:5; *T.Gad* 4:2; 6:1, 3; 7:7 for similar expressions. "To love the Lord" is found in *T.Iss.* 5:2 and 7:6, in combination with love to one's neighbour resp. to every man, compare *T.Dan* 5:3 "Love the Lord in all your life, and each other with a true heart." In *T.Dan* 5:3 we should also note the "with a true heart," compare *T.Gad* 6:3 "from the heart," and in *T.Gad* 6:1 "… in deed and word and in disposition of the soul" (cf. *T. Jos.* 10:4), also in connection with love to one's brother. In *T.Iss.* 7:6 we read: "The Lord I loved with all my strength" (cf. *T.Zeb.* 10:5; *T.Ash.* 5:4); here we find the word ἰσχύς as in Mark 12:30, 33 and Luke 10:27—whilst Deut. 6:5 (LXX) uses δύναμις.

Turning now to the passages where love/fear of God and love to one's neighbour/brother etc. (expressed in compassion, forgiveness etc.) are mentioned together, we shall begin with *T.Issachar, T.Zebulun* and *T.Dan*. In the following subsection we shall deal with *T.Benjamin* and *T.Joseph*, together with some other passages in which Joseph's attitude towards his brothers plays an important role.

2.3.2. *T.Iss.* 5:1-2 brings us right to the heart of the paraenesis in this testament:

> Keep, therefore, the law of God, my children,
> and acquire simplicity,
> and walk in guilelessness,
> not meddling with the commandments of the Lord,
> and the affairs of your neighbour.
> But love the Lord and your neighbour,
> show mercy to the poor and the weak.

The two great commandments are the most adequate expression of the law of God; they are directly connected with the central virtue of the testament: ἁπλότης. Next, love to one's neighbour has to show itself in mercy (ἐλεᾶτε) to the poor and the weak. Ἁπλότης means: simplicity, singleness (of heart), integrity, complete devotion to God and to his will. In 3:1, 4 and 4:6 it is used together with "uprightness" (εὐθύτης), in 5:1 with "guilelessness" (ἀκακία). This simplicity leads to a pure, simple life, in *T. Issachar* that of a farmer. Clearly Gen. 49:14-15 LXX influenced the author(s) here and made him (them) establish a connection with the positive appreciation of the life and the virtues of the simple farmer in Greek and Hellenistic popular philosophy. Issachar, in his integrity, keeps far from evil thoughts and desires; he is rewarded and aided by God (chapters 3-4).

His simplicity reveals itself also in his sharing the good things of the earth with everyone who is poor and oppressed (3:8,[21] cf. 5:2).

Here we may also point to Zebulun, the fisherman, counterpart of Issachar, the farmer. He shows "compassion and mercy" (εὐσπλαγχνία καὶ ἔλεος), towards Joseph (chapters 2 and 4) and next towards all people in need. The passage 5:5-7:4 gives many examples of Zebulun's compassion, expressing itself in sharing what he possessed with people in distress. All people are helped by him, without discrimination. Hence the patriarch exhorts his children:

> And now, children, I declare to you,
> to keep the commandments of the Lord,
> and to show mercy towards all,
> not only towards men, but also towards beasts. (5:1)

> Have, therefore, yourselves also, my children,
> compassion towards every man with mercy. (8:1)

"Neighbour" means everyone, so much is clear.[22] This also applies to *T. Issachar*—see 7:6, found in a concluding passage[23] in which the patriarch describes the sins he avoided and the "piety and truth" he practised:

> The Lord I loved with all my strength,
> likewise, I loved also every man as my children.

In *T.Zeb.* 8:1-2 and in *T.Iss.* 7:7 the final exhortations of the patriarch are combined with a promise concerning the future. The exhortation in *T.Zeb.* 8:1 is first followed by "… that the Lord also may show compassion and mercy to you." God will treat a person in accordance with that person's treatment of his neighbour (see also v. 3 and 5:3; 6:6, and cf. *T.Iss.* 3:7; 4:1). This will also become apparent in "the last days" when "God will send his compassion on earth, and wheresoever he finds feelings of mercy, he dwells in him" (v. 2). We may compare here *T.Napht.* 4:5 that speaks about "the compassion of the Lord" appearing in the form of "a man working righteousness and

---

[21] Compare also the ὁ μεταδιδοὺς ἐν ἁπλότητι in Rom. 12:8, cf. 2 Cor. 8:2; 9:11, 13.

[22] See also M. Konradt, "Menschen- oder Bruderliebe? Beobachtungen zum Liebesgebot in den Testamenten der Zwölf Patriarchen," *ZNW* 88 (1997), 296-310.

[23] After a final exhortation to his sons: "walk in the simplicity of your father" (5:8), and a "Sin-Exile-Return" passage in which the future sins of his offspring are characterized as forsaking simplicity and leaving farm work.

working mercy unto all who are far off and who are near" (cf. Isa. 57:19 LXX referred to in Eph. 2:17). As the explicitly Christian *T.Levi* 4:4 shows, both in *T.Zeb.* and in *T.Napht.* the coming of Jesus Christ is referred to. The same applies to the phrase "having with you the God of heaven, walking together with men in singleness of heart" in *T.Iss.* 7:7 (and to *T. Jud.* 24:1; *T.Napht.* 8:3; *T.Benj.* 9:2).

A little earlier in *T.Iss.* 7:7 we hear: "every spirit of Beliar will flee from you." Spirits of evil, wicked men and beasts have no hold on the virtuous man—so also *T.Napht.* 8:4; *T.Benj.* 3:3-5; 5:1-2; cf. 6:1. This will become fully apparent in the eschatological future, as we read in *T.Sim.* 6:6; *T.Levi* 3:3; 18:12; *T.Jud.* 25:3; *T.Zeb.* 9:8; *T.Dan* 5:10-11; cf. *T.Benj.* 3:8.

Finally, we turn to *T.Dan* 5:1-3, a passage which ends with another reference to the two great commandments. Before that, it shows, again, how God is with those who avoid sin and practise love; indeed he dwells with such people (so also *T.Jos.* 10:2-3; *T.Benj.* 6:1, 3, 4).

> Observe, therefore, my children, the commandments of the Lord
> and keep his law;
> and depart from anger and hate lying,
> that the Lord may dwell in you
> and Beliar flee from you.
> Speak truth each one with his neighbour
> and so you will not fall into pleasure and confusions,
> having the God of peace,
> and no war will prevail over you.
> Love the Lord in all your life
> and each other with a true heart.

A complex eschatological passage follows, combining several "patterns" used in the Testaments. It ends, in 5:13, with an eschatological promise comparable to the one found in T.Iss. 7:7 (plus the passages just quoted, and *T.Levi* 5:2):

> ... because the Lord will be in the midst of it,
> living together with men,
> and the Holy One of Israel,
> reigning over them in humility and poverty.

2.3.3 This survey of the place of the two great commandments in the paraenesis of *T.Issachar*, together with *T.Zebulun*, and in *T.Dan* shows how difficult it is to describe the *Testaments* as "Jewish" or "Christian," let alone as "first Jewish and later Christian." It is perfectly natural and meaningful that a paraenesis focussing on ἁπλότης leads to a reference to the coming of Jesus Christ as "walking together with men in singleness of heart" (*T.Iss.* 7:7) or, in an other context, to portraying him as embodying God's compassion (*T.Zeb.* 8:2; *T.Napht.* 4:5). He may be called " a man working righteousness and mercy" (*T.Napht.* 4:5) or "walking with the sons of man in righteousness and peace" (*T. Jud.* 25:3), or he may be said to be "reigning over them in humility and poverty" (*T.Dan* 5:13). It is quite arbitrary to deny that these passages are Christian or to bracket them as later interpolations. At the same time the substance of the paraenesis is Hellenistic-Jewish, and for the passages speaking about God dwelling in virtuous persons one can find Hellenistic *and* Christian parallels.[24] To do full justice to the *Testaments*, it seems to me, we have to treat the paraenesis found in them as early Christian, and, particularly, as an example of the continuity in ethical thought between Hellenistic Judaism and early Christianity.

2.4.1 Before we discuss the combination of the two great commandments in *T.Jos.* 11:1 and *T.Benj.* 3:3-4 we turn for a moment to *T.Zeb.* 8:4-6 and *T.Sim.* 4:4-7, where Joseph's forgiving attitude towards his brothers is mentioned as a supreme example of love for one's fellow-man.[25] *T. Zeb.* 8:4-6 follows on 8:1-3 discussed above. Joseph is introduced as a very special example of a person filled with "compassion and mercy." When his brothers came to Egypt he did not only have compassion for Zebulun (who had been compassionate towards him—see 2:4; 4:2) but he also "bore no malice" against all his brothers (οὐκ ἐμνησικάκησεν, v. 4; cf. Gen. 50:15 LXX). In this he is an example for others. In v. 5 Zebulun exhorts his children:

> To whom taking heed,
> do you also yourselves, behave without malice, my children

---

[24] See the note on *T.Benj.* 6:4 in Hollander and De Jonge, *Commentary*, 428. We may mention Rom. 8:9-11; 1 Cor. 3:16; 6:19; 2 Tim. 1:14; Jas. 4:5; *Barn.* 16:6-10; *Hermas, Man.* 10,1,6, but also passages in Philo about the soul as house of the Lord. On Philo see also D. Winston, *The Wisdom of Solomon* (AB 43; Garden City, New York: Doubleday, 1979), 102 (on Wis. 1:4). Winston speaks of "a favorite conception of the Late Stoa ... frequently used by Philo."

[25] Konradt, "Menschen- oder Bruderliebe?" rightly emphasizes that the (natural) use of the word "brother" in the pasages about Joseph does not suggest a limitation of love and forgiveness to an "inner circle."

> and love one another,
> and do not reckon, each one of you, the evil of his brother.

The same theme is found earlier in *T.Sim.* 4:4-7, in connection with warnings against envy (the principal vice in this testament) and exhortations "to walk in singleness of soul and with a good heart" and "to love each one his brother, with a good heart" (see vv. 5 and 7). In v. 5 we find the following description of Joseph:

> But Joseph was a good man
> and he had the spirit of God in him;
> being compassionate and merciful
> he did not bear malice against me,
> but he loved me as his other brothers.

To this v. 6 adds:

> All his days he did not reproach us concerning this affair,
> but he loved us as his own soul,
> and beyond his own sons he glorified us ....

2.4.2 These themes return, as might be expected, in Joseph's own testament, in particular in the more general hortatory passages. First, *T.Jos.* 10:1-11:1, found between the story of Joseph's struggle with the Egyptian woman (3:1-9:5) and the second story about Joseph's slavery and imprisonment (11:2-16:6), and, next, *T.Jos.* 17-18 at the end. *T.Jos.* 10:1-4 looks back on Joseph's steadfast attitude towards his mistress. The patriarch tells his children to notice the great effect of endurance/patience (ὑπομονή), and of prayer and fasting. He urges them to observe self-control and temperance (σωφροσύνη) and to remain pure, patient and humble. God dwells in such people (cf. also *T.Sim.* 4:4) and guards them against evil (cf. *T.Dan* 5:1; *T.Iss.* 7:7). Also he exalts those who do not exalt themselves. This last theme is developed in 10:5-6 which introduces the second story, in which Joseph keeps silent about his origin when he is sold.[26] From childhood onwards he feared God, did not exalt himself and honoured his brothers—which implied keeping silent, however much he had to endure because of that. This leads in 11:1 to the exhortation:

---

[26] Also when he is resold to an Egyptian merchant. Moreover he holds his peace when a eunuch cheats the wife of Petephres, "lest the eunuch be exposed" (16:6).

You also, therefore,
have the fear of God in all your work before the eyes
and honour your brothers;
for everyone who works the law of the Lord will be loved by him.

It is taken up in 17:1-2, after the second story, in the words:

You see, children, how great things I endured,
that I should not put my brothers to shame.
Do you also, therefore love one another
and with patience hide one another's faults.

This exhortation is underscored with another, almost exuberant, de-scription of Joseph's loving attitude towards his brothers, when they came to Egypt as well as after Jacob's death (vv. 4-7). Again the humiliation-exaltation theme returns in v. 8:

And I did not exalt myself in arrogance because of my worldly glory,
but I was among them as one of the least.

So Joseph's children will also be exalted and blessed by good things forever, if they walk in the commandments of the Lord (18:1, cf. vv. 3-4; cf. *T.Sim.* 4:5). The most important commandment of all is to love one's enemies, as we read in v. 2:

And if anyone wants to do evil to you,
do well to him and pray for him,
and you will be released by the Lord from all evil.

2.4.3 Chapters 3-6 of *T. Benjamin* dealing with "the good/holy man" and "the good/pure mind" sum up the most important features of the paraenesis of the *Testaments*. Here, too, we find statements on the two commandments and Joseph's exemplary love for his brothers. Benjamin's children have to follow the example of the good and holy man Joseph (3:1, and later 4:1, followed by 5:3; see earlier *T.Sim.* 4:4; *T.Dan* 1:4). A good man has a good mind and "sees all things rightly" (3:2).[27] The theme of God's help against evil spirits and the attacks of men returns (3:3-5; 5:2-3; 6:1, 4, 6), illustrated again by the case of Joseph (3:3; cf. the contrast "humiliation-exaltation" in 5:5). I quote 3:3-5:

[27] The section *T.Benj.* 3-6 ends in 6:5-7 by confronting "doubleness" with ἁπλότης.

> Fear the Lord
> and love your neighbour,
> And even though the spirits of Beliar ask for you
> to be delivered up to every evil of tribulation,
> yet no evil of tribulation will have dominion over you,
> even as it had not over Joseph my brother.
> How many men wished to kill him, and God shielded him!
> For he who fears God
> and loves his neighbour
> cannot be smitten by the spirit of the air of Beliar,
> because he is shielded by the fear of God;
> nor can he be ruled over by the plot of men and beasts,
> because he is helped by the love of the Lord which he has towards his neighbour.[28]

Another example of Joseph's love for his brothers follows. He asks his father to pray for his sons "that the Lord would not reckon to them whatever they had devised regarding him" (v. 6, cf. *T.Zeb.* 8:5). Jacob is overcome by Joseph's goodness (v. 7) and cries out:

> In you will be fulfilled the prophecy of heaven
> concerning the Lamb of God and Saviour of the world,
> that a blameless one will be delivered up for lawless men
> and a sinless one will die for ungodly men
> in the blood of the covenant,
> for the salvation of the Gentiles and Israel,
> and will destroy Beliar and those who serve him (v. 8).

The prophecy concerned is no doubt Isa 52:13-53:12, read by Christians as referring to life and death of Jesus Christ. The vocabulary of this verse shows standard early Christian terminology.

More could be said about chapters 4-6, but I mention just a few statements in line with what we found before. Thus, in 4:1-3 the good man is said to show "mercy to all men, even though they are sinners" and to overcome evil by doing good (cf. also 5:3-5); and in 4:4 we

---

[28] Note here the terminology in the final clause, to be compared with "…that you may flee hatred and cleave to the love of the Lord in *T.Gad* 5:2. The author(s) want(s) to emphasize that a person who fears/loves the Lord will love his neighbour with a love inspired by God. For a yet fuller picture of love for one's neighbour one should analyse *T.Gad* 3-7, warning against hatred. See in particular *T.Gad* 6:1-7:6, beginning with "love each one his brother and put away hatred from your hearts" and ending with "put away, therefore, hatred from your souls, and love one another with uprightness of heart."

read "on the poor man he has mercy; with the weak man he feels sympathy."

2.4.4 Looking back on the paraenesis in this subsection, we conclude again that it makes little sense to distinguish between "Jewish" and "Christian" elements in the paraenesis of the passages concerned. Nor is it easy to decide whether the descriptions and characterizations of Joseph's love for his brothers have to be attributed to Christians who regarded him as a type of Jesus Christ, or whether they were subsequently (to a greater or lesser extent) remodelled in order to support this typology. *T.Benj.* 3:8 is unequivocally Christian, and fits completely in its context. As I said before (see 1.1) we cannot be certain that it was only inserted at a later stage of transmission.

Other passages may be mentioned in support of Christian influence on the picture of Joseph presented in the Testaments. When, in *T.Jos.* 17:8, the patriarch asserts that he did not exalt himself in arrogance because of his wordly glory, but "was among them as one of the least," one is reminded of Luke 22:24-29 (and, as to terminology, of 1 Cor. 15:9; Matt. 25:40, 45). In *T.Zeb.* 4:4 we hear that Joseph spent "three days and three nights" in the pit, this provides a parallel to Jonah's three days and three nights in the belly of the fish (Jon. 2:1)—in Matt. 12:40 connected with Jesus' death and resurrection. Somewhat more complicated is the detail in *T.Gad* 2:2 that Gad and Judah[29] sold Joseph to the Ishmaelites for thirty pieces of gold, "and hiding them, we showed the twenty to our brothers." In Gen. 37:28 LXX the price is twenty pieces of gold, against twenty pieces of silver in the Hebrew. The number of thirty may simply emphasize the covetousness of the two brothers ($\phi\iota\lambda\alpha\rho\gamma\upsilon\rho\iota\alpha$ is a major theme in *T. Judah*). Yet it remains remarkable that just the number thirty was chosen; it reminds of Judas's selling of Jesus for thirty pieces of silver (Matt. 26:15; 27:9-10, cf. Zech. 11:12-13).

Admittedly, the evidence of these three passages is cumulative at best, and we need the hermeneutical key provided by *T.Benj.* 3:8. This situation seems to me typical of the *Testaments* as a whole. The clearly Christian passages should not be discarded as later interpolations, but as clues to a true understanding of the document as we

---

[29] So MS *b* (cf. *chj*); in Gen. 37:26-28 Judah is the one who sells Joseph. MSS *gldeaf* read "Simean," in accordance with *T.Zeb.* 2:1; 3:2; 4:2.

have it, as the result of a complex process of transmission—a process of which the earliest stages cannot be reconstructed with certainty.

CONCLUDING REMARKS

I set out to emphasize the intricacy of the relationships between the pseudepigrapha of the Old Testament and early Christianity, and I pointed out the complex history of their transmission in diverse Christian circles over a considerable period of time. I illustrated this with an analysis of the statements in the *Testaments of the Twelve Patriarchs* concerning the commandments to love God and to love one's neighbour, and on forgiveness as supreme example of love. In my analysis I argued that Charles's assessment of the paraenesis of the *Testaments* as an essential link between the ethical teaching of the Old Testament and that of the New Testament rests on a dubious literary-critical analysis—inspired by a too great confidence in our ability to discard later Christian interpolations, and to distinguish between different stages in the Jewish transmission of the book.

It is right and helpful to compare the ethics of the *Testaments* with those of Hellenistic popular philosophy and Hellenistic-Jewish sources. At the same time it must be asked how the ideas found in the *Testaments* fit in with those of early Christian authors of the second and third centuries living in Hellenistic surroundings and trying to take seriously the Jewish heritage of Christianity (including the teachings of the "Old Testament"). All along I have shown that it is very difficult (if not impossible) to distinguish between (Hellenistic-)Jewish and Christian elements in the *Testaments*, but also that such a distinction does not render full justice to the *Testaments* in their present form. Rather than earmarking the overtly Christian elements as later interpolations, we may use them as pointers to the meaning and the relevance of the *Testaments* for early Christians.

I realize that this approach to the *Testaments of the Twelve Patriarchs* leaves many questions unanswered. It does not help us to determine who first combined the two great commandments as a summary of the law. Nor does it provide an answer to the question of the specificity of early Christian ethics vis-à-vis Hellenistic and Jewish ethics. Seen in a broader perspective, this approach does not solve the problem of the existence and contents of possible pre-Christian stages in the transmission of the *Testaments*. Perhaps the dilemma "composition or thorough redaction by Christians?" is indeed unsoluble. Comparison with indubitably Jewish material, for instance in the case of *T.Levi* and related Qumran material,[30] highlights the centrality of the Christian elements in the present *Testaments*. But how traditional Jewish material reached those responsible for their composition, and exactly in what form, cannot (yet?) be traced.

In any case the *Testaments of the Twelve Patriarchs* tell a fascinating story about the struggle within early Christianity to understand the relevance of those parts of the Jewish scriptures dealing with the period of the patriarchs (and of Jewish interpretations of Genesis) for Christians. One thing is evident: we should take the so-called pseudepigrapha of the Old Testament seriously as part of early Christian literature, before trying to use them, one way or another, as witnesses to Judaism in the period around the beginning of the Common Era.[31]

[30] See chapters 7 and 8 above.
[31] See chapter 6, section 3.4.

CHAPTER TEN

LIGHT ON PAUL FROM THE
TESTAMENTS OF THE TWELVE PATRIARCHS?
THE TESTAMENTS AND THE NEW TESTAMENT

Approaching the *Testaments of the Twelve Patriarchs* as a document transmitted by Christians in order to be read (at least primarily) by Christians, has its implications for the assessment of parallel passages in the *Testaments* and the writings of the New Testament. We can no longer simply assume that authors of New Testament writings knew the *Testaments* in some (Hellenistic-)Jewish form. On the other hand it is not always evident that parallels in thought and diction should be explained by literary dependence of the *Testaments* on any of the writings of the New Testament. This chapter will illustrate the complexity of the situation, in a discussion of a number of passages in the letters of Paul.

I. LISTS OF PARALLELS

1.1 One of the features of the 26th edition of Nestle-Aland's *Novum Testamentum graece* (hereafter N.-A.) is the expansion of the number of references to the pseudepigrapha of the Old Testament in the outer margin in comparison with the 25th. On p. 81* of the English introduction to N.-A.[25] we find a list of abbreviations of the books of the Bible (including the deuterocanonical/apocryphal books of the Old Testament), followed by the statement: "Besides these occur: Ps(almi) Sal(omonis), Ascensio Isaiae, Ass(umptio) Mosis, Apc (Apocalypsis) Eliae, 4 Esra, Henoch; Aratus (Act 17,28), Epimenides (Tit 1,12), Menander (1 K 15,33)." A similar list is given on pp. 67*-68* of N.-A.[26], but this time the books are divided between those of the Old Testament (with special mention of LXX-titles) and of the New Testament with a special section "Apocrypha and Pseudepigrapha of the Old Testament" in between. As pseudepigrapha are listed *Jubilees, Martyrdom of Isaiah, Psalms of Solomon, Enoch, Assumption of oses, Apocalypse of Baruch, Testaments of the Twelve Patriarchs* (cited individually), *Life of Adam and Eve,* plus the *Apocalypse of Elijah* (according to Origen).

At the end of N.-A.[25] there is an "Index locorum" with Old Testament texts quoted in the New Testament or mentioned in the margin for other reasons. In N.-A.[26] we find Appendix III "Loci citati vel allegati," divided into two sections: A. "Ex Vetero Testamento" and B. "E Scriptoribus Graecis." The Old Testament section mentions first the books of the Hebrew Bible, next those only found in the LXX plus *4 Ezra,* and finally, somewhat surprisingly, the so-called pseudepigrapha of the Old Testament. For the editors of N.-A.[26] texts from the Old Testament pseudepigrapha mentioned in the outer margin are clearly of a comparable nature and of the same exegetical value as texts found in the Hebrew and the Greek Bibles.[1]

Appendix III just mentioned gives 16 passages from the *Testaments of the Twelve Patriarchs* as parallels to 18 passages from the New Testament (pp. 774-775). In twelve cases they appear in the margin of texts in the Letters of Paul (ten of them in Romans), otherwise two are in Acts, one in Hebrews, three in the Letter of James. This distribution makes a one-sided impression, and one wonders why particularly Paul's Letter to the Romans received special attention.[2]

1.2 One of the best-known lists of parallels between the writings of the New Testament and the *Testaments of the Twelve Patriarchs* is found on pp. lxxviii-xcii of R.H. Charles's Translation and Commentary on the *Testaments.*[3] He gives them in § 26 under the heading "Influence of the Testaments on the New Testament," adding as § 27 a survey of the "Teaching of the Author on Forgiveness, the Two Great Commandments, Universalism, the Messiah, the Resurrection, the Antichrist, and its Influence on the New Testament" (pp. xcii-

---

[1] The pseudepigrapha are not specially mentioned in the short section on Appendix III in K. Aland and B. Aland, *Der Text des Neuen Testaments* (Stuttgart: Deutsche Bibelgesellschaft 1982; 2nd ed. 1989).

[2] Nine of the ten parallels to Romans can be found in Ernst Käsemann's notes on the texts concerned in his *An die Römer* (HNT 8a; Tübingen: Mohr [Siebeck], 1973).The exception is *T.Benj.* 4:3f. at Rom. 12:21; at Rom. 1:4 K. refers to *T Levi* 18:11 instead of 18:7, mentioned in N.-A.[26]. Käsemann mentions, however, many more passages from the Testaments that are not mentioned in Nestle-Aland.

[3] R.H. Charles, *The Testaments of the Twelve Patriarchs translated from the editor's Greek text and edited with introduction, notes and indices* (London: A. and C. Black, 1908).

xcix). The list in § 26 gives parallels to twenty passages in Matthew, thirteen in Luke, five in Acts, three in John, thirty-eight in the Pauline[4] and Deutero-Pauline Epistles (plus a long list of words common to the Testaments and the Pauline Epistles, but not found in the rest of the New Testament), ten in the Catholic Epistles (four of which in James[5]), five in the Apocalypse.

For Charles, as for the editors of N.-A.[26], the *Testaments* are a Jewish writing comparable to the Apocrypha of the Old Testament, like other pseudepigrapha. He realized, of course, that there are a number of clearly Christian passages, but those he regarded as Christian interpolations which could be identified easily. In his much-used edition of the text he put them between brackets.[6] Parallels found in these interpolations are not included in his list; those taken from the rest of the document are self-evidently regarded as having influenced the ideas of the New Testament authors. On Paul, Charles writes: "From the evidence presently to be adduced, it will be clear that St. Paul was thoroughly familiar with the Greek translation of the Testaments" (p. lxxxv).[7] In two instances, 1 Thess. 2:16 /*T.Levi* 6:11 and Rom. 1:32/*T.Ash* 6:2, he speaks of direct quotations from the Testaments.

1.3 Before 1884, when F. Schnapp in his *Die Testamente der Zwölf Patriarchen* returned to the thesis of J.E. Grabe, the editor of the *editio princeps* (1698) that the *Testaments* were originally Jewish, but had been interpolated by a Christian (and won the day), many scholars treated this writing as a Christian document.[8] They, too, paid attention to the parallels with the New Testament writings, trying to establish which of those had influenced the authors of the *Testaments* in particular. There was a lot of discussion on the question whether the *Testaments* should be regarded as a product of Jewish Chris-

---

[4] The parallels on Rom. 12:1; 12:21 and 15:23 agree with those found in the margin of N.-A.[26].

[5] Here there is agreement between Charles and the margin of N.-A.[26] in the case of Jas 4:7.

[6] R.H. Charles, *The Greek Versions of the Testaments of the Twelve Patriarchs* (Oxford, Clarendon Press, 1908), reprinted several times.

[7] Charles not only assumes that the Greek was translated from the Hebrew, but also that the two families of the Greek text which he distinguishes go back to two different versions of a Hebrew text—a highly speculative theory.

[8] F. Schnapp, *Die Testamente der Zwölf Patriarchen untersucht* (Halle: Max Niemeyer, 1884).

tianity (Ebionite or Nazarene) or as belonging to Pauline Christianity.[9] One of the authors belonging to the pre-Schnapp period, J.M. Vorstman, whose Leiden dissertation *Disquisitio de Testamentis XII Patriarcharum Origine et Pretio* of 1857[10] has played only a modest role in subsequent discussions (no doubt because of its limited circulation), devoted a considerable part of his book to the subject "De Testamentorum XII Patriarcharum pretio in interpretatione librorum N.F." (pp. 101-178), and to this we now turn.

In the section just referred to Vorstman lists "loquendi formulas, quae, observatione dignissimae, et in N.T. et apud Testamentorum auctorem inveniuntur." He mentions twenty-four passages in Matthew, three in Mark, sixteen in Luke, nine in John, three in Acts, fifty-three in the Pauline Epistles, and the Deutero-Pauline writings, four in Hebrews, nineteen in the Catholic Epistles (four of which in James, seven in the Johannine epistles mentioned under a separate heading) and, finally, six in the Apocalypse (pp. 101-147). He adds a list of *hapax legomena* and very rare words in the New Testament which are also found in the *Testaments* (pp. 147-168), and concludes with a list of grammatical observations on a number of expressions found in the N.T writings as well as in the Testaments (pp. 168-178). Notwithstanding the wealth of parallels adduced Vorstman does not think literary dependence of the Testaments on any of the writings of the New Testament can be proved, except in the case of 1 Thess. 2:16/*T.Levi* 6:11 which he discusses at some length (p. 146, cf. pp. 22-26).

1.4 The limitation of references in the margin of N.-A.[26] remains difficult to explain, because the suggested parallels are of the same nature as those found in the lists given by Charles and Vorstman. Between Charles and Vorstman there is only a limited overlap; fourteen of Charles's thirty-eight Pauline and Deutero-Pauline passages,

---

[9] See H.D. Slingerland, *The Testaments of the Twelve Patriarchs. A Critical History of Research* (SBLMS 21; Missoula: Scholars Press, 1971), particularly chapter II "The Testaments of the Twelve Patriarchs from the Beginning of Research until 1884" (pp. 5-18).

[10] Published by P.C. Hoog, Rotterdam. On Vorstman's place in contemporary research see W.A. van Hengel, "De Testamenten der Twaalf Patriarchen op nieuw ter sprake gebracht," *Godgeleerde Bijdragen* 34 (1860), 881-970. In this article Van Hengel (1779-1871), who was professor of New Testament at Leiden from 1824 to 1849, gives a detailed review of Vorstman's book, interspersed with many observations of his own, clearly the result of extended study of the *Testaments*.

for instance, figure in Vorstman's list.[11] Apart from the basic dis-
agreement on the question whether the *Testaments* were influenced
by the writings of the New Testament or *vice versa*, there is clearly
difference of opinion on the degree of agreement in terminology and
ideas required to make it worthwhile to list the instance concerned in
a list of parallels.

The aim of the present paper is to illustrate the issues involved by
means of a discussion of the limited selection of parallels found in
the margins of the Epistles of Paul in N.-A.[26]. I shall, however, also
have to say something about Rom. 1:32/*T.Ash.* 6:2 important to
Charles; 1 Thess. 2:16/*T.Levi* 6:11 important to Charles and Vorstman; and about *T Benjamin* 11, a passage in the *Testaments* referring
to the apostle Paul—who was a Benjaminite, as he tells us in Phil.
3:5.

II. SOME PARAENETIC PASSAGES

In a number of cases, found in paraenetic passages, we find the use of
similar notions and expressions.

2.1 In Rom. 1:26 Paul uses the expression πάθη ἀτιμίας ("degrading
passions" NRSV). A comparable (but not identical) use of πάθος
with a genitive is found in *T.Jos.* 7:8, "For when someone has sub-
mitted to the passion of an evil desire (πάθει.....ἐπιθυμίας πονηρᾶς)."
In fact, "being a slave of two passions (πάθη) contrary to the
commandments of God" one "cannot obey God" *(T.Jud.* 18:6). Passions and sins are closely connected (cf. *T.Jos.* 3:10 with 7:8, and
T.Ash. 3:2 with *T.Jud.* 18:6).

2.2 In Rom. 2:15 Paul speaks about the function of conscience.
"They show that what the law requires is written on their hearts, to
which their own conscience also bears witness (συμμαρτυρούσης
αὐτῶν τῆς συνειδήσεως)." Here Nestle-Aland's margin refers to the
only instance of συνείδησις in the Testaments, *T.Reub.* 4:3, "even
until now my conscience presses me hard on account of my sin." In

---

[11] Among them the three passages mentioned in note 4. The N.-A.[26] margin and Vorstman
also agree in the case of Rom. 1:4 and 5:4.

two other passages in the Testaments the expression "his own heart" is used (*T.Jud.* 20:5; *T.Gad* 5:3) with a comparable meaning.

2.3 In Rom. 2:17-24 Paul reproaches the Jews, instructed in the law and relying on their relation to God, for not practicing what they teach; they are no longer a guide to the blind nor a light to those who are in darkness. Here at v. 22 Nestle-Aland's margin mentions *T.Levi* 14:4, "What will all the Gentiles do, if you are darkened through ungodliness and bring a curse upon our race..." Levi's reproach to his offspring resembles that of Paul, but it is expressed differently.[12]

2.4. In Rom. 5:3-4 Paul tells his readers that "suffering produces endurance (ὑπομονή), and endurance produces character (δοκιμή) and character produces hope." Here we are referred to a number of other New Testament texts (among which Jas 1:2-4), as well as to *T.Jos.* 10:1. In this testament Joseph concludes the elaborate story about his temptations and sufferings because of Potiphar's wife in chapters 3-9 with a disquisition in 10:1-4 which begins with the words: "You see, therefore, my children, how great things patience (ὑπομονή) works and prayer with fasting."[13] Also the second story about Joseph's troubles in 11:2-16:6 is followed by a reference to his patience and endurance in 17:1: "You see, children, how great things I endured, that I should not put my brothers to shame." Both ὑπομονή and μακροθυμία are central virtues in this testament—see also 2:7: "In ten temptations he (God) showed that I was approved (δόκιμος) and in all of them I endured (ἐμακροθύμησα), for endurance (μακρο-θυμία) is a mighty remedy, and patience (ὑπομονή) gives many good things."[14]

---

[12] In their present form and context *T.Levi* 10, 14-15 and 16 are clearly directed against Israel's priestly leaders who opposed Jesus Christ—see chapter 8, section 1.3, and my "Levi, the sons of Levi and the Law in Testament Levi X, XIV-XV and XVI," originally published in *Mélanges Cazelles* (1981), reprinted in *Jewish Eschatology, Early Christian Christology and the Testaments of the Twelve Patriarchs: Collected Essays* (ed. H.J. de Jonge; NovTSup 63; Leiden: Brill, 1991), 180-190. One may note that MSS *chij* in *T.Levi* 14:4 characterize the Gentiles as "living in blindness" (cf. Rom 2:19).

[13] For the combination of ὑπομονή and prayer see also Rom. 12:12 "rejoice in hope, be patient in suffering, persevere in prayer."

[14] For further details see the introduction to *T.Joseph* in *Commentary*, 362-365.

2.5. In 1 Cor. 6:18 we find the exhortation φεύγετε τὴν πορνείαν ("shun fornication") which is also found in *T.Reub.* 5:5.[15] Comparable expressions are "...that you may flee hatred and cleave to the love of the Lord" in *T.Gad* 5:2 and "flee the malice of Beliar" in *T.Benj.* 7:1 (cf. also *T.Benj.* 8:1; *T.Ash.* 3:2). The opposite is ἐγγίζετε δὲ τῷ θεῷ ("draw near to God") in *T.Dan* 6:2;[16] this verse is therefore mentioned in Nestle-Aland's margin at Jas 4:8, "draw near to God, and he will draw near to you." This follows on verse 7, "submit yourselves to God. Resist the devil and he will flee from you," where *T.Napht.* 8:4 is referred to, which reads "... and the devil will flee from you and the wild beasts will flee from you and the Lord will love you, and the angels will cleave to you." Wherever God's commandments are obeyed, Beliar and evil spirits will flee *(T.Iss.* 7:7; *T.Dan* 5:1; *T.Benj.* 5:2; cf.3:3-5). In the end Beliar and all evil spirits will be destroyed completely (*T.Sim.* 6:6; *T.Levi* 3:3; 18:12; *T.Jud.* 25:3; *T Zeb.* 9:8). And concerning God: Dan admonishes his sons to keep his commandments "that the Lord may dwell in you and the devil may flee from you" (*T.Dan* 5:1; cf. *T.Jos.* 10:2-3; *T.Benj.* 6:4[17]). In fact, "you will be in peace having the God of peace, and no war will prevail over you" (*T.Dan* 5:2). Further, in the eschatological future God will be near those who obey him *(T.Dan* 5:13; *T.Iss.* 7:7; *T.Zeb.* 8:2; *T.Napht.* 8:3).

2.6. *T.Dan* 5:2, just quoted, is mentioned in the margin of Rom. 15:33, "the God of peace will be with all of you." Interestingly the expression ὁ θεὸς τῆς εἰρήνης is only found in this passage in the Testaments and in several places in Paul, as a somewhat solemn expression used in blessings, assurances and wishes—see Rom. 16:20; 1 Cor. 14:33; 2 Cor. 13:11; Phil. 4:9; 1 Thess. 5:23; cf. also 2 Thess. 3:16 ("the Lord of peace") and Heb. 13:20.[18] *T.Dan* 5:2 combines an

---

[15] See now also B. S. Rosner, "A Possible Quotation of Test. Reuben 5:5 in 1 Corinthians 6:18A," *JTS* NS 43 (1992), 123-127. Rosner finds also similarities (in thought) between *T.Jos.* 10:1-3 and 1 Cor. 6:19, and *T.Jos.* 8:5 and 1 Cor. 6:20.

[16] Compare the (vain) declaration of the Egyptian woman in *T.Jos.* 6:7 "I do not come near to idols but to the Lord alone" and the characterisation of πορνεία in *T.Reub.* 4:6 as "separating it (the soul) from God and bringing it near to the idols," and *T.Sim.* 5:3, "separating from God and bringing near to Beliar." See also the note on *T.Reub.* 4:6 in *Commentary*, 100.

[17] See *Commentary*, 428, note on *T.Benj.* 6:4.

[18] See G. Delling, "Die Bedeutung 'Gott des Friedens' und ähnliche Wendungen in den Paulusbriefen," in E.E. Ellis and E. Grässer (eds.), *Jesus und Paulus. Festschrift für W.G.*

exhortation with an assurance, and thus is nearest to 2 Cor. 13:11 and Phil. 4:9.[19] In the Testaments we find also the expression "the angel of peace" (ὁ ἄγγελος τῆς εἰρήνης). His functions are to conduct Israel and to protect it against falling into the extremity of evils (*T.Dan* 6:5, cf. v. 2); to guide the soul of the good man *(T.Benj.* 6:1); and to comfort with life the man who dies quietly and in joy *(T.Ash.* 6:5-6). Here we may point to Rom. 16:22: "The God of peace will shortly crush Satan under your feet."

2.7 Also in the last instance to be mentioned in this section there is a particularly close connection between the New Testament text and a passage in the *Testaments*. In Rom. 12:21 Paul exhorts his readers: "Do not be overcome with evil, but overcome evil with good (νίκα ἐν ἀγαθῷ τὸ κακόν)." With this corresponds *T.Benj.* 4:3 which says about the good man "by doing good he overcomes the evil (οὗτος ἀγαθοποιῶν νικᾷ τὸ κακόν), because he is shielded by the good"; comparable notions are found in *T.Benj.* 5:2, 4 and *T.Jos.* 18:2—the good man is modelled upon Joseph— but *T.Benj.* 4:3 gives the nearest parallel to the Pauline expression.[20] Hence it figures prominently in the commentaries on Rom. 12:21 which mention hardly any further paralells.[21]

2.8 How do we explain these similarities in thought and diction between Paul (and James) and the *Testaments*? Discussing the ethics of the *Testaments* in section 3.3 of chapter 6, and in chapter 9, we have stressed that the exhortations of the Testaments contain little that is distinctively Jewish or Christian. They obviously want to teach what is universally good and to warn against vices which all persons, Jews and non-Jews, Christians and non-Christians should abhor. They testify to the continuity in ethical thought between Hellenistic-Jewish and early Christian circles and there is little point in trying to determine the actual provenance ("Hellenistic," "Jewish," "Christian")

Kümmel zum 70. Geburtstag (Göttingen: Vandenhoeck & Ruprecht, 1975), 76-84. There is no Old Testament equivalent, but see Num. 6:26; Judg. 6:24.

[19] So Delling, "Bedeutung," 80, who also points to Amos 5:14 and 1 Kgs 11:38. Compare also *Herm. Sim.* 9, 32,2, "Dominus habitat in viris amantibus pacem, ei enimvero pax cara est."

[20] See also *T.Gad* 6-7, an elaboration of Lev 19:17-18.

[21] *Commentary,* 423 on *T.Benj.* 4:2 points to Hippolytus, *Haer.* IX 23 describing the Essenes: μηδένα δὲ μήτε ἀδικοῦντα μήτε ἐχθρὸν μισήσειν, προσεύχεσθαι δὲ ὑπὲρ αὐτῶν ("and show hatred neither to any wrongdoer nor enemy but offer prayers on their behalf").

of the wording of individual sayings. However, it is quite probable, that the close agreements between Paul and the *Testaments* in the last two cases point to influence of Pauline terminology on the *Testaments* in their present form—but this cannot be proved with absolute certainty.

III. PARALLELS WITH THE TESTAMENT OF LEVI

In four cases in Paul (and one in Hebrews) Nestle-Aland[26] mentions parallels from the *Testament of Levi*. This testament is different from the other eleven, in so far as it contains much specific material. As was discussed in chapters 7 and 8, it has long been noticed that parallels to this material are found in Aramaic fragments found (first) in the Cairo Genizah and (later) at Qumran, as well as Greek additions to MS Athos, Koutloumous 39 (= *e*) of the *Testaments*. It is clear that *T.Levi* represents an abbreviated and heavily redacted version of the Levi-material, preserved in the various fragments of the Aramaic Levi Document. The references in Nestle-Aland are, however, to two passages to which no direct Aramaic or Greek parallels are extant, chapter 18, the announcement of a new priest, and chapters 2-3, the description of a heavenly journey of the patriarch.

3.1 At Rom. 1:4 "declared to be Son of God with power according to the spirit of holiness (κατὰ πνεῦμα ἁγιωσύνης) by resurrection of the dead" the reader is referred to *T.Levi* 18:7 "And the spirit of understanding and sanctification (ἁγιασμοῦ) will rest upon him (= the new priest) in the water"; other commentators have pointed to v. 11, where this new priest is said to "give to the saints to eat from the tree of life, and the spirit of holiness (πνεῦμα ἁγιωσύνης) will be upon them." *T.Levi* 18:6-7 and its counterpart *T.Jud.* 24:2 are clearly influenced by the story of Jesus' baptism in the Gospels. In both passages the Saviour figure not only receives the Spirit of God, but also gives it to those who put their trust in him (*T.Jud.* 24:2 ".. and he will pour out the spirit of grace upon you").

In fact, whatever text may lie behind *T.Levi* 18, in its present form it has undergone heavy Christian redaction, just as *T.Judah* 24.[22] One should note that, although Levi, as priest, occupies a central position

---

[22] See also chapter 7, section 1 above.

in Israel, his priesthood is limited (5:2); he "will proclaim concerning him who will redeem Israel" (2:10) and he has to instruct his sons concerning Jesus Christ (4:5). It is against Jesus that Levi's sons will sin—see 4:4-6 and the Sin-Exile-Return passages in chapters 10, 14-15 and 16. Also *T.Levi* 18 follows on a S.E.R. passage in 17:8-10. Next, 17:11 mentions new priestly sins and 18:1 new divine punishment, and 18:2 announces: "Then the Lord will raise a new priest to whom all the words of God will be revealed." Nowhere is it stated that he will be a Levitical priest, whereas the parallel passage in *T.Judah* 24 declares that the one who will receive "the blessing of the spirit of the Holy Father" will arise from Judah's seed.

As commentaries on Romans do not fail to notice, the expression πνεῦμα ἁγιωσύνης only occurs in Rom. 1:4 and *T.Levi* 18:11. In view of the heavy Christian stamp on this chapter it is probable that the diction of *T.Levi* 18:11 was influenced by that of Rom. 1:4, and not the other way round.[23]

3.2 Paul's mention in 2 Cor. 12:2 of his being caught up to the third heaven, has been compared by many exegetes to the description of the heavens seen by Levi on his heavenly journey in *T.Levi* 2-3; hence *T.Levi* 2 figures in Nestle-Aland's margin at this verse. The corresponding Aramaic fragment speaks about a vision of heaven(s), but breaks off before giving any details. The majority of Greek MSS gives a complicated picture of seven (three plus four) heavens, both in 2:7-9 and, in far more detail, in chapter 3. This text is difficult and probably the result of a complicated process of redaction, but it is internally consistent. MSS *(n)chij* reduce the number of heavens to three in 2:7-9, as well as in 3:1-4; (another?) three heavens are described in 3:5-8. But the connection between these and the ones previously mentioned is not clear in this group of manuscripts. Elsewhere I have argued in favour of the theory that the *(n)chij*-text is secondary compared to that found in the other manuscripts.[24] Moreover, if the *stemma codicum*, painstakingly constructed during the

---

[23] Another part of the description of the blessings granted by the new priest, "during his priesthood all sin will fail" (*T.Levi* 18:9), is referred to in the margin of Heb. 9:26, "he has appeared once and for all at the end of the age to remove sin by the sacrifice of himself." It should be noted that *T.Levi* 18 does not connect the new priesthood with any sort of sacrifice or with the self-sacrifice of the new priest.

[24] See my "Notes on Testament of Levi II-VII," *Studies*, 247-260, especially 248-251.

preparation of the Leiden edition of 1978, and consistently applied during the reconstruction of the oldest attainable text, is taken seriously, no reading found in *nchij* alone can be regarded as representing the oldest text.

Other scholars, from R.H. Charles (who held *chi* in high esteem) to J.H. Ulrichsen,[25] favour the *chij*-reading in 2:7-9 and regard it as nearer to the original text behind the complicated picture in *T.Levi* 2-3 than the text found in the other manuscripts. In my opinion, however, the reference to *T.Levi* 2 in commentaries on 2 Corinthians[26] and in Nestle-Aland's margin, is to a late, secondary version of this passage.

3.3 The second heaven described in *T.Levi* 3:2 is said to contain "fire, snow and ice ready for the day of the ordinance of the Lord in the righteous judgment of God (εἰς ἡμέραν προστάγματος κυρίου ἐν τῇ δικαιοκρισίᾳ τοῦ θεοῦ)." This text is mentioned in the margin of Rom. 2:5, "... you are storing up wrath for yourself on the day of wrath, when God's righteous judgment will be revealed (ἐν ἡμέρᾳ ὀργῆς καὶ ἀποκαλύψεως δικαιοκρισίας τοῦ θεοῦ)." Clearly, the use of the word δικαιοκρισία in both texts in connection with the last judgment,[27] is regarded as being of some significance, but this parallel does not enable us to draw any conclusions as to the relationship between Paul and the *Testaments*.

3.4 In Rom 12:1 Paul exhorts his brothers "to present your bodies as a living sacrifice (θυσίαν), holy and acceptable to God, which is your spritual worship (τὴν λογικὴν λατρείαν ὑμῶν)." To this corresponds the description of the angels of the presence of the Lord in *T.Levi* 3:(5-)6 who "offer to the Lord a pleasant odour, a reasonable and bloodless offering (λογικὴν καὶ ἀναιμάκτον προσφοράν)." Here the

---

[25] *Die Grundschrift der Testamente der Zwölf Patriarchen. Eine Untersuchumg zu Umfang, Inhalt und Eigenart der ursprünglichen Schrift* (Acta Univ. Upsaliensis; Hist. Rel. 10; Uppsala, 1991),190-192.

[26] So still V.P. Furnish, *II Corinthians* (AB 32A; Garden City, New York: Doubleday, 1984), 525.

[27] It is also used in *T.Levi* 15:2, and compare 2 Thess. 1:5 ἔνδειγμα τῆς δικαίας κρίσεως τοῦ θεοῦ. On the use of δικαιοκρίτης for God, see *Commentary, 137* on *T.Levi* 3:2 (add there *Sib. Or.* 3:704).

dependence is clearly on the part of *T.Levi*, for the combination of terms found there is quite common in early Christian texts.[28]

IV. ISRAEL AND THE GENTILES: THE CASE OF ROMANS 11:25-26

The last Pauline passage with a parallel in the *Testaments* mentioned in Nestle-Aland[26] is Rom. 11:25-26, a crucial text in Paul's argument concerning God's relation to Israel and the Gentiles.[29] Paul writes: "I want you to understand this mystery: a hardening has come upon part of Israel, until the full number of the Gentiles has come in. And so all Israel will be saved (καὶ οὕτως πᾶς Ἰσραὴλ σωθήσεται)." Here Nestle-Aland's margin mentions "Test Seb fin" without specifying the exact verse. E. Käsemann refers to *T.Zeb.* 9:6-9; U. Wilckens to *T.Zeb.* 9:8, where he probably follows the longer text found in MSS *bkgldm*.[30]

T.Zeb. 9:5-7 forms one of the many Sin-Exile-Return passages in the *Testaments*. On the Return part of it in verse 7 follows a long, complicated and clearly Christian passage in verse 8, in which the clause "and he will convert all the nations to zeal for him (εἰς παρα-ζήλωσιν αὐτοῦ) is of particular interest in view of Rom. 11:25-26. One should note that it is followed by the prophecy of new sins and new punishment in v. 9, "And again through the wickedness of your

---

[28] See *Commentary,* 138, note on *T.Levi* 3:6.

[29] In passing we have also briefly discussed the non-Pauline passages Heb. 9:26; Jas 1:3; 4:7-8. The only other instance to be noted is the reference to *T.Jos.* 8:5 in the margin of Acts 16:23-25. Acts tells us how Paul and Silas in the prison of Philippi "were praying and singing hymns to God and the prisoners were listening to them." In *T.Jos.* 8:5 it is Joseph who sings hymns to the Lord in the prison of Pharaoh, and the Egyptian woman who listens to him. The agreements are general rather than particular. Vorstman, *Disquisitio,* 115 remarks that ἐπ-ακροᾶσθαι used in Acts 16:25 is a *hapax legomenon* in the New Testament. So it is in the Testaments, but this fact is hardly sufficient to prove interdependence between the two texts mentioned.

[30] See Käsemann, *An die Römer,* 299-230, partly following a complicated and rather far-fetched theory by Chr. Müller about a tradition about a "Völkersturm" against Jerusalem/Israel, radically reinterpreted by Paul—see his *Gottes Gerechtigkeit und Gottes Volk. Eine Unter-suchung zu Römer 9-11* (FRLANT 86; Göttingen: Vandenhoeck & Ruprecht, 1964), 38-43. U. Wilckens, *Der Brief an die Römer* II (EKK VI/2; Zürich, Einsiedeln, Köln: Benziger/Neukir-chen-Vluyn: Neukirchener, 1980), 255, especially n. 1145, refers to the tradition of the "Völ-kerwallfahrt" to Sion. On the much debated question of the originality of the longer or the shorter text in *T.Zebulun* 5-9 see my "Textual Criticism and the Analysis of the Composition of the Testament of Zebulun," *Studies,* 144-160, especially 149-152. In this essay I argue in favour of the longer text found in MSS *bkgldm*.

words you will provoke him, and you will be cast away until the time of consummation (ἕως καιροῦ συντελείας)." At the time of consummation, as the next chapter tells us, the patriarch will rise in the midst of his sons, "as many as have kept the law of the Lord and the commandments of Zebulun their father" *(T.Zeb.* 10:2).

T.Zeb. 9:6-9 can only be properly understood if read alongside other passages in the *Testaments* where the Sin-Exile-Return pattern is repeated, particularly *T.Asher* 7 and *T.Levi* 17:8-18:14 (mentioned above).[31] The present text of *T.Zebulun* 9 and 10 clearly represents a Christian view on the history of Israel, ultimately dependent on views like that expressed by Paul in Romans 9-11. In the *Testaments* there is great concern for Israel's final salvation, and the definite promise that Israel will share in God's salvation if it obeys God's commandments and/or believes in Jesus Christ."[32] In *T.Benj.* 10:11, at the very end of the exhortations in the *Testaments* the patriarch—after having remarked that Israel will be convicted through the chosen ones of the Gentiles (v. 10)—concludes:

> But you, if you walk in holiness before the face of the Lord,
> you will again dwell safely with me
> and all Israel will be gathered together unto the Lord
> (καὶ συναχθήσεται πᾶς Ἰσραὴλ πρὸς κύριον).

V. SOME OTHER PASSAGES

We now turn to the three passages in the *Testaments* mentioned above, that are not mentioned by Nestle-Aland, but were considered of some importance in earlier treatments of the relationship between Paul and the *Testaments*.

5.1 Charles's theory that in Rom 1:32 Paul quoted from *T.Ash.* 6:2 rests upon a wrong textcritical decision and a highly questionable conjecture. In *T.Ash.* 6:1-2 the patriarch's children are exhorted to keep the commandments of the Lord "with a single face (μονοπροσ-

---

[31] On this see also my "The Future of Israel in the Testaments of the Twelve Patriarchs," in *Collected Essays,* 164-179.

[32] See Chapter 6, section 4.

ὥπως), because people with a double face (οἱ διπρόσωποι[33]) receive a double punishment." Hence the exhortation: "Hate the spirits of deceit which strive against men." The reason for this double punishment is not given, but a parallel in *Herm. Sim.* 9,18,2 helps us, which says: "but those who have knowledge of God ... and act wickedly, will be punished doubly (δισσῶς κολασθήσονται)." Some scribes felt they had to clarify the issue by emending the text; after "double punishment" they added "for they both do the evil thing and have pleasure in them that do it" (see now MSS *dmeafchj*), a phrase reminiscent of that of Paul in Rom. 1:32. In the present context it does not make any sense; also not if one reads the following clause as "following the example of the spirits of deceit" (with *eafchj*[34]). Even Charles is not happy with the longer version of the text as it stands. In his comments on this verse, both in his edition and his commentary, he states that this is not a matter of double punishment but of double guilt. He therefore assumes a misreading of the Hebrew underlying the text[35] resulting in a wrong Greek translation. This high-handed dealing with the text results in the English translation, "For they that are double-faced are guilty of a twofold sin; for they both do the evil thing and they have pleasure in them that do it."

5.2 A very intriguing case is presented by the parallel between 1 Thess. 2:16 and *T.Levi* 6:11 which, though not listed by Nestle-Aland, has received much, sometimes even detailed, attention in commentaries on 1 Thessalonians.[36] Paul, writing about the opposition of the Jews against the prophets, Jesus and those sent out by him (including Paul preaching to the Gentiles) concludes: "Thus they have constantly been filling up the measure of their sins, but God's

---

[33] Μονοπρόσωπος corresponds with ἁπλοῦς, a prominent feature of good people in the Testaments; διπρόσωπος has two meanings, one negative (here, and in *T.Ash.* 3:1-2; 4:1) and one neutral, "having two aspects" (so in 2:2,3,5,7,8; 4:3,4)—see the Introduction to *T.Asher* in *Commentary*, 338-341.

[34] *chj* continue with "and striving against humankind."

[35] We should remember that he assumes that each of the two families of the Greek text which he distinguishes goes back to a Hebrew original (see note 7).

[36] See especially E. von Dobschütz, *Die Thessalonicher-Briefe* (MeyerK; Göttingen: Vandenhoeck & Ruprecht, [7]1909; repr. with add. 1974), 115 and B. Rigaux, *Saint Paul. Les épîtres aux Thessaloniciens* (Ebib; Paris: Gabalda/Gembloux: Duculot, 1956), 455-456. A recent contribution to the discussion is found in T. Baarda, "The Shechem Episode in the Testament of Levi: A Comparison with Other Traditions," in J.N. Bremmer and F. García Martínez (eds.), *Sacred History and Sacred Texts in Early Judaism. A Symposium in Honour of A.S. van der Woude* (Kampen: Kok Pharos, 1992), 11-73, esp. 59-73.

wrath has overtaken them forever" (1 Thess. 2:16; NRSV marg.). The meaning of the last clause ἔφθασεν δὲ ἐπ' αὐτοὺς ἡ ὀργὴ εἰς τέ–λος has been the subject of much discussion, but there is no doubt that it forms an integral part of the text. Paul follows here a pattern of thought used by him and other early Christians to explain Jesus' death as that of the final prophet sent by God to Israel and killed by the people—a horrible event calling for the eschatological judgment in the near future (compare also Mark 12:1-9 and Luke 11:49-51 par. Matt. 23:34-36[Q]).[37]

In T.Levi 5-6 the last verse, 6:11, sums up why Levi and his brother Simeon had to kill the inhabitants of Shechem: "the wrath of God had come upon them, definitely (ἔφθασε δὲ ἡ ὀργὴ κυρίου ἐπ' αὐτοὺς εἰς τέλος)."[38] This points back to 6:8 where Levi explains that he had to go against his father's wishes because he saw that "God's sentence upon Shechem was for evil." The inhabitants of that city had wanted to treat Sarah as they treated Dinah, and they had perse-cuted Abraham and maltreated other strangers (6:8-10). In fact, the whole episode in the Testaments starts with an express command to Levi to execute vengeance on Shechem because of Dinah (5:3), given by the angel who accompanied Levi on his heavenly journey. And, anticipating the story that follows, Levi tells his readers: "I destroyed (συνετέλεσα) the sons of Hamor at that time, as is written in the heavenly tables" (5:4). The angel identifies himself in v. 6 as "the an-gel who intercedes for the race of Israel that God will not smite them utterly, for every evil spirit attacks it." In T.Dan 6:5 we read that "the angel of peace hinself will strengthen Israel that it may not fall into the extremity of evils (εἰς τέλος κακῶν)." God may punish the child-ren of Israel, but he will not allow them to be destroyed forever, like the inhabitants of Shechem for whose sins there is no pardon (see also T.Levi 7). On this point this story in the Testaments is quite clear, and in keeping with what is found elsewhere.[39] Paul and other Christians, however, were so appalled by what their fellow-Israelites had done to Jesus Christ (and were doing to those who preached the

---

[37] On this see, for instance, my *Jesus, The Servant-Messiah* (New Haven: Yale University Press, 1991), 34-37.

[38] In *T.Reub.* 4:4 the expression ἡ ὀργὴ κυρίου is used for God's punishment of Reuben for his sin with Bilhah.

[39] See also Amos 9:8 LXX; 2 Chr. 12:12; Ps. 103 (102):9; Dan. 3:34 LXX and Theod.; Jdt 7:30; Wis. 16:5, 6.

Gospel) that they interpreted this as the culmination of Israel's sins against God, bound to bring about a final and definitive judgment —on Israel.

How is the close relationship in thought and diction between 1 Thess. 2:16 and *T.Levi* 6:11 to be explained? Direct dependence one way or the other is difficult to prove. Dependence on a common source would be possible, but already Vorstman, raising this possibility, added "quamvis fontem non possim indicare,"[40] and no one after him has been successful in finding one.[41] Do we, then, have to assume use of a current Jewish expression in similar contexts (but with a different application) by both Paul and the Testaments? This is possible, but the measure of agreement in terminology remains striking.[42] On the basis of what is found elsewhere I am inclined to think that the present wording of *T.Levi* 6:11 did indeed undergo influence from 1 Thess. 2:16.[43]

5.3 The last passage to be discussed under this heading, *T.Benjamin* 11, follows immediately on *T.Benj.* 10:11 already mentioned above. When all the sons of Benjamin will dwell safely with their father, and all Israel will be gathered unto the Lord, says Benjamin,

> I shall no longer be called a ravening wolf on account of your ravages,
> but a worker of the Lord, distributing food to those who work that which is good;
> and there will arise from my seed in later times a beloved of the Lord,
> hearing his voice upon earth
> and doing the pleasure of his will (11:1-2a).

The first two lines allude to Gen. 49:27 LXX; the first part refers to the sins of the Benjaminites (and of Israel as a whole); the second

---

[40] *Disquisitio*, 23.

[41] In his commentary on the text of this verse Charles follows H. Rönsch (in his *Das Buch der Jubiläen oder die kleine Genesis* [Leipzig: Fues's Verlag, 1874], 390-391 and, in more detail, in *ZWTh* 18 [1875], 278-283) in assuming that *T.Levi* 6:11 and 1 Thess. 2:16 go back to an (otherwise unattested) reading "and the wrath of God came upon them" in Gen. 35:5.

[42] Much attention has been given to variant readings in both texts, but I think that it is very difficult to prove that these are interrelated. We should note that the omission of *T.Levi* 6:11 in one branch of the Armenian version is due to the fact that the verse is defective in the rest of the Armenian witnesses—see M.E. Stone, *The Testament of Levi* (Jerusalem: St. James Press, 1969), 77.

[43] Aramaic Levi fragments referring to the Shechem episode are extant, but unfortunately so defective that nothing can be said about an equivalent of the verse under discussion.

part to the preaching of the gospel among the Gentiles—clearly by
the Benjaminite Paul[44] who in the following lines is called "a beloved
of the Lord" (cf. Deut 33:12), arising "from my seed in later times."
This makes perfect sense in its present context.

There are significant textual variants. MS *c* brings this passage in
line with the other Levi-Judah passages at the end of a number of testaments[45] by reading in verse 2 "there will arise from the seed of
Judah and Levi," and breaking off in the middle of this verse, continuing with a conventional report about the patriarch's death and
burial. MS *c* is clearly secondary here.[46] Next there is a very short
text in the Armenian version (which omits many passages particularly towards the end of the individual testaments, and even more so in
the last testament, that of Benjamin). Scholars have argued in favour
of progressive "christianization" of the short text represented by the
Armenian; why should the Armenian translator have omitted a reference to Paul? Perhaps because he wanted to shorten whatever text
he had in front of him, or because this text had become mutilated by
accident. In any case the Armenian passage is so short and so un-
explicit, that it is difficult to see how the text in the Greek MSS could
have arisen out of an original like the text now found in Armenian.

The text of the Greek MSS (with the exception of *c*) continues in
11:2b-5 with a further description of Paul's activities. It cannot be
discussed in detail, but three features call for some comment. First
we find another allusion to Gen. 49:27 LXX, when Paul is said to be
"ravening from them (=Israel) like a wolf, and giving to the gathering of the Gentiles." The two parts of the verse from Genesis are no
longer opposed to one another, but both refer here to actions of
Paul.[47] Second, there is a clear reference to the Christian Holy Scriptures in general, and the Book of Acts in particular, in verse 4 where
it is said that Paul "will be inscribed in the holy books, both his work
and his word." The chapter ends with a reference to a word of Jacob
concerning Paul, "He will supply the needs of your tribe"—using

---

[44] As (different) marginal notes in MSS *k, l* and *d* explicate.

[45] For a survey see *Commentary*, 56-61.

[46] At the crucial point, the change of "from my seed" to "from the seed of Judah and Levi,"
c is not followed by the New Greek version, the only witness belonging to its group left at this
stage.

[47] On the early Christian interpretation of Gen. 49:27 in its various forms—none of them
entirely agreeing with the two found in the *Testaments*—see *Commentary*, 443, note on 11:2.

Pauline terminology (1 Cor. 16:17; 2 Cor. 9:12; 11:9; Phil. 2:30; Col. 1:24).

In view of the complexity of the chapter and the unevennesses in it, we may not exclude that the present text is the result of a process of redaction—which we can no longer unravel—during which new features were added. Already at the oldest stage, however, Paul, the Benjaminite, must have been mentioned as preacher to the Gentiles.

CONCLUSIONS

a. The selection of passages from the *Testaments* in the margin of Nestle-Aland's 26th edition is very limited, and unevenly distributed. Yet inclusion in our investigation of the cases listed by Vorstman or Charles would not lead to a substantially different picture.

b. Many parallels simply illustrate the continuity in content and diction between Hellenistic-Jewish and early Christian paraenesis.

c. If we take seriously that the present *Testaments* are a Christian writing, we can no longer use them to illustrate the background of Paul or, indeed, other writers of books preserved in the New Testament, in those cases where the *Testaments* reflect Christian ideas and terminology.

d. It is often difficult to prove that the authors of the *Testaments* had specific New Testament texts in mind.

e. It should be borne in mind that the *Testaments of the Twelve Patriarchs* are just one of many "pseudepigrapha of the Old Testament" which have come down to us exclusively through Christian channels; we shall have to take this fact into account when using parallels from other "pseudepigrapha" in interpreting the New Testament.

PART THREE

THE CASE OF THE GREEK LIFE OF ADAM AND EVE

THE CHRISTIAN ORIGIN OF THE GREEK LIFE OF ADAM AND EVE

I. THE GREEK LIFE OF ADAM AND EVE AND THE OTHER VERSIONS

Among the many problems which beset the study of the *Life of Adam and Eve* the most difficult one is that of its origin and date—if only because its solution presupposes answers to a great number of other questions, in particular the problem of the relationships between the different versions that have come down to us.

The present attempt to find a place for this writing in the history of Judaism and Christianity goes back to the analyses and the overall approach in *The Life of Adam and Eve and Related Literature,* written by J. Tromp and myself a few jears ago.[1] It will be argued that the short form of the Greek *Life* delineated by M. Nagel is the oldest written version available. We should take this as the starting point of our investigations. This text presents a number of unclarities and leaves a number of things unsaid; it makes use of many traditions also found elsewhere without always succeeding to forge them into a coherent whole. The final redaction has not been very thorough—and this is the reason why the other, later versions tried to improve the story by changes in wording and by omissions and additions.

The point of departure for all serious study of the Greek *Life* is still M. Nagel's *La Vie d'Adam et d'Ève (Apocalypse de Moïse)* of 1974.[2] It gives a description and thorough analysis of (nearly) all Greek witnesses and the major versions, as well as a diplomatic transcript of the Greek manuscripts available. Nagel divides the Greek witnesses into four groups. The first, found in MSS DS and V, gives the shortest text and is clearly original. The second is closely related to the first but gives a longer text, corresponding to that of all

---

[1] See M. de Jonge and J. Tromp, *The Life of Adam and Eve and Related Literature* (Guides to Apocrypha and Pseudepigrapha; Sheffield: Sheffield Academic Press, 1997). See also M. E. Stone, *A History of the Life of Adam and Eve* (SBLEJL 3; Atlanta: Scholars Press, 1992).

[2] A doctoral thesis for the Catholic Faculty of the University of Strasbourg in 1972, published by the "Service de réproduction, Université Lille III" two years later.

the versions. A third group, consisting of two manuscripts, is dependent on the second, and related to the Slavonic version. A fourth group is dependent on the first but independent of the second and the third; its manuscripts give a rather free text.

Nagel died before he could publish a critical text, but he provided a preliminary one which can be found in the *Concordance grecque des pseudépigraphes d'Ancien Testament* by A.-M. Denis.[3] It is mainly based on the manuscripts belonging to the second group. This text has been reprinted in the first column of *A Synopsis of the Books of Adam and Eve*, edited by Gary A. Anderson and Michael E. Stone.[4] In this synopsis we find the texts of the Greek, the Latin and the Slavonic versions together with those of the Armenian *Penitence of Adam*[5] and the Georgian *Book of Adam*[6]—all with English translations. This little book is an indispensable tool for all study of the relationships between the versions.

There is agreement among scholars on a number of points. The Slavonic, dependent on a secondary form of the Greek text, cannot be of much help to reach the oldest stage in the development of the *Life*. The Latin version is certainly secondary vis-à-vis the Greek, and also compared to the Armenian and the Georgian, with which it shares the stories of the penitence of Adam and Eve, the fall of Satan and the birth of Cain, found in chapters 1-21 of the Latin Vita. Until recently the Latin version was remarkable for not having (unlike the Armenian and the Georgian) an equivalent of the chapters 15-30 in the Greek (the so-called "Testament of Eve"); a new manuscript, however, has turned up in which this speech is found, albeit in a much shorter and clearly secondary form.[7]

---

[3] Louvain-la-Neuve: Institut Orientaliste, 1987. The text is printed on pp. 815-818. Otto Merk could use a thoroughly corrected copy, sent to him by the author, for his translation and commentary in O. Merk and M. Meiser, *Das Leben Adams und Evas* ((JSHRZ 2, 5; Gütersloh: Gütersloher Verlagshaus, 1998), 733-870,—see p. 751, n. 75.

[4] First published in 1994 (SBLEJL 5; Atlanta: Scholars Press). A second substantially revised edition appeared in 1999.

[5] See the text (and translation) in M.E. Stone, *The Penitence of Adam* (CSCO 429-430; Louvain: Peeters, 1981).

[6] See the edition of the Georgian by C'. K'urc'ikidze in *P'ilologiuri Dziebani* 1 (1964), 97-136. Revised translation by J.-P. Mahé, who earlier gave a French translation in *Studies in Gnosticism and Hellenistic Religions* (Festschrift G. Quispel, eds. R. van den Broek and M.J. Vermaseren; EPROER 91; Leiden: Brill, 1981), 227-260.

[7] See J.-P. Pettorelli, "Deux témoins latins singuliers de la *Vie d'Adam et Ève* Paris, BNF, lat. 3832 & Milan, B.Ambrosiana, O 35 sup.," *JSJ* 33 (2002), 1-27 —going back to earlier

The position of the Armenian and the Georgian versions, both going back to a common Greek ancestor, is disputed. In the present author's view this ancestor, closely related to the Greek manuscripts of the second group, gives a text which is secondary compared to that of the hyparchetype of the group—a group that, in all likelihood, does not give the most original form of the Greek text.[8] The addition of the stories at the beginning, as in Latin, is also secondary, however old (much of) that material, no doubt once extant in Greek, may be. Stone and Anderson disagree; they are of the opinion that in many instances the oldest version of the Greek text has to be found with the help of the Armenian and the Georgian.[9]

All this means that we have to concentrate on the Greek text found in the manuscripts of the first group—a form of the text that is unfortunately not easily available.[10] The Armenian and the Georgian versions are important for the reconstruction of the text behind chapters 1-21 in Arm.-Georg.-Latin. It is evident that we may never exclude the possibility that elements in later forms of text go back to older traditions. Finally, there is growing agreement that there is no conclusive evidence for the existence of a Hebrew or Aramaic original.

For the solution of the problem in hand this means two things: first, that we cannot determine the origin and date of the *Life of Adam*

publications in *Archivum Latinitatis Medii Aevi* 56 (1998), 5-104 and 57 (1999), 5-52. Pettorelli has traced no less than 106 manuscripts (see his "La Vie latine d'Adam et Ève. Analyse de la tradition manuscrite," *Apocrypha* 10 [1999], 220-320). For an assessment of the new evidence see J. Tromp, "The Textual History of the *Life of Adam and Eve* in the Light of a Newly Discovered Latin Text-Form," *JSJ* 33 (2002), 28-41. The history of the Latin version was obviously even more complicated than could be surmised on the basis of the manuscripts published earlier. The Paris MS enables us to go further back to a text-form strongly resembling that of the Armenian and the Georgian, not yet characterized by typical inner Latin developments (Tromp, p. 41).

[8] See my "The Literary Development of the *Life of Adam and Eve*," in G.A. Anderson, M.E. Stone and J. Tromp (eds.), *Literature on Adam and Eve. Collected Essays* (SVTP 15; Leiden, Brill, 2000), 239-49, taking up a number of points discussed in the Guide of 1997.

[9] See Stone, *A History*, 69 and, in particular, G.A. Anderson, "The Original Form of the Life of Adam and Eve. A Proposal," *Literature on Adam and Eve. Collected Essays,* 215-31.

[10] We shall have to wait for the critical edition of the Greek *Life of Adam and Eve* which is being prepared by J. Tromp. D.A Bertrand, *La vie grecque d'Adam et Ève* (Recherches Intertestamentaires 1; Paris: A. Maisonneuve, 1987) who uses Nagel's work diligently and follows his assessment of the manuscript evidence, gives, in the end, an eclectic Greek text, to be used with the same caution as that of Nagel printed in the *Concordance* and the *Synopsis* mentioned above.

and Eve unless we study the versions separately. There is, for instance, no point in using passages in the Greek and the Latin versions indiscriminately, as scholars have often done because these were the ones readily available. Next, comparing individual texts with those in other early Jewish and Christian writings does not carry us very far. We may note the use of common traditions, but will not be able to determine literary dependence one way or another. The popular theory that the *Life of Adam and Eve* has to be dated somewhere in the first century CE, because it has a number of things in common with Jewish sources like *4 Ezra* and *2 Baruch* and in particular with Paul in Rom. 5:12-21 and 1 Cor. 15:21-22, 45-49, is not really convincing.[11] Individual parallels in other Jewish or Christian sources can never give decisive proof. We shall have to look for common patterns, or parallels for determinative elements in the *Life,* that point to literary dependence one way or another, or to a common approach to the problems posed by the biblical story of Adam and Eve that may indicate a historical connection.

II. DETERMINATIVE ELEMENTS
IN THE GREEK LIFE OF ADAM AND EVE

The question then is: What are the features that make the Greek *Life of Adam and Eve* (henceforth: *GLAE*) to what it wants to be? Notwithstanding the deficiencies of the final redaction the short Greek text presents a clear structure.

Its core is a "Testament of Eve" (chs. 15-30) retelling the story of Genesis 3 in a special way. It ends with the words: "Now then, children, I have shown you the way in which we were deceived. But take heed that you yourselves do not forsake the good" (30:1). It is preceded by an overall introduction in chs. 1-4, a brief account by the dying Adam about what happened in Paradise (chs. 5-8) and the story of the failed attempt by Eve and Seth to get "the oil of mercy" from the Garden, to alleviate Adam's pains.

The sin of Adam and Eve is seen as a transgression of God's commandment (8:2; 10:2; 14:3; 23:3; 24:1, 4; 25:1). Eve in particular is to blame and she realizes that (9:2; 10:2; 14:3; 25:1, 3). It is the

---

[11] See chapter 13 below. The reason for the popularity of this theory is, of course that it enables scholars to explain Paul's views on Adam as reactions on contemporary Jewish ideas.

central point in Eve's description of what happened in the Garden. But also Adam is held responsible and he explicitly acknowledges his fault (27:2-3). Their common enemy is Satan, acting through the serpent (chs. 15-20) in order to deceive Eve. He also uses Eve to deceive Adam (21:3). In accordance with Genesis 3 God curses the serpent (not Satan) in ch. 26. Until the last judgment there will be enmity between him and Eve's offspring (see also 12:1). Humankind should beware of Satan as the archenemy (2:4; 7:2; 15:1; 25:4; 28:4).

GLAE does not end with chapter 30. An account of Adam's death and departure follows. God shows mercy; Eve and Seth see how angels bring Adam to the Paradise in the third heaven and how his body is buried with that of Abel, near the earthly Paradise (chs. 32-41). The picture given in these chapters is very complex and not always internally consistent, but one thing is clear: Adam is pardoned, he shares in heavenly bliss, and he is promised a share in the resurrection to come "with all persons belonging to your seed" (41:3). Six days after Adam Eve dies; she is buried with Adam and shares Adam's lot (chs. 42-43).

Chapters 27-29, at the end of Eve's testament, prepare the reader for these developments. Adam confesses his sin and asks for forgiveness. He is punished, for God's judgment and punishment are righteous. But when God refuses Adam access to the tree of life, he tells him: "… if you, after your departure from Paradise, guard yourself from all evil, prepared (rather) to die (then to transgress), I shall raise you at the time of the resurrection. From the tree of life will be given to you and you will be immortal for ever" (28:3-4). In 37:5 this promise is confirmed when God grants Adam a glorious *post mortem* existence until the day of God's reckoning, when God will raise him with the entire human race descended from him (37:5).

The story of Adam and Eve is the story of all human beings; the actions of the protoplasts affected their offspring. Their transgressions, their penitence, their attempts to follow God's commandments in the rest of their life, and, in the end, their sharing in the eternal life bestowed on them by God in his mercy, are related as a warning and a promise for all readers who know Genesis 3 and want to take seriously what is said there.

I would like to maintain that the essential elements of *GLAE* are to be sought in its final section, chs. 31-43, the part of the writing that relates what is not told in Genesis 3. The *Life of Adam and Eve* in its

Greek form wants to make clear that God, the creator of heaven and earth, who brought the protoplasts into being and put them into the Garden of Eden, is righteous and merciful for all who try to live in accordance with his commandments and are prepared to repent wholeheartedly when they sin.

III. JEWISH OR CHRISTIAN?

All versions of the *Life of Adam and Eve*, including the Greek, have come down to us in Christian manuscripts. The great differences between the versions, and between the manuscripts of each version, show that the text has often been handled very freely. The fact that it was transmitted by so many people in so many ways indicates that the story as told here, was and remained meaningful for Christians who took Genesis 3 seriously.

Scholars have often remarked that it seems to have nothing particularly Christian. If it were, one would expect a hint that the consequences of Adam's transgression and disobedience had to be undone by Jesus Christ's act of righteousness and obedience, as Paul maintains in Rom. 5:12-20. Nor is there any trace of the recapitulation theory developed by Irenaeus—in which Jesus Christ, the Son of God, features as the new and true Adam and the virgin Mary as the new Eve (see *Adversus Haereses* 3. 21,10-23,8).[12] Also is Gen. 3:15 not presented as a proto-gospel, as in *Adv. Haer.* 3. 23,7 (cf. 4. 40,3).

On the other hand, there are indications of Christian redaction of *GLAE*, already in its oldest form known to us. First there is the mention of the Acherusian Lake as the place where Adam is washed three times before being conducted to God's throne (37:3); this points to a Christian origin of this essential feature in the story told in chs. 33-37.[13] In this connection one may also note that in 36:3 God is called ὁ πατὴρ τῶν φώτων, an epithet only found in Christian sources.[14]

If the *GLAE* is not typically Christian, it is not typically, let alone exclusively, Jewish either. Jesus is not mentioned, but neither is Mo-

---

[12] We find this theory already *in nuce* in Justin, *Dial.* 100:3-6; cf. 84:12; 103:6.

[13] See De Jonge and Tromp, *Guide,* 73-74, and, in detail, chapter 12 below.

[14] See Jas 1:17; the expression is also found in 38:1 in MSS NIJQZ. The *Thesaurus Linguae Graecae* on cd-rom mentions only this text and a number of instances in later Christian authors (mainly in quotations or allusions to the passage in the Epistle of James).

ses. The paraenesis of the book remains quite general: "do not forsake the good," "guard yourself from all evil" (30:1; 28:4); it is too
general to be used in the discussion of provenance at all.

Summing up: there is little that is typically Jewish or Christian in
GLAE. Given the complex nature of the work, which incorporates
many older traditions, individual parallels in other Jewish and Christian sources do not help us to determine its origin and date. But the
few indications we have suggest that it originated in Christian circles.

The question should now be asked whether there are Christian
writers who, in dealing with Genesis 3, pay special attention to God's
mercy for Adam and Eve. There are at least three, at the end of the
second and the beginning of the third century: Theophilus of Antioch, Irenaeus and Tertullian. To these we now turn.

IV. IRENAEUS

I begin with Irenaeus *(fl.* 177), to whose recapitulation theory reference has just been made. In *Adv. Haer.* 3. 22,4 he concludes his
disquisition on this subject by describing the Lord as *ipse initium vi-
ventium factus, quoniam Adam initium morientium factus est.* He
adds: *Sic autem et Evae inobaudientiae nodus solutionem accepit per
obaudientiam Mariae. Quod enim alligavit virgo Eva per increduli-
tatem, hoc virgo Maria solvit per fidem.*

Irenaeus could have ended here, but finds it necessary to devote an
extra chapter to the fate of Adam personally. In 23,1-2 he argues at
some length that God had created Adam in his own image with the
intention that he would live. If Adam, hurt by the corrupting serpent,
had been condemned to death for ever, the malice of the serpent
would have been more powerful than the will of God. God is, however, invincible as well as magnanimous; therefore he saw to it that
man after being subjected to punishment would finally be liberated
by "the Second Man" coming to bind the Strong One (i.e., the Devil;
see Mark 3:27 and par.) and destroy death (2 Tim. 1:10). Among the
victims captured by the Enemy, above all the first victim Adam, the
father of all human beings, would be liberated; and this is only just.
"For God is neither weak nor unjust; he came to the rescue of man
and restored him to his original freedom" (*neque enim infirmus est*

Deus neque iniustus qui opitulatus est homini et in suam libertatem restauravit eum) (23,2).

Irenaeus then proceeds to show that God's mercy towards Adam is already evident in Genesis 3. God transferred the curse to the earth, in order that it would not remain on man.[15] Everything God said in Gen. 3:16-19 served as rebuke and punishment, so that Adam and Eve would realize whom they had to obey. God did not intend them to perish forever. God cursed the serpent (Gen. 3:15), that is the devil, the *princeps apostasiae et princeps abscessionis*. The eternal fire mentioned in Matt. 25:41 is destined for him, all apostate angels under his command, and all humans who do not repent and persist in evil works (23,3). One of those is Cain who did not show any compassion for his brother or reverence for God; he, therefore, is cursed forever (23,4).

Adam behaves quite differently. He realizes that, after transgressing God's commandment, he is no longer worthy to appear in God's presence. "The fear of God is the beginning of knowledge" (Prov. 1:9); in this case knowledge led to repentance and *paenitentibus autem largitur benignitatem suam Deus*. That Adam and Eve, after having lost "the robe of sanctity received from the Spirit"[16] put on fig leaves, a very disagreeable form of body-cover, shows how humbly they wanted to live. God showed his mercy by giving them garments of skin (Gen. 3:21). Once again Irenaeus assures his readers: God's curse was on the serpent who seduced Adam, but he pitied the one who was seduced (*eum enim odivit Deus qui seduxit hominem, ei vere qui seductus est sensim paulatimque misertus est*) (23,5).

Man was banned from paradise and forced to live far from the tree of life. Not because God begrudged him the fruit of that tree, as some people dare to maintain (*non invidens ei lignum vitae, quemadmodum audent quidam dicere*) but out of pity. Man should not remain a sinner for ever, death should put an end to sin, so that Adam, after having died to sin, would start to live for God (23,6).

Finally, Irenaeus turns to Gen. 3:15, reading it as a prophecy of the final victory by Christ over the forces of evil: ... *quoadusque venit semen praedestinatum calcare caput eius, quod fuit partus Ma-*

---

[15] Irenaeus ascribes this view to *ex veteribus quidam*.

[16] Different in *GLAE* 20:1-2; 21:6, where we find the expressions "naked of the righteousness"; "estranged from the glory of God."

riae. Reference is made to Rom. 5:14, 17; Rev. 20:2; 12:9 and 1 Cor. 15:54-55. Irenaeus concludes: All this could not legitimately be said, if he who was the first to be dominated by death, would not be liberated. *Illius enim salus evacuatio est mortis. Domino igitur vivificante hominem, id est Adam, evacuata est mors* (23:7).

The chapter ends, in 23,8, with a vehement attack on those who deny that Adam shares in God's salvation, with all human beings—especially on Tatian. He was the first to introduce this completely wrong opinion, which betrays his ignorance and blindness. Irenaeus refers back to *Adv. Haer.* 1. 28,1 where he mentions Tatian together with other heretics, Valentinus, Marcion, Saturninus and the Encratites.[17] According to Irenaeus Tatian stood alone with his theory about Adam; he simply wanted to find a point on which his school would be distinct from others. Unfortunately, no writing by Tatian survives which could corroborate Irenaeus's claim. But heresiological tradition may be right when it describes Tatian, after his separation from the main church as "inclining towards encratism and accentuating his pessimism over the problem of the fall of mankind until he ended by maintaining the doctrine of the damnation of Adam."[18]

Irenaeus, in any case, regarded Tatian's opinion as completely wrong and took pains to refute it. In his argumentation he tries to show how the Old Testament and the New agree on the matter of Adam's salvation, but it is evident that his emphasis is on showing that already in Genesis 3 God is depicted as magnanimous and merciful, as well as righteous. God reproached Adam, called him to order, punished and disciplined him, but did not give him over to eternal damnation. This special attention for Genesis 3 suggests that others—amongst them the *quidam* of 23,6[19]—had a different opinion of the Creator-God mentioned in that chapter, and that Irenaeus wanted to counter their influence too.

---

[17] The passage is preserved in Greek in Eusebius, *H.E.* 4. 29,2-3. Compare Ps. Tertullian, *Adv. omnes haereses* 7, where it is said about Tatian: *Totus enim secundum Valentinum sapit, adiciens illud, quod Adam negat salutem consequi posse, quasi non, si rami salvi fiunt, et radix salva sit.*

[18] See F. Bolgiani, art. "Tatian," *Encyclopedia of the Early Church* (Cambridge: Clarke, 1992), vol.2. 815 (whom I quote here).

[19] See also Theophilus, *Ad Autolycum* 2. 25.

V. Tertullian

From the many works of Tertullian I select a few passages (written in the first decade of the third century) that may help us to get a fuller picture. First we may note how in *De Paenitentia* 2,2-5 Tertullian stresses how fear of God, penitence and mending one's ways (*emendatio*) together produce what God intended: man's salvation. God, confronted with human transgression from Adam onward, condemned man, chased him from Paradise and subjected him to death. Later, however, God regretted his anger and undertook to forgive the one whom he formed in his image.[20] From that point onward God aimed at gathering a people on which he bestowed his good gifts, however often it showed itself ungrateful—as the prophets and John the Baptist have made clear. For God all centers around the salvation of humankind. *Horum bonorum unus est titulus, salus hominis, criminum pristinorum abolitione praemissa; haec paenitentiae causa, haec opera, negotium divinae misericordiae curans; quod homini proficit, Deo servit* (3,7).

This saving activity of God includes the work of Christ and the Spirit, and, for instance, the institution of baptism. Yet *De Paenitentia* ends, in 12,9, with a remarkable statement that suggests that Adam was restored to Paradise after confessing his transgression to God. Tertullian writes: "Adam himself, the author of the human race and also of sin against God (*stirpis humanae et offensae in Dominum princeps Adam*), does not keep silent (about the subject of repentance), once he is restored through confession to his paradise (*exomologesi restitutus in paradisum suum*)." This calls to mind *GLAE* 37 that describes Adam's elevation to Paradise in the third heaven, after God has forgiven him and he has been washed in the Acherusian Lake; he is to stay there until the last judgment. Alternatively we may think of Adam's burial near Paradise on earth, recounted in chapter 40 (cf. Latin *Vita* 48).

Anne Marie Sweet has suggested that this reference to Adam is "perhaps indicative of Tertullian's knowledge of the traditions reflected in the Vita and/or Bios (= *GLAE*, M.d.J.)."[21] Charles Munier

---

[20] *ignoscere pactus operi et imagini suae* (2,3), cf. *GLAE* 33:5; 35:2; 37:6.

[21] See A.M. Sweet, *A Religio-Historical Study of the Greek Life of Adam and Eve* (unpublished Ph.D. Dissertation, Notre Dame, 1992), 144, n. 64.

mentions the possibility of direct dependence on the *Vita Adae et Evae,* but prefers a different interpretation.[22] Referring to *De Anima* 38,2; *De Patientia* 5,13 and *De Monogamia* 17,5 Munier argues that Paradise stands here for "l'état de sainteté, d'intégrité, d'amitié avec Dieu" enjoyed by Adam before the Fall. However attractive it may be to think of dependence of Tertullian and *GLAE* on common traditions, Munier's interpretation seems preferable. Even so, the direct connection between Adam's confession of sins and return to Paradise remains striking.

Some further references to Adam are found in the second book of *Adversus Marcionem.*[23] These are important because they show how for Tertullian the right assessment of the relation between God and Adam is crucial for a proper view on God's righteousness and mercy. After having argued (in Book 1) that Marcion's God is not a God in any acceptable sense of the term, Tertullian (in Book 2) sets out to prove that the Creator God is really God, and completely good and just. In an interim summary he says: "These facts thus expounded show how God's whole activity as judge is the artificer and, to put it more correctly, the protector of his all-embracing and supreme goodness" (2. 17,1).

All Marcion's remarks about the contradictions in the Old Testament, and his objections against the God whom he sees at work there, are discussed. The Creator is not powerless, nor does he lack foresight. He cannot be accused of pettiness, weakness, inconsistency or malignity. If read properly, the Old Testament reveals the one God, who combines goodness with judgment.

The references to Genesis 3 fit into this context. Right in the beginning Tertullian warns his readers that God's greatness surpasses human understanding. Did not Paul remind us that God's judgments are unsearchable and his ways inscrutable? (cf. Rom. 11:33). Heretics are shortsighted, they want to know better than God. Adam may be

---

[22] See C. Munier, *Tertullian, La Pénitence* (SC 316; Paris: Éd. du Cerf, 1984), 239-240. Munier refers to *Vita* 40; he may mean 42:5. This, however, is part of a late form of an additional passage, that is not found in the oldest form of *GLAE* and is shared by the *Vita* and the Latin version of the *Gospel of Nicodemus.*

[23] I have used the edition and translation by E. Evans in his *Tertullian Adversus Marcionem* (2 vols.; Oxford: Clarendon, 1972). See also E.P. Meijering, *Tertullian contra Marcion. Gotteslehre in der Polemik. Adversus Marcionem I-II* (Philosophia Patrum III; Leiden: Brill, 1977).

called the first heretic, because he chose his own judgment in preference to God's.

> Even so, Adam never said to his Maker, "Thou hast not moulded me
> skilfully." He admitted the beguilement and did not conceal her who
> had done the beguiling. A very inexperienced heretic was he. He was
> disobedient; yet he did not blaspheme his Creator, nor accuse his Ma-
> ker: for since his own first beginning he had found him kind and su-
> premely good (*a primordio sui bonum et optimum invenerat*); and if he
> was a judge, it was Adam who had made him so (2. 2,7).

In 2. 10,1 Tertullian discusses the role of the devil who, after all,
incited man to sin *(instinctorem delicti)*. Could not God have fore-
seen man's sin and the devil's evil influence? The Creator created the
devil as an angel and granted him a free will, just as Adam; but he
turned himself into a devil, that is an accuser. It is interesting to see
how Tertullian then turns to Genesis 3 to show the falseness of the
devil's accusations in the Garden: "... first that God had forbidden
them to eat of every tree, and next that if they did eat they would not
die, and thirdly that God had selfishly denied them divinity (*quasi
deus illis invidisset divinitatem*)." We are reminded here of the accu-
sation of *invidia*, φθόνος, in Irenaeus, *Adv. Haer.* 3. 23,6 and in
Theophilus, *Aut.* 2. 25 (to be discussed presently). In particular we
should note the parallel in *GLAE* 18:4 where it is the devil speaking
through the serpent who tells Eve: τοῦτο δὲ γινώσκων ὁ θεὸς ὅτι
ἔσεσθε ὅμοιοι αὐτοῦ ἐφθόνησεν ὑμῖν καὶ εἶπεν· οὐ φάγεσθε ἐξ
αὐτοῦ.

A third interesting passage is *Adv. Marc.* 2. 25. When God asked
Adam: "Where are you?" (Gen. 3:9), he did not say this because he
did not know where Adam was or what he had done. "God asks a
question, as though in doubt, because here too it was his purpose to
prove that man has freedom of choice, and in a case which admitted
of either denial or admission to give him the opportunity of willingly
confessing his sin, and on that account making it less grievous (...
daret ei locum sponte confitendi delictum et hoc nomine relevandi)"
(25,3). In contrast to Cain who would later not seize the opportunity
and was cursed by God, Adam acknowledged his sin, and though he
was delivered to death, his hope was saved (*deditus morti est, sed
spes ei salva est*) (25,4). This Tertullian deduces from the two statements in Gen. 3:22, where God "indicates that he has given a tempo-

ral and temporary extension of life; and that is why he put no curse upon Adam and Eve in themselves, for they were candidates for restoration, being raised to their feet by confession (... *ut restitutionis candidatos, ut confessione relevatos*)" (25,5).

It is evident that both Irenaeus and Tertullian attach great importance to a correct interpretation of Genesis 3. They emphasize that God dealt fairly with Adam, and never intended that he should perish for ever, and they present Adam as a penitent sinner, God-fearing and ready to obey God's commandments in the future. The Old Testament no less than the New reveals us the one God, who is merciful and just, and whose aim is the salvation of humankind. At the end of the second century it was clearly thought necessary to defend the Old Testament against those who, as Marcion and his followers, disparaged it, and maintained that it only speaks about a weak, inconsistent and malignant God.

Accepting the Law, the Prophets and the Writings as part of the Holy Scriptures of the Church was a prerequisite for all true belief in God and in Christ. That is how Irenaeus and Tertullian saw it, just as Theophilus of Antioch, to whom we now turn.

VI. THEOPHILUS OF ANTIOCH

Theophilus of Antioch, one of the Apologists, wrote his three books *Ad Autolycum* around 180, roughly at the time Irenaeus composed his *Adversus Haereses*, and some twenty-five years before Tertullian's *Adversus Marcionem*.[24] Theophilus is of particular interest for our purpose because, in his second book, he gives the first Christian commentary on the beginning of Genesis, and because he presents a soteriology in which Jesus Christ is never mentioned explicitly.[25]

---

[24] I have used the edition and translation by Robert M. Grant, *Theophilus of Antioch, Ad Autolycum* (Oxford: Clarendon, 1970) and consulted M. Marcovich, *Theophili Antiocheni Ad Autolycum* (PTS 44; Berlin-New York: Walter de Gruyter, 1995). On Theophilus see R.M. Grant, *Greek Apologists of the Second Century* (Philadelphia: Westminster/London: S.C.M., 1988), 140-174, particularly "Theophilus and the Bible" (157-164) and "The Theology of Theophilus" (165-174). On pp. 156-159 Grant tries to show that Theophilus' exegesis of Genesis is essentially Jewish in origin, by comparing it with *Bereshit Rabbah* and Philo's *Questions on Genesis*.

[25] See also J. Bentivegna, "A Christianity without Christ by Theophilus of Antioch," in E.A. Livingstone (ed.), *Studia Patristica*, vol. 13 (TU 116; Berlin: Akademie-Verlag, 1975), 107-129.

Eusebius *(H.E.* 4. 24) tells us that he, too, wrote a book against Marcion, but that has not survived.

Of course Theophilus writes as a Christian, and there are several
echoes of, and even some quotations from, the writings of the New
Testament. These also belonged to the Holy Scriptures, written by
"those inspired by the Spirit" (2. 22). But when it comes to refuting
the ideas of Greek poets and philosophers about the creation of the
world by God, he turns first of all to Moses and the prophets. Moses
is "our prophet and the minister of God" (3. 18), the Hebrews are regarded as "our forefathers." Theophilus adds: "From them we possess the sacred books which are older than all other writers" (3. 20,
cf. 3. 1).[26] For a true record of the beginning of the world one has to
use the Holy Scriptures. As he says in 2. 33: " …it is plain that all the
rest were in error and that only the Christians have held the
truth—we who are instructed by the Holy Spirit who spoke in the
holy prophets and foretold everything."

Theophilus deals with Genesis 1:1-2:7 in 2. 10-19. In chs. 20-21
he quotes Gen. 2:8-3:19 *in extenso* and he comments on it in chapters
22-28. Ch. 29 speaks about Cain (and Abel); the story of the descendants of Cain and Seth, and that of cities after the Deluge are dealt
with summarily in chs. 30-33.

If we concentrate on Theophilus' treatment of Genesis 3, we note
the following points: In ch. 24 he explains man's duty to work in Paradise and to guard it as implying "no other task than keeping the
commandments of God." Man should not destroy himself, but he did,
through sin. God commanded him to eat of all fruits including those
of the tree of life, but with the exception of those of the tree of
knowledge. He was "created in an intermediate state, neither entirely
mortal nor entirely immortal" (just as Paradise was intermediate between heaven and earth). In this way God gave man "an opportunity
for progress (ἀφορμὴ προκοπῆς) so that by growing and becoming
mature (τέλειος) he might ascend to heaven, being declared god (θεὸς
ἀναδειχθείς).

In ch. 27 Theophilus returns to the question of man's mortality
and immortality. God did not create him immortal, that would have
made him god. Nor did God create him mortal; that would have made

---

[26] Several times we find quotations from the Sibylline Oracles. The Sibyl is regarded as "a
prophetess for the Greeks and the other nations" (2. 36).

God responsible for man's death. Man was created responsible for his own immortality and his own death. This holds true also after the Fall. "What man acquired for himself through his neglect and disobedience (δι' ἀμελείας καὶ παρακοῆς), God now freely bestows on him through love and mercy. For as by disobedience man gained death for himself, so by obedience to the will of God whoever will can obtain eternal life for himself (οὕτως ὑπακούσας τῷ θελήματι τοῦ θεοῦ ὁ βουλόμενος δύναται περιποιήσασθαι ἑαυτῷ τὴν αἰώνιον ζωήν)."

The parallel with Rom. 5:18-19 is striking; there are more echoes of New Testament texts in this chapter.[27] But it is equally significant that Theophilus does not speak about Adam's disobedience and Jesus Christ's obedience, but of the disobedience and obedience of man, represented by Adam, on his way to eternal life thanks to God's grace. The correspondence with the message contained in the story of *GLAE* is evident.

It is now time to return to chs. 25-26. With his command not to eat from the tree of knowledge God wanted to test Adam. As an infant Adam had to show that he obeyed the God and Father of the universe. "It is not the law which results in punishment but the disobedience and the transgression." Adam, the protoplast, was responsible for the pain and suffering that fell to his lot, and for the fact that he fell victim to death. It was not the tree that contained death, "as some suppose," nor was it God's jealousy (οὐχ ὡς φθονῶν) that led to the order not to eat from the tree, "as some suppose."

When God expelled Adam from Paradise he conferred a great benefit on man. It was God's intention "that through this punishment he might expiate his sin in a fixed period of time and after chastisement might be recalled (ὅπως διὰ τῆς ἐπιτιμίας τακτῷ ἀποτίσας χρόνῳ τὴν ἁμαρτίαν καὶ παιδευθεὶς ἐξ ὑστέρου ἀνακληθῇ)." Genesis tells twice that God put man in the Garden of Eden (Gen. 2:8 and 15). Theophilus makes this refer to Adam's sojourn in Paradise ánd to the time after judgment and resurrection.

Like Tertullian in *Adv. Marc.* 2. 25 Theophilus explains the question "Where are you, Adam?" in Gen. 3:9 as a sign of God's patience

---

[27] See also Grant, *Greek Apologists,* 171-173.

(and not of ignorance).[28] He gave Adam an occasion for repentance and confession (ἀφορμὴν ...... μετανοίας καὶ ἐξομολογήσεως)." In ch. 28 Theophilus speaks about Eve, formed by the same God as Adam, and intimately united with her husband (Gen. 2:23-24). He holds marriage in high esteem and clearly does not advocate Encra-tite views. Eve was deceived by the serpent and became the pioneer of sin (ἀρχηγὸς ἁμαρτίας). It was "the maleficent demon," also known from Rev. 12:9 (who was originally an angel) who spoke through the serpent.[29]

It is evident that Theophilus' interpretation of Genesis 3 is not only, perhaps even not primarily, directed against pagan unbelievers, but against Christian opponents with different views on the creation and the role of the Creator God. We may think of Marcion and the Marcionites; in their notes on this section of Book 2 of *Ad Autolycum* Grant and Marcovich repeatedly refer to statements by Marcion's follower Apelles preserved in *De Paradiso* of Ambrosius. The evidence for Apelles was collected and his views reconstructed by Adolf von Harnack in his classic study of Marcion.[30] He was opposed to Marcion's dualism and admitted only one supremely good God; he went much further than Marcion by repudiating the Old Testament, which was for him without value, contradictory and unreliable.[31]

If we look, for instance, at the two cases in ch. 25 where Theophilus atttacks the opinions of others (ὡς οἴονταί τινες). He contests that the tree contained death. According to *De Paradiso* 7. 35 Apelles raised the question whether death came from the nature of the wood or, in fact, from God *(unde mors accideret Adae, utrum a natura ligni an vero a Deo)*. Ambrosius holds man himself, in his obedience, responsible—like Theophilus. And with regard to God's φθόνος we are referred to *De Paradiso* 6. 30 where Apelles maintains that it is a good thing to know good and bad—just as God knows good and bad. If that is so, God has no right to refuse humankind that knowledge *(videtur qui interdicit eam hominibus non recte interdicere)*.

---

[28] In ch. 22 Theophilus emphasizes that God is not confined to any place; it was his Logos who was present in Paradise in the role of God and conversed with Adam.

[29] He calls the woman "Eve" Ἐυάν)—identified by Theophilus with the Bacchic cry "Euan" (see also Clement of Alexandria, *Protreptikos* 12. 2).

[30] *Marcion. Das Evangelium vom fremden Gott* (Leipzig: Hinrichs [2]1924; repr. [together with *Neue Studien zu Marcion*], Darmstadt: Wiss. Buchgesellschaft, 1960), 77-196; 404*-420*.

[31] On Apelles and the Old Testament see especially E. Junod, "Les attitudes d'Apellès, disciple de Marcion à l'égard de l'Ancien Testament," *Augustinianum* 22 (1982), 113-133.

Particularly in the last case (where there are parallels in Irenaeus and Tertullian, as we have seen) Theophilus may also have had other opponents in mind. In *The Testimony of Truth*, found in Nag Hammadi Codex IX, there is in 45,23-50,11 a passage on the serpent in Genesis 3 which presents an interesting parallel.[32] According to its commentator Birger Pearson it is older than comparable passages in *The Hypostasis of the Archons* 88,24-91,7 and *On the Origin of the World* 118,17-121,27.

The statements on God's φθόνος in the last two texts were the subject of a special study by W.C. van Unnik as early as in 1972, in which he also pointed to Theophilus, *Aut.* 2. 25, Irenaeus, *Adv. Haer.* 3. 23,6 and *GLAE* 18.[33] He makes the important observation that the Greek word under discussion does not indicate here an affect experienced by a "have-not" towards one who possesses many goods but, on the contrary, the attitude of a "have" over against a "have-not." According to the Gnostic texts just mentioned the serpent maintains that God, out of jealousy, begrudges man the true gnosis and real life. Over against this interpretation of Genesis 3 the authors belonging to what would definitely become the main stream in Christianity, defend God's righteousness and goodness, his ἀφθονία. Irenaeus says clearly *invidia enim aliena est a Deo (Adv. Haer.* 5. 24,4).[34]

As Van Unnik points out, the one who was really jealous is the serpent/devil. This idea occurs in Wis. 2:23-24 ("... through the devil's envy death entered the world"), Josephus, *Ant.* 1. 41 and *Gr. Apoc. Bar.* 4:8, and it is also found in Irenaeus, *Adv. Haer.* 4. 40,3; 5. 24,4, and *Epideixis* 16. Theophilus takes this idea up in ch. 29, in connection with Cain, who also here is the counterpart of Adam in not accepting the opportunity for repentance an confession offered him by God in his mercy. The murder on Abel was instigated by Satan "overcome by envy (φθόνῳ φερόμενος) because he was not strong enough to put them (= Adam and his wife) to death."

---

[32] See the edition and translation by B.A. Pearson and Søren Giversen in B.A. Pearson, *Nag Hammadi Codices IX and X* (NHC 15; Leiden: Brill, 1981), 122-210. Introduction by B.A. Pearson (who also wrote the notes to the text) on pp. 101-120.

[33] See his "Der Neid in der Paradiesgeschichte nach einigen gnostischen Texten," in M. Krause (ed.), *Essays on the Nag Hammadi Texts in Honour of Alexander Böhlig* (NHC 3; Leiden: Brill, 1972). He does not discuss the passage in *Testim. Truth* (that still lacked a satisfactory edition at the time).

[34] On this see also W.C. van Unnik, *ΑΦΘΟΝΩΣ ΜΕΤΑΔΙΔΩΜΙ* (MVAW.L 33,4 [1971]) and *De ἀφθονία van God in de oudchristelijke literatuur* (MNAW.L N.R. 36,2 [1973]).

An interesting feature of *The Testimony of Truth* is that it polemicizes with emerging mainstream Christianity as well as with other Gnostic schools.[35] Pearson dates it at the end of the second or the beginning of the third century. In this document then, we hear, at first hand, the arguments of at least some of those whose theories were rejected by Theophilus and his colleagues. For *The Testimony of Truth* the serpent is the revealer of life and knowledge, whereas the Creator God is portrayed as an ignorant and malevolent being. The author(s) comment(s):

> What sort of a God is this? First [he] was envious (φθονεῖν) of Adam that he should eat from the tree of knowledge (γνώσεως). And secondly he said, "Adam, where are you?' So God did not have foreknowledge (πρόγνωσις)? That is, he did not know this from the beginning? And later he said, 'Let us throw him out of his place lest he eat from the tree of life and live forever.' Thus he has shown himself to be a malicious (βάσκανος) envier (φθονεῖν). What sort of a God is this? Indeed, great is the blindness of those who have read (this) and have not recognized him!" (47,14-48,4; transl. Luttikhuizen).

It is clear what is at stake. The author(s) regard(s) the Creator God as a demonic figure. For the "mainstream" Christians the identity of the God revealed by Jesus Christ and the Creator of heaven and earth was a central and indispensable part of their faith.

VII. THE GREEK LIFE OF ADAM AND EVE

It would be possible to extend the search for interpretations of Genesis 3 in "Catholic" and "heretic" Christianity in the second and third century CE. Our investigation in sections 4-6 has made sufficiently clear, however, how crucial the exegesis of that chapter was

---

[35] See also G.P. Luttikhuizen, "A Resistant Interpretation of the Paradise Story in the Gnostic *Testimony of Truth* (Nag Hamm. Cod. IX.3) 45-50," in G.P. Luttikhuizen (ed.), *Paradise Interpreted. Representations of Biblical Paradise in Judaism and Christianity* (Themes of Biblical Narrative. Jewish and Christian Traditions 2; Leiden: Brill, 1999), 140-152. He stresses the polemic with other Christians as decisive factor in the origin of this document. The central question is the value of the "Old Testament" for the knowledge of the true God. B. Pearson finds many Jewish haggadic traditions in this section of *The Testimony of Truth* and argues for an inner-Jewish origin of ancient Gnostic terminology. See also his "Jewish Haggadic Traditions in *The Testimony of Truth* from Nag Hammadi (CG IX,3)," in *Ex Orbe Religionum. Studia Geo Widengren Oblata*, vol. 1 (NumenSup 21; Leiden: Brill, 1972), 457-470.

for many Christians in their search for dependable knowledge of a God who would bestow eternal life upon frail and foolish human beings. For "mainstream" Christianity it was essential to emphasize that the God who punished Adam and Eve and expelled them from Paradise, did not condemn them to death for ever. He really intended the well-being of humankind, opening the way to eternal life. The controversy about the interpretation of Genesis 3 was part of the struggle about the place of the Law, Prophets and Writings of the Jews in Christianity and their acceptance as "Old Testament," an essential part of the Holy Scriptures of the Church.

Those Christians who accepted the Old Testament as part of Holy Writ, became interested in what could further be known about figures who played a prominent role in the books of the Old Testament. That is how the so-called "pseudepigrapha of the Old Testament" received a place in early Christianity.

With regard to the *Greek Life of Adam and Eve* I come to the following conclusion on the basis of our present investigation: There is insufficient evidence that the authors mentioned knew a (Jewish) *Life of Adam and Eve*, or that, the other way round, the author(s) of *GLAE* were familiar with any of the writings analysed above. There are simply not enough indications for literary dependence one way or another. Our findings show, however, in what time the *Life of Adam and Eve* in its oldest Greek form may have originated, and against what background it may be understood. An author (or authors), belonging to the circles of "mainstream" Christianity decided to retell the story of Genesis 3; in doing so they added a supplement in order to make clear, once and for all, that Adam and Eve repented, were pardoned, taken up into heaven and would rise again at the last judgment. What happened to them as the ancestors of humankind, would be the lot of all their descendants, on the condition that they, too, repented, mended their ways and obeyed God's Law.

As I remarked earlier (at the end of chapter 3) the *Life of Adam and Eve* could have been meaningful in a different, possibly earlier, Jewish setting. The problem is, however, how we are to determine that context and reconstruct the presumably different form of the writing that fitted into it. Even if we would come up with a more or less acceptable solution, however, we would still have to answer Robert Kraft's question quoted in that context: "I can create a believable non-Christian Jewish context that could have produced this material, but must I do so? Should I do so?"[36]

[36] In two recent publications the view defended in this chapter is rejected. T.A. Knittel, in his *Das griechische 'Leben Adam und Evas'. Studien zu einer narrativen Anthropologie im frühen Judentum* (TSAJ 88; Tübingen: Mohr [Siebeck], 2002) regards the *Life* as Jewish on the basis of the too simplistic argumentation that explicitly Christian elements are absent and Jewish parallels can be found to most concepts included in it. In his *Dying Adam with his Multiethnic Family. Understanding the* Greek Life of Adam and Eve (SVTP 16; Leiden: Brill, 2001), 260-264, M. Eldridge emphasizes the differences between *GLAE* 31-43 and the approach to Genesis 3 found in the writings of Irenaeus, Tertullian and Theophilus; for that reason he sticks to the theory that the Greek *Life* is of Jewish provenance. Earlier, A.M. Sweet, in her *A Religio-Historical Study of the Greek Life of Adam and Eve,* defended a second century dating as *terminus a quo* (p. 26). She repeatedly finds indications that *GLAE* is familiar with Gnostic traditions. In her view it takes up those elements in the Genesis story distorted in the Gnostic tradition and affirms the conventional approach in its own reworking of the biblical text (p. 90). The examples Sweet adduces show the non-Gnostic, but not the anti-Gnostic character of *GLAE*. This holds also true in the case of the Gnostic passages on God's jealousy (mentioned on p. 93; she omits the text from *The Testimony of Truth*).

CHAPTER TWELVE

THE WASHING OF ADAM IN THE ACHERUSIAN LAKE
(GREEK LIFE OF ADAM AND EVE 37:3)
IN THE CONTEXT OF EARLY CHRISTIAN NOTIONS
OF THE AFTERLIFE

Marinus de Jonge and L. Michael White[1]

INTRODUCTION

The last section of the *Greek Life of Adam and Eve (GLAE),*[2] consisting of chapters 31-43, tells about events surrounding the deaths of Adam and Eve. In chapters 31-37 Adam, penitent and humble, departs to meet his Maker. Immediately after his death the angels and even the sun and the moon offer incense and prayers to God that he may have mercy on Adam (33, 35). The events are observed by Eve and Seth by means of a vision (34-36). Eve questions what she sees, but Seth explains why the sun and the moon, who are also praying over Adam's body, look like "black Ethiopians," since they are not able to shine before the "Father of Lights."[3] After this we read in chapter 37:

> (1) While Seth was saying this to his mother Eve, an angel sounded the trumpet and all the angels who were lying on their faces stood up and cried with a fearful voice, saying: (2) "Blessed be the glory of the Lord on the part of his creatures, for he has had mercy on Adam, the work of his hands." (3) When the angels had cried these words, one of the seraphs with six wings came, seized Adam and carried him off to

---

[1] This essay started as a commentary on the *Greek Life of Adam and Eve* 37:3 by Marinus de Jonge in which he tried to demonstrate the Christian origin of the text. To this end, J. Tromp and R. Buitenwerf provided helpful discussion of some difficult passages. It then led Michael White to investigate further the Greek traditions concerning the Acherusian Lake (and the river Acheron) and the different forms in which this motif was taken up in Early Christianity.

[2] The work is still often called the "Apocalypse of Moses," but this is a misnomer (found in earlier editions of the work) based on the wording in a "preface" that was added to the Greek text. This preface introduces the text as "The narrative and life of Adam and Eve ... *revealed to Moses* by God."

[3] Cf. Jas 1:17.

the Acherusian Lake; he washed him three times (καὶ ἀπήγαγεν αὐτὸν εἰς τὴν Ἀχερουσίαν λίμνην καὶ ἀπέλουσεν αὐτὸν τρίτον) and brought him in the presence of God. (4) He lay there for three hours. After that the Father of all, sitting on his throne, stretched out his hand, raised Adam up, and handed him over to the archangel Michael, saying to him: (5) "Take him up to Paradise, to the third heaven, and leave him there till that great day when I shall establish order in the world." (6) Then Michael took Adam away and left him where God had told him. And all the angels sang an angelic hymn, marveling at the pardon granted to Adam.

There are a number of variant readings (including omissions) in the Greek MSS, but it is not difficult to reconstruct the oldest attainable text. This restored original formed the basis for the translation given above. It is supported by the Georgian version (with variants). The chapter is not found in the Armenian which omits the whole of 33:1-38:1. Because Georgian is present here, we may be sure that it existed in the common ancestor of the Armenian and the Georgian. The Slavonic section corresponding to the chapter 37 in the Greek follows at a greater distance, but mentions the threefold washing in the Acherusian Lake.

The Latin version presents a complicated picture. Meyer's edition gives an abbreviated story.[4] Michael tells the mourning Seth that God has had mercy on Adam. All angels sound the trumpet blessing God for his mercy on his creature. Then Seth sees the extended hand of God, delivering Adam over to Michael with the words:

> Let him be in your custody until the day when I shall establish order in punishment (*usque in diem dispensationis in suppliciis*),[5] until the last

---

[4] See W. Meyer, "Vita Adae et Evae," *Abhandlungen der königlich bayerischen Akademie der Wissenschaften, Philosophische-philologische Klasse* 14 (Munich: Verlag der K. Akademie, 1878). Meyer's text is reprinted in M.E. Stone and G.A. Anderson, *A Synopsis of the Books of Adam and Eve* (SBLEJL 5; Atlanta: Scholars, 1994), now in a second, revised edition (SBLEJL 17; Atlanta: Scholars, 1999).

[5] 47:3 in the Latin *Vita*. J. Tromp (orally) points to a variant word order in the edition of J.H. Mozley, "The Vita Adae," *JTS* 30 (1929), 121-49: *in suppliciis usque ad diem dispensacionis*. Because it is strange that Adam should be continually punished after God has shown his mercy on him, Tromp suggests that *supplicium* (above translated "punishment") should be taken in the sense of *supplicatio* ("entreaty, humble prayer"), referring to Adam's state while in Michael's custody.

years when I will turn his sorrow into joy. Then he shall sit on the throne of him who overthrew him.[6]

One manuscript, Paris BNF, lat. 3832, recently published by J. Pettorelli,[7] has a longer text, nearer to the Greek, and particularly near to the Georgian. *Pone eum in paradiso in tertio caelo, usque in diem dispensationis qui dicitur economia, quando faciam omnibus misericordiam per dilectissimum filium meum.* This is much closer to the Greek than the text found in the other Latin witnesses. It is particularly close to the Georgian version which reads: "Take him to the third heaven, to the Garden, and leave him before the altar until the day of the 'oikonomia' which I contemplate concerning all the fleshly (beings) with my well-beloved son" (transl. Stone/Anderson). The new manuscript also has an equivalent of Gr. 37:3 in which we read: *Ecce subito uenit seraphim sex alas habens et rapuit Adam, duxitque eum in stanno cerosio, ibique eum baptizauit. Deinde eum adduxit in conspectu domini dei...* Here *stannum* will stand for *stagnum*; *cerosio* must go back to a misreading at some stage, of Acheron (or perhaps one of its cognate forms, e.g. Acheros or Acherusia.[8]

The washing of Adam in the Acherusian Lake comes as a surprise. Known from Greek sources, including Homer and Plato, the Acherusian Lake was a principal landmark in the mythical landscape of Hades, the realm of the dead. Hence, the question arises what the presence of such a typically Greek notion tells us about the background and the origin of the pseudepigraphic tradition in the *Life of Adam and Eve*. To answer this question we shall have to look for parallels in Jewish and Christian writings.

---

[6] The end of this passage from "when I will turn..." onwards, has a parallel in *GLAE* 39:2.

[7] "Vie latine d'Adam et d'Ève. La recension de Paris, BNF, lat. 3832," *Archivum Latinitatis Medii Aevi* 57 (1999), 5-52. See also chapter 11, section 1.

[8] We should note that four of the Greek MSS. omit the initial "A"; the Georgian version speaks of "the lake of cheron" and the Slavonic of the "sea of gerusia"; so G.A. Anderson and M.E. Stone, *A Synopsis of the Books of Adam and Eve* (second revised edition: SBLEJL 17; Atlanta: Scholars, 1999). Compare also the orthographic variant *Acerosius*, discussed below at n. 26.

I. CHAPTERS 31-37: THEIR LITERARY CONTEXT
IN THE GREEK VERSION

The first major part of *GLAE* is the so-called "Testament of Eve" in chapters 15-30. Its contents and function are summed up in the final verse: "Now then, children, I have shown you the way in which we were deceived. But take heed that you yourselves do not forsake the good" (30:1). Eve's testament is preceded by a short overall introduction (chs. 1-4), a brief account by Adam of the events in Paradise (chs. 5-8), and a story of a failed attempt by Eve and Seth to get the "oil of mercy" from the Garden in order to alleviate Adam's pains (chs. 9-13). Because Adam is unable to relate the full story of deception and sin in Paradise, Eve tells it (14:1-2; 31:1).

Eve's story is concerned with the events narrated in Genesis 3. It dwells on the actions of the serpent as an instrument of Satan, the archenemy of humankind. He tries to deceive Eve and Adam through her; of course, he ultimately succeeds (chs. 15-21, cf. Gen. 3:1-7). Immediately after this, God descends to Paradise and pronounces judgment (chs. 22-29, cf. Gen. 3:8-24). The sin of Adam and Eve consists in their transgression of God's commandment (14:3; 24:1, 4; 25:1). Eve is particularly to blame, as she acknowledges (25:1, 3), but Adam is also responsible, as he explicitly confesses (27:2-3).

Adam's confession of sin (followed by that of Eve in 32:2) is accompanied by a request for forgiveness. In his righteousness God punishes Adam, refuses him access to the tree of life, and expels him from Paradise (27:4-28:3; cf. ch. 29). At the same time, however, he tells him: "If you, after your departure from Paradise, guard yourself from all evil, prepared (rather) to die (than to transgress), I shall raise you at the time of the resurrection. From the tree of life will be given you, and you will be immortal for ever" (28:4).

This promise points to all that will be narrated in the final chapters (beginning at ch. 31) that follow Eve's testament. Neither the promise nor the scene narrated in chapters 31-43 is found in Genesis 3; therefore, it may be argued that in *GLAE* the emphasis falls on these final chapters. *GLAE* wants to show that God the Creator, who brought the protoplasts into being and put them in the Garden of Eden, is righteous and merciful toward all who, like Adam and Eve, repent wholeheartedly when they sin and who are prepared to live henceforth in accordance with his commandments.[9]

The final section of *GLAE,* consisting of chapters 31-43, is very complex—too complex to be analyzed here in detail.[10] For the purpose of the present study it is sufficient to note that two related but distinct vignettes are combined. One is about Adam's heavenly afterlife, in a Paradise located in heaven. It ends in 37:6, and is followed by another account of the burial of Adam in the earthly Paradise, that emphasizes the promise of an eschatological resurrection (38:1-42:2). The transition between the two is rather clumsy. After a request by Michael concerning Adam,[11] God again descends to earth, where the body of Adam still lies (ch. 38). He next addresses Adam's body about the latter's disobedience to his commandment, but promises him that he will be brought back to his dominion and will sit on the throne of the devil (ch. 39). Then, the angels Michael, Gabriel, and Uriel prepare Adam's body for burial. They simultaneously prepare Abel's body, which still lies unburied since his murder by Cain (ch. 40). Once again God calls to Adam's body, which answers: "Here I am, Lord" (cf. Gen. 3:8). God now promises Adam's own resurrection and that of all people (ch. 41, cf. earlier 10:2; 28:4). Finally, God seals Adam's grave, and all the heavenly beings return to their abode (42:1-2).

Despite the clumsiness, there is no reason to suppose that there ever existed a form of the *GLAE* (older than the present Greek version) that contained only one of these two vignettes. In both vignettes the central issue is the future fate of Adam, and no clear distinction is made between Adam's body and his spirit. Death is regularly said to

---

[9] Cf. M. Meiser, "Sünde, Buße und Gnade in dem Leben Adams und Evas," in G.A. Anderson, M.E. Stone and J. Tromp (eds.), *Literature on Adam and Eve. Collected Essays* (SVTP 15; Leiden: Brill, 2000), 297-313.

[10] For what follows see the analysis in J. Tromp, "Literary and Exegetical Issues in the Story of Adam's Death and Burial *(GLAE* 31-42)," in J. Frishman and L. Van Rompay (eds.), *The Book of Genesis in Jewish and Oriental Christian Interpretation* (Traditio Exegetica Graeca 5; Louvain: Peeters, 1997), 25-41.

[11] The most original Greek text of 38:1 probably has to be understood as follows: "After the future joy of Adam (had thus been announced), Michael cried to the Father concerning (the body of) Adam." The first clause is omitted by a number of manuscripts which clearly did not know what to make of it. Ms. B, often very free, gives an obviously secondary version of the entire verse. Surprisingly it is followed by a number of modern translators (see Tromp, "Literary and Exegetical Issues," 27-28).

come about when Adam leaves his body,[12] and the surviving part of Adam is called spirit in some passages,[13] but soul in others.[14] At the same time Adam's body is said to lie down (33:3; 37:4; cf. 35:2), and we hear how it is washed (37:3). Earlier, Seth was portrayed as kneeling over his father's body in grief (34:2; 35:1). Finally Michael brings him into the third heaven to Paradise (37:5-6), and yet there is a body still to be buried (38-41).

Adam in the heavenly Paradise awaits the day of the final judgement (37:5), elsewhere called the day of the resurrection (10:2, cf. 28:4; 41:3 and also 39:2-3). Meanwhile, Adam's body is buried in the earthly Paradise; and so dust returns to dust (40:6-41:2, cf. Gen. 3:19). Not only the surviving part of Adam in heaven, but also the body that will be raised can be designated as Adam (38:1; 40:3, 5, cf. 42:3-4). God addresses the body as "Adam" and it is able to answer (41:1). The final chapters of *GLAE* are concerned with Adam, as well as Eve and her burial (particularly in 42:3-43:4), and, through them, with the future fate of all human beings. These chapters are not interested, however, in any precise anthropology, or in the location(s) of Paradise.

II. THE ACHERUSIAN LAKE IN JEWISH AND CHRISTIAN LITERATURE

In a very informative article Erik Peterson has gathered most of the important parallels to the passage concerning the Acherusian Lake (*GLAE* 37:3) and discussed them in detail.[15] In particular, he was trying to trace this motif back to Jewish origins. No one can afford to neglect this study, though there is room for criticism of his overall approach to the matter.

2.1 *The* Apocalypse of Peter

The first text to be mentioned is at the beginning of *Apocalypse of Peter* 14. Since the *Apocalypse of Peter* is twice quoted by Clement

---

[12] So 31:1, 4; 32:4: cf. earlier 13:6 and later 42:8, speaking about the death of Eve.

[13] In 31:4 and 32:4.

[14] In 13:6; cf. 43:3.

[15] "Die 'Taufe' im Acherusischen See" *VC* 9 (1955), 1-20, reprinted in the collection of his essays *Frühkirche, Judentum und Gnosis* (Rome, Freiburg,Vienna: Herder, 1959,) 310-32. The reprint was used in the preparation of this study.

of Alexandria,[16] it must therefore have been written in the second century CE. The text is only preserved otherwise in an Ethiopic version translated from a Greek original. Parts of this Greek original are known from a fragmentary papyrus MS from Akhmim.[17] The passage relating to the Acherusian Lake is also known in Greek from the so-called Rainer fragment (from the third or fourth century).[18] The Greek reads:

> I will give to my called and my elect whomever they request of me from out of punishment. And I will give them a beautiful baptism in salvation from the Acherusian Lake which is said to be in the Elysian field (καὶ δώσω αὐτοῖς καλὸν βάπτισμα ἐν σωτηρίᾳ ’Αχερουσίας λίμ–νης ἣν καλοῦσιν ἐν τῷ ’Ηλυσίῳ πεδίῳ), a share in righteousness with my saints. And I and my elect will go, rejoicing with the patriarchs into my eternal kingdom, and I will fulfill for them my promises which I and my Father in heaven promised them.[19]

We note that the righteous elect are allowed to make intercession for others who after being saved by a baptism in the Acherusian Lake (situated in the Elysian field) are allowed to enter into the heavenly bliss with the holy ones.

2.2 *The* Sibylline Oracles

A similar picture is found in *Sib. Or.* 2:330-338, where we read:

> To these pious ones the imperishable God, the universal ruler, will also give another thing. Whenever they ask the imperishable God to save men from the raging fire and deathless gnashing, he will grant it, and he will do this. For he will pick them out again from the undying

---

[16] *Eclog.* 41.2 and 48-49. There is also a possible allusion to the text in Theophilus of Antioch, *Ad Autolycum* 2.19, which, if true, would push *the terminus ante quem* some twenty years or so earlier.

[17] Which includes the section quoted by Clement in *Eclog.* 41.2.

[18] For a survey of witnesses, see J.K. Elliott, "The Apocalypse of Peter," *The Apocryphal New Testament* (Oxford: Clarendon, 1993), 593-615 and C.D.G. Müller, "Offenbarung des Petrus," *Neutestamentliche Apokryphen* (ed. E. Hennecke and W. Schneemelcher; 2 vols.; Tübingen: Mohr; fifth edition, 1987-1989), 2. 562-78.

[19] Here following the translation by D.D. Buchholz, *Your Eyes Will Be Opened. A Study of the Greek (Ethiopic) Apocalypse of Peter* (SBLDS 97; Atlanta: Scholars, 1988), 345. See also Elliott, *The Apocryphal New Testament*, 609, n. 40, who adapts the translation of M. R. James published in "The Rainer fragment of the Apocalypse of Peter," *JTS* 32 (1931), 270-9. The Ethiopic text is here clearly secondary; so, in particular, Buchholz, *Your Eyes Will Be Opened,* 342-62.

flame and set them elsewhere and send them on account of his own people to another eternal life with the immortals in the Elysian plain where are the long waves of the deep perennial Acherusian Lake (ὄθι οἱ πέλε κύματα μακρὰ λίμνης ἀενάου ’Αχερουσιάδος βαθυκόλπου).[20]

Books 1 and 2 of the *Sibylline Oracles* belong together and are generally considered Christian.[21] J.K. Elliott, following the example of M.R. James, includes a translation of the entire section of *Sib. Or.* 2:190-338 as an appendix to *the Apocalypse of Peter* on the grounds that the former seems to be dependent on the latter.[22] Again the emphasis is on the prayer of the righteous for (an unspecified category of) sinners who are thereby saved from punishment and receive eternal life with God's people. One should note, however, that this passage in the *Sibyllines* speaks of a raging fire and an undying flame, and that it does not mention an ablution in the Acherusian Lake; we hear only of its "great/long billowing waves" (κύματα μακρά) and its location in the Elysian field. Other passages within the *Sibylline Oracles,* including one clearly Jewish passage, mention an alternative name, the river Acheron.[23]

2.3 *The* Apocalypse of Paul

A third passage which mentions the Acherusian Lake is *Apocalypse of Paul* 22-23. Of its many versions the longer form of the Latin

---

[20] Translation by J.J. Collins in J.H. Charlesworth (ed.), *The Old Testament Pseudepigrapha,* (2 vols.: GardenCity, New York: Doubleday, 1983-1985), 1. 352 (slightly altered).

[21] See E. Schürer, G. Vermes, F. Millar, and M. Goodman, *The History of the Jewish People in the Age of Jesus Christ (175 B.C.-A.D. 135)* (4 vols.; Edinburgh: T.& T. Clark, 1986), 3.1, 645; A. Kurfess and J.D. Gauger, *Sibyllinische Weissagungen* (Düsseldorf/Zürich: Artemis und Winkler, 1998), 418-9. Collins, *Old Testament Pseudepigrapha,* 1. 330 regards *Sib. Or.* 1-2 as Jewish, with interpolations by a Christian redactor.

[22] Elliott, *The Apocryphal New Testament,* 613 referring to M.R. James, *The Apocryphal New Testament* (Oxford: Clarendon, 1924), 521-4. Peterson ("Die 'Taufe' im Acherusischen See," 311) agrees: "Bekanntlich hat das zweite Buch der Oracula Sibyllina grosse Teile der Petrus-Apokalypse poetisch wiedergegeben."

[23] *Sib. Or.* 1:283-306 describing the sixth generation, "a good, an excellent one," tells that the "happy men to whom Sabaoth gave a noble mind," will "go away to Acheron, in the halls of Hades, and there they will have honour" (1:304, cf. 302). In *Sib. Or.* 5:484-485, a Jewish passage quoted by Clement of Alexandria *(Protr.* 4.50.3), the Sibyl addresses Isis as "thrice-wretched goddess, you will remain by the streams of the Nile alone, a speechless maenad on the sands of Acheron." In the latter, the poetic parallelism seems to equate the traditional Egyptian symbol of burial as "crossing the Nile" with crossing the Acheron in Hades. For the name of the river, Acheron, as part of the landscape of Hades, see also below.

(L1), also called the *Visio Pauli,* is generally regarded as the earliest one, translated from a second edition of the now lost Greek original (dating to the mid-third century).[24] In the passage concerned an accompanying angel conducts Paul to a river of which the waters are "whiter than milk" *(super lac).*[25] The angel tells him:

> This is the Acherusian Lake where is the City of Christ, but not every man is permitted to enter that city; for this is the journey which leads to Christ (two MSS: to that city). And if anyone is a fornicator and impious, and is converted and will repent and bear fruits worthy of repentance, at first when he has gone out of the body, he is brought and worships God (two MSS omit: he is ... God) and thence, by command of God (the Paris MS only), he is delivered to the angel Michael, and he baptizes him in the Acherusian Lake *(et baptizat eum in Acerosium lacum).* Then he leads him into the City of Christ alongside those who have never sinned.[26]

[24] See Elliott, "The Apocalypse of Paul," *The Apocryphal New Testament,* 616-44; H. Duensing and A. Aurelio de Santos Otero, "Apokalypse des Paulus," *Neutestamentliche Apokryphen* 2. 644-75. See now T. Silverstein and A. Hilhorst, *Apocalypse of Paul. A New Critical Edition of three Long Latin Versions* (Cahiers d'Orientalisme 21; Genève: P. Cramer, 1997). According to these two author*s* (*ibid.,* 11-21) the longer Latin recension (L1 and L3, preserved in the four earliest Latin MSS; see the next note) represent a version made between 450 and 530 from a "second edition" of the apocalypse in Greek to be dated in the beginning of the fifth century CE. Silverstein and Hilhorst think that the lost "first edition" of the Greek must have existed in Egypt around the middle of the third century CE. A different view of the dating and the transmission is suggested by C. Carozzi, *Eschatologie et au-delà: Recherches sur l'*Apocalypse de Paul (Aix-en-Provence: Université de Provence, 1994), 165-6.

[25] We shall return to this passage in the concluding section of this study. The text of the *Apocalypse of Paul* is difficult to establish. The longer Latin version is preserved in four MSS. which Silverstein and Hilhorst consider to be the most important witnesses to the text. They include the MSS. from Paris and St. Gall (designated L1), which were used in the older editions, including those of Carozzi and Deunsing-Otero in *Neutestamentliche Apokryphen.* These have now been supplemented by two other MSS from the Escorial (classed with L1) and Arnhem (designated L3) in the edition of Silverstein and Hilhorst. Both Carozzi and Silverstein-Hilhorst also print the text of a shorter Latin recension (L2) known from three mss. of Vienna, Graz, and Zurich; however, on the whole these are not very helpful for establishing the earliest text. At present there is no critical edition of the *Apocalypse of Paul,* so readings must take account of variations in the four main MSS (see next note). See also the review of Silverstein and Hilhorst by J. Tromp in *VC* 52 (1998), 213-17.

[26] Here we have adapted Elliott's translation in *The Apocryphal New Testament,* 629-30 on the basis of the Latin texts in the edition of Silverstein and Hilhorst. The manuscript from the Escorial does not mention the baptism in the Lake; it is clearly confused towards the end: "... at first when he has gone out of the body, he is led to that city by angels and delivered to the archangel Michael." The spelling varies; the St. Gall ms. reads *Acherusius/-m* consistently, while the Paris (Fleury) ms. reads *Aceriosus* in the first instance and *Acerosium* in the second. The first should be taken as metathesis, so that the proper nominative should be *Acerosius* in the

The angel, standing on the Acherusian Lake, provides a golden ship to take Paul to the City of Christ. Three thousand hymn-singing angels accompany Paul, until he arrives in the city. A little later (ch. 31) the angel and Paul return by the same route and again cross the Acherusian Lake.[27] We note that nothing is said about intercession by the righteous, but that the conversion, repentance, and acts of penitence of the sinner get much attention. It is interesting that Michael is the one who baptizes the repentant sinner in the Lake.[28]

2.4 *The* Book of the Resurrection of Christ

There is yet another Christian text that deserves our attention, the *Book of the Resurrection of Jesus Christ by Bartholomew the Apostle*.[29] Here we find a sort of excursus (chapters 21-22) that explains why Thomas was absent during the meeting of the risen Christ with the apostles (cf. John 20:24). Thomas had received news of the death of his son Siophanes. When he arrives, his son has already been buried, but Thomas raises him from the dead. Siophanes tells him about all he saw in heaven after his soul had left his body. He was conducted by Michael, who made him cross a river of fire and ascend to heaven; there he brought him to the Lake of Acheron,[30] and submerged him three times in the water (21.5-6). Directly afterwards he was admitted to the heavenly Paradise.

---

orthography of the Fleury ms. This form also occurs at the beginning of chap. 23 in this ms. using the spelling *Acerosium [lacum]*. The Arnhem ms. has *Acerusius/o/um* three times and the Escorial ms. twice, using the orthography *Agerusius* and *Agerosium*. The latter also confuse *locus* for *lacus*.

[27] The Acherusian Lake is also mentioned at these same two points in the text of a (later) Greek version published by C. Tischendorf, *Apocalypses Apocryphae* (Leipzig: H. Mendelssohn, 1866; repr. Hildesheim: G. Olms, 1966) 34-69, the passage is on 51-52. It has a slightly different version and leaves off the latter part of chap. 22, even though the mention of the Acherusian Lake is clearly preserved. The second reference, parallel to the Latin given above, reads: ὅταν δὲ μετανοήσῃ καὶ μεταστάθῃ τοῦ βίου, παραδίδοται τῷ Μιχαήλ, καὶ βάλλουσιν αὐτὸν εἰς τὴν ἀχέρουσαν λίμνην.

[28] In the two manuscripts which have this detail, the soul is brought to worship God before being handed to Michael.

[29] Now to be consulted in J.-D. Kaestli and P. Chérix, *L'évangile de Barthélemy d'après deux écrits apocryphes* (Turnhout: Brepols, 1993). The second section (143-241) is devoted to the Coptic *Book of the Resurrection*, which is dated by its translators in the fifth or sixth century CE (so esp. 170, 172).

[30] Note that in this text the name of the river has become that of the lake, see below.

2.5 *Other Christian Parallels*

Peterson mentions two further texts. Around 400 CE Prudentius speaks in his *Cathemerinon liber,* hymn 5 *(ad incensum lucernae* or "at lamp lighting") about "that night in which the holy God returned from the waters of Acheron to those living on earth" (5.127-8: *illa nocte, sacer qua rediit Deus stagnis ad superos ex Acherunticis).* That night, just before Easter, the spirits of those who sinned and suffer punishment, enjoy a brief rest and reprieve (cf. 5.125-36).[31] Quite different is a Coptic magical text preserved in London MS. Or. 5987.[32] Here seven important spirits are said to dwell near Antioch, at a place called "Acherusian Lake," flowing from underneath the throne of Jao Sabaoth (lines 18-24). The editor of this text thinks that the places mentioned here are located in heaven.[33]

The uncertainties, in some cases, surrounding their transmission notwithstanding, the first four texts mentioned in this section, with all their differences, show several features which seem to be consistent in all of them. These shed light on the following points in *GLAE* 37: Adam's repentance, the intercessory prayers in heaven, the cleansing—three times—by an angel in the Acherusian Lake, and the admission to Paradise in heaven. What these texts leave unclear is how one goes from the earth to Acherusian Lake, traditionally located in the underworld, to the Paradise in heaven. The geography of the afterlife has not yet been fully mapped out.

Peterson[34] notes these parallels when he looks for possible Jewish conceptions behind the apocalypses of Peter and Paul. He has to admit, however, that *GLAE* 37 is not free from Christian redaction, and he is not able to find any clearly Jewish text which mentions the Acherusian Lake.[35] The obvious conclusion is that all the texts dis-

---

[31] See text, translation and note in M. Lavarenne, *Prudence I, Cathemerinon Liber (Livre d'heures),* (Collection Budé; Paris: Les Belles Lettres, 1943) 30-1.

[32] The text was edited and translated by A.M. Kropp, *Ausgewählte Zaubertexte* (2 vols.; Bruxelles: Fondation Égyptologique Reine Elisabeth, 1931), 1:22-28 and 2:149-160.

[33] In passing I note that *Gr. Ap. Bar.* 10 speaks about a great lake in the third (fourth) heaven where the souls of the righteous assemble. This clearly resembles the Acherusian Lake, but it is not called by that name. See D.C. Harlow, *The Greek Apocalypse of Baruch (3 Baruch) in Hellenistic Judaism and Early Christianity* (SVTP 12; Leiden: Brill, 1996), 142-6. Harlow interprets this apocalypse as both a Jewish and a Christian text.

[34] See especially "Die 'Taufe' im Acherusischen See," 319-23.

[35] Note, however, the anomalous reference to Acheron in *Sib. Or.* 5:484-485, which Peterson does not seem to have known. See above n. 23.

cussed so far, including the *GLAE,* represent early *Christian* appro-
priations of the Greek traditions about the Acherusian Lake. In support of this, it may be useful to look for a moment at the Greek sources for this tradition, especially Plato's *Phaedo,* before turning to
some commentaries by early Christian authors.

III. THE ACHERUSIAN LAKE: FROM HOMER TO PLATO

Plato's statements about the Acherusian Lake are found in a long
disquisition of Socrates (*Phaedo* 107c-115a; cf. 80e-82b) on the future destination of the soul. The tradition of the Acherusian Lake,
however, goes back to Homer, where it became well known as one of
the key elements of the landscape of Hades. In Homeric tradition Hades, the realm of the dead, was separated from the world of the living
by a kind of no-man's land. The shades of the dead haunt this no-
man's land until proper burial has occurred, and then—and only
then—are they allowed to cross the body of water (either lake or
river) which marks the entrance into Hades proper.[36] The body of
water is simply called "river" (ποταμός) in *Iliad* 23.71-4, but is identified as the Styx in *Iliad* 8.369. In *Odyssey* 10.508-15 (cf. 11.155-9)
the rivers have multiplied to include Oceanus, Styx, Pyriphlegethon,
Cocytos, and Acheron. Oceanus marks the boundary to Hades'
house. On the other side stands the grove of Persephone with its trees
and vegetation. The four rivers are there: Cocytus is designated as a
branch of the Styx; Cocytus and Pyriphlegethon are said to flow into
the river Acheron; and a large boulder stands at this confluence of the
rivers. This proliferation of names and details corresponds with an
elaboration of the underworld landscape already at work in the later
Archaic period.[37] By the fifth century BCE, one finds an even more

---

[36] This summary of the early Greek tradition, is based on the recent, in-depth study of C.
Sourvinou-Inwood, *'Reading' Greek Death to the End of the Classical Period* (Oxford: Claren-
don, 1995), 61-3, and the extensive bibliography provided. A useful survey of the views of
afterlife in Greek and Roman tradition is also given by Alan E. Bernstein, *The Formation of
Hell: Death and Retribution in the Ancient and Early Christian Worlds* (Ithaca: Cornell Univ.
Press, 1993), 21-129. The study of Emily Vermeule, *Aspects of Death in Early Greek Art and
Poetry* (Berkeley: Univ. of California Press, 1979) remains very useful as well. Also for a re-
view essay on earlier studies of death and afterlife in the Greek world see Peter Green, "On the
Thanatos Trail," in *Classical Bearings: Interpreting Ancient History and Culture* (London:
Thames and Hudson, 1989), 63-76.

[37] Sourvinou-Inwood, *'Reading' Greek Death,* 61.

extensive geography, but now it is the river Acheron and/or the lake, Acherusia, that usually mark the border, where one must board the ferry of Charon to make the crossing.[38]

In the Classical period, a *nekyomanteion* (an oracle or evocation of the shades of the dead) became a regular feature of the crossing into Hades. It was particularly associated with the Acherusian Lake and probably helps explain why this name became the most prominent.[39] Hence, a key feature of the Greek conception of the rite of passage from life to death included an appearance of the shade(s) at the Acherusian Lake. Eventually, this mythical landscape, conceived as a parallel "world" to the land of the living above, was the source of further commentary and interpretation down into Hellenistic and Imperial times.[40] The most influential of these was Plato's, who concluded that the river Acheron flowed into the lake Acherusia, which then lay at the edge of the Elysian fields, the realm of the blessed. Of the four rivers[41] of Hades, Acheron and the lake into which it feeds, are clearly the most benign (*Phaedo* 112e-113a). So we turn to the disquisition of Socrates.

Socrates remarks: "It is right to think then, gentlemen, that if the soul is immortal, it requires our care not only for the time we call life, but for the sake of all time, and that one is in terrible danger if one does not give it that care (107c)."[42] The disquisition takes the form of a myth, a travelog of the underworld. Of this Socrates says:

---

[38] Compare Aeschylus, *Sept. contra Theb.* 856; Theocritus 17.47; Pausanias 10.28.4; Euripides, *Alcest.* 252-3; 443; 900-2; Aristophanes, *Ranae* 181-3; 193; 471; Sophocles, *Elec.* 137-8; Aeschylus, *Agam.* 1160; Thucydides 1.46; Xenophon, *Anab.* 6.2.2. The names Acheron and Acherusia are not always given.

[39] So Porphyry's commentary on a reference in Sophocles *Polyxena.* See the discussion of this period in Sourvinou-Inwood, *'Reading' Greek Death,* 307-8.

[40] Compare Cicero, *Tusc. disp.* 1.16.37; 1.21.48; Vergil, *Aen.* 6. 298-304; 384-94; *Anthol. Pal.* 5.240; 7.67- 68; 7.365; Apuleius, *Metam.* 6.18; Lucian, *Dial. mort.* 20.1; *Necyomantia* 10; *Contemplantes* 7; *De luctu* 3. In the Latin tradition the name Styx, used both of the river and the lake, sometimes holds the place of Acheron in Plato's account. In *Aeneid* book 6, where Aeneas makes his journey to the underworld, Acheron is mentioned clearly as a part of the realm dominated by the geography of the Styx.

[41] So 112e-113c, but in actuality there are five named by Plato; he mentions Oceanus separately and treats Cocytus only in conjunction with the Styx (the fourth), even though both are named.

[42] Here and elsewhere we follow the translation of G.M.A. Grube, *Plato's Phaedo* (Indianapolis: Hackett, 1977), unless otherwise noted.

No sensible man would insist that those things are as I have described them, but I think it is fitting for a man to risk the belief—for the risk is a noble one—that this, or something like this, is true about our souls and their dwelling places, since the soul is evidently immortal, and a man should repeat this to himself as if it were an incantation, which is why I have been prolonging my tale.[43]

In order to describe the destination of the departed souls Plato gives an elaborate picture of the entire cosmos, which is much vaster than humans on earth can perceive. The subterranean world is surrounded by the waters of Oceanus, while the different realms of Hades are defined by the four rivers, Acheron, Pyriphlegethon, Cocytus, and Styx (112e-113c). Most of the dead wind up at the shores of the Acherusian Lake (113a). The worst go to Tartarus, the pit of Hades full of fire and torment which is fed by the two raging rivers Pyriphlegethon[44] and Cocytus (113b-c). Criminals and scoundrels are hurled into Tartarus never to emerge from it (113e). Only those who have led eminently pious lives make their way, presumably passing by the Acherusian Lake, to a pure dwelling place above and dwell upon the earth (114b). Among these, the ones who have further purified themselves by philosophy will live without a body, in "even more beautiful abodes" which cannot be described (114c).

It is in connection with the souls of the majority of people, those who have lived an average life, that Plato first mentions the Acherusian Lake (112e-113b). To it "the souls of the majority come after death and, after remaining there for a certain appointed time, longer for some, shorter for others, they are sent back to birth as living creatures" (113a). In a second passage Plato mentions "vessels" or

---

[43] *Phaedo* 114d. See Dorothea Frede, "Der Mythos vom Schicksal der Seelen nach dem Tod," *Platons 'Phaidon'* (Darmstadt: Wiss. Buchgesellschaft, 1999), 152-67. Elsewhere, for instance in *Gorgias* 523a-527a, *Republ.* 614a-621b and *Phaedrus* 245b-249d, Plato uses other myths in discussing similar subject matter. Cf. also P. Habermehl's treatment of the Greek "Klassische Zeit" (278-82) in C. Colpe, E. Dassmann, J. Engemann, P. Habermehl, and K. Hoheisel, "Jenseits (Jenseitsvorstellungen)," *RAC* 17 (1996), 246-407.

[44] Plato is also interested in "scientific" explanations of natural phenomena that can be correlated with this map of the cosmos. So for example, the third river, Pyriphlegethon (which means "blazing with fire"), is said to run at times close to the surface of earth and is the source of volcanic activity, since "offshoots of it are the lava flows that spout forth wherever they happen on the earth" (113b).

"boats" (ὀχήματα), undoubtedly based on the image of Charon's skiff,[45] to transport the dead down the river Acheron to the lake:

> Now when the dead have come to the place where each is led by his genius (δαίμων), first they are judged, those who have lived good and uprightly lives and those who have not. And those who seem to have lived intermediately (οἳ μὲν ἂν δόξωσι μέσως βεβιωκέναι) [i.e., neither fully good nor fully bad] go upon the Acheron, embarking on vessels provided for them, and are borne in these (vessels) to the lake, and there they dwell; and, if they have done any wrong, being purified (καθαιρόμενοι) of wrongs by paying a penalty (διδόντες δίκας), they are redeemed (ἀπολύονται), while for their benevolent deeds they acquire honors (τῶν τε εὐεργεσιῶν τιμὰς φέρονται), according to the merits of each.[46]

Very interesting is what he says next about "those who are deemed to have committed great but curable crimes... but who have felt remorse for the rest of their lives" (113e). They must be thrown into Tartarus, but every year the underworld rivers Cocytus and Pyriphlegethon carry them past the Acherusian Lake, where the rivers run near by but do not merge (cf. 113b).[47] As those in torment pass by they are able to cry out across the expanse to the ones they have killed or otherwise maltreated, asking them to forgive them. If their supplications are successful their punishment comes to an end. If not, they are taken back into Tartarus and have to try again at a later time (114a-b). So now we learn that their victims, like most others, also dwell at the Acherusian Lake. In the Greek geography of Hades, it must be remembered, the underworld was the final abode of both good and bad. Only the exceptionally good, as we saw, had prospects of a better abode somewhere beyond. Yet that "place" remained unspecified, at least in Plato, and could only be accessed by journeying first through Hades.

---

[45] The figure of Charon was actually a later entry into the picture of the underworld's operations, introduced perhaps in the early Classical period from Magna Graecia; cf. Green, "On the Thanatos Trail," 68.

[46] 113d-e. The translation has been adapted to bring out the phrasing of the Greek.

[47] Notice that this is quite different than the picture of the rivers in *Od.* 10.508-15; see above at n. 36.

IV. EARLY CHRISTIAN COMMENTARY ON PLATO'S DESCRIPTION

4.1 *Clement of Alexandria*

At the beginning of the third century CE Clement of Alexandria refers to several passages of Plato, when he argues that the notion of chastisement after death and punishment through fire was taken over by Greek poets and philosophers from the philosophy of the non-Greeks, including the Jews.[48] One of the passages discussed in this regard is *Phaedo* 112-113, taken up in the context of the immortality of the soul by correlation with a quotation from Ps. 104:4 (103:4 LXX):

> As it says, "the one who makes his angels spirits and the flaming fires his ministers" (τοὺς λειτουργοὺς αὐτοῦ πῦρ φλέγον). It follows then that the soul is immortal. For that which is punished or corrected (κολαζόμενον ἢ παιδευόμενον) with sensation, inasmuch as he is said to suffer, is alive. What then? Did not Plato know both the rivers of fire and the depths of the earth (καὶ πυρὸς ποταμοὺς καὶ τῆς γῆς τὸ βάθος), poetically naming Tartarus what is called Gehenna by the barbarians, as well as the Cocytus, the Acheron, and the Pyriphlegethon, even introducing them as some punishments for chastening to correction (καὶ τοιαῦτά τινα εἰς τὴν παίδευσιν σωφρονίζοντα παρεισάγων κολαστήρια)?[49]

One of the key points of Clement's argument is the correlation between fire and punishment, thus allowing him an easy connection to Gehenna in the Jewish tradition.[50] It is interesting to note that for Clement the most important element of the passage is the corrective function of the different forms of punishment in conjunction with the immortality of the human soul. This is why the angels "seize and punish the wicked."[51]

---

[48] *Strom.* 5.90.4-91.5; cf. 5.90.1 and 1.15. For this argument compare also Arnobius, *Adv. Nationes* 2,14. The basic argument, of course, goes back to Hellenistic-Jewish apologetic, especially Artapanus and Philo.

[49] *Strom.* 5.90.6-91.2. In this passage, some MSS of Clement read "prophetically" for "poetically," but the latter is supported by Eusebius' quotation of this passage, to be discussed below.

[50] So, it should be noticed that the long rhetorical question regarding the passage from Plato is a chiasm which makes explicit the following equations: "the depths" (βάθος) = Tartarus = Gehenna, while "the rivers of fire" = Cocytus, Acheron, and Pyriphlegethon. For Gehenna as the place of fiery punishment, see *inter alia* Matt. 5:22; 18:9; 23:33.

[51] *Strom.* 5.90.6.

4.2 *Eusebius of Caesarea*

About a century later Clement's remarks would be taken over by Eusebius of Caesarea in his *Praeparatio Evangelica*. First, in *Praep. Ev.* 11.38 he quotes *Phaedo* 113a-114c *verbatim*. Here he wants to show how Plato, in accordance with the Hebrew Scriptures, mentions divine judgement, the different dwelling places of the pious, and the various punishments of the ungodly. Eusebius also quotes a number of passages from the scriptures to show the correlation with the sacred word. In 11.38.9 the life of the pious without bodies (ἄνευ σωμάτων) of *Phaedo* 114c is altered—without comment—to a life "without troubles" (ἄνευ καμάτων).[52] Eusebius is also eager to interpret the vessels used on the Acheron and the lake (ὀχήματα in *Phaedo* 113d) as the bodies (σώματα)[53] in which the souls receive punishment, according to the rules of the Hebrews (11.38.10). Then in *Praep. Ev.* 13.13.6 he quotes the passage from Clement (given above). Eusebius next returns to *Phaedo* 113d and 114c in *Praep. Ev.* 13.16.14-15 at the end of a critical discussion of Plato's ideas about the soul.

The use of the *Phaedo* passage clearly became standard in early Christian efforts to prove that Plato, too, spoke about a future judgement and places of chastisement. Theodoretus of Cyrus († 466), in his *Graecarum affectionum curatio* 11.19-24, quotes the same passage as Eusebius (parts of which are only summarized).[54] He criticizes Plato for having the souls chastised without a body, and for his theory of the transmigration of souls. All this, he says, has more to do with the teaching of Pythagoras than that of the apostles (11.33-39).

The way the *Phaedo* passage functions in early Christian apologetic differs considerably from the use of the tradition of the Acheru-

---

[52] See G. Favrelle's commentary on this passage in G. Favrelle and É. des Places, *Eusèbe de Césarée, La préparation évangélique. Livre XI* (SC 292; Paris: Cerf, 1982), 382-385.

[53] Eusebius' alterations here reflect differing interpretations and usages of the day. For example, in a variation on the saying of Plato, the fifth cent. CE neoplatonist Hierocles calls the "body the paltry vessel of the soul" (σῶμα ... ψυχῆς λεπτὸν ὄχημα), so the *Carmen Aureum* 26, in, *Fragmenta Philosophicorum Graecorum*, ed. by F. Mullach (3 vols.; Paris: XXXX, 1861-81) 1, 478m. Compare the usage of the term also by the neoplatonist Proclus, *Inst.* 205-210 which says that each different type of soul has its own particular kind of "vessel" (ὄχημα), a conveyance for its ability to descend and ascend into the divine realm, but these "vessels" are not material (208).

[54] He follows Eusebius's reading in *Phaedo* 114c.

sian Lake in the *Greek Life of Adam and Eve* and other apocalyptic writings discussed in the previous section of this essay. Both types of texts show, however, that this section of the *Phaedo* (together with other Greek traditions about Hades) played an important role in early Christian theological reflection on life after death.

V. SHIFTING SANDS ON THE ACHERUSIAN SHORES

Since we have earlier argued that the passage in *GLAE* 37:3 already reflects Christian origins, we may now suggest some possibilities regarding the changing lines at work here. Let us begin by dividing the traditions into two distinct groups. Group 1 comprises what we shall call the apocalyptic tradition and is represented by the passages in *GLAE* 37:3, *Apocalypse of Peter* 14, and its close parallel in *Sib. Or.* 2.330-338.[55] Group 2 comprises a *platonizing tradition* seen chiefly in Clement and Eusebius.[56]

Chronologically all three texts in Group 1 seem to come from the second century CE. One emphasis within this group of texts is bodily resurrection as a way of conceptualizing the afterlife. It is worth noting, therefore, that one of the contemporary Christian apologists, Theophilus of Antioch, explicitly refuted Plato's belief in the immortality of the soul from the *Phaedo*.[57] We noted the emphasis on resurrection especially in conjunction with the story of Adam's washing in the Acherusian Lake in parallel with the preparation of his body for burial. Only now the angels have replaced Hermes and Charon as the guides for the dead. Even so, the washing scene has strong resonances of ancient mortuary ritual,[58] but in earlier Christian

---

[55] The passage noted above from the *Book of the Resurrection of Christ* may well reflect later lines of this tradition, but the sparing usage of others is less clearly so.

[56] The passage noted above from Theodoret of Cyrus also marks this trajectory.

[57] *Ad Autolycum* 3.7; cf. 2.38; the former may be a direct allusion to the argument of the *Phaedo* (see esp. 80d, 81e-82a, and 88d; the first and the last are closely tied to the passage in 112-114).

[58] As Sourvinou-Inwood (*'Reading' Greek Death*, 62-4) shows, the mapping out of Hades corresponded to the gradual reconciliation of burial ideas and practices with a growing notion of the afterlife. In the later Classical traditions, she also shows (308-20) that Charon is understood as a benign figure, whose role is to ease the transition to (and thereby alleviate fear of) the underworld. Hermes led the souls down to Charon, who welcomed them (in friendly or familial manner) and ferried them across. The sealing of the tomb at the completion of the mortuary ritual was thought to signal the beginning of this final passage.

usage, of course, washing, burial, and resurrection were all symbolized in baptism.

Whether there is a more direct literary connection between *GLAE* and the other two texts cannot presently be demonstrated. It may be suggested, however, that the introduction of the Acherusian Lake into the scene derives in some measure from midrashic expansions (or corrections) to *1 Enoch*'s tours of Sheol, where the fallen angels and the souls of the dead await the final judgment.[59] Secondary harmonization of *1 Enoch* to the Greek tradition in Christian texts is also suggested by the allusion in 2 Pet. 2:4: ὁ θεὸς ἀγγέλων ἁμαρτη-σάντων οὐκ ἐφείσατο ἀλλὰ σειραῖς ζόφου ταρταρώσας παρέδωκεν εἰς κρίσιν τηρουμένους ... ("God did not spare the angels when they sinned but having cast them into Tartarus he delivered them to chains of gloom for keeping until judgment ...").[60] The texts of Group 1 show a significant correlation of the traditional apocalyptic elements with the Greek tradition also reflected in Plato; however, lacking in these texts is any direct indication of the discussion of the Acherusian Lake in *Phaedo* 112-113.[61]

At the same time, it must also be remembered that the text of *Apocalypse of Peter* was known both to Clement of Alexandria and to Eusebius, who picked it up from Clement if not other sources.[62] Clement also shows an awareness of the *Sibylline Oracles* and even quotes from it one of the passages on the river Acheron.[63] With these trajectories in mind we may turn to Group 2. Despite their clear awareness of the apocalyptic tradition (Group 1), the documents in Group 2 (chiefly Clement and Eusebius) show a markedly different interest in the Acherusian Lake tradition. Focusing explicitly on the

---

[59] So *1 Enoch* 17:4 ; 21:7; 22:4-6. Note also 22:7 where Abel's spirit wanders in Sheol.

[60] We should perhaps also give attention to the parallel in Jude 6: ἀγγέλους τε τοὺς μὴ τηρήσαντας τὴν ἑαυτῶν ἀρχὴν ἀλλὰ ἀπολιπόντας τὸ ἴδιον οἰκητήριον εἰς κρίσιν μεγάλης ἡμέρας δεσμοῖς ἀϊδίοις ὑπὸ ζόφον τετήρηκεν ("And the angels who did not keep their own position, but left their proper dwelling, he has kept in *eternal* chains in deepest darkness for the judgment of the great day."). Here also we may mention the passage in Ignatius, *Eph.* 19.3.

[61] One feature that may suggest a direct awareness of the platonic tradition is the intercession of the angels (or the elect in *Apoc. Peter*) for the dead, which vaguely resembles the appeal of those in torment to the ones they have harmed in *Phaedo*, 114a.

[62] See above n. 16; for Eusebius see *H.E.* 6.14.1; cf. 3.3.2; 3.25.4.

[63] See above n. 23. Lactantius (*Inst. div.* 7.18.2-4), which cites passages from the *Corpus Hermeticum* and from books 3, 4, 5, and 8 of the Sibyllines, also includes a passage with similarities to that in *Sib. Or.* 2.330-338 (although attributed to Hystaspes).

passage from Plato (esp. *Phaedo* 112e-114a) their interest is, as we have seen, more with the immortality of the soul, punishment for sin, and the passage of the soul into heaven. There is likely a point of intersection between these two trajectories, but over time the *apocalyptic tradition* receded while the *platonizing tradition* continued and, to some extent, subsumed the former. So it must be noted that Eusebius, in contrast to Clement, seems to resist some elements of Plato's immortal soul "without body" in the afterlife even while retaining the *Phaedo* passage transmitted by Clement. This trend is even more explicit in the passage noted above from Theodoret of Cyrus. Augustine and others, however, would eventually seek a different solution in explaining the body-soul relationship in afterlife.[64] Generally, this platonizing turn dates from the third century CE and later, at least for the texts we know. Whether this more traditionally Greek element entered the Christian tradition earlier is impossible to determine with any precision.[65]

In this light we may conclude by looking again at the passage in the *Apocalypse of Paul* (quoted above), since it may well reveal a point of intersection between the two trajectories. It is worth remembering that this text dates from the mid-third century CE[66] but clearly continued in wide manuscript circulation, both Greek and Latin (much wider than *GLAE* or *Apocalypse of Peter*) in the fourth to seventh centuries CE. Augustine *(Ench.* 112-3) seems to know its images,[67] at just about the same time as the passage quoted above from Prudentius. The Latin version, the *Visio Pauli,* comes only

---

[64] Cf. Bernstein, *Formation of Hell,* 313-333 and P. Fredricksen, "Beyond the Body/Soul Dichotomy: Augustine's Answer to Mani, Plotinus, and Julian," in *Paul and the Legacies of Paul,* ed. by W.S. Babcock (Dallas: Southern Methodist University Press, 1990, 227-50, both with ample bibliography.

[65] These and similar Greek traditions on the geography of Hades might now be profitably explored in future studies of other early Jewish and Christian texts, including, *inter alia,* Wis 2:1; 16:13; 17:14; 4 Macc. 13:14-17; and Luke 16:23-27 (parable of Lazarus and Dives). R.F. Hock ("Lazarus and Micyllus: Greco-Roman Background to Luke 16:19-31," *JBL* 106 [1987], 447-63) discusses the history of scholarship on this passage and argues persuasively for a hitherto unrecognized classical background to the parable. Cf. Bernstein, *Formation of Hell,* 239-45.

[66] If one were to follow the second century dating of Carozzi *(Eschatologie et au-delà,* 165) then some modification of this scheme would be required, but it seems unlikely.

[67] Even though Augustine elsewhere dismisses the *Apocalypse of Paul* as apocryphal *(In Iohan. Tract.* 98), the passage in the *Enchiridion* shows a much more positive use of the traditions developed in it regarding the afterlife.

slightly later. The *Apocalypse of Paul* clearly preserves elements of the apocalyptic tradition of the Acherusian Lake (Group 1), notably the emphasis on repentance, the delivery to the angel (Michael), the *baptism* in the Acherusian Lake, and the passage into Paradise.[68] On the other hand, there is no mention of intercession in this passage, and there is more stress on the soul "leaving the body" (so 22:3: *exierit de corpore*) to make the journey. All in all, notions of resurrection seem less in evidence.

At the same time, the passage mentions some unusual features which may only come from Plato or other Greek traditions, as picked up in the Christian commentary tradition of Group 2. Here we note in particular the "golden ship" (like the vessels in Plato) by which Paul sails across the river into the City of Christ, which is said to be beside the Acherusian Lake. The latter may be taken as an equation of Paradise with the Elysian fields. It appears, therefore, that *Apocalypse of Paul*, like Clement before, was consciously harmonizing the earlier apocalyptic tradition to that of Plato.[69]

---

[68] Bernstein, *Formation of Hell*, sees the *Apocalypse of Peter* as the stark extreme of the apocalyptic tradition (282-291); he takes it as the principal source for the *Apocalypse of Paul*, even though the latter takes a different view (299-305).

[69] So note *Strom.* 5.11.77, which quotes from the *Apocalypse of Zephaniah* (so O. Wintermute in *Old Testament Pseudepigrapha*, 1. 508). The discussion here by Clement directly correlates the teaching of Plato with that of the prophets. G. Steindorff *(Die Apocalypse des Elias, eine unbekannte Apokalypse und Bruchstücke der Sophonias-Apocalypse* [TU 17.3a; Leipzig: Hinrichs, 1899]) had identified the *Apocalypse of Zephaniah* as the likely source for the passage on "the Acherusian river" as found in *Apocalypse of Paul*. So, too James (*Apocryphal New Testament*, 538 n. 1; cf. 527 n. 1) mentioned both the *Apocalypse of Zephaniah* and the *Apocalypse of Elijah* as sources for the *Apocalypse of Paul*. According to James *Apoc. Zeph.* has the departed embark on a boat accompanied by a myriad chorus of angels. This passage is found in the Sahidic fragment of *Apoc. Zeph.* and is, in fact, quoted in the Coptic version of the *Apoc. Paul* (fol. 35b); so Wintermute in *Old Testament Pseudepigrapha*, 1. 508 n. B.c. H. Duensing-A. Santos Otero (*Neutestamentliche Apokryphen*, 2, 645-646) agree that both *Apoc. Peter* and *Apoc. Zeph.* were sources for the *Apoc. Paul*. The rest of the Sahidic fragment as restored by Wintermute, however, does not contain the reference to a boat. On the other hand, the longer Akhmim fragment of *Apoc. Zeph.* does contain the reference to the boat in what appears to be the parallel passage to that of the Sahidic (chap. 8.1; cf. 7.9). While these relationships do indicate that Clement knew an earlier Greek version of the *Apocalypse of Zephaniah*, the later Coptic versions may derive additional materials from other sources; so Wintermute (*Old Testament Pseudepigrapha*, 1. 499-500), who follows Steindorff in dating the Akhmimic frag. to the end of the fourth cent. CE, and the Sahidic to the early fifth cent. CE. Both Coptic mss. also contained fragments of the *Apocalypse of Elijah*. So it must be remembered that both the *Apocalypse of Paul* and the *Apocalypse of Peter* were similarly preserved in Egyptian versions of comparable date and provenience (see above nn. 16-18; 24). What this suggests about the

This impression is strengthened further when one looks carefully at the geography of Paradise in the *Apocalypse of Paul*. Now we discover that the Acherusian Lake is in the lower heavens, or more precisely in the space just below the gates of heaven.[70] Here Paul is led on a tour of the heavenly Paradise and the pits of Tartarus.[71] The angelic guide first brings Paul to the river Oceanus, "which irrigates [var. is above] the whole earth" (21:2), and they cross into the land of promise which is lit by the lights of heaven (21:3). Paul sees "a river flowing with milk and honey" (*flumen currentem lac et mel*) along whose banks grow many lush trees (22:1).[72] Next they come to the milk-white waters which the angel identifies as the Acherusian Lake (22:5). Here, he is told, is where the good are brought to be baptized by Michael before entering into the City of Christ. After crossing the lake on the golden boat (23:1), Paul sees the great city, which is surrounded by four rivers: honey, milk, wine, and oil (23:3). Each river stands on one side of the city, and next Paul is taken on a tour of the regions of the four rivers, each of which is inhabited by specific types of individuals who are on their way into the city (25-28). In chapters 29-30 Paul is shown the city itself and its inhabitants, before he is taken back to the entrance by the same route (31:1). When they once again cross beyond the river Oceanus, Paul now finds himself in a realm without light, and there begins his tour of the rivers of fire and the pits of Tartarus, also called the Abyss (31:3-34). While the number of rivers now seems to have multiplied further, the basic geography is that of Oceanus and the four rivers of Hades known to us from Homer and Plato.

One seemingly unusual detail is the description of the Acherusian Lake, whose waters are said to be "exceedingly white, whiter than

trajectory of discussion on heavenly judgment tradition in early Egyptian (Coptic) Christianity perhaps deserves further study.

[70] *Apoc. Paul* 21:2-3: after Paul has just come back down from the third heaven, the angel leads him "up to the gates of heaven" (*duxit super ianuas caeli*—all MSS but Arnhem), while the St. Gall MS (followed closely by the Escorial MS) adds *deduxit me in c[a]elum [a]lium* ("and led me to another heaven"). See next note.

[71] The narrative of Paul's tour of heaven and hell is based on the reference to being "caught up into the third heaven" (ἁρπαγέντα ... ἕως τρίτου οὐρανοῦ) and "caught up into paradise" (ἡρπάγη εἰς τὸν παράδεισον) in 2 Cor. 12:2-4. *Apocalypse of Paul* turns this into three distinct tours: chapters 11-20 describe his tour through the three levels of heaven; chapters 21-31, the tour of the subheavenly Paradise; and chapters 32-45, the tour of Tartarus. Yet it will be seen that the second and third are connected by the traditional Greek geography of Hades.

[72] Cf. *Od.* 10.509-10; Rev. 22:1-2.

milk" (*cuius erant aquae candidae valde super lac*, 22:5).[73] Apparently it flows from the "river of milk and honey" (22:1; cf. 31:1). In effect, this seems to be the river Acheron, which flows into the Acherusian Lake. In the Latin, of course, "milk" (*lac*) and "lake" (*lacus*) form a natural wordplay.[74] So, too, the ideal of "whiteness" in relation to baptism is perhaps a natural symbolism, but there may be more at work in this subtle detail. None of the texts in the Group 1 mention the river Acheron or being conveyed by it to the lake. This aspect seems to come directly from Plato and sources of the classical period on which he was drawing.

While in *Apocalypse of Paul* the river is not explicitly called Acheron, the identification is assured both by its traditional Greek geography (flowing into the Acherusian Lake) and its description as "milk-white." For what we have here is an attribute derived from the place name. The name Acheron is etymologically connected to the name of a tree (the Ἀχερωΐς), called the "white poplar" (sometimes just called λευκή, "white") for its distinctive color.[75] It appears in Homer (*Il.* 13.389; 16.482). The etymological connection is explicated by Pausanias: "Heracles found the white poplar growing on the banks of the Acheron, the river in Thesprotia, and for this reason it is called Ἀχερωΐδα by Homer" (5.14.2). Heracles is said to have brought it to Greece. Pausanias adds that Heracles preferred to sacrifice to Zeus by burning the thighbones of his victims only over this particular wood. The mention of Heracles' exploits reminds us of another connection to Hades myths, since his journey to the underworld to retrieve Alcestis took him to the Acherusian Lake (Euripides, *Alcestis* 443; cf. 252-3; 900-2).[76] For readers steeped in classical mythology, allusions to a "milk-white" river in the world of the dead are hard to miss.[77]

[73] The text is somewhat difficult here. Only the Paris MS gives this precise reading, which Silverstein and Hilhorst emend by reading *eius* for *cuius*. But the sense is clearly supported by the Escorial and Arnhem MSS: *et vidi (f)lumen aqu(a)e candidum valde super lacte* (Arnhem). Only the St. Gall MS omits the more direct connection with the river and removes the comparison to milk, thus: *Aqua candida vidi desuper lacum*.

[74] This may well explain the alteration of the text in the St. Gall MS; see note above.

[75] The poplar is still called λευκη in modern Greek.

[76] Interestingly, in *Od.* 10.510, the trees said to line the grove of Persephone on the shores of Oceanus are said to include the "black poplar" (αἴγειροι).

[77] We must note that there is also a "river of milk" (*flumen lactis*, 23:3; *fluvius lactis*, 26) among the four rivers that surround the city. This is probably not to be equated directly with the "river of milk and honey" (22:1) or the "milk-white" Acherusian Lake (22:5); however, it may

Even so, there may be yet another allusion at work here. The phrasing of the preserved Latin version, "exceedingly white, more than milk" (*candidae valde super lac*, 22.5) may preserve in vaguer form another wordplay carried over from the Greek original. In ancient Greek the word milk was γάλα (still used today), of which the genitive form is γάλακτος . Thus its stem (*Grundform*) is *glak*, which also becomes the direct etymological root of both *lac* (gen. *lactis*) and *glacies* in Latin.[78] In Greek usage, the forms γαλακτίας and γαλαξαῖος, especially when combined with κύκλος ("circle"), became the designation for the astronomical formation which still bears this ancient symbolic name, the "Milky Way." From this common usage[79] came the derived nominal form, γαλαξίας (from which we get "galaxy"), specifically to mean the Milky Way and thereby to signify the heavenly realm.[80] Assuming that the Greek original of the *Apocalypse of Paul* used a similar formulation in 22:5, as seems likely,[81] then the symbolism of the passage takes on new dimensions.

While such symbolism does not appear in the Plato passage itself, it had become part of the pagan discussion of the afterlife by the first century BCE. So, we see it explicitly in Cicero's discussion of the soul in his "Dream of Scipio," in part his commentary on Plato's *Republic*. Cicero certainly knew of the role of the Acherusian Lake in

be surmised that these four rivers somehow flow from the lake. The reason for the names of the four rivers will be discussed below.

[78] So H. Frisk, *Griechisches etymologisches Wörterbuch* (2 vols.; Heidelberg: Carl Winter Universitätsverlag, 1960), 1. 293-294 (s.v. γάλα); cf. P. Chantraine, *Dictionnair étymologique de la langue grecque: Histoire des mots* (4 vols.; Paris: Klincksieck, 1968), 1. 206-207.

[79] See Aristotle, *Meteor.* 345a.25. A variant form is also worth noting: ἐς βάθος κύκλου ("out of the depths of the [heavenly] circle") in Aristophanes, *Aves* 1715; cf. Sophocles, *Ajax* 672. The form γαλακτίας alone came to have this meaning; so Ptolemy, *Syntaxis mathematica* 8.2.

[80] Cf. Diodorus Siculus, *Hist.* 5.23; Lucian, *Ver. hist.* 1.16; Manetho Astrol. 2.116.

[81] The original wording of the Greek for the phrase preserved in the Latin (*candidae valde super lac*) might have been something like λευκοτητά [? λαμπροτητά] τοῦ γαλάκτος, or perhaps ὑπὲρ γαλαξαῖον, but it is impossible to know for sure. The later Greek version (ed. Tischendorf, *Apocalypses Apocryphae*, 51), thought to be secondary to the shorter Latin versions, does not include this detail at 22:5, so we cannot compare the precise rendering of this motif in Greek. That it was in the Greek original, however, is indicated by the fact that the other references to a "river of milk" are retained in the later Greek version at 23:5 (καὶ ποταμοὶ τέσσαρες ἐκύκλουν αὐτήν, ῥέοντες μέλι καὶ γάλα καὶ ἔλαιον καὶ οἶνον [Tischendorf, 52]). At 26 (Tischendorf, 54) the full phrase ὁ ποταμὸς τοῦ γαλάκτος is preserved at precisely the same locus in the text where the Latin reads *fluvius lactis*. Consequently, we can be confident that some form of this word play was in the Greek original.

interpretations of the afterlife from Homer to Plato and beyond, even though the name is not used in this instance.[82] So, in the dream, Cicero reports Scipio's conversation with his departed ancestors; Scipio discovers they are still "alive" in a world beyond (*De re publ.* 6.14.14). What follows is Cicero's disquisition on the immortality of the soul. Next (6.16.16), the younger Scipio is exhorted by his dead father to live a worthy life so that he might obtain the same reward:

> But Scipio, thus imitate your grandfather here; imitate me, your father; love justice and duty (*justitiam cole et pietatem*) which are indeed strictly due to parents and kinsmen, but most of all to your fatherland. Such a life is the way into the heavens (*ea vita via est in caelum*) to that gathering of those who have completed their earthly lives and have been loosed from the body (*corpore laxati*) and who live in that place you see [yonder] (it was the circle of light which blazed most brightly among the other flames [of the sky][83]) which you folks [pl.] call, as you got it from the Greeks, the Milky Circle[84] (*quem vos, ut a Graiis accepistis, orbem lacteum nuncupatis*).

Now the heavenly reward is equated with the "milk-white" way through the stars.[85] This notable shift may help understand why in the *Apocalypse of Paul*, and later Christian tradition, the journey of the soul to the afterlife goes first through the heavens, where the Acherusian Lake is now located, before some are sent from there

---

[82] See esp. Cicero's *Tusc. disp.* 1.16.37; 1.21.48 where Acheron is used explicitly. In the first passage he quotes (in Latin) a passage from an unknown author which he links by direct reference to the pivotal passage in Homer *(Od.* 11), the *nekyomanteion* of the shades before Odysseus. In the latter, he is poking fun at other interpretations of these older myths, notably those of Epicurus. Also in 1.17.39 he mentions the views of Plato, still hard to go wrong with, he would say, but he suggests that newer ideas that place the earth in the middle of the cosmos (the Ptolemaic theory) call for further thought.

[83] The phrase here is: *erat autem is splendidissimo candore inter flammas circus elucens.* So compare "Paul's" description of the heavenly city *(Apoc. Paul 23:2): Et erat lumen eius super aeris lumen, lucens mundi huius super numerum et modum* ("Its light was brighter than that of the heavenly light, illuminating beyond the number and manner of those of the world.") This passage is not included in all the mss. of *Apoc. Paul;* however, note the use of *candor* in Cicero and *candidus* in *Apoc. Paul* 22:5.

[84] Here the Latin (*orbem lacteum)* is a direct translation of the usual form of the Greek: κύκλος γαλαξαῖος or γαλαξίας κύκλος.

[85] In *Apoc. Paul* 21:3 Oceanus, the entry into paradise, is said to be "the light of heaven which gives light to the whole land" (St. Gall: *quot lumen caeli est quod lucet omni terre illic)*; cf. 31:2.

down into the pits of Hades.[86] The geography of the afterlife has taken a new turn.

The conscious harmonization to biblical Paradise myths is explicit in the *Apocalypse of Paul*, such as when the Acheron is said to "flow with milk and honey."[87] Parallel to Plato's description of Hades, Paradise (Christ's City) is said to be vast and surrounded by "four rivers" (cf. *Phaedo* 112e), but now they are named according to the rivers of Eden (23:3; cf. Gen. 2:11-14). So, we learn that the "river of milk" is named Euphrates.[88] When Paul is once again brought out beyond Oceanus, he discovers a dark and shadowy realm, where there is a "river burning with fire" which is reserved for the lukewarm, i.e., those who pray like Christians but sin like pagans (31). Another river of fire (32) looms over a deep abyss, Tartarus (34);[89] it is reserved for the worst sinners (in a later interpolation, including errant churchmen). The pits of hell lie under Oceanus. Others whom Paul sees during his tour of the heavenly city fare far better. Some are constantly abasing themselves for their pride and sins on earth to improve their lot. In its derived Latin version, at least, the *Apocalypse of Paul* promotes the ascetic life; those who practice chastity and asceticism are said to be welcomed at the river of milk (22; 26).

It is not likely that all of these features belong to the Greek original of the *Apocalypse of Paul;* however, they do reflect at least an extension of basic elements derived from the *platonic tradition* of the afterlife; to some extent, these "platonizing" elements were already at work in the earlier stages of the text quite apart from those conveyed by the *apocalyptic tradition* that were also there. In late antiquity, the image of the Acherusian Lake may have served as a mythic axis for the synthesis of an older apocalyptic eschatology (as seen in the *Greek Life of Adam and E*ve) with Platonic notions of afterlife, now

---

[86] So *Apoc. Paul* 31-36.

[87] 22:1: *currentem lac et mel;* 31:1: *flumen lactis et mellis.* Cf. Exod. 3:8; Lev. 20:24.

[88] 23:3: *flumen lactis [dicitur] Eufrat(es),* and this may be why the name Acheron was intentionally dropped in the earlier scene, even though the symbolism is retained.

[89] Note here the equation of Tartarus with the "exceedingly deep pits" (Latin *foveas profundo valde,* 32:1) and the "abyss" *(abyssus,* 32:2). Both formulations seem to be rendered with βάθος in the abbreviated form of this passage in the later Greek version (Tischendorf, *Apocalypses Apocryphae,* 58). The same equation is made by Clement, see note 50 above.

equated with the heavenly Paradise—a synthesis that would eventually come to dominate the new Christian worldview.[90]

---

[90] Cf. T. Silverstein, "Did Dante know the Vision of St. Paul?" *Harvard Studies and Notes in Philology and Literature* 19 (1937), 231-47.

CHAPTER THIRTEEN

THE GREEK LIFE OF ADAM AND EVE AND THE WRITINGS OF THE NEW TESTAMENT

INTRODUCTION

In his important book *The Theology of Paul the Apostle* James Dunn devotes his third chapter to "Humankind under Indictment." This begins with a long section on Adam which deals mainly with Adam in the Epistle to the Romans, but discusses briefly "Adam in Jewish Scripture" and "Adam in post-biblical Jewish Tradition" before turning to Paul.[1] In Dunn's opinion it is not really possible to speak of a Jewish scriptural tradition of the "fall" of Adam and Eve, but the situation is different in the Jewish writings of the post-biblical ("intertestamental") period. If we study these writings with regard to their views on Adam and Eve and the consequences of their actions for humanity, it becomes evident "that Paul was entering into an already well-developed debate and that his own views were not uninfluenced by its earlier participants."

Like others before him Dunn draws on a variety of sources to support his thesis. He uses Ben Sira (pointing to Sir 25:24 in particular), Wisdom of Solomon (e.g., Wis. 2:23-24), *Jubilees*, Philo, Josephus, the *Life of Adam and Eve* (both in its Greek version called the *Apocalypse of Moses* and the Latin *Vita Adae et Evae)* and the two apocalypses *4 Ezra* and *2 Baruch* which reflect the destruction of the Jerusalem Temple in 70 CE. However great the variety in detail, there is a striking unity of perspective on two points, according to Dunn. Genesis 1-3 invites an interpretation which takes seriously the play between Adam and *'adam* ("humankind"); and next: the Genesis story leads to speculation on the relationship between sin and death, and on the nature of the transgressions of the protoplasts.

---

[1] James D.G. Dunn, *The Theology of Paul the Apostle* (Grand Rapids—Cambridge: Eerdmans/Edinburgh: T.&T. Clark, 1998), 82-84 and 84-90. The quotation at the end of this paragraph is from p. 90.

Dunn's approach is by no means uncommon and can be found in a number of monographs and commentaries before him.[2] It is also not uncommon to include the *Life of Adam and Eve* among the writings that may have influenced Paul's view on Adam and Eve as ancestors of the human race. Recent study of the *Life of Adam and Eve* in its different versions[3] has led me, however, to question this common assumption. The present chapter is an attempt to show why one should be hesitant to use this pseudepigraphon in the interpretation of the letters of Paul or other writings of the New Testament.

To return to Dunn for a moment: according to him the *Life of Adam and Eve* emerged probably a little after Paul, but it shows some striking parallels with Paul. Dunn mentions the Greek and Latin versions, and follows M.D. Johnson[4] (and others) in assuming an original Hebrew text behind those—to be dated between 200 BCE and 100 CE There may well have been a version prior to Paul and our current texts therefore reflect traditions and speculations about Adam and Eve known to him. Yet much remains uncertain, and it is not surprising that M.D. Johnson, after enumerating a number of interesting parallels, concludes: "In spite of these parallels it is impossible to determine whether there is a relationship between the New Testament and our texts."

[2] See the bibliography in Dunn, *Theology of Paul*, 79, n.1. Note especially Jacob Jervell, *Imago Dei. Gen. 1, 26f. im Spätjudentum, in der Gnosis und in den paulinischen Briefen* (FRLANT N.F. 58; Göttingen: Vandenhoeck & Ruprecht, 1960); E. Brandenburger, *Adam und Christus. Exegetisch-religionsgeschichtliche Untersuchungen zu Römer 5, 12-21 (1 Kor. 15)* (WMANT 7, Neukirchen: Neukirchener Verlag, 1962); R. Scroggs, *The Last Adam. A Study in Pauline Anthropology* (Philadelphia: Fortress, 1966). See also the article by J.L. Sharpe III, "The Second Adam in the Apocalypse of Moses," *CBQ* 35 (1973), 35-46. Commentaries on Romans usually deal with the matter under discussion at 3:23; 5:12-21 and/or 7:7-12. See especially the excursuses "Sünde und Tod, Erbtod und Erbsünde" in O. Kuss, *Der Römerbrief übersetzt und erklärt*, vol. 1 (Regensburg: F. Pustet, [2]1963), 241-275, and "Adam bei Paulus" in H. Schlier, *Der Römerbrief* (HTKNT 6; Freiburg-Basel-Wien: Herder, 1977), 179-189.

[3] See M. de Jonge and J. Tromp, *The Life of Adam and Eve and Related Literature* (Guides to Apocrypha and Pseudepigrapha; Sheffield: Sheffield Academic Press, 1997).

[4] In his contribution "Life of Adam and Eve," in J.H. Charlesworth (ed.), *Old Testament Pseudepigrapha*, vol. 2 (Garden City, New York: Doubleday, 1985), 249-295. The quotation at the end of this paragraph is from p. 255. D.A. Bertrand, in his *La vie grecque d'Adam et Ève* (Recherches Intertestamentaires 1; Paris: Maisonneuve, 1987), 29-31, regards Ben Sira as *terminus a quo* for the Greek *Life* and the Epistles of Paul as *terminus ad quem*.

H.F.D. Sparks, in *The Apocryphal Old Testament*,[5] is (rightly)
even more cautious. There is nothing Christian in the Greek version
of the *Life*; references to the Old Testament betray dependence on the
Septuagint and a Semitic original is therefore unlikely. He concludes:
"All that can safely be said about it is that the author, whether Jew or
Christian, constructed his narrative making use of such Jewish traditions or written sources as were known to him; that he almost certainly wrote in Greek; and that in all probability he is to be dated
within the first three Christian centuries."

The most recent translation with introduction and annotations of
the *Life of Adam and Eve* is O. Merk's and M. Meiser's volume in
the series "Jüdische Schriften aus hellenistisch-römischer Zeit."[6]
Although they, like others before them, only translate the Greek and
Latin versions and print them in parallel columns, they note the
complicated relationships not only between these two, but also with
three additional forms of text: the Armenian "Penitence of Adam,"
the Georgian version (both published recently) and the Slavonic
version (known for a long time). Together these writings contain a
great variety of traditions about Adam and Eve. It is very difficult to
determine how the documents are related to one another but,
according to Merk and Meiser, in all probability the Greek version
represents one of the oldest stages of development, and the Latin text
the last one.[7]

Merk and Meiser note that all versions of the *Life of Adam and
Eve* have come down to us in Christian manuscripts, but that they are
not genuinely Christian (apart from easily detectable later additions).
It is not easy to date them; for the Greek *Life* they finally choose the
period between short before the beginning of the common era and the
end of the first century. The decisive factor for them are the parallels
with Paul's letters.[8]

This raises (again) the question of the nature of these parallels. Do
they really show that Paul, and perhaps other authors of New Testa-

---

[5] See his Introduction to M. Whittaker's translation of the Latin *Life of Adam and Eve* plus
part of the *Apocalypse of Moses*, in H.F.D. Sparks, *The Apocryphal Old Testament* (Oxford:
Clarendon, 1984), 141-167. The quotation in the text is from p. 142.

[6] *Das Leben Adams und Evas* (JSHRZ 2, 5; Gütersloh: Gütersloher Verlagshaus, 1998),
733-870.

[7] See their sections "Literarkritik" (pp. 755-756) and "Quellenkritik" (pp. 757-764).

[8] See "Datierung und religionsgeschichtliche Verortung" (pp. 764-769). The Latin version
must be considerably later.

ment writings, knew the Greek *Life of Adam and Eve,* the oldest version of the document handed down to us (as was argued in chapter 11)? That is: did take up important, determinative elements in this form of the *Life?*

I. THE STORY OF ADAM AND EVE AS THE STORY OF HUMANKIND

In chapter 11, section 2 we have seen that the structure of the *Greek Life of Adam and Eve (GLAE)* is similar to the pattern of a farewell discourse (often called "testament"). After the introductory chapters 1-4 which introduce the *dramatis personae,* Adam, 930 years old and very ill, assembles his children. He tells them briefly about what happened in Paradise (chs. 5-8). He sends Eve and Seth to the Garden to ask for "the oil of mercy" that may alleviate his pains. Michael refuses to give it. Seth is to go back to his father who will die in three days; he will witness Adam's fearful upward journey, as his soul departs (chs. 9-13). Adam then asks Eve to tell their children and children's children "how we transgressed." Thus Eve relates how the devil, through the serpent, seduced her; how she persuaded Adam to eat from the tree; and how God had them expelled from Paradise—in fact, she retells the story found in Genesis 3 in her own special way. Her "testament" (chs. 15-30) ends with the words; "Now then, children, I have shown you the way in which we were deceived. But take heed that you yourselves do not forsake the good" (30:1).

An account of Adam's death and departure from the earth follows. Adam is confident that God will not forget him, "the vessel that he made." He will give back his spirit into the hands of the one who gave it to him. Eve has to pray for him, for human beings do not know how they will meet their maker, whether he will be angry with them or merciful (ch. 31). God shows mercy; Eve and Seth are allowed to behold how angels bring Adam to the Paradise in the third heaven and how is body is buried with that of Abel, near the earthly Paradise (chs. 32-41). The picture given in these chapters is very complex and not always internally consistent,[9] but one thing is clear:

---

[9] See on this J. Tromp, "Literary and Exegetical Issues in the Story of Adam's Death and Burial (GLAE 31-42)," in J. Frishman and L. Van Rompay (eds.), *The Book of Genesis in Jewish and Oriental Christian Interpretation* (Traditio Exegetica Graeca 5; Leuven: Peeters, 1997), 25-41. See also chapter 12, section 1.

Adam is pardoned, he shares in heavenly bliss, and he is promised a share in the resurrection to come "with all persons belonging to your seed" (41:3). Six days after Adam Eve dies; she is buried with Adam and shares Adam's lot (chs. 42-43).

The story of Adam and Eve is the story of all human beings; what the protoplasts did directly affected their offspring. Their transgressions, their penitence, their attempts to follow God's commandments in the rest of their life, and, in the end, their sharing in the eternal life bestowed on them by God in his mercy, are related as a warning and a promise for all readers who know Genesis 3 and want to take seriously what is said there.

Going a little more into detail, we note that the sin of Adam and Eve is seen as basically a transgression of God's commandment (8:2; 10:2; 14:3; 23:3; 24:1, 4; 25:1). Eve in particular is to blame and she realizes that (9:2; 10:2; 14:3; 25:1, 3; it is the central point in Eve's description of what happened in the Garden). At Adam's departure from the earth Eve utters an impressive prayer of confession and repentance (ch. 32). But also Adam is held responsible and he explicitly acknowledges his fault (27:2-3).

The consequences of their sin are illness (chs. 5-13), leading to death (7:1; 14:2). Adam and Eve are definitely refused access to the tree of life (chs. 27-29). Adam will have to labour hard in order to eke out a living (ch. 23), and Eve will suffer many pains in giving birth to her children (25:2). Humankind will no longer be able to keep the animals under control (24:4; cf. chs. 10-12). Adam's and Eve's state before the Fall is only hinted at in 20:1, 2 where Eve, after eating from the fruit of the tree, realizes that she is "naked of the righteousness" with which she had been clothed. She sees herself as "estranged from the glory." Adam echoes this when he, realizing that he stands naked, abuses Eve, calling her an "evil woman" and reproaches her for having estranged him from the glory of God (21:6).

The common enemy of Adam and Eve is Satan, acting through the serpent (chs. 15-20) in order to deceive Eve. He also uses Eve to deceive Adam (21:3). In accordance with Genesis 3 God curses the serpent (not Satan) in ch. 26. Until the last judgment there will be enmity between him and Eve's offspring (see also 12:1). Humankind should beware of Satan as the archenemy (2:4; 7:2; 15:1; 25:4; 28:4).

Only at the end of days the archdeceiver will be removed from his throne, and this throne will then be given to Adam (39:2-3).

God's judgment and punishment are righteous, as is expressly underscored in ch. 27. But when God punishes Adam by refusing him access to the tree of life, he tells him: "But if you, after your departure from Paradise, guard yourself from all evil,[10] prepared (rather) to die (then to transgress), I shall raise you at the time of the resurrection. From the tree of life will be given to you and you will be immortal for ever" (28:3-4; cf. 13:3-5 in MSS ALCR, belonging to the second and third groups, only). In 37:5 this promise is confirmed when God grants Adam a glorious *post mortem* existence until the day of God's reckoning, when God will raise him with the entire human race descended from him (37:5).

The *Greek Life of Adam and Eve* is essentially a retelling of Genesis 3, making an attempt to get across the message of this part of the Scriptures, as perceived by its author(s). There is much interest in what happened, and what went wrong; the consequences of the transgression of the protoplasts, for themselves as well as for their offspring, are of great importance. The story does not end with the expulsion from Paradise, however; it tells what happened many years later when Adam and Eve had come to the end of their earthly life. The final section, chs. 31-43, spells out, in great variety of detail, how God, in his mercy, then granted heavenly bliss and eternal life to Adam (and also to Eve). After they had repented they had refrained from evil and led a good life, so much is clear.

The story as told here, is potentially meaningful for everyone who takes Genesis 3 seriously, whether Jew or Christian (see chapter 11, section 3). It has often been remarked that it seems to have nothing particularly Christian. There is no reference to the salvation brought by Jesus Christ. Nor is there, as we have seen in chapter 11, section 4, any trace of the recapitulation theory which Irenaeus developed.

On the other hand, the mention of the Acherusian Lake as the place where Adam is washed three times before being conducted to God's throne (37:3), does point to a Christian origin of this essential feature in the story told in chs. 33-37, and the expression ὁ πατὴρ τῶν φώτων used for God in 36:3 is an epithet only found in Christian

---

[10] Compare Eve's equally general closing admonition: "do not forsake the good" in 30:1.

sources. This is, at the very least, an indication of Christian redaction of the *GLAE*, already in its oldest form known to us.

If *GLAE* is not typically Christian, it is not typically Jewish either, and certainly not exclusively Jewish. Parallels with Jewish writings, including those with rabbinic sources, have been noted by many commentators. But those parallels do not necessarily point to Jewish provenance of the writing under discussion.[11] One has argued that the book is non-rabbinic; but this does not mean that it is pre-rabbinic (a rather vague term anyway)—and thus relatively early—or that it is Hellenistic Jewish. As we have seen, its paraenesis remains quite general: "do not forsake the good, refrain from evil (30:1; 28:4); it is too general to be used in the discussion of provenance at all.

We may add that there is also no clear link between the *Life of Adam and Eve* and the documents found near Qumran. In a paper for a recent congress devoted to the apocrypha and pseudepigrapha in light of the Dead Sea Scrolls, M.E. Stone has pointed out that there are many documents in the Qumran Library that try to explain the origin of evil and, consequently, the causes of the flood by the myths about Enoch, the Watchers, the giants etc. Adam apocrypha and legendary developments of the Adam stories in the Bible are strikingly absent from Qumran, while there are many works associated with the axis from Enoch to Noah.[12]

Reviewing all this, one has to conclude that there remains some uncertainty about the provenance of the *Life of Adam and Eve* in its earliest Greek form. However, the few indications we have suggest that it originated in Christian circles, and the burden of proof lies with those who want to defend Jewish provenance of the document, in its present or an earlier form. Given the complex nature of the writing, which incorporates many older traditions, individual parallels in other Jewish or Christian sources do not help us very much, unless, of course, we are able to discover common patterns, or parallels for determinative elements in *GLAE*, that point to a literary dependence one way or the other.

---

[11] On this see also Stone, *A History of the Life of Adam and Eve* (SBLEJL 3; Atlanta: Scholars, 1992), 56-61.

[12] See his "The Axis of History at Qumran," in E.G. Chazon, M.E. Stone, A. Pinnick (eds.), *Pseudepigraphic Perspectives: The Apocrypha and Pseudepigrapha in Light of the Dead Sea Scrolls* (STDJ 31; Leiden: Brill, 1999), 133-149. Compare also E.G. Chazon, "The Creation and Fall of Adam in the Dead Sea Scrolls," in *The Book of Genesis* (see n. 9), 13-23.

II. THE GREEK LIFE OF ADAM AND EVE
AND CHRISTIAN SOURCES OF THE FIRST CENTURY CE[13]

Parallels from the *Greek Life of Adam and Eve* have been connected with a number of passages of the New Testament, although not with very many. Most of the discussion has centered around the Pauline passages speaking about Adam (Rom. 5:12-21; 1 Cor. 15:21-22, 45-49).

The two passages about Eve, 2 Cor. 11:3 and 1 Tim. 2:13-14 have also drawn the attention of scholars. The first mentions her, not Adam, as the victim of deception by the serpent ("... the serpent deceived Eve by its cunning"), and the second elaborates this point: "For Adam was formed first, then Eve; and Adam was not deceived, but the woman was deceived and became a transgressor..." This has been connected with the prominence of Eve's part in the process of deception and transgression in *GLAE*. Yet there is little that could not have been derived from Genesis 3 independently—as is shown by a number of apparently unrelated further parallels. One may note Sir. 25:24, "From a woman sin had its beginning, and because of her we all die"; *Syr. Bar.* 48:42-43, "O, Adam, what was it that you did to all your posterity? And what should be said to Eve who first listened to the serpent?" and *Barn.* 12:5, "...for the transgression took place in Eve through the serpent."[14] Moreover, although *GLAE* mentions Eve's sins more often than that of Adam, both protoplasts are held responsible, and are punished and pardoned.

In support of the connection of 2 Cor. 11:3 with *GLAE* some scholars have pointed out that a little further on, in v. 14, Paul warns his readers that "even Satan disguises himself as an angel of light."[15] As a parallel they mention *GLAE* 17:1-2 where Eve in the garden,

---

[13] For the reasons given in the previous section, I shall concentrate on the Greek *Life* and not pay attention to passages in the Latin *Vita* figuring prominently in earlier studies of the subject (the Armenian and Georgian have not played any role so far).

[14] Compare Wis. 2:23-24 which ascribes the death of humankind, created for incorruption, to the envy of the devil (very probably a reference to Genesis 3), and Rev. 12:7 where the great dragon (who endangers the woman and her child) is referred to as "that ancient serpent, who is called Devil and Satan, the deceiver of the whole world."

[15] Compare *Vit. Ad.* 9:1, where Satan in his second (equally successful) attempt to seduce Eve, while she is doing penitence in the Tigris, changes into an angel. The Greek text of this passage, found in MSS R and M after *GLAE* 29:6, speaks here of λαβὼν σχῆμα ἀγγέλου (or: ἀγγελικόν). A reference to *Vit. Ad.* 9 in the margin at 2 Cor. 11:14 is the only one to any version of the *Life of Adam and Eve* found in Nestle-Aland[26/27].

sees Satan in the likeness of an angel; he has taken on the form of an angel in order to join in the daily worship of the angels. This report is awkwardly inserted into a context where Satan operates through the serpent. One should ask, however, whether this connection does not point to a common acquaintance with a particular tradition rather than to any form of literary dependence.[16]

Even less can be concluded from the reference in 2 Cor. 12:2-4 to Paradise in the third heaven. "A person in Christ" (Paul himself) was caught up there, "and heard things that are not to be told, that no mortal is permitted to repeat." In *GLAE* 37:5 (cf. 40:1) Adam is brought to Paradise in the third heaven to remain there until the last day.[17] The only other writing mentioning Paradise in the third heaven is *2 Enoch* (see chapters 8-9)—unfortunately a document with a very complex textual history and disputed origin and date. In view of the complexity of the situation it is certainly too simple to assume dependence of Paul on *GLAE* 37:5.[18]

Commentators disagree on the meaning of Rom. 3:23. Does the ὑστεροῦνται τῆς δόξης τοῦ θεοῦ refer to the glory of God that all human beings, sinners without any exception, will not attain, "fall short of" (so NRSV), or to the glory which they no longer possess and are now "deprived of" (REB)? Those who prefer the second option, or think that Paul may have at least alluded to the human situation before the Fall, often refer to *GLAE* 20:1-2; 21:5-6.[19]

As we have seen above, the state of the protoplasts before the Fall is (at the most) only hinted at in the passages concerned. *GLAE* does not seem to be interested in the subject; nor does it present a consistent picture of Adam's exalted state after his death or at the end of

---

[16] In *Did.* 16:4 the "deceiver of the world" appears as Son of God. K. Niederwimmer, *Die Didache* (Göttingen: Vandenhoeck & Ruprecht, 1989), 262, n.7 points to the parallel in the late *Apoc. Elijah* 3:16-18 (34:3-9), where the son of lawlessness will transform himself for all who see him; he will become a child and an old man. In *Test. Job* 6:4 Satan disguises himself as a beggar.

[17] In 35:2 Eve and Seth see *seven* heavens ("firmaments") opened. A scheme of seven heavens is the one found most frequently (see H. Traub, *TWNT* 5, 511-512) and M. Himmelfarb, *Ascent to Heaven in Jewish & Christian Apocalypses* (New York/Oxford: Oxford U.P., 1993), 32.

[18] Paul's account in 2 Corinthians 12 gave the cue for the composition of the Apocalypse of Paul; see J.K. Elliott, *The Apocryphal New Testament* (Oxford: Clarendon, 1993), 616-644. Here Paul sees "the places of the just" in the third heaven and meets Enoch and Elijah (chs. 19-20). One should note that *Ap. Paul* 22 mentions the Acherusian Lake (see also chapter 12).

[19] See e.g. Sharpe, "Second Adam" (see n. 2), 37-40.

days. Important is that Eve realizes that she has lost her righteousness (20:1), and that, consequently, she is estranged from her glory[20]—just as Adam sees that he is naked and has been estranged from the glory of God (21:5-6). In 21:2 the words that Eve (or rather the Satan through Eve) spoke to Adam at the occasion are qualified as "the words of transgression (παρανομία) that brought us down from great glory" (cf. 39:1). Transgression of God's commandment(s) leads to loss of righteousness and estrangement. In the Old Testament estrangement from God is often associated with apostasy and idolatry (e.g. Ez. 14:5, 7; Hos. 9:10). In Col. 1:21-22 those "estranged and hostile in mind, doing evil deeds" are said to have been "reconciled" (by Christ). In *GLAE* 31-45 another, similar word is used: συγχώρησις, forgiveness—see 33:5; 35:2; 37:6 (cf. 27:3). The angels appeal to God to forgive Adam, because he is his image and the work of his hands. God does have mercy for Adam, he stretches his hand out to Adam and has him brought to Paradise in the third heaven (37:4-6). All emphasis is on the severance and restoration of the relations between God and the human beings which he created.

GLAE 19:3 (just before 20:1) tells how the serpent puts "his poison of evil, that is of covetousness" on the fruit which he gives Eve to eat. Particularly the comment that follows in MSS ATLC (cf. B) ἐπιθυμία γὰρ ἐστι κεφαλὴ πασῆς ἁμαρτίας has drawn the attention of New Testament scholars. They have connected it with Jas 1:14-16 and with Rom. 7:7-12 where Paul seems to regard "covetousness" as the principal sin. A number of commentators suggest that Paul had here Adam and Eve in mind,[21] and that he may have been influenced by the picture given in *GLAE* 19:3. I doubt whether this can ever be proven convincingly, moreover because the reading in the manuscripts just mentioned is clearly secondary to that found in all other groups. So MSS S and V read ἐπιθυμία γὰρ ἐστι πασῆς ἁμαρτίας. This should be translated as "(this is) a longing for all sin"—an effort at explaining the juxtaposition of κακία and ἐπιθυμία in the preceding clause.[22] In that case there is no suggestion that "covetousness" would be the root of all evil.

---

[20] Only MSS ALCRM add here "with which I had been clothed," repeating the clause used with "righteousness" in the preceding verse.

[21] Compare the use of ἐξηπατήσεν in v. 11.

[22] In their commentary Merk and Meiser also prefer this reading (p. 830). Yet they translate: "Begierde ist Ursache der Sünde" and refer to Rom. 7:7.

The central element in Paul's view on Adam and Christ is cogent-
ly expressed in 1 Cor. 15:21-22: "For since death came through a human being, the resurrection of the dead has also come through a human being; for as all die in Adam, so all will be made alive in
Christ." This is elaborated in the much-discussed passage Rom 5:12-
21, which begins with: "Therefore, just as sin came into the world
through one man, and death came through sin, and so death spread to
all because all have sinned ..." in v. 12, and ends with v. 21 that
confronts the dominion of sin and death with that of grace through
righteousness leading to eternal life in Jesus Christ. Essential is the
idea of participation through incorporation. Grace and life are for all
who are "in Christ," just as all human beings share in sin and death
"in Adam."

Paul states that the bitter lot of humankind is due to the transgression of Adam. Eve is not mentioned here, but that is not surprising because Paul's argument centers around the antithetic parallel
between Christ and Adam. In *GLAE* the emphasis is on Eve's sin.
Adam reproaches Eve for having "brought upon us great wrath,
which is death ruling over all our race" (14:2; cf. 7:1; 9:2). She
herself acknowledges: "... all sin in creation has come about through
me" (32:2).[23] The sin of the protoplasts has its lasting effects on their
offspring; so much is clear in the *GLAE*, just as in Genesis 2-3 (see
2:17; 3:19), but the corporate nature of the bond between Eve, and
Adam, with humankind does not receive any special attention.

This becomes particularly clear when we examine the passages in
GLAE dealing with the future. Of course, Adam and Eve function as
prototype of all human beings, also when they receive forgiveness,
are exalted to heaven and share in the resurrection at the end of days.
The children of Adam and Eve will share in all this if they keep
God's commandments diligently, do not sin and repent if they have
sinned, but *not because of* Adam's repentance or obedience. One
should note the references to Adam's resurrection in 28:4; 37:5 and
41:3. Only the last one mentions Adam's offspring: "Now I promise
you the resurrection; I shall raise you in the resurrection with all
persons belonging to your seed." Adam's offspring will rise together
with him, not because of him.

---

[23] Compare Eve's complaint in 10:2: "Woe is me! For when I come to the day of the resurrection, all who have sinned will curse me, saying: 'Eve did not keep the command of God.'"

The *Greek Life of Adam and Eve* is concerned with Adam and Eve as much as with all human beings after them and like them. Paul is, strictly speaking, not interested in Adam himself; he speaks not about Adam's salvation, but about that of those children of Adam who believe in Christ and are united with Christ as the Last Adam. In his "The Second Adam in the Apocalypse of Moses" Sharpe has tried to demonstrate that in the *Life* the "sinful Adam" and the "exalted Adam" function similarly to the "First Adam" and the "Last Adam" in Paul's letters. According to him this is so because the apostle used the characteristics of the exalted eschatological Adam to describe the resurrected Christ. This theory is not only far-fetched, but also unconvincing in detail.[24]

CONCLUSION

The examination of the parallels between the writings of the New Testament and the *Greek Life of Adam and Eve* does not point to a direct relationship between any of these writings and *GLAE*, although (as might be expected) common or similar traditions have been used. This means that also the theory that *GLAE* should be dated in the first century CE cannot be substantiated.

For patterns and determinative elements common to *GLAE* and other Christian writings we shall have to look elsewhere. As I argued in chapter 11, a case can be made for dating *GLAE* at the end of the second century CE on the basis of a comparison with Theophilus of Antioch, Irenaeus and Tertullian. In *Ad Autolycum* 2. 20-28, for instance, Theophilus tries to show that God the Creator did not deal unfairly with Adam. He wanted to test him, to see whether he would be obedient to his command (2. 25). When God called Adam and said: "Where are you Adam?", it was because he was patient and gave him an occasion for repentance (2. 26). Without any special emphasis on the redemptive work of Christ, Theophilus teaches that by obedience to the will of God, whoever will can obtain eternal life for himself (2. 27). Irenaeus, in *Adv. Haer.* 3. 23, tries to show that there is certainly also forgiveness and salvation for Adam personally; in 3. 23. 8 he strongly attacks Tatian for denying this. And Tertullian, at

---

[24] For this see also A.M. Sweet, *A Religio-Historical Study of the Greek Life of Adam and Eve* (unpublished Ph.D. Dissertation, Notre Dame, 1992), 147-148.

the end of his *De Paenitentia* (12, 9), speaks of *stirpis humanae et offensae in Dominum princeps Adam* as one who is *exomologesi restitutus in paradisum suum.*

BIBLIOGRAPHY

Special Abbreviations

Charles, *APOT*	R.H. Charles, *The Apocrypha and Pseudepigrapha of the Old Testament* (2 vols.; Oxford: Clarendon, 1913).
Charlesworth, *OTP*	JH. Charlesworth (ed.), *The Old Testament Pseudepigrapha* (2 vols.; Garden City, New York: Doubleday, 1983 and 1985).
Collected Essays	M. de Jonge, *Jewish Eschatology, Early Christian Christology and the Testaments of the Twelve Patriarchs. Collected Essays of Marinus de Jonge* (ed. H.J. de Jonge; NovTSup 63, Leiden, (1991).
Commentary	H.W. Hollander and M. de Jonge, *The Testaments of the Twelve Patriarchs. A Commentary* (SVTP 8; Leiden: Brill, 1985).
Edition	M. de Jonge (in cooperation with H.W. Hollander, H.J. de Jonge, T. Korteweg), *The Testaments of the Twelve Patriarchs. A Critical Edition of the Greek Text* (PVTG 1,2; Leiden: Brill, 1978).
JSHRZ	Jüdische Schriften aus hellenistisch-römischer Zeit (Gütersloh: Gütersloher Verlagshau Gerd Mohn).
Kautzsch, *APAT*	E. Kautzsch, *Die Apokryphen and Pseudepigraphen des Alten Testaments* (2 vols.; Tübingen: Mohr, 1900).
Studies	M. de Jonge (ed.), *Studies on the Testaments of the Twelve Patriarchs* (SVTP 3; Leiden: Brill, 1975).

K. Aland and B. Aland, *Der Text des Neuen Testaments* (Stuttgart: Deutsche Bibelgesellschaft 1982; 2nd. ed. 1989)

C. Albeck (ed.), *Midrash Bereshit Rabbati* (Jerusalem, 1940).

M.C. Albl, *'And Scripture Cannot Be Broken'. The Form and Function of the Early Testimonia Collections* (NovTSup 96; Leiden: Brill, 1999).

G.A. Anderson, "The Original Form of the Life of Adam and Eve. A Proposal," in G.A. Anderson, M.E. Stone and J. Tromp (eds.), *Literature on Adam and Eve. Collected Essays,* (SVTP 15; Leiden: Brill, 2000) 215-31.

— and M.E. Stone, *A Synopsis of the Books of Adam and Eve* (SBLEJL 5; Atlanta: Scholars, 1994; second revised edition SBLEJL 17; 1999).

A. Aschim, Review of R.A. Kugler, *From Patriarch to Priest, JBL* 117 (1998) 353-355.

T. Baarda, "The Shechem Episode in the Testament of Levi: A Comparison with Other Traditions," in *Sacred History and Sacred Texts in Early Judaism. A Symposium in Honour of A.S. van der Woude* (ed. J.N. Bremmer and F. García Martínez; Kampen: Kok Pharos, 1992), 11-73.

M. Baillet,"[3Q]7.Un apocryphe mentionnant l'ange de la Présence," in M. Baillet, J.T. Milik and R. de Vaux, *Les "Petites Grottes" de Qumrân* (DJD 3; Oxford: Clarendon, 1962), 99.

—, "484. Testament de Juda (?)" in M. Baillet, *Qumrân Grotte 4.III. 4Q 482-4Q520* (DJD 7; Oxford: Clarendon, 1982),3.

J. Barton, *The Spirit and the Letter. Studies in the Biblical Canon* (London: SPCK, 1997).

P. Batiffol, "Le livre de la prière d'Aséneth," *Studia Patristica: Études d'ancienne littérature chrétienne* (Paris: Leroux, 1889-90), vols 1-2,1-160.

R. Bauckham, *Jude, 2 Peter* (WBC, 50; Waco TX: Word, 1983).

J. Becker, *Untersuchungen zur Entstehungsgeschichte der Testamente der Zwölf Patriarchen* (AGJU 8; Leiden: Brill, 1970).

—, *Die Testamente der Zwölf Patriarchen*, JSHRZ 3,1 (1974; second edition 1980), 16-163.

R.T. Beckwith, "Formation of the Hebrew Bible," in M.J. Mulder and H. Sysling (eds.), *Mikra. Text, Translation, Reading and Interpretation of the Hebrew Bible in Ancient Judaism and Early Christianity* (CRINT, 2,1; Assen-Maastricht: Van Gorcum/Philadelphia: Fortress, 1988), 39-86.

G. Beer, "Das Martyrium des Propheten Jesaja," in Kautzsch, *APAT* 2, 119-127.

J. Bentivegna, "A Christianity without Christ by Theophilus of Antioch," in E.A. Livingstone (ed.), *Studia Patristica*, vol. 13 (TU 116; Berlin: Akademie-Verlag, 1975).

T.A. Bergren, *Fifth Ezra: The Text, Origin and Early History* (SBLSCS 25; Atlanta: Scholars, 1990).

—, "Christian Influence on the Transmission History of 4, 5 and 6 Ezra," in J.C. VanderKam and W. Adler (eds.), *The Jewish Apocalyptic Heritage in Early Christianity* (CRINT 3,4; Assen: Van Gorcum/Minneapolis:Fortress,1996), 102-127

—, *Sixth Ezra: The Text and Origin* (New York/Oxford: Oxford U.P., 1998).

A.E. Bernstein, *The Formation of Hell: Death and Retribution in the Ancient and Early Christian Worlds* (Ithaca: Cornell Univ. Press, 1993).

M.J. Bernstein, "Pseudepigraphy in the Qumran Scrolls: Categories and Functions," in E.G. Chazon, M.E. Stone, A. Pinnick (eds.), *Pseudepigraphic Perspectives. The Apocrypha and Pseudepigrapha in Light of the Dead Sea Scrolls* (STDJ 31: Leiden, Brill, 1999), 1-26.

D.A Bertrand, *La vie grecque d'Adam et Ève* (Recherches Intertestamentaires 1; Paris: Maisonneuve, 1987).

P. Bettiolo, A. Giambelluca Kossova, C. Leonardi, E. Norelli, L. Perrone, *Ascensio Isaiae. Textus. Commentarius* (2 vols.; Turnhout: Brepols, 1995).

K. Beyer, *Die aramäischen Texte vom Toten Meer* (Göttingen: Vandenhoeck & Ruprecht, 1984).

—, *Die aramäischen Texte vom Toten Meer. Ergänzungsband* (Göttingen: Vandenhoeck & Ruprecht, 1994).

G. Bohak, *Joseph and Aseneth and the Jewish Temple in Heliopolis* (SBLEJL 10; Atlanta: Scholars, 1996).

F. Bolgiani, art. "Tatian," *Encyclopedia of the Early Church* (Cambridge: Clarke, 1992), vol.2, 815.

W. Bousset, "Die Testamente der XII Patriarchen, 1. Die Ausscheidung der christlichen Interpolationen," *ZNW* 1 (1900), 141-175.

E. Brandenburger, *Adam und Christus. Exegetisch-religionsgeschichtliche Untersuchungen zu Römer 5, 12-21 (1 Kor. 15)* (WMANT 7, Neukirchen: Neukirchener Verlag, 1962).

M. Braun, *History and Romance in Graeco-Oriental Literature* (Oxford: Blackwell, 1938).

S.P. Brock, Review of J.H. Charlesworth, *The Old Testament Pseudepigrapha*, *JJS* 35 (1984), 200-209 and 38 (1987), 107-114.

G.J. Brooke, "4Q Testament of Levi[d](?) and the Messianic Servant High Priest," in M.C. de Boer (ed.), *From Jesus to John. Essays on Jesus and New Testament Christology in Honour of Marinus de Jonge* (JSNTSup 84; Sheffield: Sheffield Academic Press, 1993), 83-110.

D.D. Buchholz, *Your Eyes Will Be Opened. A Study of the Greek (Ethiopic) Apocalypse of Peter* (SBLDS 97; Atlanta: Scholars, 1988).

C. Burchard, *Untersuchungen zu Joseph und Aseneth. Überlieferung—Ortsbestimmung* (WUNT 8; Tübingen: Mohr [Siebeck], 1965).

—, "Zur armenischen Überlieferung der Testamente der zwölf Patriarchen" in C. Burchard, J. Jervell and J. Thomas, *Studien zu den Testamenten der Zwölf Patriarchen* (BZNW 36; Berlin: Töpelmann, 1969), 1-29.

—, *Joseph und Aseneth*, JSHRZ 2,4 (1983), 575-735.

—,"Joseph and Aseneth," in Charlesworth, *OTP* 2, 177-247.

—, "Der jüdische Asenethroman und seine Nachwirkung. Von Egeria zu Anna Katharina Emmerick oder von Moses aus Aggel zu Karl Kerényi," in W. Haase (ed.), *Aufstieg und Niedergang der römischen Welt* II. 20. 1 (Berlin-New York: De Gruyter, 1987), 658-667, updated in *Gesammelte Studien*, xix-xxiii, 321-436.

—, *Gesammelte Studien zu Joseph and Aseneth* (SVTP 13; Leiden: Brill, 1996).

—, "Zum Stand der Arbeit am Text von Joseph und Aseneth," in M. Becker and W. Fenske (eds.), *Das Ende der Tage und die Gegenwart des Heils* (FS H.-W. Kuhn; AGAJU 44; Leiden: Brill, 1999), 1-28.

—, "Character and Origin of the Armenian Version of *Joseph and Aseneth*," in V. Calzolari Bouvier, J.-D. Kaestli and B. Outtier (eds.), *Apocryphes arméniens: transmission-traduction-création-iconographie* (Publications de l'Institut romand des sciences bibliques 1; Lausanne: Éditions du Zèbre, 1999),73-90.

— (ed.), *Joseph und Aseneth kritisch herausgegeben* (PVTG 5; Leiden: Brill, 2003).

—, "The Text of *Joseph and Aseneth* Reconsidered" (forthcoming in *JSP* 2003).

H. von Campenhausen, *Die Entstehung der christlichen Bibel* (BHT 39; Tübingen: Mohr [Siebeck], 1968).

A. Caquot, "Les testaments qoumrâniens des pères de sacerdoce," *RHPR* 78/2 (1998), 3-26.

C. Carozzi, *Eschatologie et au-delà: Recherches sur l'*Apocalypse de Paul (Aix-en-Provence: Université de Provence, 1994.

R.H. Charles, *The Ascension of Isaiah* (London: A. and C. Black, 1900)

—, *The Greek Versions of the Twelve Patriarchs* (Oxford: Clarendon, 1908).

—, *The Testaments of the Twelve Patriarchs Translated from the Editor's Greek Text* (London: A. and C. Black, 1908).

—, *The Apocrypha and Pseudepigrapha of the Old Testament* (2 vols.; Oxford: Clarendon, 1913).

—, "The Martyrdom of Isaiah," in Charles, *APOT* 2, 155-162.

P. Chantraine, *Dictionnaire étymologique de la langue grecque. Histoire des mots* (Paris: Editions Klincksieck, 1968), 4 vols.

J.H. Charlesworth, *The Pseudepigrapha and Modern Research* (SBLSCS 7; Missoula MT: Scholars, 1976; second expanded edition 1981).

—, "Christian and Jewish Self-Definition in Light of the Christian Additions to the Apocryphal Writings," in E.P. Sanders, A.I. Baumgarten and A. Mendelson (eds.), *Jewish and Christian Self-Definition, vol 2. Aspects of Judaism in the Graeco-Roman Period* (London: SCM, 1981), 27-55.

— (ed.), *The Old Testament Pseudepigrapha* (2 vols.; Garden City, New York: Doubleday, 1983 and 1985).

—, *The Old Testament Pseudepigrapha and the New Testament* (SNTSMS 54; Cambridge: Cambridge UP, 1985; new edition with new preface [pp. vii-xxiv], Harrisburg:Trinity International, 1998).

—, "Pseudepigrapha of the Old Testament," *Anchor Bible Dictionary* (New York: Doubleday, 1992), 5, 537-540.

—, "In the Crucible. The Pseudepigrapha as Biblical Interpretation," in J.H. Charlesworth & C.A. Evans (eds.),*The Pseudepigrapha and Early Biblical Interpretation* (JSPSup 14; Sheffield: Sheffield Academic Press, 1993), 20-43.

E.G. Chazon, "The Creation and Fall of Adam in the Dead Sea Scrolls," in J. Frishman and L. Van Rompay (eds.), *The Book of Genesis in Jewish and Oriental Christian Interpretation* (Traditio exegetica graeca 5; Leuven: Peeters, 1997), 13-23.

R.D. Chesnutt, *From Death to Life: Conversion in Joseph and Aseneth* (JSPSup 16; Sheffield: Sheffield Academic Press, 1995).

J.J. Collins, "Sibylline Oracles," in Charlesworth, *APOT* 1, 317-472.

—, *Between Athens and Jerusalem. Jewish Identity in the Hellenistic Diaspora* (New York: Crossroad, 1983; revised edition: Grand Rapids: Eerdmans, 2000).

F.C. Conybeare, "On the Jewish Authorship of the Testaments of the Twelve Patriarchs," *JQR* 5 (1893), 375-398.

D. Cook, "Joseph and Aseneth," in *The Apocryphal Old Testament* (ed. H.F.D. Sparks), 465-503.

C.H. Cosgrove, "Justin Martyr and the Emerging Christian Canon. Observations on the Purpose and Destination of the Dialogue with Trypho," *VC* 36 (1982), 209-232.

B. Dehandschutter, "Pseudo-Cyprian, Jude and Enoch. Some notes on 1 Enoch 1:9," in J.W. van Henten *et al.* (eds.), *Tradition and Re-interpretation in Jewish and Early Christian Literature* (FS J.C.H. Lebram; SPB 36; Leiden: Brill, 1986), 114-120.

G. Delling, "Die Bedeutung 'Gott des Friedens' und ähnliche Wendungen in den Paulusbriefen," in E.E. Ellis and E. Grässer (eds.), *Jesus und Paulus. Festschrift für W.G. Kümmel zum 70. Geburtstag* (Göttingen: Vandenhoeck & Ruprecht, 1975), 76-84.

A.-M. Denis, *Fragmenta pseudepigraphorum quae supersunt graeca* (PVTG 3; Leiden: Brill, 1970).

—, *Introduction aux pseudépigraphes grecs d'Ancien Testament* (SVTP 1: Leiden: Brill, 1970).

—, *Concordance grecque des pseudépigraphes d'Ancien Testament* (Louvain-la-Neuve: Institut Orientaliste, 1987)

—, *Concordance latine des pseudépigraphes d'Ancien Testament* (Turnhout: Brepols, 1993).

— (et collaborateurs, avec le concours de J.-C. Haelewyck), *Introduction à la littérature religieuse judéo-hellénistique* (2 vols.; Turnhout: Brepols, 2000).

A. Díez Macho *et al.* (eds.), *Apócrifos del Antiguo Testamento* (5 vols.; Madrid: Ediciones Cristianidad, 1983-1987).

E. von Dobschütz, *Die Thessalonicher-Briefe* (MeyerK; Göttingen: Vandenhoeck & Ruprecht, [7]1909; repr. with add. 1974).

H. Duensing and A. Aurelio de Santos Otero, "Apokalypse des Paulus," *Neutestamentliche Apokryphen* (ed. E. Hennecke and W. Schneemelcher; Mohr [Siebeck] 1989), 2, 644-75.

J.D.G. Dunn, *The Theology of Paul the Apostle* (Grand Rapids—Cambridge: Eerdmans/ Edinburgh: T. & T. Clark, 1998).

A. Dupont-Sommer, "Le Testament de Lévi (XVII-XVIII) et la secte juive de l'Alliance," *Sem* 4 (1952), 33-53.

—, *Nouveaux aperçus sur les manuscrits de la Mer Morte* (Paris: Adrien-Maisonneuve, 1953).

— and M. Philonenko (eds), *La Bible. Écrits Intertestamentaires* (Bibliothèque de la Pléiade 337; Paris: Gallimard, 1987).

R.H. Eisenman and M. Wise, *The Dead Sea Scrolls Uncovered* (Shaftesbury: Element, 1992).

M. Eldridge, *Dying Adam with his Multiethnic Family. Understanding the* Greek Life of Adam and Eve (SVTP 16; Leiden: Brill, 2001).

T. Elgvin, "4Q474—A Joseph Apocryphon?" *RevQ* no 69, vol. 18 (1997), 97-107.

J.K. Elliott, "The Apocalypse of Peter," *The Apocryphal New Testament* (Oxford: Clarendon, 1993), 593-615.

—, "The Apocalypse of Paul (Visio Pauli)," *The Apocryphal New Testament* (Oxford: Clarendon, 1993), 616-644.

E.E. Ellis, "The Old Testament Canon in the Early Church," in M.J. Mulder and H. Sysling (eds.), *Mikra. Text, Translation, Reading and Interpretation of the Hebrew Bible in ancient Judaism and Early Christianity* (CRINT, 2,1; Assen-Maastricht: Van Gorcum/Philadelphia: Fortress, 1988). 653-690.

E. Evans, *Tertullian Adversus Marcionem* (2 vols.; Oxford: Clarendon, 1972.

J.A. Fabricius, *Codex apocryphus Novi Testamenti* (Hamburg, 1703; second edition 1719).

—, *Codex Pseudepigraphus Veteris Testamenti* (2 vols.: Hamburg, 1713; second edition 1722-1723).

G. Favrelle and É. des Places, *Eusèbe de Césarée, La préparation évangélique. Livre XI* (SC 292; Paris: Cerf, 1982).

Peter W. Flint, "'Apocrypha', Other Previously-Known Writings, and 'Pseudepigrapha' in the Dead Sea Scrolls," in P.W. Flint and J.C. VanderKam (eds.), *The Dead Sea Scrolls after Fifty Years. A Comprehensive Assessment* (Leiden: Brill, 1999), vol. 2, 24-66.

D. Frede, "Der Mythos vom Schicksal der Seelen nach dem Tod," *Platons 'Phaidon'* (Darmstadt: Wissenschaftliche Buchgesellschaft, 1999), 152-67.

P. Fredricksen, "Beyond the Body/Soul Dichotomy: Augustine's Answer to Mani, Plotinus, and Julian," in W.S. Babcock (ed.), *Paul and the Legacies of Paul* (Dallas: Southern Methodist University Press, 1990), 227-50.

H. Frisk, *Griechisches etymologisches Wörterbuch* (Heidelberg: Carl Winter Universitätsverlag, 1960), 2 vols.

V.P. Furnish, *II Corinthians* (AB 32A; Garden City, New York: Doubleday, 1984).

J.G. Gager, *Moses in Greco-Roman Paganism* (SBLMS 16; Nashville-New York: Abingdon, 1972).

F. García Martínez, "Estudios Qumránicos 1975-1985: Panorama Crítico (III)," *EstBib* 46 (1988), 325-374.

— and E.J.C. Tigchelaar, *The Dead Sea Scrolls Study Edition* (2 vols.; Leiden: Brill, 1997-1998).

— and A.S. van der Woude, *De rollen van de Dode Zee* (2 vols.; Kampen: Kok, 1994-1995).

M. Gaster, "The Hebrew Text of one of the Testaments of the Twelve Patriarchs," *Proceedings of the Society of Biblical Archaeology* 16 (1893-1894), 33-49, 109-117.

H.E. Gaylord, "3 (Greek Apocalypse of) Baruch," in Charlesworth, *OTP* 1, 653-679.

J.E. Grabe, *Spicilegium SS. Patrum et ut Haereticorum I*, Oxoniae, 1698.

R.M. Grant, *Theophilus of Antioch, Ad Autolycum* (Oxford: Clarendon, 1970).

—, *Greek Apologists of the Second Century* (Philadelphia: Westminster / London: S.C.M., 1988).

P. Green, "On the Thanatos Trail," in *Classical Bearings: Interpreting Ancient History and Culture* (London: Thames and Hudson, 1989), 63-76.

J.C. Greenfield and M.E. Stone, "Remarks on the Aramaic Testament of Levi from the Genizah," *RB* 86 (1979), 214-230.

—, Appendix III, "The Aramaic and Greek fragments of a Levi Document," in Hollander and de Jonge, *Commentary*, 457-469.

—, "Two Notes on the Aramaic Levi Document," in H.W. Attridge   *et al.* (eds.), *Of Scribes and Scrolls. Studies on the Hebrew Bible, Intertestamental Judaism and Christian Origins presented to John Strugnell* (Lanham: University Press of America, 1990), 153-161.

—, "The Prayer of Levi," *JBL* 112 (1993) 247-266.

—, "The First Manuscript of *Aramaic Levi Document* from Qumran," *Le Muséon* 107 (1994), 257-281.

—, "Aramaic Levi Document," in G.J. Brooke *et al.* (eds.), *Qumran Cave 4. XVII. Parabiblical Texts, Part 3* (DJD 22; Oxford: Clarendon, 1996), 1-72.

P. Grelot, "Notes sur le Testament de Lévi," *RB* 86 (1956), 391-406.

G.M.A. Grube, *Plato's Phaedo* (Indianapolis: Hackett, 1977).

P. Habermehl, "Klassische Zeit" in C. Colpe, E. Dassmann, J. Engemann, P. Habermehl, and K. Hoheisel, "Jenseits (Jenseitsvorstellungen)," *RAC* 17 (1996), 246-407, esp. 278-82.

J.-C. Haelewyck, *Clavis Apocryphorum Veteris Testamenti* (Corpus Christianorum; Turnhout: Brepols, 1998).

R.G. Hall, "*The Ascension of Isaiah*: Community, Situation, Date and Place in Early Christianity," *JBL* 109 (1990), 289-306.

E. Hammershaimb,"Das Martyrium Jesajas," JSHRZ 2,1 (1973),15-34.

D.R.A. Hare, "The Lives of the Prophets," in Charlesworth, *APOT* 2, 379-399.

D.C. Harlow, *The* Greek Apocalypse of Baruch (3 Baruch) *in Hellenistic Judaism and Early Christianity* (SVTP 12; Leiden: Brill, 1996).

—, "The Christianization of Early Jewish Pseudepigrapha: The Case of *3 Baruch*," *JSJ* 32 (2001), 416-444.

A. von Harnack, *Marcion. Das Evangelium vom fremden Gott* (Leipzig: Hinrichs [2]1924; repr. [together with *Neue Studien zu Marcion*], Darmstadt: Wissenschaftliche Buchgesellschaft, 1960).

B. Heininger, "Totenerweckung oder Weckruf *(Par. Jer.* 7, 12-20)? Gnostische Spurensuche in den Paralipomena Jeremiae," *SNTSU* A 23 (1998), 79-112.

W.A. van Hengel, "De Testamenten der Twaalf Patriarchen opnieuw ter sprake gebracht," *Godgeleerde Bijdragen* 34 (1860), 881-970.

J.W. van Henten and B. Schaller, "Christianization of Ancient Jewish Writings," *JSJ* 32 (2001), 369-370.

J. Herzer, *Die Paralipomena Jeremiae: Studien zur Tradition und Redaktion einer Haggada des frühen Judentums* (TSAJ 43; Tübingen: Mohr [Siebeck], 1994).

—, "Paralipomena Jeremiae—eine christlich-gnostische Schrift? *JSJ* 30 (1999), 25-39.

—, "Direction in Difficult Times: How God is Understood in the *Paralipomena Jeremiae*," *JSP* 22 (2000), 9-30.

M. Himmelfarb, "R. Moses the Preacher and the Testaments of the Twelve Patriarchs," *AJS Review* 9 (1984), 55-78.

—, *Ascent to Heaven in Jewish & Christian Apocalypses* (New York/Oxford: Oxford U.P., 1993)

R.F. Hock, "Lazarus and Micyllus: Greco-Roman Background to Luke 16:19-31," *JBL* 106 (1987), 447-63.

H.W. Hollander, *Joseph as an Ethical Model in the Testaments of the Twelve Patriarchs* (SVTP 6, Leiden: Brill, 1981).

—, "Israel and God's Eschatological Agent in the Testaments of the Twelve Patriarchs" in P.W. van der Horst (ed.), *Aspects of Religious Contact and Conflict in the Ancient World* (Utrechtse Theologische Reeks 31; Utrecht: Faculteit de Godgeleerheid, 1995), 91-104.

—, "The Portrayal of Joseph in Hellenistic, Jewish and Early Christian Literature," in M.E. Stone and T.A. Bergren (eds.), *Biblical Figures outside the Bible* (Harrisburg, Pa: Trinity Press International, 1998), 237-263.

— and M. de Jonge, *The Testaments of the Twelve Patriarchs. A Commentary* (SVTP 8; Leiden: Brill, 1985).

T. Holtz, "Christliche Interpolationen in "Joseph und Asenath," *NTS* 14 (1967-8), 482-497, also in T. Holtz, *Geschichte und Theologie des Urchristentums. Gesammelte Aufsätze* (eds. E. Reinmuth and C. Wolf; Tübingen: Mohr (Siebeck), 1991), 55-71.

P.W. van der Horst, *Die Prophetengräber im antiken Judentum* (Franz-Delitzsch-Vorlesung 2000; Münster: Institutum Judaicum Delitzschianum, 2001).

—,"The Tombs of the Prophets in Early Judaism" in his *Japheth in the Tents of Shem. Studies on Jewish Hellenism in Antiquity* (Leuven: Peeters, 2002), 119-138.

A. Hultgård, *L'eschatologie des Testaments des Douze Patriarches.* Vol. 1 *Interprétation des textes*; vol. 2 *Compostion de l'ouvrage, textes et traductions* (Acta Universitatis Upsalienses: Historia Religionum 6 and 7, Uppsala 1977 and 1982)

E.M. Humphrey, *Joseph and Aseneth* (Guides to Apocrypha and Pseudepigrapha; Sheffield: Sheffield Academic Press, 2000).

J.W. Hunkin, "The Testaments of the Twelve Patriarchs," *JTS* 16 (1915), 80-95.

M.R. James, *The Apocryphal New Testament* (Oxford: Clarendon, 1924).

—, "The Rainer fragment of the Apocalypse of Peter," *JTS* 32 (1931), 270-9.

J. Jeremias, *Heiligengräber in Jesu Umwelt (Mt 23,29; Lk 11,47). Eine Untersuchung zur Volksreligion der Zeit Jesu* (Göttingen: Vandenhoeck & Ruprecht, 1958)

J. Jervell, *Imago Dei. Gen. 1, 26f. im Spätjudentum, in der Gnosis und in den paulinischen Briefen* (FRLANT N.F. 58; Göttingen: Vandenhoeck & Ruprecht, 1960).

—, "Ein Interpolator interpretiert. Zu der christlichen Bearbeitung der Testamente der Zwölf Patriarchen," in C. Burchard, J. Jervell and J. Thomas, *Studien zu den Testamenten der Zwölf Patriarchen* (BZNW 36; Berlin: Töpelmann, 1969), 30-61.

M.D. Johnson, "Life of Adam and Eve," in Charlesworth, *APOT* 2, 249-29.

H.J. de Jonge, "Les fragments marginaux dans le MS. *d* des Testaments des XII Patriarches," *JSJ* 2 (1971), 19-28, reprinted in *Studies*, 87-96

—, "Die Textüberlieferung der Testamente der zwölf Patriarchen," *ZNW* 63 (1972), 27-44, reprinted in *Studies*, 45-62.

—, "La bibliothèque de Michel Choniatès et la tradition occidentale des Testaments des XII Patriarches," *Nederlands Archief voor Kerkgeschiedenis* 53 (1973), 171-180, reprinted in *Studies*, 97-106.

—, "Die Patriarchentestamente von Roger Bacon bis Richard Simon (mit einem Namenregister)," *Studies*, 3-42.

—, "Die Textüberlieferung der Testamente der Zwölf Patriarchen," *Studies* 45-62.

—, "The Earliest Traceable Stage of the Textual Tradition of the Testaments of the Twelve Patriarchs," *Studies,* 63-86.

—, "Additional notes on the history of MSS. Venice Bibl. Marc. Gr. 494 (*k*) and Cambridge Univ. Libr. Ff. 1.24 (*b*)," *Studies*, 107-115.

M. de Jonge, *The Testaments of the Twelve Patriarchs. A Study of their Text, Compostion and Origin* (Assen: Van Gorcum, 1953; second edition 1975).

—, "Christian Influence in the Testaments of the Twelve Patriarchs," *NovT* 4 (1960), 182-235, reprinted in *Studies*, 193-246.

—, "Christelijke elementen in de Vitae Prophetarum," *Nederlands Theologisch Tijdschrift* 16 (1961-1962), 161-178.

—, *Testamenta XII Patriarcharum edited according to Cambridge University Library MS Ff. 1.24, fol. 203a-261b with short notes* (PVTG 1; Leiden: Brill, 1964; second revised edition 1970).

—, "Notes on Testament of Levi II-VII," in M.S.H.G. Heerma van Voss *et al.* (eds.), *Travels in the World of the Old Testament* (Studies presented to Professor M.A. Beek; Assen, Van Gorcum, 1974), 132-145, reprinted in *Studies*, 247-260.

— (ed.), *Studies on the Testaments of the Twelve Patriarchs* (SVTP 3; Leiden: Brill, 1975).

—, "The Greek Testaments of the Twelve Patriarchs and the Armenian Version," *Studies*, 120-139.

—, "Textual Criticism and the Analysis of the Composition of the Testament of Zebulun," *Studies*, 144-160.

—, "The Interpretation of the Testaments of the Twelve Patriarchs in Recent Years,"   *Studies*, 183-192

—, "Testament Issachar als 'typisches' Testament," *Studies*, 290-316.

— (in cooperation with H.W. Hollander, H.J. de Jonge, T. Korteweg), *The Testaments of the Twelve Patriarchs. A Critical Edition of the Greek Text* (PVTG 1,2; Leiden: Brill, 1978)

—, Review of H.D. Slingerland, *The Testaments of the Twelve Patriarchs: A Critical History of Research, JSJ* 9 (1978), 108-111.

—, Review of A. Hultgård, *L'eschatologie des Testaments des Douze Patriarches* vol. 1, *JSJ* 10 (1979), 100-102.

—,"The Main Issues in the Study of the Twelve Patriarchs," *NTS* 26 (1980), 508-524, reprinted in *Collected Essays*, 147-163.

—, "Levi, the sons of Levi and the Law in *Testament Levi* X, XIV-XV and XVI," in J. Doré *et al.* (eds.), *De la Tôrah au Messie. Mélanges H. Cazelles* (Paris-Tournai: Desclée & Cie, 1981), 513-523, reprinted in *Collected Essays*, 180-190.

—, Review of A. Hultgård, *L'eschatologie des Testaments des Douze Patriarches* vol. 2, *JSJ* 14 (1983), 70-80.

—, "The Testaments of the Twelve Patriarchs: Christian and Jewish. A Hundred Years after Friedrich Schnapp," *Nederlands Theologisch Tijdschrift* 39 (1985), 265-275, reprinted in *Collected Essays*, 233-243.

—, "Hippolytus' 'Benedictions of Isaac, Jacob and Moses' and the Testaments of the Twelve Patriarchs," *Bijdragen* 46 (1985), 245-260, reprinted in *Collected Essays*, 204-219.

—, "Two Interesting Interpretations of the Rending of the Temple-veil in the Testaments of the Twelve Patriarchs," *Bijdragen* 46 (1985), 350-362, reprinted in *Collected Essays*, 220-232.

—, "The Pre-Mosaic Servants of God in the Testaments of the Twelve Patriarchs and in the writings of Justin and Irenaeus," *VC* 39 (1985), 157-170, reprinted in *Collected Essays*, 263-276.

—, "Two Messiahs in the Testaments of the Twelve Patriarchs?" in J.W. van Henten, H.J. de Jonge *et al.* (eds.), *Tradition and Re-Interpretation in Jewish and Early Christian Literature* (FS J.C.H. Lebram; SPB 36; Leiden: Brill, 1986), 150-162, reprinted in *Collected Essays*, 191-203.

—, "The Future of Israel in the Testaments of the Twelve Patriarchs," *JSJ* 17 (1986), 196-211, reprinted in *Collected Essays*, 164-179.

—, "The Testaments of the Twelve Patriarchs: Central Problems and Essential Viewpoints," in W. Haase (ed.), *Aufstieg und Niedergang der römischen Welt* II. 20. 1 (Berlin-New York: De Gruyter, 1987), 359-420.

—, "The Testament of Levi and 'Aramaic Levi'," in F. García Martínez and E Puech (eds.), *Mémorial Jean Carmignac, RevQ* 49-52; vol. 13 (1988), 367-385; reprinted in *Collected Essays,* 244-262.

—, "Die Paränese in den Schriften des Neuen Testaments und in den Testamenten der Zwölf Patriarchen. Einige Überlegungen," in H. Merklein (ed.), *Neues Testament und Ethik. Für Rudolf Schnackenburg* (Freiburg-Basel-Wien: Herder, 1989), 538-550, reprinted in *Collected Essays*, 277-289.

—, "Test. Benjamin 3:8 and the Picture of Joseph as 'A Good and Holy Man,'" in J. W. van Henten (ed.), *Die Entstehung der jüdischen Martyrologie* (SPB 38; Leiden: Brill, 1989), 204-214, reprinted in *Collected Essays*, 290-300.

—, "Rachel's Virtuous Behavior in the Testament of Issachar," in D. Balch *et alii* (eds.), *Greeks, Romans and Christians. Essays in Honor of A. J. Malherbe* (Minneapolis: Fortress and Augsburg , 1990), 340-352, reprinted in *Collected Essays,* 301-333.

—, *Jewish Eschatology, Early Christian Christology and the Testaments of the Twelve Patriarchs. Collected Essays of Marinus de Jonge* (ed. H.J. de Jonge; NovTSup 63, Leiden: Brill, 1991).

—, *Jesus, The Servant-Messiah* (New Haven: Yale University Press, 1991), 34-37.

—, "Robert Grosseteste and the Testaments of the Twelve Patriarchs," *JTS* N.S. 42 (1991), 115-125.

—, Review of J.H. Ulrichsen, *Die Grundschrift der Testamente der Zwölf Patriarchen, JSJ* 23 (1992), 295-302.

—, "The Transmission of the Testaments of the Twelve Patriarchs by Christians," *VC* 47 (1993), 1-28.

—, "Light on Paul from the Testaments of the Twelve Patriarchs?" in L.M. White and O.L. Yarbrough (eds.), *The Social World of the First Christians. Essays in Honor of Wayne A. Meeks* (Minneapolis, Fortress Press, 1995), 100-115.

—, "The so-called Pseudepigrapha of the Old Testament and Early Christianity," in P. Borgen and S. Giversen (eds.), *The New Testament and Hellenistic Judaism* (Aarhus: Aarhus University Press, 1995; reprint: Peabody, Mass.: Hendrickson, 1997), 59-71.

— and J. Tromp, "Jacob's Son Levi in the Pseudepigrapha of the Old Testament and Related Literature," in T.A. Bergren and M.E. Stone (eds.), *Biblical Figures Outside the Bible* (Minneapolis: Fortress, 1997), 203-236.

— and J. Tromp, *The Life of Adam and Eve and Related Literature* (Guides to Apocrypha and Pseudepigrapha; Sheffield: Sheffield Academic Press, 1997).

—, "Levi in Aramaic Levi and in the Testament of Levi," in E.G. Chazon, M.E. Stone and A. Pinnick (eds.), *Pseudepigraphic Perspectives: The Apocrypha & Pseudepigrapha in Light of the Dead Sea Scrolls. Proceedings of the International Symposium of the Orion Center for the Study of the Dead Sea Scrolls and Related Literature* (STDJ 31; Leiden: Brill, 1999), 71-89.

—, "The Testaments of the Twelve Patriarchs and related Qumran Fragments," in R.A. Argall, B.A. Bow, Rodney A.Werline (eds.), *For a Later Generation. The Transformation of Tradition in Israel, Early Judaism and Early Christianity* (Festschrift for G.W.E. Nickelsburg; Harrisburg, Pa.: Trinity Press International, 2000), 63-77.

—, "Remarks in the Margin of the Paper 'The Figure of Jeremiah in the *Paralipomena Jeremiae*,' by J. Riaud," *JSP* 22 (2000), 45-49.

—, "The Literary Development of the *Life of Adam and Eve*," in G.A. Anderson, M.E. Stone and J. Tromp (eds.), *Literature on Adam and Eve. Collected Essays* (SVTP 15; Leiden: Brill, 2000), 239-249.

—, "The Christian Origin of the *Greek Life of Adam and Eve*," in G.A. Anderson, M.E. Stone and J. Tromp (eds.), *Literature on Adam and Eve. Collected Essays* (SVTP 15; Leiden: Brill, 2000), 347-363.

—,"The Greek Life of Adam and Eve and the Writings of the New Testament," in A. von Dobbeler, K. Erlemann, R. Heiligenthal (eds.), *Religionsgeschichte des Neuen Testaments. Festschrift für Klaus Berger zum 60. Geburtstag* (Tübingen /Basel: Francke, 2000), 149-160.

—, "Testamentenliteratur," *TRE* 33 (2001), 110-113.

—, "The Two Great Commandments in the Testaments of the Twelve Patriarchs," *NovT* 44 (2002), 371-392.

—, "The Authority of the 'Old Testament' in the Early Church: The Witness of the 'Pseudepigrapha of the Old Testament,'" in J.-M. Auwers and H.J. de Jonge (eds.), *The Biblical Canons* (BETL 163; Leuven, Peeters, 2003), 457-484.

— and L.M. White, "The Washing of Adam in the Acherusian Lake (Gr. *Life of Adam and Eve* 37:3) in the Context of Early Christian Notions of the Afterlife," in J.T. Fitzgerald, T.H. Olbricht and L.M. White (eds.), *Early Christianity and Classical Culture: Comparative Studies* (NovTSup; Leiden: Brill, 2003), forthcoming.

E. Junod, "Les attitudes d'Apellès, disciple de Marcion à l'égard de l'Ancien Testament," *Augustinianum* 22 (1982), 113-133.

J.-D. Kaestli and P. Chérix, *L'Évangile de Barthélemy d'après deux écrits apocryphes* (Turnhout: Brepols, 1993).

E. Käsemann, *An die Römer* (HNT 8a; Tübingen: Mohr [Siebeck], 1973).

J.J.A. Kahmann and B. Dehandschutter, *De Tweede Brief van Petrus en de Brief van Judas* (Boxtel: KBS, 1983).

E. Kautzsch, *Die Apokryphen and Pseudepigraphen des Alten Testaments* (2 vols.; Tübingen: Mohr, 1900).

—, "Das Testament Naphtalis aus der hebräischen Chronik Jerachmeels," in Kautzsch, *APAT* 2, 489-492.

M.A. Knibb, "Martyrdom and Ascension of Isaiah," in Charlesworth, *OTP* 2, 143-176.

—,"The Martyrdom of Isaiah," in M. de Jonge (ed.), *Outside the Old Testament* (Cambridge Commentaries on Writings of the Jewish and Christian World, vol. 4; Cambridge: C.U.P., 1985), 178-192.

—, "Messianism in the Pseudepigrapha in the Light of the Scrolls," *DSD* 2 (1995), 181-184.

—,"Perspectives on the Apocrypha and Pseudepigrapha. The Levi Traditions," in F. García Martínez and E. Noort (eds.), *Perspectives in the Study of the Old Testament & Early Judaism. A Symposium in Honour of Adam S. van der Woude on the Occasion of His 70th Birthday* (VTSup 73; Leiden: Brill, 1998), 197-213,

—, "Christian Adoption and Transmission of Jewish Pseudepigrapha: The Case of *1 Enoch,*" *JSJ* 32 (2001), 396-415.

J. Knight, *The Ascension of Isaiah* (Guides to Apocrypha and Pseudepigrapha; Sheffield: Sheffield Academic Press, 1995).

T.A. Knittel, *Das griechische 'Leben Adam und Evas'. Studien zu einer narrativen Anthropologie im frühen Judentum* (TSAJ 88; Tübingen: Mohr [Siebeck], 2002).

D.-A. Koch, "Schriftauslegung. II. Neues Testament," *TRE* 30 (1999), 457-471.

M. Konradt, "Menschen- oder Bruderliebe? Beobachtungen zum Liebesgebot in den Testamenten der Zwölf Patriarchen," *ZNW* 88 (1997), 296-310.

T. Korteweg, "The Meaning of Naphtali's Visions," *Studies,* 261-290.

R.S. Kraemer, *When Aseneth met Joseph: A Late Antique Tale of the Biblical Patriarch and His Egyptian Wife Reconsidered* (New York: Oxford U.P., 1998).

R.A. Kraft, "The Multiform Jewish Heritage of Early Christianity," in J. Neusner (ed.), *Christianity, Judaism and other Greco-Roman Cults* (FS Morton Smith; Leiden: Brill, 1975), vol. 3, 174-199.

—, "Reassessing the Recensional Problem in Testament of Abraham," in G.W.E. Nickelsburg (ed.), *Studies in the Testament of Abraham* (SBLSCS 6; Missoula MT: Scholars, 1976), 121-137.

—, "Christian Transmission of Greek Jewish Scriptures: A Methodological Probe," in A. Benoît (ed.), *Paganisme, Judaïsme, Christianisme. Mélanges offerts à Marcel Simon* (Paris: Éd. E. de Boccard, 1978), 207-226.

—, "The Pseudepigrapha in Christianity," in J.C. Reeves (ed.), *Tracing the Threads. Studies in the Vitality of Jewish Pseudepigrapha* (SBLEJL 6; Atlanta: Scholars, 1994), 55-86.

—, "Setting the Stage and Framing some Central Questions," *JSJ* 32 (2001), 371-395.

— and A.-E. Purintun, *Paraleipomena Jeremiou* (SBL Texts and Translations, Pseudepigrapha Series 1; Missoula MT; Scholars, 1972).

G. Kretschmar, "Die Bedeutung der Liturgiegeschichte für die Frage nach der Kontinuität des Judenchristentums in nachapostolischer Zeit" in M. Simon (ed.), *Aspects du Judéochristianisme* (Paris: Presses Universitaires de France, 1965), 113-13.

—, "Die Kirche aus Juden und Heiden. Forschungsprobleme der ersten christlichen Jahrhunderte," in J. van Amersfoort and J. van Oort (eds.), *Juden und Christen in der Antike* (Kampen: Kok, 1990), 9-43.

A.M. Kropp, *Ausgewählte Zaubertexte* (2 vols.; Bruxelles: Fondation Égyptologique Reine Elisabeth, 1931).

R.A. Kugler, *From Patriarch to Priest. The Levi-Priestly Tradition from* Aramaic Levi *to* Testament of Levi (SBLEJL 9; Atlanta: Scholars, 1996).

—, *The Testaments of the Twelve Patriarchs* (Guides to the Apocrypha and Pseudepigrapha; Sheffield: Academic Press, 2001).

C'. K'urc'ikidze, "Adamis apokripu'li c'xovrebis k'art'uli versia," *P'ilologiuri Dziebani* 1 (1964), 97-136.

O. Kuss,"Sünde und Tod, Erbtod und Erbsünde," *Der Römerbrief übersetzt und erklärt,* vol. 1 (Regensburg: F. Pustet, second edition 1963), 241-275.

M. Lavarenne, *Prudence I. Cathemerinon Liber (Livre d'heures)* (Collection Budé; Paris: Les Belles Lettres, 1943).

A. Lehnardt, *Bibliographie zu den jüdischen Schriften aus hellenistisch-römischer Zeit* (JSHRZ 6,2; Gütersloh: Gütersloher Verlagshaus, 1999).

B.W. Longenecker, *2 Esdras* (Guides to Apocrypha and Pseudepigrapha; Sheffield: Sheffield Academic Press, 1995).

G.P. Luttikhuizen, "A Resistant Interpretation of the Paradise Story in the Gnostic *Testimony of Truth* (Nag Hamm. Cod. IX.3) 45-50," in G.P. Luttikhuizen (ed.), *Paradise Interpreted. Representations of Biblical Paradise in Judaism and Christianity* (Themes of Biblical Narrative. Jewish and Christian Traditions 2; Leiden: Brill, 1999), 140-152.

R.S. MacLennan, *Early Christian Texts on Jews and Judaism* (Brown Judaic Studies; Atlanta: Scholars, 1990).

J.-P. Mahé, "Le livre d'Adam géorgien," in R. van den Broek and M.J. Vermaseren (eds.) *Studies in Gnosticism and Hellenistic Religions* (Festschrift G. Quispel; EPROER 91; Leiden: Brill, 1981), 227-260.

M. Marcovich, *Theophili Antiocheni Ad Autolycum* (PTS 44; Berlin-New York: Walter de Gruyter, 1995).

E.P. Meijering, *Tertullian contra Marcion. Gotteslehre in der Polemik. Adversus Marcionem I-II* (Philosophia Patrum III; Leiden: Brill, 1977).

M. Meiser, "Sünde, Buße und Gnade in dem Leben Adams und Evas," in G.A. Anderson, M.E. Stone and J. Tromp (eds.), *Literature on Adam and Eve. Collected Essays* (SVTP 15; Leiden: Brill, 2000), 297-313.

O. Merk and M. Meiser, *Das Leben Adams und Evas*, JSHRZ 2,5 (1998), 733-870.

T. Mertens, "Geestelijke testamenten in de laatmiddeleeuwse Nederlanden. Een verkenning van het genre," in G.R.W. Dibbets and P.W.M. Wackers (eds.), *Wat duikers vent is dit! Opstellen voor W.M.H. Hummelen* (Wijhe: Uitg. Quarto, 1989), 75-89.

N. Messel, "Ueber die textkritisch begründete Ausscheidung vermeintlicher christlicher Interpolationen in den Testamenten der Zwölf Patriarchen," in *Festschrift W.W. Baudissin* (BZAW 33 [1918]), 355-374.

B.M. Metzger, *The Canon of the New Testament. Its Origin, Development and Significance* (Oxford: Clarendon, 1987).

W. Meyer, "Vita Adae et Evae," *Abhandlungen der königlich bayerischen Akademie der Wissenschaften, Philosophische-philologische Klasse* 14 (Munich: Verlag der K. Akademie, 1878), 185-250.

J.-P. Migne, *Dictionnaire des Apocryphes* (2 vols; Paris, 1856 and 1858; reprint Turnhout: Brepols, 1989).

J.T. Milik, "Le Testament de Lévi," in D. Barthélemy and J.T. Milik, *Qumran Cave I* (Oxford: Clarendon, 1955), 87-91.

—, "Le Testament de Lévi en araméen. Fragment de la grotte 4 de Qumrân," *RB* 62 (1955), 398-406.

—, "'Prière de Nabonide' et autres récits d'un cycle de Daniel. Fragments araméens de Qumrân 4," *RB* 63 (1956), 407-415.

—, "Problèmes de la littérature hénochique à la lumière des fragments araméens de Qumrân," *HTR* 64 (1971), 333-378..

—, *The Books of Enoch. Aramaic Fragments of Qumrân Cave 4* (Oxford: Clarendon, 1976).

—, "Écrits préesséniens de Qumrân: d'Hénoch à 'Amram," in M. Delcor (ed.), *Qumrân. Sa piété, sa théologie et son milieu* (BETL 46; Paris-Gembloux: Duculot/Leuven: University Press, 1978) 91-106.

U. Mittmann-Richert, *Einführung zu den historischen und legendarischen Erzählungen* (JSHRZ 6,1.1; Gütersloh: Gütersloher Verlagshaus, 2000).

J.H. Mozley, "The Vita Adae," *JTS* 30 (1929), 121-47.

C. Müller, *Gottes Gerechtigkeit und Gottes Volk. Eine Untersuchung zu Römer 9-11* (FRLANT 86; Göttingen: Vandenhoeck & Ruprecht, 1964).

C. Munier, *Tertullian, La Pénitence* (S.C. 316; Paris: Ed. du Cerf, 1984).

M. Nagel, *La vie d'Adam et d'Ève (Apocalypse de Moïse)* (Diss. Strasbourg 1972; Université Lille III: Service de réproduction, 1974).

G.W. Nebe, "Qumranica I: Zu unveröffentlichten Handschriften aus Höhle 4 von Qumran," *ZAW* 106 (1994), 307-322.

G.W.E. Nickelsburg, *Jewish Literature between the Bible and Mishnah* (Philadelphia: Fortress, 1981).

—, *1 Enoch 1. A Commentary on the Book of 1 Enoch, Chapters 1-36; 81-108* (Hermeneia; Minneapolis: Fortress, 2001).

—, "Enoch, First Book of," *Anchor Bible Dictionary* (New York: Doubleday, 1992), 2, 508-516.

—, "Son of Man," *Anchor Bible Dictionary* (New York: Doubleday, 1992), 6, 137-150.

K.-W. Niebuhr, *Gesetz und Paränese. Katechismusartige Weisungsreihen in der frühjüdischen Literatur* (WUNT II 28; Tübingen: J. C.B. Mohr, 1987).

K. Niederwimmer, *Die Didache* (Göttingen: Vandenhoeck & Ruprecht, 1989).

E. von Nordheim, *Die Lehre der Alten I. Das Testament als Literaturgattung im Judentum der Hellenistisch-Römischen Zeit* (ALGHJ 13; Leiden: Brill, 1980).

E. Norelli, *Ascension du prophète Isaïe* (Apocryphes. Collection de poche de l'AELAC; Turnhout: Brepols, 1993).

—, "Ascension du prophète Isaïe," in F. Bovon and P. Geoltrain (eds.), *Écrits apocryphes chrétiens*, vol. 1 (Bibliothèque de la Pléiade 442; Paris: Gallimard, 1997), 499-546.

G.S. Oegema, *Apokalypsen* (JSHRZ 6,1.5; Gütersloh: Gütersloher Verlagshaus, 2001).

B.A. Pearson, "Jewish Haggadic Traditions in *The Testimony of Truth* from Nag Hammadi (CG IX,3)," in *Ex Orbe Religionum. Studia Geo Widengren Oblata*, vol. 1 (NumenSup 21; Leiden: Brill, 1972), 457-470.

—, "Jewish Sources in Gnostic Literature," in M.E. Stone (ed.), *Jewish Writings of the Second Temple Period* (CRINT, 2,2; Assen: Van Gorcum/Philadelphia, Fortress: 1984), 443-481.

—, "Use, Authority and Exegesis of Mikra in Gnostic Literature," in M.J. Mulder and H. Sysling (eds.), *Mikra. Text, Translation, Reading and Interpretation of the Hebrew Bible in ancient Judaism and Early Christianity* (CRINT, 2,1; Assen-Maastricht: Van Gorcum/Philadelphia: Fortress, 1988), 635-652.

— and S. Giversen, "IX,3: The Testimony of Truth," in B.A. Pearson (ed.), *Nag Hammadi Codices IX and X* (NHC 15; Leiden: Brill, 1981), 101-203.

E. Peterson, "Die 'Taufe' im Acherusischen See" *VC* 9 (1955), 1-20, reprinted in *Frühkirche, Judentum und Gnosis* (Rome, Freiburg, Vienna: Herder, 1959), 310-32.

J.-P. Pettorelli, "La vie latine d'Adam et Ève," *Archivum Latinitatis Medii Aevi* 56 (1998), 5-104.

—, "Vie Latine d'Adam et d'Ève. La recension de Paris, BNF, lat. 3832," *Archivum Latinitatis Medii Aevi* 57 (1999), 5-52.

—, "La Vie latine d'Adam et Ève. Analyse de la tradition manuscrite," *Apocrypha* 10 (1999), 220-320).

—, "Deux témoins latins singuliers de la *Vie d'Adam et Ève*, Paris, BNF, lat. 3832 & Milan, B.Ambrosiana, O 35 sup.," *JSJ* 33 (2002).

M. Philonenko, *Les interpolations chrétiennes des Testaments des Douze Patriarches* (Cahiers de la RHPR 35; Paris: Presses Universitaires de France, 1960).

—, *Joseph et Aséneth. Introduction, texte critique, traduction et notes* (SPB 13; Leiden: Brill, 1968).

—, "Joseph et Aséneth," in *La Bible. Écrits intertestamentaires* (Bibliothèque de la Pléiade 337; Paris Gallimard, 1987), cxxii-cxxv, 1559-1601.

—, "Son soleil éternel brillera (4QTestLévi^{c-d} (?) ii 9," *RHPR* 73 (1993-94), 405-408.

—, "Simples observations sur les Paralipomènes de Jérémie," *RHPR* 76 (1996), 157-177.

J.-C. Picard, *Apocalypsis Baruchi Graece* (PVTG 2; Leiden: Brill, 1967), 61-96.

—, "L'apocryphe à l'étroit. Notes historiographiques sur le corpus d'apocryphes bibliques," *Apocrypha. Le champ des apocryphes* 1 (1990), 69-117.

—, *Le continent apocryphe: Essai sur les littératures apocryphes juive et chrétienne* (Instrumenta Patristica 36; Steenbrugis: In Abbatia S. Petri/Turnhout: Brepols, 1999).

E. Puech, "Le Testament de Qahat en araméen de la Grotte 4 (*4QTQah*)," *RevQ* nos. 57-58, vol.15 (1991), 23-54.

—, "Fragments d'un apocryphe de Lévi et le personnage eschatologique. 4QTestLévi[cd](?) et 4QAJa," in J. Trebolle Barrera and L. Vegas Montaner (eds.), *The Madrid Qumran Congress: Proceedings of the International Congress on the Dead Sea Scrolls, Madrid 18-21 March, 1991* (STDJ 11,2; Leiden: Brill, 1992), 2, 449-501.

J. Riaud, *Les Paralipomènes du prophète Jérémie: Présentation, texte original, traduction et commentaires* (Cahiers du centre interdisplinaire de recherches en histoire, lettres et langues 14; Angers: Université Catholique de l'Ouest, 1994).

—, "Quelques réflexions sur l'*Apocalypse grecque de Baruch* ou *III Baruch* à la lumière d'un ouvrage récent," *Semitica* 48 (1999), 89-99.

—, "The Figure of Jeremiah in the *Paralipomena Jermiae Prophetae*: His Originality; His 'Christianization' by the Christian Autnor of the Conclusion (9.10-32)," *JSP* 22 (2000), 31-44.

P. Riessler, *Altjüdisches Schrifttum ausserhalb der Bibel* (Heidelberg: Kerle Verlag/W.Rühling, 1928; (reprint Darmstadt: Wissenschaftliche Buchgesellschaft, 1966).

B. Rigaux, *Saint Paul. Les épîtres aux Thessaloniciens* (Ebib; Paris: Gabalda/Gembloux: Duculot, 1956).

H. Rönsch, *Das Buch der Jubiläen oder die kleine Genesis* (Leipzig: Fues's Verlag, 1874).

—,"Xeniologica Theologica, II.2. Die pentateuchischen Grundlagen des apostolischen Ausspruches 1 Thess. 2,16," *Z.W.Th.* 18 (1875), 278-283.

B.S. Rosner, "A Possible Quotation of Test. Reuben 5:5 in 1 Corinthians 6:18A," *JTS* NS 43 (1992), 123-127.

P. Sacchi (ed.), *Apocrifi dell'Antico Testamento* (vols. 1-2, Torino: Unione Tipografico-Editrice Torinese, 1981, 1989; vols. 3-4, Brescia: Paideia, 1999, 2000; vol. 5: Brescia: Paideia, 1997).

—, "Il problema degli apocrifi dell' Antico Testamento," *Henoch* 21 (1999), 97-129.

S. Safrai (ed.), *The Literature of the Sages. First Part* (CRINT II, 3a; Assen: Van Gorcum/ Philadelphia: Fortress, 1987).

S.G.J. Sanchez, *Justin Apologiste Chrétien. Travaux sur le Dialogue avec Tryphon de Justin Martyr* (CRB 50; Paris: Gabalda, 2000).

D. Satran, *Biblical Prophets in Byzantine Palestine. Reassessing the Lives of the Prophets* (SVTP 11; Leiden: Brill, 1995).

B. Schaller, *Paralipomena Jeremiae*, JSHRZ 1,8 (1998), 659-777.

—, "Is the Greek Version of the *Paralipomena Jeremiou* Original or a Translation?" *JSP* 22 (2000), 51-89.

T. Schermann, *Prophetarum Vitae Fabulosae* etc. (Leipzig: Teubner, 1907) and *Propheten und Apostellegenden nebst Jüngerkatalogen des Dorotheus und verwandter Texte* (TU 31,3; Leipzig: Heinrichs, 1907).

H. Schlier,"Adam bei Paulus," *Der Römerbrief* (HTKNT 6; Freiburg-Basel-Wien: Herder, 1977), 179-189.

F. Schnapp, *Die Testamente der Zwölf Patriarchen untersucht* (Halle: Alex Niemeyer, 1884).

—, "Die Testamente der 12 Patriarchen" in Kautzsch, *APAT* 2, 458-502.

E. Schürer, *Die Geschichte des jüdischen Volkes im Zeitalter Jesu Christi* (3 vols.; Leipzig: Hinrichs, fourth edition, 1901-1909).

E. Schürer, G. Vermes, F. Millar, and M. Goodman, *The History of the Jewish People in the Age of Jesus Christ (175 B.C.-A.D. 135)* (4 vols.; Edinburgh: T & T Clark, 1973-1987).

H. Schreckenberg, *Die christlichen Adversus-Judaeos-Texte und ihr literarisches und histori-sches Umfeld (1.-11. Jh.)* (Europ. Hochschulschriften 23, Bd. 172: Frankfurt a.M.-Bern-New York-Paris: Peter Lang, ²1990).

A.M. Schwemer, *Studien zu den frühjüdischen Vitae Prophetarum* (2 vols.; TSAJ 49-50; Tü-bingen: Mohr [Siebeck], 1995-1996).

—, *Vitae Prophetarum*, JSHRZ 1,7 (1997), 539-658.

R. Scroggs, *The Last Adam. A Study in Pauline Anthropology* (Philadelphia: Fortress, 1966).

J.L. Sharpe III, "The Second Adam in the Apocalypse of Moses," *CBQ* 35 (1973), 35-46.

T. Silverstein, "Did Dante know the Vision of St. Paul?" *Harvard Studies and Notes in Philol-ogy and Literature* 19 (1937), 231-47.

— and A. Hilhorst, *Apocalypse of Paul. A New Critical Edition of three Long Latin Versions* (Cahiers d'Orientalisme 21; Genève: P. Cramer, 1997).

R.A. Sinker, *Testamenta XII Patriarcharum* (Cambridge: Deighton Bell and Co, 1869).

—, *Testamenta XII Patriarcharum. Appendix* (Cambridge: Deighton Bell and Co, 1879).

O. Skarsaune, *The Proof from Prophecy. A Study in Justin Martyr's Proof-Text Tradition: Text-Type, Provenance, Theological Profile* (NovTSup 56; Leiden: Brill, 1987).

H.D. Slingerland, *The Testaments of the Twelve Patriarchs: A Critical History of Research* (SBLMS 21: Missoula MT: Scholars, 1977).

L. Sormani, *Inventaris van de Archieven van het Borger-kinderen-Weeshuis, het Arme-kinder-Weeshuis en de beide Weeshuizen te Nijmegen* (Nijmegen, Drukkerij Gebr. Jansen, 1951).

C. Sourvinou-Inwood, *'Reading' Greek Death to the End of the Classical Period* (Oxford: Clarendon, 1995).

H.F.D. Sparks, *The Apocryphal Old Testament* (Oxford: Clarendon, 1984).

A. Standhartinger, *Das Frauenbild im Judentum in der hellenistischen Zeit: Ein Beitrag an-hand von 'Joseph und Aseneth'* (AGAJU 26; Leiden: Brill, 1995).

G.N. Stanton, "Aspects of Early Christian-Jewish Polemic and Apologetic," *NTS* 31 (1985), 377-392, reprinted in his *A Gospel for a New People. Studies in Matthew* (Edinburgh: T. & T. Clark, 1992; 232-255.

—, "5 Ezra and Matthean Christianity in the Second Century," *JTS*, N.S. 28 (1977), 67-83, reprinted in *A Gospel for a New People. Studies in Matthew* (Edinburgh: T. & T. Clark, 1992), 256-277.

J. Starcky, "Les quatre étapes du messianisme à Qumrân," *RB* 70 (1963), 481-505.

G. Steindorff, *Die Apocalypse des Elias, eine unbekannte Apocalypse und Bruchstücke der Sophonias-Apocalypse* (TU 17.3a; Leipzig: Hinrichs, 1899).

M.E. Stone, *The Testament of Levi. A First Study of the Armenian MSS of the Testaments of the XII Patriarchs in the Convent of St. James*, Jerusalem (Jerusalem: St. James Press, 1969).

—, *The Armenian Version of the Testament of Joseph* (SBLTT Pseudepigrapha Series; Missoula MT: Scholars 1975).

—, "The Armenian Version of the Testaments of the Twelve Patriarchs. Selections of Manu-scripts," *Sion* 49 (1975).

—, "Armenian Canon Lists III—the Lists of Mechitar of Ayrivank' (c. 1285 C.E.)," *HTR* 69 (1976), 289-30.

—, "New Evidence for the Armenian Version of the Testaments of the Twelve Patriarchs," *RB* 84 (1977), 94-107.

—, *The Penitence of Adam* (CSCO 429-430; Louvain: Peeters, 1981).

— (ed.), *Jewish Writings of the Second Temple Period* (CRINT 2,2; Assen: Van Gorcum/ Philadelphia: Fortress, 1984).

—, "Categorization and Classification of the Apocrypha and Pseudepigrapha," *Abr-Nahrain* 24 (1986), 167-177.

—, "The *EPITOME* of the Testaments of the Twelve Patriarchs," *Revue des Études Arménien-
nes*, N.S. 20 (1986-1987), 69-107; reprinted in Stone, *Selected Studies*, 145-183.

—, *Fourth Ezra* (Hermeneia; Minneapolis: Fortress, 1990).

—, *Selected Studies in Pseudepigrapha and Apocrypha with Special Reference to the Armenian Tradition* (SVTP 9; Leiden: Brill, 1991).

—, *A History of the Life of Adam and Eve* (SBLEJL 3; Atlanta: Scholars Press, 1992).

—, "The Epitome of the Testaments of the Twelve Patriarchs in Matenadaran No. 2679," *Mus*
108 (1995), 265-277.

—, "215. 4QTestament of Naphtali," in G.J. Brooke *et al.* (eds.) *Qumran Cave 4. XVII.
Parabiblical Texts, Part 3* (DJD 22; Oxford: Clarendon, 1996), 73-82.

—, "The Genealogy of Bilhah," *DSD* 3 (1996), 20-36.

—, "The Hebrew Testament of Naphtali," *JJS* 47 (1996, 311-32,

—, "Some Further Readings in the Hebrew Testament of Naphtali," *JJS* 49 (1998), 346-47.

—, "Warum Naphtali? Eine Diskussion im Internet," *Judaica* 54 (1998), 188-191.

—, "The Axis of History at Qumran," in E.G. Chazon, M.E. Stone, A. Pinnick (eds.),
*Pseudepigraphic Perspectives: The Apocrypha and Pseudepigrapha in Light of the Dead
Sea Scrolls* (STDJ 31; Leiden: Brill, 1999), 133-149.

—, "Aramaic Levi Document and Greek Testament of Levi," in S.M. Paul, R.A. Kraft, L.H.
Schiffman and W.W. Fields (eds.), *Emanuel. Studies in Hebrew Bible, Septuagint and dead
Sea Scrolls in Honour of Emanuel Tov* (Leiden: Brill, 2003), 429-437.

— and R.A. Kraft, Reviews of H.F.D. Sparks, *The Apocryphal Old Testament* and J.H.
Charlesworth, *The Old Testament Pseudepigrapha*, *RSR* 14 (1988), 111-117.

T. Stylianopoulos, *Justin Martyr and the Mosaic Law* (SBLDS 20; Missoula MT: Scholars,
1975).

A.M. Sweet, *A Religio-Historical Study of the Greek Life of Adam and Eve* (unpublished Ph.D.
Dissertation, Notre Dame, 1992).

C. Tischendorf, *Apocalypses Apocryphae* (Leipzig: H. Mendelssohn, 1866; repr. Hildesheim:
G. Olms, 1966).

S.H. Thomson, *The Writings of Robert Grosseteste Bishop of Lincoln 1235-1253* (Cambridge:
Cambridge University Press, 1940.

C.C. Torrey, *The Lives of the Prophets. Greek Text and Translation* (SBLMS 1; Philadelphia,
1946).

H. Traub, "οὐρανός, C.II. Judentum," *TWNT* 5, 511-512.

J. Tromp, *The Assumption of Moses. A Critical Edition with Commentary* (SVTP 10; Leiden:
Brill, 1993).

—, "Two References to a Levi Document in an Epistle of Ammonas," *NovT* 39 (1997), 235-
247.

—, "Literary and Exegetical Issues in the Story of Adam's Death and Burial (GLAE 31-42)," in
J. Frishman and L. Van Rompay (eds.), *The Book of Genesis in Jewish and Oriental Christian Interpretation* (Traditio exegetica graeca 5; Leuven: Peeters, 1997), 25-41.

—, Review of T. Silverstein and A. Hilhorst, *Apocalypse of Paul*, *VC* 52 (1998), 213-17.

—, "The Textual History of the *Life of Adam and Eve* in the Light of a Newly Discovered Latin
Text-Form," *JSJ* 33 (2002), 28-41.

—, "Origen on the Assumption of Moses," (forthcoming).

J.H. Ulrichsen, *Die Grundschrift der Testamente der Zwölf Patriarchen. Eine Untersuchung zu
Umfang, Inhalt und Eigenart der ursprünglichen Schrift* (Acta Universitatis Upsaliensis:
Historia Religionum 10, Uppsala 1991).

W.C. van Unnik, *ΑΦΘΟΝΩΣ ΜΕΤΑΔΙΔΩΜΙ* (Mededelingen van de Kon. Vlaamse Acade-
mie voor Wetenschappen, Klasse der Letteren 33,4 [1971]).

—, "Der Neid in der Paradiesgeschichte nach einigen gnostischen Texten," in M. Krause (ed.), *Essays on the Nag Hammadi Texts in Honour of Alexander Böhlig* (NHC 3; Leiden: Brill, 1972).

—, *De ἀφθονία van God in de oudchristelijke literatuur* (Mededelingen der Kon. Nederlands Akademie van Wetenschappen, Afd. Letterkunde, N.R. 36,2 [1973]).

J.C. VanderKam, "1 Enoch, Enochic Motifs and Enoch in Early Christian Literature, in VanderKam and Adler (eds.), *The Jewish Apocalyptic Heritage*, 33-101.

— and W. Adler (eds.), *The Jewish Apocalyptic Heritage* (CRINT 3, 4; Assen: Van Gorcum/ Minneapolis: Fortress, 1996).

I.M. Veldman and H.J. de Jonge, "The Sons of Jacob: the Twelve Patriarchs in Sixteenth-Century Netherlandish Prints and Popular Literature," *Simiolus* 15 (1985), 176-196.

E. Vermeule, *Aspects of Death in Early Greek Art and Poetry* (Berkeley: Univ. of California Press, 1979).

A. Vögtle, *Der Judasbrief/Der zweite Petrusbrief* (EKK, 22; Solothurn-Düsseldorf: Benziger/Neukirchen-Vluyn: Neukirchener, 1994).

J.M. Vorstman, *Disquisitio de Testamentis XII Patriarcharum Origine et Pretio* (Rotterdam: P.C. Hoog, 1857).

A. Welkenhuysen, "Plantijns drukken van de Testamenten der XII Patriarchen (1561, 1564, 1566) in hun 'boekhistorische' context," *De Gulden Passer* 66-67 (1988-1989), 505-515.

U. Wilckens, *Der Brief an die Römer* II (EKK VI/2; Zürich, Einsiedeln, Köln: Benziger/Neukirchen-Vluyn: Neukirchener, 1980).

R.L. Wilken, "The Christians as the Romans (and Greeks) Saw Them," in E.P. Sanders (ed.), *Jewish and Christian Self-Definition*, vol. 1 (London: SCM, 1980), 100-125.

S.G. Wilson, *Related Strangers: Jews and Christians 70-170 CE* (Minneapolis: Fortress, 1995).

H. Windisch, *Der zweite Korintherbrief* (KEK; Göttingen: Vandenhoeck & Ruprecht, 1924; Neudruck 1970)

D. Winston, *The Wisdom of Solomon* (AB 43; Garden City, New York: Doubleday, 1979).

O.S. Wintermute, "Apocalypse of Zephaniah," in Charlesworth, *APOT* 1, 497-515.

A.S. van der Woude, *Die messianischen Vorstellungen der Gemeinde von Qumrân* (Assen: Van Gorcum, 1957).

—, *Oudisraëlitische en Vroegjoodse Literatuur* (eds. F. García Martínez and E. Noort; Kampen: Kok, 2000).

W. Wright, *Catalogue of Syriac Manuscripts*, vol. 2 (London: British Museum, 1871).

INDEX OF REFERENCES

I. OLD TESTAMENT
INCLUDING
APOCRYPHAL/DEUTEROCANONICAL
BOOKS

Genesis
1:1-2:7	194
2:8-3:19	194
2:8	195
2:11-14	226
2:15	195
2:17	238
2:23-24	196
3	184-200, 204-206, 228-240
3:1-7	204
3:8-24	204
3:8	205
3:9	192, 196
3:15	186, 188
3:16-19	188
3:19	206, 238
3:21	188
3:22	193
5:23	64
30:1-3	115
30:7-8	115
30:24	119
34	126, 137, 148
35:1-5	127
35:5	175
35:8	114
37:3-4	119
37:28	157
41:	61
45:14	117
48:22	119
49	122
49:14-15(LXX)	79, 150
49:17-18(LXX)	90
49:27(LXX)	175-176
49:33	121
50:15-21	61

Exodus
3:8	226

Leviticus
11:1-8	148
19:17-18	167
19:18	149
20:24	226

Numbers
6:26	148

Deuteronomy
6:4-5	149
6:5(LXX)	150
14:6-8	148
25:5-10(LXX)	147
33	101
33:8-11	135
33:12	176

Judges
6:24	167

2 Samuel
17:23	121

1 Kings
11:38	167

2 Kings
20:1	121

2 Chronicles
12:12	174

Psalms
96(95):10	21
103(102):9	174
104(103):4	216
110:4	126

Proverbs
1:9	188

Isaiah
52:13-53:12 156
57:19(LXX) 152

Ezekiel
14:5, 7 237

Daniel
7 65

Hosea
9:10 237

Amos
5:14 167
9:8(LXX) 174

Jonah
2:1 157

Zechariah
11:12-13 157

Maleachi
1:11 128
2:4-9 135

Tobit 11

Judith
7:30 174

Wisdom of Solomon
2-5 62
2:1 220
2:23-24 197, 228, 235
16:5, 6 174
16:13 220
17:4 220

Ecclesiasticus (Sirach) 11
25:24 228, 235

Epistle of Jeremiah 11

Additions to Daniel
3:34 (LXX&Theod.) 174

4 Maccabees
13:14-17 220

II. NEW TESTAMENT

Matthew
5:17-20 51
5:43-48 62
12:40 157
21-25 51
21:33-44 51
22:37-39 145
23:29 45, 47
23:34-38 51
23:34-36 174
25:40 157
25:41 188
25:45 157
26:15 157
26:52 62
27:9-10 157

Mark
1:9-11 112
3:27 187
12:1-9 174
12:30 150
12:33 150

Luke
10:25-27 146
10:27 150
11:47 45, 47
16:23-27 220
22:24-29 157

John
4:21 55
4:22-23 55
6 62
18:11 62

Acts 176
16:23-25 171

Romans
1:4 161, 164, 168, 169
1:26 164
1:32 162, 164, 172-173

2:5	170	13:11	166-167
2:15	164		
2:17-24	165	Ephesians	
2:19	165	2:7	152
2:22	165		
3:23	229, 236	Philippians	
5:3-4	165	2:30	177
5:4	164	4:9	166-167
5:12-21	184, 186, 229, 235, 238		
5:14, 17	189	Colossians	
5:18-19	195	1:21-22	237
7:7-12	229, 237	1:24	177
8:9-11	153		
9-11	172	1 Timothy	
11:25-26	171-172	2:13-14	235
12:1	162, 170		
12:8	151	2 Timothy	
12:12	165	1:10	187
12:17	62	1:14	153
12:21	161, 162, 167		
15:23	162	Hebrews	
15:33	166	7	126
16:20	166	9:26	169, 171
16:22	167	13:20	166
1 Corinthiams		James	
3:16	153	1:2-4	165-171
6:18	153, 166	1:14-16	237
6:20	166		
10	62	1:17	186
11:17-34	62	4:5	153
14:33	166	4:7-8	166, 171
15:9	157		
15:21-22	184, 235, 238	1 Peter	
15:45-49	184, 235	3:9	62
15:54-55	189		
16:17	177	2 Peter	
		2:4	219
2 Corinthians			
3:14	21	Jude	
8:2	151	4	64
9:11	151	6-7	20
9:12	177	6	219
9:13	151	8	66
11:3	235	9	20, 65
11:9	177	14	20, 64, 65
11:14	235		
12:2-4	222, 236	Revelation	
12:2	169	12:9	189, 196

20:2	189
22:1-2	222

III. Old Testament Pseudepigrapha and New Testament Apocrypha

Apocalypse of Elijah	221
3:16-18 (34, 3-5)	236

Apocalypse of Paul	
11-20	222
19-20	236
21-31	222
21:2-3	222
21:3	225
22-23	208-210
22	226, 236
22:1	222, 223, 226
22:3	221
22:5	222, 223, 224, 225
23:1	222
23:2	225
23:3	222, 223, 226
23:5	224
25-28	222
26	223, 224, 226
31-36	226
31	210, 226
31:1	222, 223, 226
31:2	225
31:3	222
32-45	222
32	226
32:1, 2	226
34	226

Apocalypse of Peter	
14	206-207, 218-220

Apocalypse of Zephaniah	221

Ascension of Isaiah	34, 41-43, 44
1-5	41
1:1-3:12	41
1:2b-6a, 7, 13	42
2:9	42
3:13-4:22	41, 42
3:9	54
3:13-4:22	41, 42
3:13	41, 54

3:17	54
4:13-15	54
5:1-16	41, 54
5:1a, 15-16	42
6-11	41, 42
10:7	41
11:22	54

Assumption of Moses	20
1:14	66, 67
3:12	67
6:2-6	67
9-10	67
9:7	67
10:1-2	67
11:17	67
12:6	67

2 Baruch (Syriac Apocalypse of Baruch)	48, 184
1-77	48
13:11-14:3	48
48:42-43	235
78-87	48

3 Baruch (Greek Apocalypse of Baruch)	56-58
1:6	57
1:8	57
2-16	57
4:8	197
10	211

Book of the Resurrection of Jesus Christ by Bartholomew the Apostle	
21-22	210
21:5-6	210

1 Enoch	11, 34, 63-65
1-36	63, 64
1:1-32:6	63
1:9	20, 64, 65
6-16	20
17:4	219
21:7	219
22:4-7	219
37-71	37, 63, 65
72-82	63
81:5-82:3	120
83-90	63
92-105	63, 64

97:6-104:13	63
106:1-107:3	63
2 Enoch	
8-9	236
4 Ezra	48-52, 184
7:28	49
14:49-50	49
5 Ezra	48-52
1:24	50, 51
1:30-33	51
2:10-11	50
2:42-48	51
2:45	51
2:47	51
6 Ezra	48-52
15:28-33	50
15:43-16:16	50
15:57-59	49
16:35-78	49
16:68-74	50
Joseph and Aseneth	58-62
1-21	58
4:7	62
6:3-5	62
8:5	62
8:9	62
13:13	62
15:5	62
16:16	62
18:11	62
19:5	62
19:6	62
19:8	62
19:11	62
21:4	62
21:13-14	62
21:21	62
22-29	58
23:9	62
23:10	62
28:5	62
28:14	62
29	62
29:3	62
29:4	62

Jubilees	11, 99
7:38-39	120
10:14	120
10:17	120
21:10	120
30-32	135
30:1-32:9	108
30:5-17	110, 132, 133
30:18-20	132
34:1-9	78
37:1-38:1-14	78
45:16	120
46:9-11	121
Life of Adam and Eve	34
Greek version	
1-4	184, 204, 231
2:4	185, 232
5-13	232
5-8	184, 204, 231
7:1	232, 238
7:2	185, 232
8:2	184, 232
9-13	204, 231
9:2	184, 232, 238
10-12	232
10:2	184, 205, 206. 238
12:1	185, 232
13:3-5 (MSS ALCR)	233
13:6	206
14:1-2	204
14:2	232, 238
14:3	184, 204, 232
15-30	182, 184, 204, 231
15-21	204
15-20	185, 232
15:1	185, 232
17:1-2	235-236
18	197
18:4	192
19:3	237
20:1-2	188, 232, 236
20:1	237
21:2	237
21:3	185
21:5-6	236, 237
21:6	188, 232
22-29	204
23	232
23:3	184, 232
24:1	184, 204, 232

24:4	204, 232	39:2-3	206, 232
25:1	184, 204, 232	39:2	203
25:2	232	40	190, 205
25:3	184, 204, 232	40:1	236
25:4	185, 232	40:3, 5	206
26	185, 232	40:6-41:2	206
27-29	185, 232	41	205
27	233	41:1	206
27:2-3	185, 204, 232	41:3	185, 206, 232, 238
27:3	237	42-43	185, 232
27:4-28:3	204	42:1-2	205
28:3-4	185, 233	42:3-43:4	206
28:4	185, 187, 204, 205, 206,232, 233, 238	42:3-4	206
		42:8	206
29	204	43:3	206
29:6 (add MSS RM)	235		
30:1	184, 185, 187, 204, 231, 233, 234	Latin version	
		1-21	182, 183
31-43	185, 200, 201, 204-205, 233, 237	9:1	235
		42:5	191
31-37	201, 204-206	47	202
31	231	48	190
31:1	204, 206		
31:4	206	*Lives of the Prophets*	43-48
32-41	185, 231	Life of Daniel	46
32	232		
32:2	204, 238	*Paralipomena Ieremiou*	44, 52-56, 58
32:4	206	1:1-9:9	53
33-37	186, 233	1:1-4:5	53
33	201	3:8, 15	55
33:1-38:1	202	4:6-11	53
33:3	206	4:8	55
33:5	190, 237	5	53
34	201	5:34	55
34:2	206	6:1-7:12	54
35:1	206	6:5-7	55
35:2	190, 206, 236, 237	6:13-14, 22	55
36	201	7:13-32	54
36:3	186, 233	7:17	55
37	190, 201-202, 211	7:32	55
37:3	186, 201-212, 218, 233	8	54, 55
37:4-6	237	8:9	55
37:4	206	9	54, 55
37:5-6	206	9:5	55
37:5	185, 206, 233, 236, 238	9:10-32	53
37:6	190, 205, 237	9:13	53
38	205	9:18	54
38:1-42:2	205, 206	9:20	54
38:1	186, 205, 206		
39	205	Psalms 151A, 151B, 154, 155	11
39:1	237a		

Sibylline Oracles	34, 219
1-2	208
1:283-306	208
1:302	208
1:304	208
2:190-338	208
2:330-338	207-208, 218-219
3:704	170
5:484-485	208, 211, 219
Testament of Job	122
6:4	136
Testaments of the Twelve Patriarchs	
Testament Reuben	89
2-3	97
2:1	88
2:2-9	87-88
3:8-9	147
4:3	164
4:4	174
5:5	166
6:8	147
6:9	147
6:11-12	89
Testament Simeon	89
4:4-7	153-154
4:4	155
4:5	154. 155
4:6	154
4:7	154
6:6	152, 166
8:2	121
Testament Levi	78, 79, 81, 82, 89, 99
title	126
1:1;	121, 125
2-5	109, 132
2-3	139, 168-170
2	133
2:1-6:2	136
2:1-2	126
2:3 add. in MS *e*	81, 108, 110, 129
2:3	129
2:3-5	136
2:3-4	127
2:4	129, 132, 136
2:5-5:2	126
2:6-4:1	136
2:7-9	169-170

2:10-11	125, 136
2:10	169
3:1-4	169
3:2	170
3:3	152, 166
3:5-8	169
3:5-6	170
3:6	136
4	139
4:1	100
4:2-6	136, 137
4:2-3	132
4:3	111, 112, 125
4:4-6	169
4:4	112, 125, 152
4:5-6	112
4:5	132, 169
5-6	174
5:1-6:2	136, 137
5:1-2	109
5:2 add. in MS *e*	129
5:2	100, 112, 125, 137, 152, 169
5:3-7	110, 127
5:3-4	137
5:3	174
5:4	148, 174
5:6	174
6-7	109
6:1-2	127
6:2	132, 137
6:3-7:4	126, 127, 137
6:8-10	174
6:8	137, 174
6:11	137, 162-164, 173-175
7	174
8	109, 110, 130, 133, 137, 139
8:1-17	126
8:1	137
8:11-15	137
8:14	125
8:18-19	126, 132
8:19	137
9	109, 130
9:1-2	127
9:1	129
9:3-4	127
9:5-14	127
9:6-14	137
9:6-7	137
9:6	138
9:9-11	137

9:10	137
9:12-14	137
10	109, 112, 125, 127, 130, 137, 138, 165, 169
10:1	147
10:15	147
11-12	109, 126, 127
11:7	129
12:3	133
12:5	126
12:6-7	120, 130
12:7	130
13	109, 110, 127, 130, 138
13:1	130, 138, 147
13:3	138
13:4	138
13:7	147
14-15	112, 125, 127, 138, 165, 169
14	110, 131
14:1	131
14:3-4	112
14:4	147-165
15:2	170
16	112, 125, 127, 138, 165, 169
16:1	11, 138
16:3	100
16:5	127
17-18	80, 111, 172
17:1-11	111, 125, 128, 138
17:7-10	111
17:8-11	112
17:8-10	112, 169
17:10	111
17:11	169
18	112, 125, 128, 139, 168
18:1	112, 125, 128, 139, 168
18:2-4	111, 112, 139
18:2 add. in MS e	78, 108, 129
18:2	169
18:3	112, 125
18:6-7	100, 139, 168
18:7	112, 161, 168
18:9	111, 169
18:11	161, 168, 169
18:12	152, 166
18:14	122, 125
19	128
19:1	138
19:2	128
19:4	120, 130

Testament Judah	99, 157
1:4	147
3-7	78
9	78
12:11-12	117
13:1	147
18:3	147
18:6	164
20:5	165
21:1-6a	126
21:7	90
22:2	100
23:5	89
24	112, 168
24:1-2	89
24:1	100, 125, 152
24:2	100, 168
25:1-2	117, 148, 169
25:1	90
25:3	152, 154, 166
26:1	147
Testament Issachar	79, 90
2:1	103
2:3	103
3-4	150
3:1	150
3:4	150
3:7	151
3:8	151
4:1	151
4:6	147, 150
5:1-2	150
5:1	147
5:2	149, 151
5:8	151
7:6	149, 151
7:7	151, 152, 153, 154, 166
Testament Zebulun	79, 94
2	151
2:4	153
3:4	147
4	151
4:2	153
4:4	157
5-9	171
5:1	147, 151
5:3	151
5:5-7:4	151
6:6	151

8:1-2	151	4:2	149
8:1	151	5:2	156, 166
8:2	151, 153, 166	5:3	165
8:3	151	6:1-7:6	156, 167
8:4-6	153	6:1	149, 150
8:4	153	6:3	149, 150
8:5	149, 153, 156	7:1	89
9-10	172	7:7	149
9:5-7	171	8:1	89
9:5	147		
9:8	152, 166, 171	*Testament Asher*	
9:6-9	171-172	2:2- 8	173
9:9	171	2:8-10	147
10:2	147, 148, 172	3:1-2	147, 173
10:5	150	3:2	164, 166
		4:1	173
Testament Dan	90	4:3, 4	173
1:4	155	5:4	150
5:1-3	152	6:1-2	172-173
5:1	147, 154, 166	6:2	162, 164
5:2	147, 166	6:5-6	167
5:3	146, 149, 150	7	172
5:8	90	7:2-3	89
5:10-11	152	7:3-4	89
5:13	152, 153, 166	7:5	147
6:1	147	7:6	98
6:2	166, 167		
6:5	167, 174	*Testament Joseph*	78, 99
6:10	147	1-2	79
7:2	98	1:2	119
7:3	98	1:4	119
		2:7	79, 165
Testament Naphtali		3-9	79, 99, 118, 154, 165
1:6-8	115	3:3	147
1:6-12	113	3:10	164
1:9-12	114, 115, 119	7:8	164
1:9	115	8:5	166, 171
1:10	115	10:1-11:1	79, 154
1:12	113	10:1-4	154, 165
2:2-8	88	10:1-3	166
2:8	98	10:1	165
2:9	88	10:2-3	152, 166
4:5	151,153	10:4	150,
5-7	78, 115	10:5-6	154
8:3	152, 166	10:5	119
8:4	152, 166	11-16	79, 99, 118, 119, 154, 165
		11:1	119, 147, 153, 154
Testament Gad		12:1	118
2:2	157	14:1-5	118
3-7	156	15:1-2	118
3:1	147	16:1	118

16:4-5	118
16:6	154
17:1-18:4	79, 154
17:1-2	118, 155
17:1	165
17:4-7	155
17:8	155, 157
18:1	155
18:2	155, 167
18:3-4	155
18:6	164
19:4	119
19:6	147
Testament Benjamin	90, 117
1:4-5	119
3-8	142
3-6	155
3	142
3:1	147, 155
3:2	155
3:3-5	152, 155-156, 166
3:3-4	149, 153
3:3	155
3:6-7	156
3:8	142, 152, 157
4:1-3	156
4:1	155
4:3	161, 167
4:4	156
5:1-2	152
5:2-3	155
5:2	166, 167
5:3-5	156
5:3	155
5:4	167
5:5	155
6:1	152, 155, 167
6:3	152
6:4	152, 153, 155, 166
6:5-7	155
6:6	155
7:1	147, 166
8	90
8:1	147, 166
9	148
9:2	149, 152
10	148
10:2-11	88
10:2-5	146
10:3	147

10:4-10	104
10:10	172
10:11	104, 147, 148, 172, 175
11	88, 148, 164, 175-177
11:1-2	177
11:4	176
12	88
12:3	121

IV. Aramaic Levi Document

Aramaic fragments
Fragments from the Cairo Geniza   78,
107,128, 130, 131, 168
Bodleian col. a   132, 133, 134, 135
Cambridge col. a-b 130, 131, 132, 133
Cambridge col. d   129, 133

Qumran fragments (see also 4Q540-541
among Qumran Documents)
1Q21 (1QTLevi ar)   108, 128, 135
4Q213 (4QLevia ar)   108, 110,
128, 131, 138
4Q213a (4QLevib ar)   81, 108, 110,
128, 131, 132
4Q213b (4QLevic ar)   108, 128
4Q 214, 214a, 214b (4QLevid-f ar)
108, 128

*Greek fragments in MS e (MS Athos,
Koutloumous 39)*   78, 109,
128, 130, 168
addition at T. Levi 2:3   81, 108,
110, 129, 132
addition at T. Levi 5:2   129
addition at T. Levi 18:2   107, 129

Syriac fragment   129

ALD (detailed)   11, 107-113,
119-122, 128-140
7   132
12-13   120
13-61   134, 137
16-18   135
48-50   134
50   120
57   120
58-61   134
59   135

62-81	120
67-68	120
67	135
74-77	120
78-79	133
81	120,130
82-95	130, 135, 138
82-84	120, 121
82	120, 130
88-99	120
99-100	135
*6	134
*7-8	134
*18	134, 135

V. QUMRAN DOCUMENTS
(for fragments on Levi see also Aramaic Levi Document)

1Q28b (1QSb)	112
3Q7 (3Q TJuda?)	118
4Q201-202 (4QEn^{a-b} ar)	63
4Q204-207 (4Q En^{c-f} ar)	63
4Q208-211 (4QEnastr^{a-d} ar)	63
4Q212 (4QEn^g ar)	63
4Q215 (4QTNaph)	11, 113-117, 119, 120
4Q215^a (4Q Time of Righteousness)	114
4Q252-254^a (4QcomGen A-D)	122
4Q365-365^a (Reworked Pentateuch^{b-c})	123
4Q371-373 (4QapocrJoseph^{a-c})	119
4Q378-379 (4QapocrJoshua^{a-b})	122-123
4Q474 (4Q Text concerning Rachel and Joseph)	119
4Q484 (4QpapTJud?)	118
4Q537 (4QTJacob? ar)	120
4Q538 (4QTJud ar)	11, 117, 118, 120
4Q539 (4QapocrJoseph^b ar)	11, 118, 119, 120
4Q540 (4QapocrLevi^a ar)	110-111, 113, 122, 139
4Q541 (4QapocrLevi^b? ar)	110-111, 112, 113, 120, 122, 139
4Q542 (4QTQahat ar)	11, 81, 109, 120-122, 135
4Q543-548 (4Q visions of 'Amram^{a-f} ar)	11, 81, 109, 120-122, 135

4Q554 (4Q New Jerusalem^a)	123
4Q559 (4QpapBibChronology ar)	122
11Q19 (11Q Temple)	123

VI. OTHER HEBREW AND ARAMAIC DOCUMENTS

Midrash Bereshit Rabbah	78
Midrash Bereshit Rabbati	113-117
Midrash Wayissa'u	78
Targumim on Genesis	78
Testament of Naphtali (Hebrew)	78, 113-117

VII. JEWISH AUTHORS WRITING IN GREEK

Artapanus	216
Flavius Josephus	
Antiquitates Iudaicae	
1, 41	197
Contra Apionem	
2, 190-219	103
De Bello Iudaico	
2, 1119-166	103
Philo	103, 153, 216
Hypothetica 7, 1-9	103
Ps. Phocylides	103

VIII. CHRISTIAN AUTHORS

Ambrose	
De Paradiso	
6.30	196
7.35	196
Arnobius	
Adv. Nationes	
2.14	216
Augustine	
Enchiridion	220

In Iohannem Tractatus
98 — 220

Roger Bacon
Opus Majus
Pars II, cap. XVI — 87
Pars VII, pars IV — 87

Barnabas (Epistle of)
12:5 — 235
16:6-10 — 153

Bonaventura
Commentaria in Quattuor Libros Sententiarum
IV. Dist. XXIX,Qu. — 86

Clement of Alexandria
Eclogae
41.2 — 207, 219
48-49 — 207, 219

Protrepticus
4.50.3 — 208, 219
12.2 — 196

Stromateis
1.15 — 216
5.11.77 — 221
5.90.1 — 216-220
5.90.4-91.5 — 216-220
5.90.6-91.2 — 216-220

Didache
16:4 — 236

Eusebius of Caesarea
Historia Ecclesiastica
3.3.2 — 219
3.25.4 — 219
4.24 — 194
4.26,13-14 — 20
4.29.2-3 — 189
6.14.1 — 219

Praeparatio Evangelica — 34
11.38 — 217-220
13.13.6 — 217-260
13.16. 14-15 — 217-220

Gelasius Cyzicenus
Historia Ecclesiastica
II.17.7 — 66
II.21.7 — 66

Georgius Syncellus
Chronographia — 63

Robert Grosseteste
Epistola V — 87

Hermas (Shepherd of)
Mandata
10.1.6 — 153

Similitudines
9.18.2 — 173
9.32.2 — 167

Hieronymus
Tractatus de Psalmo 15 — 98

Hippolytus
Benedictions of Isaac, Jacob and Moses — 101, 126

Refutatio Omnium Haeresium
IX.23 — 167

Irenaeus
Adversus Haereses
1.28.1 — 189
3.21.10-23.8 — 186
3.22.4 — 187
3.23.1-8 — 187-189, 239
3.23.1-2 — 187
3.23.2 — 187
3.23.3 — 188
3.23.4 — 188
3.23.5 — 188
3.23.6 — 188, 189, 192, 197
3.23.7 — 186, 189
3.23.8 — 189, 239
4.40.3 — 186, 197
5.24.4 — 197

Epideixis
16 — 197

Isidore of Seville
De Ortu et Obitu Patrum — 45

Justin Martyr
  1 Apology
  41.1-4   21

  Dialogue with Trypho
  11.2   27, 149
  12.1-3   149
  14.1-8   149
  23.1-2   26
  29.2   26
  30.1   26
  44-46   149
  45.1   149
  45.2-3   149
  45.4   105
  71-73   20, 21
  80-81   105, 149
  84.12   186
  92.5   26
  93.1-2   149
  100.3-6   186
  103.6   186
  116.3   128
  130.1-2   105

Lactantius
  Institutiones Divinae
  7.18.2-4   219

Matthaeus Parisiensis
  Chronica Majora
  IV.232-233   85
  IV.232   86
  IV.233   86
  V.284-287   85

Melito
  Ἐκλογαί   20-21

Origen
  In Librum Jesu Nave Homiliae
  15,6   97

Prudentius
  Cathemerinon Liber
  hymn 5   211, 220
  5.125-136   211
  5.127-128   211

Tertullian
  Adv. Marcionem
  1   191
  2.2.7   192
  2.10.1   192
  2.17.1   191
  2.25   196
  2.25.3-4   192
  2.25.5   193
  De Anima
  38.2   191

  De Monogamia
  17.5   191

  De Paenitentia
  2.2-5   190
  3.7   190
  12.9   190, 240

  De Patientia
  5.13   191

Ps. Tertullian
  Adv. Omnes Haereses
  7   189

Theodoretus of Cyrus
  Graecarum Affectionum Curatio
  11.19-24   217-220
  11.33-39   217-220

Theophilus of Antioch
  Ad Autolycum
  2.10-19   194
  2.19   207
  2.20-21   194
  2.22-28   194, 239
  2.22   194, 196
  2.24   194
  2.25   189, 192, 195-196, 197, 239
  2.26   195, 239
  2.27   195, 239
  2.28   196
  2.29   194, 197
  2.30-33   194
  2.33   194
  2.36   194

2.38	218
3.1	194
3.7	218
3.18	194
3.20	194

Vincent of Beauvais
Speculum Historiale — 89
Lib. II. cap. CXXV — 86

Coptic Magical Text in London MS Or. 5987
lines 18-24 — 211

Gnostic Writings
The Testimony of Truth
45.23-50.11 — 197
47.14-48.4 — 198

The Hypostasis of the Archons
88.24-91.7 — 197

On the Origin of the World
118.17-121.27 — 197

IX. OTHER GREEK AND LATIN AUTHORS

Aeschylus
Septem contra Thebes
856 — 213

Agamemnon
1160 — 213

Anthologia Palatina
5.240 — 213
7.67-68 — 213
7.365 — 213

Apuleius
Metamorphoses
6.18 — 213

Aristophanes
Aves
1715 — 224

Ranae
181-183, 193, 471 — 213

Aristotle
Meteorologica
345a.25 — 224

Cicero
De Re Publica
6.14.14 — 225
6.16.6 — 225

Tusculanae Disputationes
1.16.37 — 213, 225
1.17.39 — 225
1,21.48 — 213, 225

Diodorus Siculus
Historiae
5.23 — 224

Euripides
Alcestis
252-253, 443, 900-902 — 213, 223

Hierocles
In Carmen Aureum
26 — 217

Homer
Iliad
8.359 — 212
13.389 — 223
16.482 — 223
23.71-74 — 212

Odyssey
10.508-515 — 212, 215
10.509-510 — 222, 223
11.155-159 — 212, 225

Lucian
Contemplantes
7 — 213

Dialogi Mortuorum
20.1 — 213

De Luctu
3 — 213
Necyomantia
10 — 213

Verae Historiae
1.16   224

Manetho Astrol.
2.116   224

Pausanias
5.14.2   213
10.28.4   213

Plato
  Gorgias
  523a-527a   214

  Phaedo
  80d   218
  80e-82b   212
  81e-82a   218
  88d   218
  107-115a   212
  107c   213
  112-113   216, 219
  112e-115a   213-215, 218, 220
  113a-114c   217
  122e   226

  Phaedrus
  245b-249d   214

Respublica
614a-621b   214

Proclus
  Institutio Theologica
  205-208   217

Ptolemy
  Syntaxis Mathematica
  8.2   224

Sophocles
  Ajax
  672   224

  Electra
  137-138   213

Theocritus
17.47   213

Thucydides
1.46   213

Virgil
  Aeneid
  6.298-304, 384-394   213

Xenophon
  Anabasis
  6.2.2   213

ANALYTICAL SUBJECT INDEX

A. Pseudepigrapha of the Old Testament. General Questions

Apocrypha of the O.T. as Roman-Catholic term   9, 10, 16

Collections and handbooks (editors/authors)   9-17
    R.H. Charles   9, 29
    J.H. Charlesworth   13-14, 16, 29
    A.-M. Denis   9
    A. Díez Macho *et alii*   10
    A. Dupont-Sommer/M. Philonenko   10
    J.A. Fabricius   9
    J.-C. Haelewyck   9
    Jüdische Schriften aus hellenistisch-römischer Zeit   10, 29-30
    E. Kautzsch   9, 29
    P. Riessler   10
    P. Sacchi   10, 16
    E. Schürer   10
    H.F.D. Sparks   12-13, 16
    M.E. Stone   10-1

Selection criteria
    literary: history and words of O.T. figures   2, 12, 13, 16, 18
    historical: restiction to Jewish writings in period 200 BCE-100/200 CE   9, 13, 16
    few "pseudepigrapha" in literal sense   17

Primary textual witnesses
    great majority of Christian provenance   1, 11-13, 31-32, 39
    few among Dead Sea Scrolls   11, 31
    belief in basic continuity between old and new dispensation   28
    not overtly Christian passages need not be Jewish   27-28, 33-34, 36-39
    in some cases gradual growth: "evolving literature"   35
    few manuscripts before the tenth century   35
    importance of ancient versions   35
    importance of quotations by Christian authors   34
       special case: Hellenistic Jewish authors in Eusebius, *Praeparatio*
       Evangelica   34
    transmission in the later Byzantine period   35
    little knowledge about translation of texts from Hebrew/Aramaic into
    Greek   35
    difference in transmission of different types of text   34, 36

Methodological considerations
  necessity of "working back" to earlier stages of transmission   17, 27, 31-32, 37-38
    earlier Christian stages, and only if possible, (a) Jewish stage(s)   17, 37-38
  theories of Christian interpolation/redaction remain tenuous   12, 33-34, 37-38, 39-40
  comparison with undubitably Jewish sources   37

Remarks by scholars on criteria, sources and methods
  J.H. Charlesworth   13-14
  Jüdische Schriften aus hellenistisch-römischer Zeit   29-30
  D.C. Harlow   31
  M.A. Knibb   31
  R.A. Kraft   31-38
  J.-C. Picard (on the "continent apocryphe")   14-16
  P. Sacchi   16
  H.F.D. Sparks   12-13
  M.E. Stone   11, 14, 32
  S.G. Wilson (on Christian adaptations of Jewish apocrypha)   31

Pseudepigrapha as sources for knowledge of period 200 BCE-100 CE?   12, 13-14

Pseudepigrapha as witnesses to the authority of the Old Testament for
  Christians   14, 18-28

The "Old Testament" in Early Christianity   18-28
  "Scripture(s)" in N.T. books   18-19, 20
  canon and text   19-22
  term "Old Testament" in Ἐκλογαί of Melito   20-21
  testimonia-books/florilegia   21-22
  Gnostics: various attitudes towards O.T. texts   22
  Marcion   22-24
    Jewish Scriptures contain revelation of lower Creator-god   23
    revelation of the One true God in *Euaggelion* and *Apostolikon*   22-23
    Antitheses   23
    Marcionites; Apelles   23
    Marcion forces other Christians to reformulate their views on the
    authority of the O.T. books   23-24
  Justin Martyr   24-27
    Dialogue with Trypho defines authority of O.T. in discussion with
    Jews, Judaizers and Marcionites   24-25
    1 and 2 Apology: truth in works of philosophers dependent on Moses   25-26
    No theory concerning "New Testament"   25
    unity of Scripture defended with help of typological-allegorical
    interpretation   25
    three periods in God's giving of the commandments: a) before Moses,
    b) Mosaic Law with extra regulations for the Jews, c) new disposition
    with Jesus Christ   26-27, 105-106, 148-149

"Pseudepigrapha" witness to the authority of the books of the "Old
Testament"   18, 27-28

Transmission of individual Pseudepigrapha of the Old Testament
    Ascension of Isaiah   41-43
       account of Isaiah's martyrdom   41
       Martyrdom of Isaiah: originally separate Jewish writing?   41-42
       vision of Isaiah   41-43
       origin in Christian prophetic circles in Syria   42-42
       connection with *Vitae Prophetarum*   44
    Assumption of Moses   66-68
       Latin text (fragmentary) from sixth century   66
       quotation in Jude 9   20, 65-66
       quotations by Gelasius and Origin   66
       Herod's death last recognizable historical event   67
       emphasis on role of Moses and Levite Taxo   67
       few leads for Christian interpretation   67-68
    2 Baruch (Syriac Apocalypse of Baruch)   48
       reaction to destruction of Jerusalem/temple   48
       parallel material in *Paralipomena Ieremiou*   53
    3 Baruch (Greek Apocalypse of Baruch)   56-58
       Greek text   56
       Slavonic version made from a Greek original   56
       mourning over destruction of Jerusalem/temple   57
       heavenly journey (through five heavens)   57
       no emphasis on rebuilding of temple   57
       often considered as Jewish ànd Christian, but a Christian origin is
preferable   56-58
       connection with *Paralipomena Ieremiou*   58
    1 Enoch (Ethiopic Enoch)   63-65
       Ethiopic text   64-65
       —date of manuscripts   65
       —date of version   65
       —the *Book of Giants*   63
       Greek witnesses   63
       Qumran fragments   11, 63
       quotation in Jude 14   20, 64-65
       references to Enoch in Early Christian writings   65
       Book of Parables (chs. 37-71)   63, 65
       Son of Man traditions in *1 Enoch* and Gospels   65
    4-5-6 Ezra   48-52
    4 Ezra
       known in eight versions, going back to a Greek text   48-49
       Christian elements in versions easily detected   49
       reaction to destruction of Jerusalem/temple   48
       date: around 100 CE   48

in Latin version associated with *5 Ezra* and *6 Ezra*   49-52

5 Ezra interpretative key for *4 Ezra*   52

5 Ezra

    associated with *4-6 Ezra* around 450 CE   49

    prediction of obedient new nation after disobedience of Israel   50-51

    parallels with Gospel of Matthew   51

    date: aftermath of Bar Kochba revolt 132-135 CE   51

6 Ezra

    associated with *4 Ezra* before 400 CE   49

    prediction of impending doom, especially for "Babylon" and Asia   49-50

    parallels with Book of Revelation   50

    date: between 270 and 313   50

Joseph and Aseneth

    Greek manuscripts   59-60

    ancient versions   59-60

    longer version to be preferred to shorter version   59-60

    date archetype of available witnesses: fifth century CE   60-61

    Aseneth's encounter with Joseph, her conversion and marriage (chs 1-21)   58

    attack by Pharaoh's son, assisted by sons of Bilhah and Zilpah (chs. 22-29)   58

    Aseneth as model proselyte   61-62

    Christian phrases   62

    Christian or Jewish?   61-62

Lives of the Prophets: see *Vitae Prophetarum*

Martyrdom of Isaiah: see *Ascension of Isaiah*

Paralipomena Ieremiou   30, 52-56

    Greek witnesses (different recensions)   52-53

    ancient versions   52

    main theme: destruction of Jerusalem/temple, exile in Babylon, return to Jerusalem   52-56

    main figure: Jeremiah

    —entrusts vessels of temple to earth   53-54

    —and keys to heaven   53-54

    —leader of exile in Babylon   54

    —returns with exiles to Jerusalem   54

    —is stoned to death in temple   54

    Baruch remains in Jerusalem   53

    —sends eagle with letter to Babylon   53-54

    Abimelech sleeps for 66 years   53-54

    Christian elements evident in 9:10-32   53-54

    thorough Christian redaction   54-56:

    —return of Jerusalem stands for gathering in heavenly city   55

    —Johannine elements   57

    parallels with *2 Baruch*   53

    connection with *3 Baruch*   58

connection with *Vitae Prophetarum*   44
Testament of Moses: see *Assumption of Moses*
Vitae Prophetarum   30, 43-48
  Greek text in seven recensions   43-44
  ancient versions   43
  no proof for Hebrew/Aramaic original   44
  Anonymous Recension: oldest form of text   44
  —most ancient witness in Cod. Vat. gr. 2125 dates from seventh
  century   44
  Jewish provenance: arguments A.M. Schwemer   44-45
  —parallel short Graeco-Roman biographies   44
  —legends of martyrdom in *Ascension of Isaiah* and *Paralipomena
  Ieremiou*   44
  —geographical data reflect Hasmonean and Roman period   44-45
  —tombs of prophet martyrs mentioned in Luke 11:47 par. Matt. 23:29   45
  circumstantial evidence adduced by P.W. van der Horst   47
  —tombs of prophets as object of Jewish pilgrimage
  Christian provenance: arguments D. Satran   45-47
  —crucial redactional stage in fourth or fifth century   45-46, 47
  —*Vitae Prophetarum* used by Isidore of Seville   45
  —typical elements of Byzantine piety in *Life of Daniel*   46
  —pictures of holy men in Lives of monks of Egypt and Syria   46
  —pilgrimage to holy sites since Constantine   46

Destruction of Jerusalem/temple
  in *2 Baruch*   48
  in *3 Baruch*   57
  in *4 Ezra*   48
  in *Paralipomena Ieremiou*   52-56
Heavenly journey
  in *Ascension of Isaiah*   41
  in *3 Baruch*   57

Gnostics: see The "Old Testament" in Early Christianity

Justin Martyr: see The "Old Testament" in Early Christianity

Marcion: see The "Old Testament" in Early Christianity

B. THE TESTAMENTS OF THE TWELVE PATRIARCHS

Central message and purpose: concern with Israel's salvation; summons to
obey God's "essential" commandments, already observed by the patriarchs;
summon to accept Jesus Christ as savious of Israel and the gentiles   82-83, 105-106, 148-149

Parallels with view on commandments found in works of Justin Martyr and
others   26-27, 105-106, 148-149

Different methods of analysis
  textual criticism: see Text and versions; Transmission by Christians
  literary-critical approach   75-77
    theories of interpolations and redactions
      —F. Schnapp   75
      —R.H. Charles   75
      —J. Becker   75
      —A. Hultgård   76
      —J.H. Ulrichsen   76
      —difficulty of application of modern standards of consistency   76
  form-critical approach   76-77
    Sin-Exile-Return passages   76, 82
    Levi-Judah passages   76, 82
    —connection with Messianic expecations at Qumran?   80-81
    Saviour passages   82
    Resurrection passages   82
    form-criticism of limited value in analysis of composition process   76-77
  comparison of central elements with parallel material of clearly Jewish and
  Christian provenance (see also Related Qumran Fragments)   77-78, 79-81
    biographical elements   78-79
    —serve as illustrations for exhortations   124
    eschatological elements   77, 82, 99-102, 124-125
    —references to Jesus Christ in all types of passages dealing with the
    future   82, 99, 102
    paraenetical elements (see also Two great commandments)   77, 78-79, 102-105
    —core position in all testaments   102-105, 124
    Joseph as paradigm of virtue   78-79, 102, 153-159
    the simplicity of Issachar as farmer   79, 150-151
    continuity between Helenistic, Hell. Jewish and Early Christian
    paraenesis   102-104, 141-142, 158-15
    some paraenetic passages and N.T. parallels   164-168

Parallels with New Testament Texts (for individual passages see Index of
References)   160-177
  Lists of parallels
    in Nestle-Aland, *Novum Testamentum Graece*   160-161
    in R.H. Charles's Commentary   161-162
    in J.M. Vorstman, *Disquisitio de Testamentis XII Patriarcharum
    Origine et Pretio* (1857)   163
  paraenetic passages   164-168
  parallels to *T.Levi*   168-171, 173-175
  Israel and the gentiles (Rom. 11:25-26)   171-172
  Paul as Benjaminite   175-177

Related Qumran fragments   79-81, 107-123, 124-140
(see also Index of References)
   Studies in period 1952-1960   79-81
      on Teacher of Righteousness (Dupont-Sommer, Philonenko)   80
      on messianic expectations (Van der Woude)   80
      on Prayer of Levi (Milik)   81
   Aramaic Levi Document   107-113, 124-140
      Cairo Genizah fragments   107, 128
      Greek fragments   107, 109, 128-129
      Syriac fragment   107, 129
      Qumran fragments   108, 128-129
      4Q540 and 4Q541 and ALD   110-111, 113
      one document underlying different fragments   108, 130
      —cannot be proved to be a testament   109, 130
      order of fragments within ALD   109-110, 130-135
      parallels with Levi-priestly traditions in *Jubilees*   108, 135
      connection with 4QTQahat and 4Q'Amram   109, 119-122
      —priestly instructions handed down from generation to generation 109, 120, 122
      T.Levi dependent on written source similar to ALD   108-109, 130
      —but evidently Christian document   112, 125-128, 135-140
   Naphtali fragment 4Q 215 (genealogy of Bilhah)   113-117
      parallel with *T.Napht.* 1:6-12   113-115
      parallel in *Midr. Bereshit Rabbati*   113-115
      connection with Medieval *Hebrew T.Naphtal*i?   115-117
      4Q215 not part of testament   115-117
   Fragments attributed to a *T.Judah*   117-118
   Fragments attributed to a *T.Joseph*   118
      4Q474 part of Joseph apocryphon?   119
   4QTQahat and 4Q'Amram   119-122
   Further references to sons of Jacob/twelve tribes   122-123

Testament/farewell discourse as literary genre   116, 122, 124-125

Text and versions (see also Transmission by Christians)
   editions of Greek text
      J.E. Grabe   162
      R. Sinker   73
      R.H.Charles   71, 73
      M. de Jonge c.s.   72, 74
   stemma codicum   74, 93
   features of individual Greek manuscripts   87-90
   Armenian version   73-74, 93-97
   Latin version   84-87
   Middle Dutch versions   90-93

Transmission by Christians
    transmission in Middle Ages   84-93
        the role of Robert Grosseteste and contemporaries   84-87
        indications of copyists'attitude towards *Testaments* in Greek
        manuscripts   87-90
        interest in ethics of *Testaments* in Middle Dutch translations   90-93
    transmission prior to the tenth century   93-99
        transition from uncial to minuscule   93
        date of Armenian version   93-97
    transmission between the third and the eighth century   97-99
        references in Origen and Jerome   97-98

Two great commandments   141-159
    continuity between Hellenistic, Hellenistic Jewish and Early Christian
    paraenesis   141-142, 158-159
    R.H. Charles on influence of ethics of *Testaments* on N.T.   142-146
    Law/commandments of God   146-148
    appeal to "Enoch" or "tables of heaven"   147
    parallels with views of Justin Martyr   148-149
    T.Issachar, with *T.Zebulun* and *T.Dan*   149-153
    Joseph as paradigm of forgiveness   153-154
    Joseph as paradigm of virtue in *T.Joseph*   153-155
    the good and holy man in *T.Benjamin*   155-157
    Joseph as type of Jesus Christ   142, 156-157

War between Egypt and Canaan   121

C. The Greek Life of Adam and Eve (GLAE)

GLAE and other versions of the *Life of Adam and Eve*   181-184, 230-231
    different groups of Greek manuscripts   181-182
    edtions of Greek text
        M. Nagel   181-182
        D. Bertrand   183
        J. Tromp   183
    Armenian and Georgian versions   182-183
    GLAE 37:3 in Greek, Latin and Georgian   201-203
    Latin *Vita*   182-183
        new Latin evidence   182, 203
    Slavonic   182
    GLAE oldest from of *Life of Adam and Eve*   181-184

GLAE: structure and determinative elements   184-186, 204-206, 231-233
    Introduction (chs. 1-4)   184, 204, 231
    Adam's story of Paradise (ch. 5-8)   184, 204, 231

Eve's and Seth's quest for the oil of mercy (chs. 9-13)   184, 204, 231
illness and death consequences of sin (chs. 5-13)   232
"Testament of Eve" (chs. 15-30) basically a retelling of Genesis 3   185, 204, 231-233
Satan, acting through the serpent, is archenemy of humankind   185, 232-233
transgression of God's commandment by Eve and Adam   184, 204, 232
Eve realizes that she is to blame   184-185, 204, 232
also Adam acknowledges his fault   185, 204, 232
punishment of Adam and Eve (chs. 22-29)   185, 204, 232
God promises Adam share in final resurrection, if he guards himself from
all evil (ch. 28)   185, 204, 233
final exhortation not to forsake the good (ch. 30)   184, 231
Adam's death and departure from the earth (chs 31-43)
account of what is not told in Genesis 3   185, 204
therefore of extra importance   185, 204
main theme: God, righteous and merciful, grants heavenly bliss and a share
in the final resurrection—to Adam and Eve, and all who, like them, repent
and refrain from evil   185-186, 233
Dying Adam is confident that God will not forget him (ch. 31)   231
Eve's confession (ch. 32)   232
Adam meets his Maker, intercession by angels; Eve is a witness, with Seth
as interpreter (chs. 33-36)   205-206
God has mercy upon Adam, who is washed in the Acherusian Lake, and
brought to Paradise in the third heaven (ch. 37)   201-203, 205
another encounter between Adam and God; Adam's body is buried in
Paradise on earth, together with that of Abel (chs. 38-42)   295-206
death and burial of Eve (chs. 42-43)   206

GLAE: provenance
urges readers to take Genesis 3 seriously   186, 233
nothing typically or exclusively Jewish   186-187, 234
extensive transmission by Christians   186
no specific (earlier) Jewish setting can be reconstructed   37-38, 199-200, 234
date in first century CE questionable   184, 228-231
no influence of Rom. 5:12-20   186, 234
nor trace of recapitulation theory (Justin Martyr, Irenaeus)   186, 233
Yet: Christian elements
God as ὁ πατὴρ τῶν φώτων   186, 233-234
washing of Adam in the Acherusian Lake (37:3)   186, 233, 201-227
comparison with Early Christian comments on Genesis 3 called for   37, 38, 187

GLAE and passages in the New Testament (for individual passages see Index of
References)   235-239

GLAE and Christian authors around 200 CE   187-200, 239-240
Irenaeus   187-189
recapitulation theory   187

God's mercy towards Adam evident in Genesis 3   187-189
Adam's repentance   188
God knows no *invidia* (as some people assert)   188
attack on people who deny that Adam shares in God's salvation
(Tatian)   189
Tertullian   190-193
Adam's repentance   190, 192
Adversus Marcionem: Creator God is the true God, good and just   191, 193
—this is evident in Genesis 3   191-193
—God knows no *invidia*   193
Theophilus of Antioch   193-198
first Christian commentator on beginning of Genesis   193-194
soteriology in which Jesus Christ is not explicitly mentioned   194
comments on Genesis 3   194-197
Adam representative of man in his disobedience and obedience   195
God is merciful towards Adam   194-196
God does not know φθόνος   195-198
Genesis interpretation directed against Marcion and Marcionites   196-197
and against Gnostic opponents   197-198
Testimony of Truth about φθόνος   197-198
Conclusion   198-200
these Christian authors not dependent on *GLAE*   199
GLAE not familiar with authors   199
yet: similar concern for true interpretation of Genesis 3; this is an
essential element in the struggle about the acceptance of the "Old
Testament" by Christians   199

The washing of Adam in the Acherusian Lake (*GLAE* 37:3) and Early Christian
notions of the Afterlife
GLAE 37:3 in context   201-206
Acherusian Lake in Christian sources   206-212
Apocalypse of Peter   206-207
Sibylline Oracles 2:330-338   207-208
Apocalypse of Paul   208-210, 220-227
Book of Resurrection of Christ   210
other writings   211-212
Acherusian Lake/river Acheron from Homer to Plato   212-215
Christian commentary on Plato's description   216-227
Clement of Alexandria   216
Eusebius of Caesarea   217
Theodoretus of Cyrus   217
apocalyptic traditionn   218-219
platonizing tradition   219-220
intersection of two strands in *Apocalypse of Paul*   220-227
the "Milky Way"   222-225
Cicero's "Dream of Scipio"   224-225

STUDIA IN VETERIS TESTAMENTI PSEUDEPIGRAPHA

EDITED BY

M.A. KNIBB, H.J. DE JONGE

J.-CL. HAELEWYCK, J. TROMP

2. DELCOR, M. (ed.), *Le Testament d'Abraham*. Introduction, traduction du texte grec et commentaire de la recension grecque longue. Suivi de la traduction des Testaments d'Abraham, d'Isaac et de Jacob d'après les versions orientales. 1973. ISBN 90 04 03641 5

3. JONGE, M. DE (ed.), *Studies on the Testaments of the Twelve Patriarchs*. Text and Interpretation. 1975. ISBN 90 04 04379 9

4. HORST, P.W. VAN DER (ed.), *The Sentences of Pseudo-Phocylides*. With Introduction and Commentary. 1978. ISBN 90 04 05707 2

5. TURDEANU, É., *Apocryphes slaves et roumains de l'Ancient Testament*. 1981. ISBN 90 04 06341 2

6. HOLLANDER, H.W., *Joseph as an Ethical Model in the Testaments of the Twelve Patriarchs*. 1981. ISBN 90 04 06387 0

7. BLACK, M. (ed.), *The Book of Enoch or I Enoch*. A New English Edition with Commentary and Textual Notes. In Consultation with J.C. VANDERKAM. With an Appendix on the "Astronomical" Chapters by O. NEUGEBAUER. 1985. ISBN 90 04 07100 8

8. HOLLANDER, H.W. & M. DE JONGE (eds.), *The Testaments of the Twelve Patriarchs*. A Commentary. 1985. ISBN 90 04 07560 7

9. STONE, M.E., *Selected Studies in Pseudepigrapha and Apocrypha*. With Special Reference to the Armenian Tradition. 1991. ISBN 90 04 09343 5

10. TROMP, J. (ed.), *The Assumption of Moses*. A Critical Edition with Commentary. 1993. ISBN 90 04 09779 1

11. SATRAN, D., *Biblical Prophets in Byzantine Palestine*. Reassessing the *Lives of the Prophets*. 1995. ISBN 90 04 10234 5

12. HARLOW, D.C., *The Greek* Apocalypse of Baruch (3 Baruch) *in Hellenistic Judaism and Early Christianity*. 1996. ISBN 90 04 10309 0

13. BURCHARD, C., *Gesammelte Studien zu Joseph und Aseneth*. Berichtigt und ergänzt herausgegeben mit Unterstützung von Carsten Burfeind. 1996. ISBN 90 04 10628 6

14. STONE, M.E., *Armenian Apocrypha Relating to Adam and Eve*. Edited with Introductions, Translations and Commentary. 1996. ISBN 90 04 10663 4

15. ANDERSON, G.A., M.E. STONE & J. TROMP (eds.), *Literature on Adam and Eve*. 2000. ISBN 90 04 11600 1

16. ELDRIDGE, M.D., *Dying Adam with his Multiethnic Family*. Understanding the *Greek Life of Adam and Eve*. 2001. ISBN 90 04 12325 3

17. BUITENWERF, R., *Book III of the* Sibylline Oracles *and its Social Setting*. With an Introduction, Translation, and Commentary. 2003. ISBN 90 04 11286 1 1

18. DE JONGE, M. *Pseudepigrapha of the Old Testament as Part of Christian Literature*. The Case of the *Testaments of the Twelve Patriarchs* and the Greek *Life of Adam and Eve*. 2003. ISBN 90 04 13294 5